Milan

timeout.com/milan

Published by Time Out Guides Ltd, a wholly owned subsidiary of Time Out Group Ltd.
Time Out and the Time Out logo are trademarks of Time Out Group Ltd.

© Time Out Group Ltd 2006
Previous editions 2002, 2004.

10 9 8 7 6 5 4 3 2 1

This edition first published in Great Britain in 2006 by Ebury Publishing
Ebury Publishing is a division of The Random House Group Ltd,
20 Vauxhall Bridge Road, London SW1V 2SA

Random House Australia Pty Limited 20 Alfred Street, Milsons Point, Sydney, New South Wales 2061, Australia
Random House New Zealand Limited 18 Poland Road, Glenfield, Auckland 10, New Zealand
Random House South Africa (Pty) Limited Isle of Houghton, Corner Boundary
Road & Carse O'Gowrie, Houghton 2198, South Africa

Random House UK Limited Reg. No. 954009

Distributed in USA by Publishers Group West
1700 Fourth Street, Berkeley, California 94710

Distributed in Canada by Penguin Canada Ltd
10 Alcorn Avenue, Toronto, Ontario, Canada M4V 3B2

For further distribution details, see www.timeout.com

ISBN 1-904978-54-1 (until January 2007)
ISBN 978-1-904978-54-1 (after January 2007)

A CIP catalogue record for this book is available from the British Library

Colour reprographics by Wyndeham Icon, 3 & 4 Maverton Road, London E3 2JE

Printed and bound Cayfosa-Quebecor, Ctra. de Caldes, Km 3, 08130 Sta. Perpètua de Mogoda, Barcelona, Spain.

Papers used by Ebury Publishing are natural, recyclable products made from wood grown in sustainable forests

Time Out Guides Limited
Universal House
251 Tottenham Court Road
London W1T 7AB
Tel + 44 (0)20 7813 3000
Fax + 44 (0)20 7813 6001
Email guides@timeout.com
www.timeout.com

Editorial

Editor Lesley McCave
Deputy Editor Lisa Ritchie
Consultant Editor Roberta Kedzierski
Listings Editor Simone M Cividini
Proofreader Sylvia Tombesi-Walton
Indexer Sam Le Quesne

Editorial/Managing Director Peter Fiennes
Series Editor Ruth Jarvis
Deputy Series Editor Lesley McCave
Business Manager Gareth Garner
Guides Co-ordinator Holly Pick
Accountant Kemi Olufuwa

Design

Art Director Scott Moore
Art Editor Pinelope Kourmouzoglou
Senior Designer Josephine Spencer
Graphic Designer Henry Elphick
Digital Imaging Dan Conway
Ad Make-up Jenny Prichard

Picture Desk

Picture Editor Jael Marschner
Deputy Picture Editor Tracey Kerrigan
Picture Researcher Helen McFarland

Advertising

Sales Director Mark Phillips
International Sales Manager Ross Canadé
International Sales Executive Simon Davies
Advertising Sales (Milan) MAD & Co International
Advertising Assistant Kate Staddon

Marketing

Group Marketing Director John Luck
Marketing Manager Yvonne Poon
Marketing & Publicity Manager, US Rosella Albanese

Production

Group Production Director Mark Lamond
Production Manager Brendan McKeown
Production Coordinator Caroline Bradford

Time Out Group

Chairman Tony Elliott
Managing Director Mike Hardwick
Financial Director Richard Waterlow
TO Magazine Ltd MD David Pepper
Group General Manager/Director Nichola Coulthard
TO Communications Ltd MD David Pepper
Group Art Director John Oakey
Group IT Director Simon Chappell

Contributors

History Gregory Dowling, Roberta Kedzierski (*Coming, seeing and..., Five days that shook Milan, First things first Roberta Kedzierski*). **Milan Today** Mark Worden. **Art in Milan** Danielle Carrabino. **Food in Milan** Pamela Cuthbert. **Where to Stay** Roberta Kedzierski. **Sightseeing** Daniel Smith (*Walk on, Grand Centrale, Triennale Roberta Kedzierski*). **Restaurants** Michael Thompson. **Cafés & Bars** Rachel Roberts (*Bitter pleasures Paul French*). **Shops & Services** Valerie Waterhouse. **Festivals & Events** Derek Allen. **Children** Mark Worden. **Film** Derek Allen. **Galleries** John Moretti. **Gay & Lesbian** Jeremy Hayne. **Music** Mark Worden. **Nightlife** John Moretti. **Sport & Fitness** John Moretti. **Theatre & Dance** Mark Worden. **Getting Started** Monica Larner. **Monza & the Brianza** Lesley McCave. **Bergamo** Alexia Loundras. **Lago d'Orta** Valerie Waterhouse. **Lago Maggiore** Roberta Kedzierski. **Lago di Como** Roberta Kedzierski (*Luck be a lake tonight Paul French*). **Lago di Garda** Alexia Loundras. **Directory** Jeremy Hayne (*Further Reference Anne Hanley, Nick Funnell, Roberta Kedzierski, Vocabulary Anne Hanley, Roberta Kedzierski*). *Additional reviews Simone M Cividini.*

Maps JS Graphics (john@jsgraphics.co.uk).

The Milan transport map is used by kind permission of ATM.

Photography by Gianluca Moggi, New Press Photo, **except:** page 10 Art Archive; pages 14, 17 Bridgeman Art Library; page 18 Mary Evans Picture Library; page 25 akg-images/Electa; page 94 akg-images; page 145 Giorgio Armani; page 171 Foto Delmati; page 173 Angelo Redoelli; pages 177, 192 Andrea Lazzarini Editore; pages 180, 189, 202, 209, 210, 213, 216 Cesare Cicardini. The following images were provided by the featured establishment/artist: pages 153, 164, 181.

The Editor would like to thank Anna Agostani, Luciana Bacci, Alessandra Baldeschi, the Colombo Brothers, Valeria Lotti, Laura Macaulay, Matteo Mangosi, James Mitchell, Sue McCave, Anna Norman, Paola Ora, I Tremendi, Daniela Trovato, and all contributors to previous editions of *Time Out Milan*, whose work forms the basis for parts of this book.

Contents

Introduction

Rome has the Colosseum, Florence has *David*, Turin has the Shroud. But what about Milan? Well, it has two major masterpieces, thank you very much. Firstly, the Duomo, a majestic Gothic folly of a building that took 500 years to complete. Secondly, Leonardo da Vinci's *Last Supper*, arguably the artist's finest achievement, miraculously spared from World War II bombing as the building around it fell. But, unlike Rome or Florence, Milan does not brim with world-famous attractions. As a tourist, you're unlikely to wear yourself out, dashing from street to street trying to tick things off a list of must-see sights. Milan's charm is understated. Its pleasures lie in its dusty churches, the narrow streets of the Brera district, the courtyards glimpsed through wrought-iron gates.

But don't for a minute think that this city is dull. It may be the business capital of Italy, but where people work hard they play hard too, and nowhere is this more evident than in Milan. The locals have turned happy hour into an art form, making it a three-hour session of cocktails and upmarket snacks. (Maybe it's because of the years of practice, but no one seems to have a hangover the next day.) And the feast day of Sant'Ambrogio, the city's patron saint, is such a celebration that it also marks the opening night of La Scala's season.

And then there's the shopping, for which Milan is justly renowned. OK, so it helps if you're on good terms with your bank manager, but away from the so-called Fashion Rectangle you'll find boutiques selling the wares of local designers, whose prices will make you smile rather than gasp.

But surely it's not all good news? Well, no. Dedicated followers of fashion – whether that fashion be apparel, mobile phones or cars – must be prepared to pay the price. Until recently the Milanese were able to indulge. These days it's more difficult. Make no mistake, the city has become more expensive for those who live here – and tourists may feel the pinch too.

And what about the pollution? On a good day you'll see the Alps from the roof of the Duomo. On a bad day you'll be banned from driving into the city centre, the result of the local government's attempt to clean up. Even the smoking ban has made it here: since January 2005 it is illegal to light up in public places.

There are those who claim that, just as New York isn't like the rest of the US, Milan isn't like the rest of Italy. While there may be some truth in this, on the other hand chatty barmen serve cappuccinos with heart-shaped froth to their female customers, and vegetable vendors hawk their goods on market day, in the process bringing the countryside to Milan for a few hours and forcing the city slickers to slow to their pace for a moment.

It's just that Milan is different from its more touristy brethren. Those who look beyond the glitz and glamour will discover a city that strides out in style, moving forwards with barely a glance to the past – a fact that is sometimes regrettable. In Milan, the locals look steadfastly to the future (whatever that may hold). They just sometimes need the tourists to show them what a treasure house they have right here, right now.

ABOUT TIME OUT CITY GUIDES

This is the third edition of *Time Out Milan,* one of an expanding series of Time Out City Guides produced by the people behind the successful listings magazines in London, New York and Chicago. Our guides are all written by resident experts who have striven to provide you with all the most up-to-date information you'll need to explore the city or read up on its background, whether you're a local or a first-time visitor.

THE LIE OF THE LAND

We have divided the city into five areas that do not necessarily reflect the local names; the sightseeing chapters and many others are arranged according to these areas. All other venues elsewhere have been listed with the relevant area name. Wherever possible, a map reference is provided for every venue listed, indicating the page and grid reference at which it can be found on the street maps (*see pp248-252*).

ESSENTIAL INFORMATION

For all the practical information you might need for visiting Milan, including emergency phone numbers, visa and customs information, advice on facilities for the disabled, useful websites and details of local transport, turn to the **Directory** chapter at the back of the guide. It starts on page 218.

THE LOWDOWN ON THE LISTINGS

We've tried to make this guide as useful as possible. Addresses, telephone numbers, websites, transport information, opening times, admission prices and credit card details are all included in our listings. However, businesses can change their arrangements at any time. Also, in Milan, small shops and bars rarely keep precise opening hours, and may close earlier or later than stated. Similarly, arts programmes are often finalised very late. Before you go out of your way, we'd advise you whenever possible to phone and check opening times, ticket prices and other particulars. While every effort has been made to ensure the accuracy of the information contained in this guide, the publishers cannot accept responsibility for any errors it may contain.

PRICES AND PAYMENT

We have noted where possible to shops, restaurants, hotels and so on accept the following credit cards: American Express (AmEx), Diners Club (DC), MasterCard (MC) and Visa (V). Some shops, restaurants and attractions might also take major travellers' cheques.

TELEPHONE NUMBERS

It is necessary to dial provincial area codes with all numbers in Italy, even for local calls. Therefore, all normal Milan numbers begin 02, whether you're calling from inside or outside the city. From abroad, you must dial 0039 (the international dialling code for Italy) followed by the number given in the book – which includes the initial 02. For more information on telephones and codes, *see p232.*

MAPS

The map section at the back of this book includes a map of the Lombardy region, an overview map of the greater Milan area, a transport map and a street index. Many of the destinations featured in the Trips Out of Town section (*see pp178-216*) have detailed maps within the appropriate chapters. The street maps start on page 248 and now pinpoint specific locations of hotels (❶), restaurants (❶) and cafés, bars and *gelaterie* (❶).

LET US KNOW WHAT YOU THINK

We hope you enjoy *Time Out Milan*, and we'd like to know what you think of it. We welcome tips for places that you think we should include in future editions and take note of your criticism of our choices. There's a reader's reply card at the back of this book for your feedback, or you can email us at guides@timeout.com.

There is an online version of this book, along with guides to over 100 international cities, at **www.timeout.com**.

In Context

Late 18th-century depiction of piazza del Duomo.

History

Invaded, dominated, devastated, rebuilt… Milan has had more ups and downs than the hemlines on its catwalks.

Positioned strategically at the gateway to the Italian peninsula, Milan and the surrounding region of Lombardy have been the subject of constant disputes over the centuries. At one stage or another, Celts, Romans, Goths, Lombards, Spaniards and Austrians have all ruled the city, and that's before you include the Viscontis and the Sforzas, the two powerful families who imposed their grandiose rule over Milan between the late 13th and early 16th centuries. For the most part, the city has weathered these changes – and occasionally even fought back – and has emerged today as the undisputed economic and cultural powerhouse of a united Italy.

EARLY SETTLEMENTS

From prehistoric times up to the Roman conquest, Lombardy's earliest inhabitants, the Camun people, had settlements in the Valcamonica area in the province of Brescia. Down on the marshy plain of the Po river,

other tribes, mostly from Liguria, dwelt in stilt-houses by the side of the region's many lakes. The rest of the Italian peninsula was populated by Italic peoples and Etruscans. Gallo-Celtic tribes moved across the Alps and into the fertile plains of the Po Valley some time between the fifth and fourth centuries BC, spreading into territory occupied by Ligurians and Etruscans, and pitching camp in the vicinity of what are now Milan, Brescia, Bergamo and Lombardy's other major cities.

These Celts – particularly the Insubre tribe, whose settlement where Milan now stands had become large and dominant by this time – had their hearts set on further expansion southwards. Ultimately, however, it was the Romans who pushed their borders northwards into what they termed Cisalpine Gaul ('Gaul this side of the Alps'). In the 280s they began their slow drive across the Po Valley from the east, founding colonies as they went and conquering the town they renamed Mediolanum in 222 BC.

ROMANS AND CHRISTIANS

It was not all plain sailing for the Roman conquerors: during the Second Punic War (218-201 BC), for example, northern Italy's Celts and Ligurians rallied to the side of Hannibal, helping the great Carthaginian general's exhausted troops beat the Romans back across the Po.

It was a temporary hitch, however, and by 42 BC Rome had exerted its hold over Cisalpine Gaul sufficiently to make it officially part of its Italian territories. In his reorganisation of Italy in 15 BC, Emperor Augustus made Milan capital of the Transpadania region, which included the towns of Como, Bergamo, Pavia and Lodi, and extended as far west as Turin. No longer a mere military garrison, and with its own municipal and judicial structures, Mediolanum began to take on the importance expected of a city placed so strategically between the Italian peninsula and those areas beyond the Alps where Roman interests were widespread.

During the (relatively) peaceful times that extended from the reign of Augustus, the placid agricultural zone of northern Italy flourished: roads were built and rivers made navigable, to the benefit of both communications and trade. And though the area's elite still preferred their country villas over urban residences, towns were endowed with suitably imposing monuments.

When barbarian tribes began baying at the Roman empire's northern borders in the third century AD, Diocletian split the empire into two halves to streamline its military capacities. From AD 292 Mediolanum became the effective capital of the western emperor, Diocletian himself, while Byzantium was home to Maximian, his eastern counterpart, leaving Rome to languish.

> **'Under Diocletian and his persecuting successors, Milan chalked up nearly as many top-notch martyrs as Rome.'**

As Milan's political and military star rose, so did its importance as a centre of Christianity, which – according to local lore – was brought to the city by St Barnabus, a friend of St Paul. Under Diocletian and his persecuting successors, Milan chalked up nearly as many top-notch martyrs as Rome.

Constantine the Great (306-37), who reunified the two halves of the empire under his sole control and was only too aware of Mediolanum's strategic importance, diplomatically issued the Edict of Milan (313), putting an end to the persecution of Christians and paving the way for Christianity to become the religion of state. St Ambrose (*see p91* **Saintly vision**) was elected bishop of Milan in 374, remaining in that office until his death in 397. His legendary piety and charity conferred untold prestige on the local Church, giving his successors in the region unrivalled spiritual and temporal clout for centuries to come.

In 402 Emperor Honorius moved the seat of the empire to Ravenna, which meant that Milan was now pretty much at the mercy of waves of attacking barbarian tribes. After Attila the Hun left the city in 452, Milan was a smouldering wreck. It was partially rebuilt, only to be razed again by the Goths in 489 and 539. Most of the population had taken refuge in the countryside, and the clergy had fled to Genoa. However, by that time, the fate of the beleaguered city was of little interest to anyone. After the death in 476 of the last western emperor, Romulus Augustulus, and the collapse of the empire, Odoacer – the Latinised Goth who wielded the greatest power on the peninsula – had himself crowned king in what had become northern Italy's most important town: not Milan, but Pavia, to the south.

GERMANIC INVASIONS

For decades Goths and Byzantines alternately colluded and squabbled for control of the Italian peninsula, heedless of the threat swiftly mounting from across the Alps, where the bloodthirsty King Alboin was forging various antagonistic tribes of Germanic Lombard peoples into something like a unified front. In 568 the Lombards began their relatively challenge-free rampage through northern Italy, setting up their capital in Pavia, which fell to the invaders after a siege in 572. The region they overran was a shadow of its former self, its agriculture and infrastructure in tatters. This seemed to matter little to the ruling Lombards, who taxed and oppressed with glee, only becoming slightly less hostile after wily Pope Gregory the Great (590-604) persuaded the Lombard Queen Theodolinda to convert her people from Arianism (according to the Church, the heretical version of Christianity espoused by the Lombards) to Roman-style Christianity.

Later popes continued to clash with the ever-expanding Lombards, whose territory now extended from the myriad dukedoms of the Po Valley to the far south of mainland Italy. With the Normans of southern Italy also making life difficult for the occupant of the throne of St Peter's, outside help was sought, in the shape of the Franks. In the second half of the eighth century the head of this Germanic tribe was Charlemagne, a mighty warrior and impressive politician who, although illiterate,

Coming, seeing and...

Milan owes much of its character to the kindness (or otherwise) of strangers. The succession of people who came, saw and conquered, and then moved on (or were conquered in their turn), all left their mark on the city's landscape.

First off, Milan gets its name from one of the earliest documented settlers, the Celts, who arrived in about 388 BC. Although opinion is divided, some sources say they called it Mid-lan 'a place in between', an important centre of communications – a hub, in other words. The Celts then moved southwards in their drive to take over the Italian peninsula, encountering the Romans, who were moving northwards. In 222 BC, Mid-lan became a Roman city and its name was Latinised into Mediolanum. Apart from various artefacts in museums around the city, evidence of the Romans' presence can be traced in the basic street layout. In Roman city planning, a Decumanus Maximus intersected the Cardo or Cardus Maximus perpendicularly at the forum. In Milan, the decumanus can be seen in the line that goes from via Santa Maria alla Porta, via Santa Maria Folcorina, via del Bollo, and then towards corso di Porta Romana (and Rome, of course). The line of the Cardo goes from via Nerino, via Cantù, via Santa Margherita, piazza della Scala and along via Manzoni. The forum would have been in the area of piazza San Sepolcro, where the Pinacoteca and Biblioteca Ambrosiana are now located.

Rather more evocative of the glory that was Rome is what remains of the city walls. Take a look in via Circo, just off via Torino, and in the garden of the Civico Museo Archeologico, where one of the watch towers is still intact. Recently opened to the public is the Roman amphitheatre on via de Amicis. Built on an elliptical plan, it accommodated 35,000 spectators, and was unearthed in 1935.

Milan continued to be under Roman domination until 452 when Attila the Hun left his mark by razing the city to the ground. So did the Goths, who swept through in 489 and 539. It wasn't until 569, when the Lombards took over, that the emphasis shifted back to development rather than destruction. Among their heritage are many of the place names. Apart from Lombardy itself, there's piazza Cordusio at the end of via Dante, and many place names that end in or contain the syllable 'engo', such as the Arengario.

Over the centuries, Milan was an object of desire for several other European countries, coming under Spanish rule in 1535. The most obvious evidence of this period are the *mura spagnole*, or Spanish walls. Begun in 1548 by order of the governor Ferrante Gonzaga, they were completed in 1560 and covered 11 kilometres (almost seven miles), making them among the longest (and Milan one of the largest cities) in Europe. Although the Spanish walls were for the most part demolished in the 19th century to enable expansion, they live on in the form of a ring road, known as the *circonvallazione interna*. You can see traces, though, at Porta Romana, and on viale Beatrice d'Este.

In September 1706, as a result of the War of Spanish Succession, Milan found itself under Austrian rule. The city owes much to this period (which extended to 1859) – for example, what we now call Palazzo Reale. Just to the south of the cathedral, this handsome palazzo was built in the 1770s for Empress Maria Theresa. There's also the Botanical Gardens, the Brera Academy of Fine Arts, the Observatory, and, of course, La Scala opera house.

had established a glittering court at Aachen from where he had set out to conquer much of western Europe. In 774 Charlemagne turned his attention to Italy, where he crushed the Lombards – at the time under the leadership of King Desiderius, who was Charlemagne's own father-in-law – and added King of the Lombards to his long list of titles.

Pope Leo III awarded him yet another title – *imperator augustus*, later known as Holy Roman Emperor – in 800. In the short term, it was a sound move on the part of the pontiff, forcing Charlemagne to uphold papal rights against encroaching foes. But following Charlemagne's death in 814, no one could live up to his mighty reputation, and even before his direct family line had died out, his empire had fallen into the hands of bickering lordlings.

Northern Italy was no exception to this. Already, under Lombard and Carolingian rule, religious orders had established control over large swathes of countryside, building monasteries in the midst of rich agricultural and pastoral holdings. With Magyar invaders harrying them through the ninth and tenth centuries, the locals barricaded themselves into a series of fortified hamlets, each proclaiming its territorial rights over the surrounding countryside and laying the foundations of an extensive feudal system that would later come into conflict with the religious oligarchy.

With the end of the Carolingian line in 888, northern Italy passed under the control of a series of Frankish *reucci* (literally 'little kings'), who occasionally found themselves in conflict with the questionable characters titled *imperator augustus* by popes kept firmly under the thumbs of Roman nobles. It was the unwise attempt by kinglet Berengar II to force Adelaide, widow of his predecessor Lothar, to marry him (or possibly his son Adalbert; sources are divided) that upset this state of affairs. In 961 the eastern Frankish King Otto I responded to a plea for help from the beautiful Adelaide, who had been locked up in a tower overlooking Lake Garda by her would-be spouse (or maybe father-in-law). Otto invaded Italy, carried Adelaide off and the following year was crowned Holy Roman Emperor in Rome.

Under Ottos I, II and, in particular, the devout Otto III, Lombardy's clergy had a field day. The Church was given precedence over the landed nobility, whose uppitiness irked the emperors and whose power was consequently reduced. In Milan a building boom gave the city a succession of new Romanesque landmarks – including the basilica of Sant'Ambrogio. Allied with the *cives* – city-dwelling merchants or tradesmen – the clergy became the effective rulers of Lombardy's increasingly wealthy cities from around the start of the new millennium.

CIVE ACTION

By the end of the 11th century the *cives* were demanding a greater degree of control: in Milan a *consulatus civium* (town council meeting) was recorded in 1097. The towns of Bergamo, Brescia, Como, Cremona and Mantova followed suit in the second decade of the following century. The first of these meetings was held very much under the clergy's auspices, in the *brolo* (garden) of the bishop's palace – hence the abundance of later town halls around Lombardy called palazzo del Broletto.

But increasing civic feistiness also brought the various settlements of the Lombardy region into conflict with each other. Milan, the strongest and wealthiest, imposed its supremacy over Lodi, Cremona, Como and even Pavia, in spite of the latter's imperial connections.

This was too much for the Holy Roman Emperor of the time, Frederick Barbarossa, who marched across the Alps to bring Milan to heel. At the end of a seven-month siege in 1162, the emperor had the city's fortifications pulled down and the palaces of leading anti-imperial

agitators destroyed. Hated as Milan was by many of its neighbours, Barbarossa's heavy-handed treatment of it failed to endear him particularly to any of the wary cities of Lombardy. In 1167, at a meeting of their representatives at Pontida, the *comuni* (towns run by the people) banded together in the Lega Lombarda (Lombard League). Its symbol was a large cart (*carroccio*) with the Lombard standard flying atop it; popular lore has it that the forces of the Lombard League were rallied around this cart when they engaged with and beat back the imperial troops at the Battle of Legnano in 1176. Risorgimento (*see p19*) sentimentalists saw this battle – the subject of the eponymous opera by Giuseppe Verdi – as marking the beginning of Italian resistance to foreign tyrants; but if truth be told, it was the emperor as tax-imposer, rather than as foreign power, they were fighting against.

Statue of Vittorio Emanuele II in piazza del Duomo.

Ludovico il Moro. *See p15*.

The moment the Holy Roman Empire ceased to be a threat, the *comuni* returned to their self-interested squabbling.

The Battle of Legnano was followed by further skirmishing against the emperor's forces, but in 1183 the Peace of Konstanz at last awarded Milan the privileges of independence and self-government it had long considered itself more than worthy of. The city could now settle down happily to its own internal bickering. Most of the trouble arose from conflicts between the old aristocracy and the pushy ranks of merchants and tradesmen. The city's institutions were powerless to resolve these problems, so solutions were sought from outside, with the aristos lining up with the pro-empire Ghibelline party, and the parvenus joining the pro-papal Guelphs.

This was yet another indication of Milan's innate inability to free itself from outside interference. Admittedly, geography was against it: Lombardy was inevitably the

doorway into Italy for a stream of northern invaders. But the city's habit of wavering between outside powers ultimately sealed its fate. In 1266 Pope Clement IV summoned Charles d'Anjou from France to deal with Barbarossa's heirs in Sicily. Forced into a decision, Milan's then-dominant Guelph (that is, pro-papacy) faction, led by the Torriani family, opted to back the anti-empire movement.

But if there was one thing you could be sure of at the time, it was that popes never continued backing winners – the plan was not to let anybody become too strong. Charles conquered the south and became king of Sicily, but then the pope switched allegiance, championed a German candidate for the title of emperor, and even backed anti-papal Ghibelline forces in the north.

FAMILY RULE

Among these forces was one Ottone Visconti, an archbishop of Milan who had been ousted by the Torriani family. Ottone seized the initiative, scoring a major victory over the Torrianis in 1277. One year later he was declared *signore* (lord) of the city. The old *comune* system was over: Milan – like so many other northern Italian cities – was going the way of one-family rule.

In 1294, on payment of 50,000 florins to Holy Roman Emperor Henry VII, Ottone's great-nephew and designated successor, Matteo, was given the title of *vicario imperiale* (imperial delegate), a rank that also gave him a claim to authority over Milan's neighbours. He was driven out of Milan in 1302 by the Torriani family, but with the emperor's support he made a triumphant return in 1311. From then on the Viscontis went from strength to strength. In 1330 Azzone Visconti was proclaimed *dominus generalis* (general ruler). Within the space of a generation, the surrounding cities all acknowledged Visconti rule.

> **'There was nothing velvet-gloved about Gian Galeazzo's command. He had a chancellor accused of treachery walled up alive.'**

The family's splendour reached its zenith with the rule of Gian Galeazzo Visconti (1378-1402), who obtained the title of Duke of Milan in 1395 from Emperor Wenceslas. Two years later it was upped to Duke of Lombardy; Gian Galeazzo ruled over the second-largest *signoria* in Italy (only the kingdom of Naples was bigger), which included Milan, Pavia, Bergamo, Brescia, Como, Lodi and Cremona, among other cities. Gian Galeazzo was a man of learning and culture, but there was nothing velvet-gloved about his command. Local feudal lords who refused to recognise his authority had their castles razed and were whipped off to prison. One chancellor, accused of treachery, was walled up alive.

It was under this intelligent but ruthless despot that Milan became the largest city in Italy, with a population of around 250,000, at the turn of the 15th century. Major building projects were embarked upon in the region, including the Certosa (Charterhouse) in Pavia and the Duomo of Milan. When Visconti died of the plague in 1402, the great duchy was divided among his heirs, with his wife Caterina left as regent and tutoress.

Elsewhere in the duchy, Gian Galeazzo's death was the signal for other *signori* to raise their heads; Pandolfo III Malatesta declared himself *signore* of Bergamo and Brescia, while Facino Cane took over the territory in the west. In Milan, meanwhile, Caterina died – perhaps poisoned – just two years after her husband; and their eldest son, Giovanni Maria, was killed on his way to church. It fell to the younger son, Filippo Maria, to try to regain control of things. He had inherited his father's ambitious spirit and intelligence, along with his bookish habits and suspicious, closed character. But Milan's further-flung neighbours proved more resilient than they had been in his father's day: despite a number of wars against Florence and Venice, Filippo Maria ruled over a much-reduced duchy, with Bergamo and Brescia ceding to Venice.

A CULTURAL COURT

When Filippo Maria died in 1447, leaving no male heirs, a group of noblemen attempted to re-establish republican life, setting up the *Aurea Repubblica Ambrosiana* (literally, Golden Ambrosian Republic). Never slow to take advantage of a neighbour's weakness, Venice attacked, grabbing Piacenza and Lodi. The new authorities of Milan (foolishly) entrusted their defence to Francesco Sforza, husband of Filippo Maria Visconti's illegitimate daughter Bianca Maria and the closest thing there was to a direct Visconti heir. Francesco won back the lost cities, but then did a secret deal with the Venetians, giving them Brescia and other territories in exchange for their recognition of him as the new duke of Lombardy.

After a brief siege, Milan's republican forces capitulated in 1450. Francesco's rule was even more magnificent than that of Gian Galeazzo Visconti. He transformed the city into a powerful metropolis, building among other things the Castello Sforzesco and the Ospedale Maggiore, now Ca' Granda. On his death in 1466 he was succeeded by his pleasure-loving son Galeazzo Maria, whose determination to transform the court into a brothel-cum-circus did not endear him to all his subjects. This was made clear in 1476, when he was stabbed to death in church by three young patricians.

As his son was only seven at the time, Galeazzo Maria's wife gave the regency to a trusty minister and two of her husband's brothers. The younger, Ludovico Mauro, known as 'il Moro' (the Moor) because of his dark complexion, was clearly the dominant figure and very soon he had the reins of power securely in his hands. He proved a good ruler, encouraging agricultural development and the silk industry. Under him, the court became one of Italy's great centres of art and culture, with architects like Donato Bramante and all-round geniuses such as Leonardo da Vinci given free scope. Only the court of Mantova could compete for brilliance: there, Ludovico's sister-in-law, the urbane Isabella d'Este, had married into the Gonzaga family and reigned over a centre of high culture that included court painter Andrea Mantegna.

The life expectancy of these brilliant Renaissance courts as independent entities was, however, short. On a military plane, they hadn't a hope of vying with Europe's great powers. In a fatally flawed attempt to neutralise two birds with one cunningly thrown stone (both Naples and France had a claim on the Duchy of Milan through complicated inter-dynastic marriages), Ludovico suggested that King Charles VIII of France might wish to regain the throne of Naples, which had been seized from the French Anjous by the Spaniards. Charles, who had dreams of becoming a second Charlemagne, was just waiting to be persuaded, and in 1494 he descended into Italy, with encouragement also from Florence and the Pope.

However, after a fairly easy victory in the south, Charles embarked upon what was to become a French habit in Italy, and began looting the Kingdom of Naples. At this point he lost the approval of the Neapolitan population and also learned how short-lived papal support could be. Pope Alexander organised a Holy Alliance to drive him out, getting the backing of Ludovico as well. In 1495 Charles was defeated at Fornovo, near Parma, and returned to France.

But four years later France's new king, Louis XII, took his revenge. When he invaded Italy – determined, among other things, to claim his rights over Milan – Ludovico appealed to the Holy Roman Emperor Maximilian. The ragged army of Swiss and German mercenaries that the emperor drummed up could not match French firepower, and with the help of Mantova's

Gonzaga family, the French took il Moro prisoner in 1499; he died in France in 1508.

In the same year French-ruled Milan joined the League of Cambrai, which had been summoned by the great warrior – if not great pope – Julius II to counter the threat posed by the expansion of Venice on to the Italian mainland. The League scored a major victory against the Venetians at Agnadello (1509), after which the pope – surprise,

surprise – changed allegiance and started supporting the Venetians. In 1513 the papal armies, Venice and Spain all turned on the French, who were expelled from Lombardy, and Ludovico's son Massimiliano was put in power.

By this time, however, Lombardy's role as rugby ball in the endless scrimmages between the Great Powers – France, Austria and Spain – was firmly established: for the next three and a

Five days that shook Milan

These days the Milanese, irritated by the way the government in Rome is running things, might call for secession from the rest of Italy, but patriotism isn't entirely absent from their disillusioned hearts. To witness a swell of *orgoglio italico* (Italian pride) in even the most hard-bitten cynic, just mention the *Cinque Giornate*. These five memorable days in 1848 (18-22 March) truly changed the course of Italian history.

Fired by news that riots in Vienna had led the Austrian Emperor to offer concessions to its inhabitants, the people of Milan – who had been under Austrian rule since the Treaty of Vienna in 1815 – decided to follow suit.

In less than a week, armed with little more than the materials to make barricades, the *milanesi* succeeded in their plan. An initial demonstration on 18 March led to the capture of Palazzo del Governo (the building now known as Palazzo Reale). The vice-governor, Heinrich Graf O'Donnell, was forced to allow the rebels to institute a civic guard and order the police force to stand down. The Palazzo del Governo was soon recaptured, but not before a provisional government had been set up. This was short-lived, but over the next four days, the *milanesi* managed to seize control of the city and all its gates. Driven out at Porta Tosa – which since then has been known as Porta Vittoria – field-marshal Joseph Radetzky, his 16,000 troops and 400 cannons retreated to Lodi.

As the last Habsburg officials left the city, the *milanesi* formed a provisional government. Over the next few days the revolt extended to other cities and within a short time the Habsburgs could only count on what was known as the 'Quadrilateral', that is, the area delineated by Peschiera, Mantova, Legnano and Verona.

On 8 April the provisional government of Milan became the provisional government of Lombardy, replacing all the other ruling bodies established in the previous two weeks. On 8 June a plebiscite (a change in the constitution

brought about by public vote) resulted in Lombardy formally uniting with Sardinia. It was agreed that, until a constitutional assembly was formed, the provisional government would continue. But on 27 July the tide started to turn in favour of the Austrians and Milan was recaptured on 7 August.

The five-day revolt was a landmark in the Italians' struggle for independence. But the road was to be a long one, with Italy finally becoming a nation in 1870, when Rome joined the rest of the country that had been unified in 1859.

While the *Cinque Giornate di Milano* was an initial step on the long journey towards the creation of a united Italy, evidence of some of the uprising's more immediate consequences are still visible. Giuseppe Grandi's moving sculpture and obelisk names the fallen in the middle of piazza Cinque Giornate. A less obvious marking is at corso Venezia 13, where a good-sized chunk is missing from the hefty stone doorway of this handsome building. The explanation is provided on a brass plaque on the wall nearby, which reads: 'Marzo 1848'. To someone who knows Milan, little more needs to be said; it's evidence that the Austrian troops were not leaving quietly.

If you're visiting the Pinacoteca di Brera, you might also want to cast a glance at Palazzo Pisani Dossi (via Brera 11). Two and a half cannonballs set into the wall in the courtyard testify to less-than-peaceful Austrian retreat. The building was hit, as the plaque tells us, on 19, 20 and 21 March. Ask the doorman to get access to the courtyard (open 9am-6pm Mon-Fri). Another cannonball can be seen three metres (ten feet) above street level at via Sacchi 4.

To find out more about the *Cinque Giornate*, visit the Museo del Risorgimento (via Borgonuovo 23, 02 8846 4176). Here you can see the black hats with plumes worn by the leading members of the revolt, as well as a copy of the leaflets providing updates on the goings-on that were dropped from balloons in key areas outside the city centre.

half centuries the region was trampled over by foreign armies and swapped about among the great rulers. It was to become a pawn in the Thirty Years War (1618-48), which pitted Catholic leaders against Protestant, and the Habsburgs against just about everyone else around Europe.

SPANISH SUBORDINATION

The region enjoyed a 14-year semblance of autonomy after France's King Francis I was defeated at Pavia in 1525, his efforts to assert French hereditary rights over Lombardy stymied by imperial forces. Massimiliano Sforza's brother Francesco ruled under the tutelage of the Holy Roman Emperor Charles V (a Habsburg, and King Charles I of Spain); but when Francesco died in 1535, Charles assumed direct power. So began 170 years of Spanish domination. The once-proud independent Duchy of Milan became the neglected capital of a province: administered, guarded and taxed by foreigners.

Milan's population fell from 130,000 to 70,000; industry and agriculture wouldn't recover from the crisis until towards the end of the 17th century. When the last Gonzaga died in 1627,

another convoluted war of succession ensued, bringing invading armies, famine and disease in its wake. The plague of 1630 was especially devastating to Milan, killing thousands.

In the second half of the 17th century, Milan's religious life was given fresh vigour by the imposing Cardinal (later Saint) Carlo Borromeo. He was a leading figure of the Counter-Reformation – the movement that had arisen out of the Council of Trent (1545-63), which was convened to clean up a corrupt Catholic Church so it could hold its own against the spread of Protestantism.

The 18th century began with the impossibly complicated War of Spanish Succession (1701-14), following upon attempts by the French king Louis XIV – who was married to a Habsburg – to grab for France all the various European possessions of Spain's last Habsburg monarch, Charles II. In 1706, in the course of this war, Milan was occupied by Eugenio von Savoy (whose Italian/German/French name indicates the complexity of his background) on behalf of Emperor Joseph I of Austria; the Peace of Utrecht (1713), and then the Treaty of Rastadt (1714), confirmed the new occupation.

Defending the city during the general strike of 1898. *See p19.*

First things first

Given its catwalk credentials, it's no surprise that some of the hottest international fashion labels were born in Milan: Giorgio Armani and Gianni Versace both set up shop here in the 1970s, while in the mid '80s Miuccia Prada transformed her grandfather's somewhat staid leather-goods company into today's exclusive accessories and clothing line. But the city also lays claim to some less obvious innovations…

While it may well have been the first public library in Italy when it opened in 1609, today the Biblioteca Ambrosiana (*see p62*) is off-limits to all but bona fide scholars. The treasures therein include 500,000 printed volumes and 30,000 manuscripts. Among the former is a 1470 edition of Virgil; of the latter, the highlight is Leonardo da Vinci's *Codex Atlanticus*. You can arrange a group visit (in Italian) to the Biblioteca Ambrosiana by sending a fax with your details, including fax and phone number, to Monsignor Gianfranco Ravasi on 02 8069 2210. On the subject of firsts and the Ambrosiana, Caravaggio's *Basket of Fruit*, considered by some scholars to be Italy's first still-life painting, is probably the most important work in the Pinacoteca Ambrosiana next door to the Biblioteca.

Located in what is now the garden of the luxurious Diana Majestic Hotel (*see p47*), Italy's first public swimming pool, the Bagni di Diana, opened in 1842. It may have been named after a woman, but the pool was strictly men-only until 1930. If you want to see Milanese males taking the plunge, check out the 1896 Louis Lumière short film, *Les Bains de Diane à Milan*.

Today the Milanese are more likely to escape to the lakes for such leisurely activity, but back in the days of the Bagni di Diana there were no quick getaways. Until September 1924, that is, when the 85-kilometre (53-mile) Milan–Como motorway (*pictured*) was opened as the world's first toll motorway.

Thomas Edison, the man who perfected the light bulb, and then went on to develop domestic electricity, was born in Milan. Milan, Ohio, that is. That might be why he chose Milan, Italy, as one of the cities where his experimental two-wire system of electricity should be installed. Or perhaps those ever-enterprising Milanese had heard about the experiments taking place at Menlo Park, New Jersey, in the late 1870s and wanted to get in on the action. Indeed, Edison was besieged by people from all over the world anxious to secure rights for their respective countries. One of these was Professor Giuseppe Colombo of Milan, whose syndicate, the Italian Edison Company, secured the rights for the whole of Italy – a nation that had existed for just ten years. Among the syndicate's tasks was to create the country's – and, as it turned out, Europe's – first purpose-built electricity generating plant, which went into operation in May 1882. A plaque in via Santa Radegonda, just beside the Duomo, commemorates the spot. This pioneering system chugged on for 18 years. In February 1900 the Edison station in central Milan was superseded by a water-driven plant at Paderno, on the River Adda – the course of which was once channelled by that most famous of innovators, Leonardo da Vinci. But that's another story…

AUSTRIAN ENLIGHTENMENT

Administratively, the Austrians were a step up from the Spaniards, who had made it their business to improve as little and tax as much as possible. They implemented various reforms, one of which was to draw up a land registry for tax purposes. Suddenly, aristocratic land-owners faced an unprecedented need to make their land profitable, which helped get the economy moving.

The Austrians also did their best to alleviate some of the worst judicial abuses, abolishing ecclesiastic tribunals and the use of torture (to the dismay of some conservative Lombards). The intellectual climate brightened as well – a number of lively journals were published in Milan, and Enlightenment ideas began to trickle down through the educated classes. Numerous learned institutions were founded, including the Accademia di Brera, instituted by Empress Maria Teresa in 1776. The Teatro alla Scala was opened in 1778.

> **'If there is one thing that characterises the Milanese, it's their determination to improve on past records.'**

It was thanks to this climate of enlightenment that Napoleon, seen by many optimists at the time as embodying the spirit of democratic reform, was received so enthusiastically when he marched into Milan in May 1796. Milan became the capital of Napoleon's Cisalpine Republic. It was perhaps with rather less enthusiasm, in 1805, that the Milanese watched the French emperor assume the throne of Italy in the Duomo – the same iron crown that had once sat on the heads of the old Lombard kings.

After Napoleon's fall in 1814, the Congress of Vienna restored Lombardy to Austria. Although the region thrived culturally and economically during the 19th century, the Milanese remained largely hostile to Austrian rule. This hostility found a musical outlet in some of Verdi's early operas, but finally exploded in the heroic *Cinque Giornate* (five days) of 1848 (*see p16* **Five days that shook Milan**). Inspired by the spirit of the Risorgimento – the Italy-wide movement to create a united country – the Milanese succeeded in throwing the Austrians out of the city after five days of street fighting. However, owing to the military incompetence of Carlo Emanuele of Piedmont, to whom the generally republican leaders of the insurrection had reluctantly turned for aid, the uprising eventually failed. Austrian forces re-entered the city, which, along with the whole of the Lombardy region, was placed under the iron-fisted control of their commander-in-chief Count Joseph Radetzky.

UNIFICATION AND THE RISE OF FASCISM

Liberation didn't come until the Second War of Independence in 1859. This time, under the pressure of combined military intervention by the French and the Piedmontese – and with the decisive action of Risorgimento hero Giuseppe Garibaldi and his guerrilla troops – the Austrians were forced to cede Lombardy to Vittorio Emanuele II of Savoy, the first king of a united Italy.

Though few doubted that the seat of government had to be Rome, Milan clearly considered itself the new country's cultural and financial capital. In the years immediately after unification, the city celebrated its free status by undertaking a number of grandiose building projects, including the construction of the great Galleria Vittorio Emanuele II.

On a more practical level, the opening of the San Gottardo tunnel through the Alps facilitated trade with northern Europe, and gave another boost, if one were needed, to Lombardy's industry. The flip side of this boom was suffering and unrest among the workers. Support for socialism grew; a general strike in 1898 was repressed with extreme brutality, leaving 81 'subversives' dead and 502 injured. Immediately after World War I there were 445 strikes within the space of a single year; it was in this tumultuous climate that the Fascist party began its thuggish activities, with some of its earliest attacks being launched in Milan against the socialist newspaper *Avanti* (previously edited, curiously enough, by Mussolini himself).

> **'It was in Milan that the fallen Mussolini made his final appearance – strung up in piazzale Loreto.'**

With Fascism established, demonstrations of proletarian discontent disappeared. It was not until 1943 that Milanese workers dared manifest their displeasure once again, bringing several factories in Milan and Turin to a halt; these protests contributed to the downfall of Mussolini's regime in July the same year. In April 1945 the population of Milan rekindled the old 1848 spirit, rising up against the occupying Nazi forces and liberating the city in just three days. If there is one thing that characterises the Milanese, it's their determination to improve on past records.

Galleria Vittorio Emanuele II.
See p19.

And it was in Milan that the fallen Mussolini made his grisly final public appearance. Having been captured in Dongo on Lake Como and executed by partisans in 1945, Mussolini and his mistress Claretta Petacci were strung up for all to behold in Milan's piazzale Loreto.

POST-WAR PROSPERITY

At the end of World War II, Lombardy was instrumental in the boom that transformed Italy from an agricultural country to an industrial world leader. If over nine million Italians moved from one part of the country to another in search of work between 1955 and 1971, many, if not most, ended up in Milan and the larger cities of Lombardy, where work was plentiful. Alongside heavy industry, such as steelworks, car manufacturing and railway construction, the area provided opportunity for anyone with a good idea and plenty of energy to set up their own small concern. As they expanded to become players on the international stage, these small, often family-run companies found they needed help promoting their businesses. Milan soon developed into the capital of Italy's media-related industries, including PR and advertising. Long the home of most of the country's book and magazine publishers, the city also provided the base for the birth of commercial television. (Silvio Berlusconi caught this wave in the early 1970s when he founded Telemilano.)

Despite urban terrorism in the late 1970s and early '80s, Lombardy's new industries continued to gain momentum. In 1975, trying to secure his place in the country's burgeoning fashion industry, which was finding its focus in Milan, Piacenza-born Giorgio Armani sold his Volkswagen to finance his business. Having left his home in Reggio Calabria for Paris, Gianni Versace returned to Italy in 1978 and started plying his trade – in Milan.

By the 1980s Lombardy – one of Italy's 20 regions – was generating 20 per cent of the country's GDP. The spectacular wealth that Milan had accumulated proved too tempting; in 1992 a scandal was exposed, showing that businesspeople were having to provide kick-backs (*tangenti*) to government officials if they wished to win contracts. Led by judge Antonio di Pietro, a six-year investigation – dubbed *Tangentopoli* – followed. Arrests were many, but convictions were few, the statute of limitations saving many from jail sentences. Being nothing if not resilient, however, Lombardy as a whole, and Milan in particular, was able to absorb the blow to its reputation as the 'moral capital of Italy' and, through to the end of the 20th century and into the 21st, the city continued to grow and prosper.

Key events

EARLY SETTLEMENTS

5th-4th centuries BC Celtic tribes cross Alps from Gaul to Po Valley occupied by Ligurians.

ROMANS AND CHRISTIANS

280s BC Romans begin conquest of Po Valley.
222 BC Romans conquer Mediolanum (Milan).
218-201 BC Second Punic War: Celts back Hannibal, beat Romans back across the Po.
42 BC Romans control Cisalpine Gaul.
15 BC Emperor Augustus makes Milan capital of Transpadania.
1st & 2nd centuries AD Relatively peaceful times. Agricultural northern Italy flourishes.
3rd century Barbarians threaten; Diocletian splits the empire into two halves and makes Mediolanum capital of Western Empire (292).
4th century Empire reunited under control of Constantine the Great (306-37).
313 Edict of Milan legalises Christianity.
374-97 St Ambrose is bishop of Milan.
452 Attila the Hun razes Milan.
476 Odoacer, a Goth, is crowned king in Pavia.

GERMANIC INVASIONS

568 Lombards begin rampage through Italy.
572 Lombards make Pavia capital.
774 Charlemagne defeats Lombards.
800 Charlemagne made Holy Roman Emperor; after his death (814) empire collapses.
9th-10th centuries *Reucci* (minor kings) bicker for control.
961 Frankish King Otto I invades; named Holy Roman Emperor in 962; clergy more powerful.

CIVE ACTION

Late 11th century *Consulatus civium* (town council meeting) held in Milan 1097.
Early 12th century Milan takes control over several Lombard towns, including Lodi, Cremona, Como and Pavia.
1162 Holy Roman Emperor Frederick Barbarossa (1152-90) lays siege to Milan.
1167 Lombard *comuni* band together in the anti-imperial Lega Lombarda.
1176 Lega beats imperial forces at Legnano.
1183 Peace of Konstanz grants Milan independence; pro-Empire Ghibellines squabble with pro-pope Guelphs.

FAMILY RULE

1277 Ottone Visconti's Ghibelline forces beat Guelphs; Ottone declared *signore* of Milan.
1294 Matteo Visconti controls all Milan area.
1330s Viscontis take control of Bergamo and other nearby towns.

1395 Gian Galeazzo Visconti (1378-1402) made Duke of Milan; Milan is Italy's largest city, population 250,000.
1402 Gian Galeazzo dies; cities break away.

A CULTURAL COURT

1447 Filippo Maria Visconti dies with no male heir; Milanese republic set up; Filippo Maria's son-in-law Francesco Sforza leads, then betrays, republicans.
1450 Francesco becomes Duke of Lombardy.
1476 Francesco's brother Ludovico il Moro becomes duke; court is centre of culture.
1499 France's King Louis XII invades Italy, takes il Moro prisoner.
1513 French expelled from Lombardy; Ludovico's son Massimiliano placed in power.

SPANISH SUBORDINATION

1525 Francesco Sforza rules under tutelage of Holy Roman Emperor Charles V.
1535 Francesco dies, Charles V assumes power; 150 years of Spanish rule begins.
1560 Carlo Borromeo made archbishop of Milan; gives religious life new vigour.

AUSTRIAN ENLIGHTENMENT

1706 Milan is occupied by Austria.
1796 Napoleon invades, makes Milan capital of Cisalpine Republic; crowned King of Italy (1805).
1814 Lombardy restored to Austria.
1848 Milanese rise up against Austrians in *Cinque Giornate* rebellion; revolt quashed.

UNIFICATION AND THE RISE OF FASCISM

1859 Second war of independence: Austrians cede Lombardy to Vittorio Emanuele II of Savoy, united Italy's first king.
1898 81 die, 502 injured in general strike protests in industrially booming Milan.
Post-1918 Fascist party emerges.
1943 Milanese workers strike, contributing to Mussolini's downfall.
April 1945 The Milanese liberate city from German control in three-day uprising.

POST-WAR PROSPERITY

1960-70s Lombardy is the driving force behind Italy's 'economic miracle'.
1992 *Tangentopoli* scandal erupts in Milan.
2001 Coalition led by Lombard lad Silvio Berlusconi wins general election.
2006 Berlusconi's Forza Italia party defeated by Romano Prodi's centre-left coalition.

Milan Today

A city in crisis or one that's on the up? Opinions are divided.

In the 1980s it was one of the world's hippest and most affluent cities, but Milan has lost a lot of its lustre in recent years. The whole of the euro zone has been going through hard times, but in Italy the process appears to have been particularly acute. Indeed, according to a March 2006 article by the *Financial Times* correspondent Tony Barber, 'Italy has replaced Germany as the euro zone's unofficial sick man'.

Freelance journalist and author Giuseppe Fumagalli, on the other hand, believes that 'Italy is undergoing a transformation not unlike that which the British economy faced in the 1970s'. Fumagalli admits to being both a Berlusconi supporter and 'an optimist', while for most Milanese residents the expression of choice is '*la crisi*' (the crisis). And, in spite of the particularly heated recent election campaign, many observers, both Italian and foreign, agreed that a change in government was unlikely to bring about much of an improvement in the Italian economy. The population is growing older and employment prospects for the young generation are bleak.

Quite how this situation affects Milan, which is Italy's richest and most dynamic major city, is hard to tell. There are no visible signs of crisis on a night out in the city's bars and restaurants, but the retail scene is more revealing. Closing-down sales have become a more common sight, and the end-of-season sales last longer than ever. Nevertheless some sectors – in particular the high end of the market – remain healthy.

This is confirmed by Vincenzo Chierchia, retail correspondent for *Il Sole 24 Ore*, Italy's main business paper. For him, the situation is essentially one of 'polarisation'. The smaller shops are going to the wall (not least because much of the younger generation has no desire to carry on running the family business when their parents retire), but luxury stores continue to do well, whether it be for food or fashion. Large media stores like Feltrinelli and FNAC are thriving. Indeed, the success of the French-owned FNAC, along with that of Japanese-owned Muji, would suggest that foreign companies are moving in and enjoying success.

You might be forgiven for thinking that the frequent sales offer shopping bargains for tourists, were it not for the fact that Italian prices have – as in the rest of the euro zone – risen dramatically since the advent of the new currency. Quite why this happened is the subject of much debate, but many claim that the confusion caused by the introduction of the euro was exploited, not only by retailers, bars and restaurants, but also by their suppliers. In Italy's case, many prices effectively doubled: when the euro was introduced in January 2002, the official exchange rate was just under 2,000 lira, but the euro's buying power was often about half that. The Berlusconi government tended to see the advent of the euro – something that had been desired by his nemesis, former European Commission president Romano Prodi – as the cause of Italy's economic problems. Prodi and his allies countered that Berlusconi was merely using the euro as a scapegoat for his government's poor economic performance. As is often the case in politics, there were elements of truth in both views.

The euro has undoubtedly prevented Italian governments from resorting to their favourite cure whenever the going got tough: devaluing the lira. With a currency that depends on the Central European Bank, this is no longer an option, leaving Italian manufacturers at the mercy of cheaper competition from such countries as China. This state of affairs has been particularly disastrous for textiles and furniture and a fear of China has almost become a theme of Italian life.

'Most people see the future as being grim, or borderline grim.'

In the case of Milan, this is exacerbated by immigration. The Chinese have lived in and around the city's Porta Volta area since the 1950s, but this community has been expanding rapidly of late, taking over both shops and real estate. This, combined with the SARS scare, means that the Chinese have virtually replaced the Albanians and the Arabs as the immigrant community locals are most wary of, even if this anxiety is economic rather than social.

The Russian community is also growing quickly and Milan's large numbers of Filipinos, South Americans and Africans means that the city has become something of a melting pot – a miniature New York.

The comparison also extends to the business world. Just as Wall Street is famously located in New York, Italy's stock exchange and financial community are in Milan. It is also the capital of Italy's newspaper, magazine and book publishing industries, not to mention design, fashion, music and advertising. The Milanese themselves are akin to New Yorkers, being ambitious, hard-working and self-obsessed. As Giuseppe Fumagalli, a native of Bergamo, says, 'Milan really is the place to go if you want to make it in Italy, as it offers opportunities that can't be found in other cities.' Fumagalli qualifies the New York comparison by quoting a conversation he once had with the late, great Italian soccer journalist Gianni Brera, whom he profiled for a book: 'I suggested to Brera that Milan was a mini New York, but he retorted by saying that it was really a gigantic Lodi [a nearby small provincial town where everyone knows each other].'

Quite where Milan – or indeed Lodi and Italy as a whole – is headed is anyone's guess. Eric Sylvers, Italian correspondent for the *New York Times* and the *International Herald Tribune* is optimistic: 'Most people see the future as being grim, or borderline grim, but I have a feeling that the situation can improve. Italy may lag behind its European neighbours, but things can only get better.'

Certainly, Milan has risen from the ashes before. Like Germany and Japan, it was bombed heavily during World War II, only to enjoy an impressive post-war boom. And when industry began to fade in the 1970s, the city rapidly re-invented itself through the service sector boom of the 1980s. This process has been chronicled in an excellent book by John Foot, *Milan Since the Miracle: City, Culture and Identity.* Foot, who divides his time between Milan and London, where he is a lecturer in Italian at University College, is also an expert on football, having recently written *Calcio: A History of Italian Soccer*, a sociological study of the game and its wide-reaching effects in Italian society.

Both books include lengthy sections on Silvio Berlusconi, who is typically Italian, in that he used football to achieve other things (his ownership of the successful AC Milan team was the springboard for his entry into politics in the early 1990s), and typically Milanese in that he was a self-made man.

Even though his political activities would subsequently take him to Rome, Berlusconi's business career unfolded in Milan, where he was born in 1936. After graduating from university here, he entered the property business. He received considerable help in his career from an influential Milanese friend, the Socialist politician (and later prime minister) Bettino Craxi, who died in 2000 in Tunisia, where he had fled in order to avoid assorted trials for corruption. Craxi and his allies also played a part in helping Berlusconi to build his

Taking to the streets, Milan-style.

vast and controversial television empire, which he refused to abandon on becoming prime minister, first in 1994 and again in 2001. During the 1980s Berlusconi even considered running as the Socialist party's candidate for Milan mayor, which is odd in light of the fact that visceral anti-communism was to become one of the key elements of the right-wing Forza Italia party that he founded the following decade.

Although Berlusconi resides at an over-the-top villa in nearby Arcore (where he has built a mausoleum for himself and his most devoted colleagues), Milan is his real HQ. It is also the source of his greatest difficulties: corruption trials similar to those that destroyed his former protectors in the Christian Democrat and Socialist parties. In early 2006 the British public was to get an idea of Berlusconi's misdeeds when the lawyer David Mills (husband of Blair cabinet minister, Tessa Jowell) was accused of receiving a bribe from Berlusconi in order to commit perjury in one of the latter's trials. A piece by Martin Jacques in *The Guardian* around the same time even had the headline: 'New Labour must recognise that Berlusconi is the devil.' Berlusconi tends to dismiss investigators and judges as a bunch of communists and one of the recurrent themes in his political career has been the avoidance of prosecution. As prime minister, he promoted legislation that had direct consequences for his trials.

Berlusconi's fear of what would happen to him if he lost the 2006 election became increasingly apparent as the campaign progressed. Indeed his left-wing opponents were at pains to point out that there would be

no vendetta. One of them even commented that 'there won't be another Piazzale Loreto'. This was a reference to the Milan piazza where the corpse of Mussolini was displayed in 1945. Mussolini's political career also began in Milan (where he worked as a journalist before entering politics) and it was here, after his death, that it came to its particularly gruesome end. Even if it has never been Italy's capital, Milan has often been its most important city. The Milanese themselves consider it the country's 'moral capital' (here, it might be explained, moral means deserved, as in moral victory, rather than suggesting that Milan is the country's capital of morality).

For the rest of Italy, Milan is a city of all work and no play. And, indeed, the Milanese like nothing more than to get away from their industrious home. One of the city's greatest geographical advantages is its proximity to both the mountains (for winter) and the lakes and seaside (for summer). Given the current financial climate it is not quite as easy to get away as it was in the past – which is reflected, perhaps, by the trend for travel agents to offer loans to their customers for exotic holidays.

It may surprise those who associate Italy with sensual pleasures (not all of them healthy) that they can no longer light up in bars, restaurants or offices; in fact it was one of the first European countries to impose a ban on smoking in public places (in January 2005). This also came as a shock to residents. As the witty singer-songwriter Robyn Hitchcock told his audience during a performance at Milan's Scimmie Club: 'After the show is over we'll be going back to England for a cigarette.'

Caravaggio's **Basket of Fruit**. *See p29.*

Art in Milan

A modern metropolis, Milan struggles to match the quantity of historic masterpieces offered by other Italian cities.

Fashion and finance capital it may be, but when it comes to world-famous art, Milan has long been overshadowed by its Italian siblings – Rome, Florence and Venice, in particular. But banish all notions of a Grand Tour, and any thoughts of endless lists of must-see pieces, you'll be pleasantly suprised at what there is to see in both the city and its environs.

Milan's shortage of important artworks can be traced to a variety of factors. The city's long-standing position as underdog and also-ran is one. It's true that Milan was a capital under Diocletian during the late Roman Empire, but Rome had already marked off its territory in terms of artistic and architectural style several centuries before, and Milan simply became a ready receptacle for Roman work, such as the portrait head of Maximinus or the torso of Hercules, both in the Civico Museo Archeologico (*see p93*).

In the 14th century, under its Visconti rulers, Milan was an important centre of the International Gothic. But art historians have never been comfortable with the idea of the International Gothic as a high point of western art; and even Milan's most famous landmark, the Duomo, supposed to be a celebration of this highly ornate style, took over 500 years to build, which meant that, by the time it was completed, its proposed architectural purity had been tainted by a variety of styles.

In the 15th century, Milanese ruler Ludovico il Moro Sforza had the taste and the ambition to create a city as splendid as Renaissance Florence. He surrounded himself with the most renowned artists of the era, but his plans were nipped in the bud when he was taken prisoner by the French in 1499.

From the early 1500s until it became part of the Kingdom of Italy in the 19th century, Milan was ruled by foreigners. It's understandable, therefore, that indigenous qualities that could be held up as standards for posterity are difficult to spot.

In addition, Milan never had an artistic Golden Age like Florence in the 15th century, or Rome in the 16th. In the days of the Grand Tour it was largely left off travel itineraries, and remains that way in the era of the package tour. *The Last Supper* aside, 'don't miss' pieces are generally not found here.

The dearth of 'high' art can also be attributed to a tendency to turn greatness into something else. This is a truly Lombard characteristic: an exasperating urge not to create *ex novo*, but to add on, remodel or cover with whitewash. The city has always been all too glad to bury its past.

'*The Last Supper* shows how far ahead of his time Leonardo was.'

FROM CAVEMEN TO CHRISTIANITY

Lombardy's earliest artistic expression can be seen in the prehistoric caves and rock art in the Valcamonica (*see p28* **Art outside Milan**). The Museo della Preistoria e Protostoria in the Castello Sforzesco (*see p67*) and the collections in the Musei Civici in the Villa Mirabello in Varese also contain fine examples of prehistoric art.

The arrival of the Romans turned Milan – ancient Mediolanum – into the region's most important city. Yet only in the last century – with the construction of the *metropolitana* (the underground) – did its (very few) ruins emerge. When Mediolanum became the main city of Augustus's XI *regio* in 15 BC, it took the form of a Roman city with walls, *cardo* and *decumanus* and a forum where the church of San Sepolcro (*see p62*) now stands. Many great monuments were built at the end of the third century AD, when Diocletian made Milan the capital of the western half of the Empire, and again as the city emerged as a focal point of early Christianity.

When the charismatic Ambrose became bishop in 374, he embarked on a Christian building campaign that included five basilicas around the city walls and two cathedrals in the centre – among them, San Simpliciano (*see p69*). Though most of these were remodelled during the Romanesque period, the fifth-century chapel of Sant'Aquilino in San Lorenzo (*see p84*) still has mosaics that reveal the pictorial tastes of the age.

Modern historiography no longer looks upon the early medieval period as the Dark Ages; for Milan, however, it was as black as could be. Humbled and razed by successive waves of barbarian invaders, impoverished Milan was sidelined in favour of flourishing neighbouring towns. The Germanic Lombards, who held sway from the sixth to the ninth centuries, favoured Monza and Pavia – the crown of Lombard Queen Theodolinda is in the treasury of Monza cathedral (*see p180*).

In the 1100s, however, bishops Angilbert II and Anspert ushered in a new age of monumental splendour for Milan with a burst of building activity and new city walls. The church of Sant'Ambrogio (*see p89*) is home to the most important artistic works from this period: the ciborium (with recycled Roman porphyry columns and capitals), Angilbert II's gold altarpiece (depicting scenes from the life of Christ and St Ambrose) and the mosaics in the funerary chapel of San Vittore in Ciel d'Oro.

The reconstruction of Sant'Ambrogio in the 11th and 12th centuries inaugurated the great Romanesque period in Milan. The Byzantine, Islamic and Lombard influences on proto-Romanesque sculpture are clearly visible in the decoration on the capitals of the columns and the polychrome-and-gilt stucco of the canopy. Much of the work of the time was destroyed by later invaders, or subjected to heavy restoration at the end of the 19th century. But luckily, bits and pieces of many no-longer-extant buildings have been preserved in the sculpture museum of the Castello Sforzesco (*see p66*), including an early 'ideological' relief, *St Ambrose Expelling the Arians*, which is signed by **Gerardo** and **Anselmo**, two master stone cutters from the Campione area between the lakes of Lugano and Como. Other examples of this period's prosperity include the construction of the church of Santa Maria di Brera – now incorporated into the Pinacoteca di Brera (*see p69*), and the abbey at Viboldone (*see p28* **Art outside Milan**).

FAMILY AFFAIRS

By the 1330s the powerful Visconti family had put an end to the free commune of Milan and seized power. Azzone Visconti ushered in a 150-year era of Gothic luxury that turned the city into a centre of art and culture – and, briefly, a rival to Florence. The wealth of artistic schools represented in Milan at the time can be seen in the Pinacoteca di Brera (*see p69*).

Azzone was responsible for importing another great Gothic master, **Giovanni di Balduccio**, who brought the imposing sculptural/architectural Pisan style of funerary monument to Milan. His masterpiece – the tomb of Stefano Visconti – is in the church of Sant'Eustorgio (*see p85*), while his sculptural decoration on the Porta Ticinese (*see p84*) is still *in situ*. Azzone's successor, Bernabò Visconti, favoured sculptor **Bonino da Campione**: his massive equestrian statue of Bernabò in the Castello Sforzesco matched his commissioner's ego.

Pinacoteca di Brera, one of Lombardy's most important art galleries. *See p26 and p69.*

In painting, the International Gothic flourished in Milan under Bernabò's nephew Gian Galeazzo Visconti. His favourite artist was **Giovannino de' Grassi**, one of the many stone cutters and architects to work on the city's immense Duomo from 1386 onwards: his sculptures can be seen on the portals in the south sacristy and on St Catherine's altar in the left nave. Other examples of the refined Milanese culture of the period include **Bonifacio Bembo**'s *Tarocchi* in the Pinacoteca Accademia Carrara in Bergamo (*see p183*), and the **Zavattari brothers**' frescoes in the chapel of Queen Theodolinda in Monza's Duomo (*see p180*).

> **'Ludovico il Moro had different ideas, and strove to make the city a centre of Renaissance style.'**

The rule of the Visconti gave way to that of the Sforza dynasty, which aimed, at first, to conserve the city's International Gothic tradition. But both the first Sforza duke, Francesco, and his successor, Galeazzo Maria, were aware of the artistic goings-on in central Italy, which by then was on to its second generation of Renaissance painters (including **Piero della Francesca**, whose Montefeltro altarpiece is in the Brera; *see p69*). What emerged was a sort of Lombard-Tuscan pastiche, both in architecture and painting.

The leading artist of the age was **Vincenzo Foppa**, who blended Mantegnesque and Tuscan influences in his masterpiece *Scenes from the Life of St Peter the Martyr*, held in the Cappella Portinari, in Sant'Eustorgio (*see p85*).

Galeazzo Maria's half-brother Ludovico il Moro Sforza had very different ideas: while extending the territory under Milanese control

well into present-day Switzerland, he strove to make the city a true centre of Renaissance style. To that end, he summoned the most highly acclaimed men of letters, musicians and artists of the time, including **Donato Bramante** and **Leonardo da Vinci**, to his court.

Though Bramante is best known for his buildings in Milan (Santa Maria delle Grazie, *see p93*, and Santa Maria presso San Satiro, *see p62*), he also left his mark in frescoes: his *Portraits of Illustrious Men*, now in the Brera (*see p69*), show how extensively the humanistic culture of central Italy had penetrated Lombard territory.

Leonardo was commissioned to make a vast equestrian monument to Francesco Sforza, but the sculpture failed to get past the planning stage. The model for it was destroyed by French troops after Ludovico was ousted, but a reconstruction by sculptor Nina Akamu can be seen at the Ippodromo, piazzale dello Sport 15.

The most famous ducal commission, however, remains Leonardo's *Last Supper* (*Il Cenacolo*; *see p94* **Supper time**) in the refectory of Santa Maria delle Grazie, Ludovico's favourite church. In spite of being ravaged by time and by Leonardo's unfortunate experimental technique, the fresco still shows how far ahead of his time Leonardo was, especially in comparison with **Donato da Montorfano**'s fresco of the crucifixion on the opposite wall.

THE COUNTER-REFORMATION AND BAROQUE

Leonardo and Bramante had already left the city by the time Ludovico il Moro fell in 1499, but the Lombard tradition that had taken root there continued for two more decades. The prolific **Ambrosio da Fossano (Il Bergognone)** was its chief representative, leaving behind a prodigious amount of work at the Certosa di Pavia (*see p28* **Art outside Milan**) and in Milan itself (*The Coronation of the Virgin* in the apsidal conch of San Simpliciano and a series of Christ and the Apostles in the sacristy of Santa Maria della Passione, *see p78*). Great convent and monastery churches were built within the city walls, and decorated by the likes of **Giovanni Boltraffio** and **Bernardino Luini**.

Holy Roman Emperor Charles V had works by his Venetian favourite **Titian** (including *The Flagellation*, which was later carried off to Paris by Napoleon) installed in Milanese churches. Towards the middle of the century, another important Venetian work arrived in Milan: **Tintoretto**'s *Christ Disputing with the Elders in the Temple*, now in the Museo del Duomo (*see p52*; currently closed for restoration).

The more austere spirit of the Counter-Reformation – personified in Milan by the all-powerful archbishop cousins Carlo and Federico Borromeo – brought the first traces of the late Renaissance style, Mannerism. No area of artistic output in the region in the late 16th and early 17th centuries escaped the cousins' influence. Among their favourites was the Cremonese painter **Bernardino Campi**, whose work is cloyingly pious, while brothers **Vincenzo** and **Antonio Campi** from Cremona (but no relation to Bernardino) also found fertile terrain in Milan, as did **Simone Peterzano** from Bergamo. But the Lombard Mannerist artist *par excellence* was **Gaudenzio Ferrari** from Valsesia. He appeared on the scene in 1544-5, painting frescoes in Santa Maria della Pace (now in the Brera; *see p69*) and in Santa Maria delle Grazie (*see p93*).

Art outside Milan

The artistic itinerary in Lombardy beyond Milan is replete with little-known marvels, many of them beautifully located within the natural splendour of the region.

The earliest example of art in Lombardy is situated outside Brescia (96 kilometres/ 60 miles) to the east of Milan, in the glacial complex of the **Valcamonica Valley**, which is home to more than 300,000 petroglyphs, dating back 10,000 years. The **Parco Nazionale delle Incisioni Rupestri** (0364 42140, www.sopraintendenzaarcheologica lombardia.tremila.it), a UNESCO World Heritage Site, is in the town of Capo di Ponte, 75 kilometres (47 miles) north of Brescia.

A visit to the **Abbazia di Viboldone** (www.viboldone.it), just to the south-east of Milan, is worthwhile. Although only the church of the original complex remains, Viboldone abbey is one of the most important Gothic monuments in Lombardy. Inside is a *Last Judgement*, attributed to Giusto de' Menabuoi, plus other frescoes by followers of Giotto.

Architecture-lovers, meanwhile, will delight in the **Certosa di Pavia**, 40 kilometres (25 miles) south of Milan (via del Monumento 5, 0382 925 613), a mix of Romanesque, Gothic and Renaissance styles. This large-scale Carthusian monastery was originally conceived as a family tomb by Gian Galeazzo Visconti in 1396 and continued to grow until the 16th century to include a church, convent buildings and two cloisters. It remains one of the most important monuments in Lombardy thanks to its decoration by Renaissance masters Perugino, Bernardino Bergognone, Macrino d'Alba and Cristoforo Solari.

Several museums are also worth a trip from Milan. One of the highlights is the **Pinacoteca Accademia Carrara** in Bergamo (*see p183*) is the room of portraits by Lombard artist Giovan Battista Moroni. The **Museo Civico Ala Ponzone** (Palazzo Affaitati, via Ugolani Dati 4, 0372 407 269/0372 31 222) in Cremona, 91 kilometres (57 miles) south-east of Milan, houses a *Who's Who* of Lombard artists: well-known masters such as Caravaggio and the Campi brothers are joined by lesser-known greats such as Sofonisba Anguissola, one of the few female Renaissance artists, and the eccentrically delightful Giuseppe Arcimboldo.

One of Italy's artistic gems is the Lombard town of **Mantova**, 153 kilometres (95 miles) south-east of Milan. Thanks to the architects and artists employed by the Gonzaga court, present-day Mantova retains much of its medieval and Renaissance appearance. The **Palazzo Ducale** (0376 352 100) was decorated by the likes of Pisanello in the early 15th century and later by Andrea Mantegna, whose Camera degli Sposi is a study in Renaissance perspectival illusionism and realistic portraiture. The quintessential Renaissance architect Leon Battista Alberti also left his mark in Mantova, most notably in his two churches with classically inspired mid 15th-century façades: **San Sebastiano** (0376 328 504) and **Sant'Andrea** (0376 328 504). In 1524 Duke Federico II Gonzaga entrusted the construction of the **Palazzo Te** (0376 323 266) to architect and painter Giulio Romano. This tour-de-force of Mannerist design and decoration culminates in the Sala dei Giganti.

Around the same time, **Michelangelo** was working on his *Rondanini Pietà* (1555-64), now in the Castello Sforzesco. It is unfinished (Michelangelo worked on it right up until his death), but is nonetheless extremely appealing to the contemporary eye. Later, another Michelangelo would make his mark on the city: **Caravaggio** (real name Michelangelo Merisi). Probably born in Milan (in 1571), he grew up in the village of Caravaggio near Bergamo. Although he left Milan for Rome when he was 20, his work was already influenced by other Lombard painters who were experimenting with figurative art based on a faithful reproduction of reality. Caravaggio embraced naturalism wholeheartedly, creating paintings unlike anything seen before. Few of his works are left in Milan: *Basket of Fruit* (**photo** *p25*) is in the Pinacoteca Ambrosiana (*see p62*), while *Supper at Emmaus* is in the Pinacoteca di Brera (*see p69*). Both these paintings perfectly capture the essence of Caravaggio's mature art, displaying the dramatic sense of naturalism he was renowned for and his mastery of the technique of chiaroscuro, which he achieved by placing his partially illuminated subjects against a dark background, thereby creating a dramatic contrast between light and dark.

Baroque hit Milan while Federico occupied the archbishop's throne (1595-1631), and a new generation of Milanese painters emerged: **Giovanni Battista Crespi** (aka **Il Cerano**), **Giulio Cesare Procaccini**, **Il Morazzone** (Pier Francesco Mazzucchelli) and **Daniele Crespi**. A series of canvases with *Scenes from the Life of St Charles Borromeo* (1602-10) by Il Cerano and Procaccini is still exhibited in the Duomo from early November until 6 January each year. But the single greatest symbol of the cultural spirit of the age is the Pinacoteca Ambrosiana (*see p62*), founded in 1618 when Federico's own art collection was donated to the Biblioteca Ambrosiana.

ROMANTIC ROCOCO

During Milan's first stint under Austrian rule (1706-96), mature baroque and extravagant rococo flourished. The archetypal rococo dabbler, **Giambattista Tiepolo**, was called on to decorate many Milanese residences in the 1740s; the Venetian's paintings can be seen in Palazzo Clerici (*see p57*). Frescoes by a precursor of Tiepolo, **Sebastiano Ricci**, adorn the vault of San Bernardino alle Ossa (*see p80*).

The second period of Austrian rule (1815-59) brought Milan closer to the spirit of northern Europe; its open attitude towards liberal ideas made it a capital of the Romantic era, a role epitomised in **Francesco Hayez**'s *Il bacio* (*The Kiss*) in the Brera.

CONTEMPORARY CONNECTIONS

Milan's annexation into the Kingdom of Italy in 1805 magnified its two-fold image as European city and Italian economic success story. Liberal-leaning private enterprise created great works such as the Cimitero Monumentale (*see p71*), and, later, the Galleria Vittorio Emanuele II (*see p52*).

In the arts, an eclectic movement of Lombard historicism sprang up, wandering from the Romanesque-Gothic to the Bramantesque styles of painting. Simultaneously, the avant-garde **Scapigliatura** school (comprising Federico Faruffini, Luigi Conconi and the sculptor Giuseppe Grandi) paved the way for the energetic celebration of modernism: futurism.

While **Filippo Tommaso Marinetti**, author of *The Futurist Manifesto*, held his famous salon in his home on corso Venezia (a plaque marks the spot), **Alessandro Mazzucotelli** and his **Società Umanitaria** were forging a socialist *arte nuova* in applied arts. Out of this came **Pelizza da Volpedo**'s *Fourth State*, a symbol of artistic commitment to the forces of social change, now in the **Museo dell'Ottocento** at Villa Belgiojoso Bonaparte (*see p74*).

The Milan of the interwar years was a political and cultural contradiction. At the centre of humanitarian socialism, the city was also the birthplace of fascism. The construction of the Palazzo d'Arte (*see p70*) in 1932-3 as permanent headquarters for the Triennale exhibition demonstrated the city's connection with contemporary art at an early date.

The Palazzo d'Arte became a reference point for the first **Novecento** group, whose greatest exponents were the ex-futurists **Carlo Carrà** and **Mario Sironi**, as well as the **Chiaristi**, with their neo-impressionist painting, and the young expressionist artists of the **Corrente**, such as **Aligi Sassu** and **Ernesto Treccani**. These last two organised their own gallery, Il Milione, where the first Italian abstract artists met. This period also saw the birth of great collections of contemporary art in Milan, the most famous of which is the PAC (Padiglione d'Arte Contemporanea; *see p156*).

INTO THE 21ST CENTURY

Milan has continued to be a centre for showing and producing art. Among the city's main post-war avant-garde movements are **Fronte Nuovo**; the abstract **MAC**; the 'spatial' and 'nuclear' groups of **Lucio Fontana**; urban-existential neo-realism gravitating around the **Centro dei Gesuiti di San Fedele**; **Piero Manzoni**'s conceptual and behavioural art; and the 'pop' art of **Valerio Adami** and **Emilio Tadini**.

Cotoletta alla milanese. See p31.

Food in Milan

An A-Z of mouth-watering morsels.

Milan is a city of fashion and industry, but it's also the heart of a region rich in culinary pleasures. Distinguished British food writer Anna Del Conte (OK, she's originally from Milan) pronounced Lombardy 'the most interesting region of Italy' in terms of gastronomy. Its diverse topography (Alpine mountains, fertile valleys and expansive flatlands) dictate what's on offer, while occupations by Etruscans, Romans, Austro-Hungarians, French and Spanish have all influenced the region's menus over the centuries.

Overall, expect to find a taste for things rich and creamy in spite of the nationwide love of olive oil and the classic Mediterranean diet. Lots of butter, plenty of veal, double-cream cheeses and decadent desserts are still *alla moda* around here. And, surprisingly, given that it is land-locked, this area also serves a banquet of fish, some caught in local lakes and rivers, and much brought in from neighbouring Liguria, the Veneto and Emilia Romagna.

So, take a deep breath, and tuck in.

Alla milanese

When you see this on a menu, the meat or fish will have been dipped in egg, coated in breadcrumbs and then fried, traditionally in butter and oil.

Amaretti

These crisp biscuits made with bitter and sweet almonds, apricot kernels and egg whites become sticky as they melt in the mouth. The name derives from *amaro*, meaning bitter. The most famous ones are packaged in a red tin box by producer Lazzaroni under the name Amaretti di Saronno – the Lombard town where they were first made in the 1600s. The popular amaretto liqueur, Disaronno, has been made since 1525 from a secret recipe including burned sugar, fruit and herb essences soaked in apricot kernel oil.

Arborio

One of the long-grain varieties of top-quality rice grown in Lombardy and preferred for making the regional dish, risotto.

Bergamo (Alta)

This beautiful Renaissance city, 45 kilometres (28 miles) north-east of Milan, is a pastry lover's paradise. Check out the pretty *pasticcerie* for *polenta con osei*. Once a delicacy featuring tiny roasted fowl, these are now lovely polenta cakes topped with marzipan fantasies in the form of little birds. *See also p188* **Corn star**.

Bitto

It's the name of a river, a valley, an annual fair and, most famously, a mountain cow's milk cheese from the Valtellina region. Fragrant and slightly sour when young, and bold when aged for up to ten years, the best of *bitto* is a prestigious treat with a DOP designation, the food equivalent of DOC for wine.

Bresaola di Valtellina

Another delicacy from the mountains, this lean, dried beef is best when sliced thin and splashed with oil, black pepper and lemon.

Campari

Milan is rightly proud of its cochineal-based aperitif made of mysterious ingredients, and even if some call it cough syrup with booze, others sip it happily with a spritz of Prosecco, soda, a splash of gin or orange juice. *See also p116* **Bitter pleasures**.

Cheese banks

There's an old saying: for every church in Rome, there's a bank in Milan – and in some of these institutions, curds and whey took the place of bills and coins. 'Cheese banks', established in a handful of Lombardy's small cities and towns, allowed producers to drop off their unripened cheeses in cold-storage rooms (instead of safes) in exchange for money. Once the product was ripe and ready for market, the cheese maker returned to take away the aromatic stuff lying in wait and then repaid the loan in cash.

Cotechino di Cremona

One of the few sausages of Lombardy, this fatty pork salami is traditionally boiled in pig casing. A ceremonial offering eaten with lentils for luck on New Year's Day, it's also a filling, inexpensive dish served year-round.

Cotoletta alla milanese

Popular history claims this breaded veal chop is derived from Austria's Wiener Schnitzel. Not so. Served on the bone and from a different cut of meat, the Milanese version is fried in butter and not lard. More to the point, Milan's veal chop dates back to at least the 1100s, and 700 years later was the subject of letters written by Field Marshal Joseph Radetzky, who imported the dish to Vienna. So there!

Dal Pescatore

A bit of a trek, but worth it, this restaurant is located on the outskirts of Mantova, in the south-east corner of Lombardy. Here chef Nadia Santini and her husband Antonio have been making culinary news around the world with the restaurant that his family started in 1925. French star chef Paul Bocuse declared it 'the best restaurant in the world'. Big words for a humble establishment that has earned its three Michelin stars with such plates as pike with polenta and braised *asino* (donkey). Reserve in advance, expect to pay in accordance with the experience – but not excessively – and sit back to let the owners guide you through their seasonal best. *See also p179* **Food and travel**.

Ethnicity

Milan is one of Italy's most multicultural cities, which means you can find a good curry (both Indian and Thai), some respectable sushi and decent Szechuan at restaurants here. Even Eritrean gets a look-in.

The bigger the better: *panettone*. See p34.

Fish

Although many of Lombardy's waterways are polluted – especially the industrial-burdened shores of the River Po – they nonetheless teem with excellent freshwater fish. The Po has pike and perch, while the lakes have a range of small and larger catch, including tiny *alborelle* (bleak) and the elusive and highly sought-after trout of Lake Como (*persico*).

Franciacorta

This is one of the few wine-making regions of note in Lombardy, its sparkling white made mostly from chardonnay grapes with a little pinot noir and pinot blanc (instead of the pinot meunier of Champagne). Produced in a microclimate tucked into the hills of Lago d'Iseo, these wines were the first Italian bubbly to get a DOCG denomination, thanks to the vision of producer Guido Berlucchi.

Futurist Manifesto

Better known for their propaganda to steer new political and cultural movements in the 1920s, Filippo Tommaso Marinetti and fellow Futurists set the stage for ruin when they tried to eliminate pasta from the Italian diet. Worse still was their idea of a good nosh, with parsimonious, one-bite dishes, some intended only for sniffing but not for eating. A fascist failure, the culinary revolutionaries were beaten back by fork-wielding traditionalists demanding their right to eat spaghetti.

Galleria Vittorio Emanuele II

From its opening in 1867, the Galleria has been a meeting place for drinking coffee or sipping Campari while scrutinising passers-by and taking part in that favourite Milanese pastime, gossiping.

Gorgonzola

You're travelling on the Milan metro, searching for your stop on the map overhead, when suddenly you have a craving for a nice piece of gorgonzola cheese. No wonder: you're looking at the name on the map. Before it became a suburb of the ever-sprawling city, this was the town where the creamy blue cow's milk cheese originated – and it is still where some of the best farmhouse stuff is made.

Gremolata or *gremolada*

Any *ossobuco* worth its salt comes topped with this traditional paste – made from pounded lemon, garlic, parsley and (usually) anchovy – that explodes with flavour.

Happy hour

Having become a tradition in recent years, this post-workday ritual is honoured with little more than stale crisps in some bars. However, many places in Milan do it with characteristic flair, offering generous buffets to go with your drinks. After sampling complimentary platters of olives, small sandwiches, savoury dips, salads and nuts, you might want to skip dinner altogether. *See also p119* **Get happy**.

In the slow lane

When a group of left-leaning journalists in Piedmont learned that McDonalds was planning to set up shop in the heart of historical Rome in the mid 1980s, they held an urgent meeting at their neighbourhood *osteria*. The result was a manifesto that celebrates conviviality, promotes local, seasonal ingredients and counters 'the degrading effects of fast food'. Thus the Slow Food movement was born.

The philosophy swept from one Italian region to another, taking hold with vigour in Milan and Lombardy. Little wonder: the agricultural backbone of Lombardy combines with the gastronomic spirit of Milan to create fertile territory where Slow Food restaurants, shops and products now thrive.

After a successful start at home, the dynamic, ever-growing movement went international in 1989, just as foodies sprouted organic consciences en masse.

While fast food was busy producing an overweight population as numerous as the under-nourished, Slow Food has embraced 100,000 members, from America to Asia. With greed and feed working together to mess up the world's food supply, Slow Food's message may be more relevant now than ever before.

In Italy the organisation generally operates as a grass-roots collective. Volunteers around the world open local chapters and work with their members to create events that promote good things to eat and other food issues.

If you're looking for a slow approach to eating in Milan, the movement's series of books, such as *Osterie d'Italia*, offers restaurant and shop listings, notes, menus and tours. Two local eateries with a Slow Food approach include **Osteria delle Vigne** and **Osteria Grand Hotel** (for both, *see p111*). There are also related events year-round in Lombardy. See also www.slowfood.com.

Krapfen
These sweet little doughnuts of leavened pastry, baked or fried and then filled with jam or cream, were passed down from Austria and are now made across northern Italy.

Lemons
The Italian taste for citrus dates back millennia. During the Renaissance, palaces built along the warmer shores of the Lombard lakes came with a separate greenhouse, a *limonaia*, where the fruit trees were stored in winter. Today the lemon trees along Lake Garda are a fragrant reminder of the past.

Lesso misto
This northern version of assorted boiled meats, *bollito misto*, relies on good-quality beef for a simple meal of broth followed by a bowl of long-cooked meat. Not a vegetable in sight.

Mascarpone
The main ingredient in *tiramisù* and other rich desserts, this luscious cream cheese is good eaten plain or with a little cocoa and sugar on top.

Minestrone alla milanese
Rice replaces the usual pasta in the standard Italian veggie soup. Other typical ingredients are green vegetables, pancetta and onion.

Missoltino
More than a tasty little shad from Lake Como, this fish is a cult. A festival held each September celebrates it as a symbol of local, traditional foods – complete with souvenir T-shirts featuring the sardine-like image.

Navigli
The network of Milan's canals built in the 1100s turned the city into a hub of imported goods from around the area and as far away as the Mediterranean Sea. Today the area is home to popular bars, cafés and *osterie*.

Offelle
Made with *pasta frolla* (sweet pastry) and baked either plain or sweetened with apricot jam, these little biscuits have been capping Milanese meals alongside coffee and fruit since the 1500s.

Ossobuco
This defining dish of Lombardy reflects the region's love of slowly stewed veal. Thick slices of shank – *ossobuchi* – from milk-fed calves are tied into bundles, browned in butter and then cooked with wine. Some people add tomatoes, but purists disapprove. The marrow at the centre of the shank makes the dish rich and velvety.

The fruits (and veg) of Mother Nature.

Herring
Not a local speciality, but a Germanic taste adopted here as a popular *antipasto*, especially if the fish is smoked or pickled.

Indigestion
This is something the affluent crowds in the heyday of La Scala must have experienced, wining and dining to excess in their red velvet boxes, while keeping at least half an eye on the show. In fact, these Bacchus-worshippers were the picture of modesty compared to the so-called 'big eaters' of medieval Milan, when 50-course banquets were all the rage.

Jam
The Lombards love their preserves, whether spicy chutneys or pungent jams. Look out for ones made with elderberries or blueberries.

Panettone

Literally 'big bread', Milan's own fragrant Christmas fruitcake, distinctive for its dome shape, is an oversized brioche scented with citrus peel, laced with eggs and butter and flecked with plump raisins. *Colomba* ('dove') is the Easter edition, crowned with toasted almonds and moulded in the shape of a bird.

Peck

In a city of fancy food shops where delicacies are displayed like jewels, this food emporium is a gastronome's Tiffany's. Opened in 1892 by Franz Peck, a butcher from Prague, the original cheese and meat store has since evolved into a foodie mecca dedicated to top Italian products. *See also p107* **The taste maker**.

Polenta

Among Italians, the pejorative term for Lombards is 'polenta eaters'. Once at the bottom of the food chain – you ate polenta if you couldn't afford bread – the pap was a kind of porridge made from spelt, millet and buckwheat. Polenta rose in status through literature, most famously in Manzoni's *I promessi sposi* (*The Betrothed*), and until only a few decades ago most households had a polenta copper pot. Today most polenta is made with cornmeal and is instant. Look for the real stuff in good restaurants – either boiled, grilled or fried – especially in Bergamo (*see p188* **Corn star**).

Quail

In keeping with the local penchant for pretty edible things is the pairing of braised quail (*quaglia*) with creamy risotto.

Rice

Introduced in the 14th century to Lombardy by an otherwise wayward member of the ruling Visconti family, rice soon became a local staple. The flatlands of the Po Valley easily flooded and were adapted into rice paddies. Arborio and carnaroli are the best varieties for making the beloved risotto, a 19th-century invention whereby rice is sautéed in butter and onions and then cooked slowly in stock.

San Pellegrino

The salty, mineral-saturated waters of this spa town north of Bergamo have been drawing thirsty travellers for centuries. It's the source for the effervescent bottled water of the same name.

Stracchino

This family of cheeses used to be made only in the autumn when tired (*stracche*) cows were milked after their long descent from the mountains to the flatlands. Gorgonzola is a member of the group, as is *crescenza*, a super-white fresh *stracchino*.

Taleggio

Although farmhouse versions are still available in all their nutty glory, this rich cow's milk cheese can also be found in its industrially produced and packaged form in supermarkets. In Bergamo it is served at the end of a meal with preserved fruit.

Torrone di Cremona

This nougat of egg whites, toasted almonds and candied fruits was first made in Cremona in the image of the local bell tower for the 15th-century wedding banquet that joined the region's most powerful families, the Sforzas and Viscontis.

Umido

Describes Lombardy's typical recipes for meats braised in small amounts of liquid as well as the weather: foggy in winter and sticky in summer.

Valtellina

Not only a DOC designation for pleasant, light-bodied red wines, but also the Alpine valley that is home to traditional cheeses, including the best *bitto*, and cured meats such as *bresaola*.

Veal

The Milanese are known for their refined and decadent taste, so it's little wonder that the milk-fed calf is at the centre of the classic meat dishes *ossobuco* and *cotoletta alla milanese*.

Villa d'Este

This luxurious award-winning inn on the shores of Lake Como (*see p204*) offers a breakfast buffet of such generous and exquisite proportions that Joseph Heller was moved to immortalise his experience with a memorable, mouth-watering essay, *Just Coffee, Thanks*.

Weight gain

Milan is undoubtedly a food-lover's paradise, but you must pace yourself if you're trying to watch your figure. Remember: three courses are optional, not obligatory!

Yellow

The colour of *risotto alla milanese*, one of the city's most famous dishes. The Spanish ruled Milan for nearly two centuries, starting in the 1500s, and left behind saffron (*zafferano*), which provides the risotto's deep golden stain.

Zucca

The famous *tortelli di zucca* from Mantova is a sweet pasta that comes stuffed with *zucca* (pumpkin), mustard-like chutney and crushed amaretti biscuits; it's then sprinkled with grated cheese. Zucca is also an alcoholic drink, not made with pumpkin but with rhubarb, and named after its creator, Ettore Zucca of Milan.

Where to Stay

Where to Stay

Designer pads, budget B&Bs and historic grandes dames – take your pick.

As Milan is, on the whole, more commercial centre than tourist magnet, it makes sense that much of its accommodation is geared towards corporate travellers. Around 80 per cent of the Italian HQs of international companies are based here, or in the immediate area – which creates a lot of executive traffic.

What does this mean for the visitor looking for a place to stay? For a start, a preponderance of large establishments in the upper price brackets and a shortage of small, inexpensive options. On the upside, because Milan hotels are at a premium Monday to Friday, there's usually plenty of room available on the weekends, often at special rates (although you may have to ask).

Finding accommodation can be a challenge. In addition to the constant flow of business travellers, for most of the year thousands from all over Italy, and further afield, descend on Milan to attend trade fairs. These are held at the massive new fairgrounds complex at Rho, as well as the 'old' Fiera, in the north of the city. Firstly, the fashion elite converge four times a year for the shows (late February and late September for the womenswear collections, and mid January and late June for menswear). Then, during mid April, even more of the city's beds are monopolised by those attending the annual furniture fair (Salone Internazionale del Mobile). Regular attendees have running bookings and latecomers have been known to commute in from as far afield as Verona.

Milan also suffers from a chronic shortage of parking spaces. Few hotels have their own car park (throughout this chapter, we have indicated where this is the case). To compensate, many have deals with local garages for overnight parking. The price of this service varies considerably but can be as high as €50. Needless to say, don't come by car if you can help it – you won't need one anyway, as Milan is a compact city with an efficient and comprehensive public transport system.

STANDARDS AND PRICES

As the well-travelled are aware, hotel star-rating systems vary from country to country. Italy is no exception. Opting for a three-star or above is likely to reduce the risk of unpleasant surprises. That said, the three-star category covers a vast range. One establishment may charge the same or more than its refurbished neighbour. In our listings, we have categorised hotels according to price.

Pensione is not an official term and is used to describe one- and two-star hotels; these are usually family-run affairs where rooms tend to be functional and you may have to share a bathroom. There's a huge difference between the best and worst deals in this category – higher prices do not guarantee better service. But this disparity can also work the other way, translating into great value for money. We've listed what we consider the best budget options below. A *locanda* was traditionally a cheap place to eat and sleep; nowadays it usually signifies a fancy *pensione* with olde-worlde charm.

The best Hotels

For celeb-spotting
Principe di Savoia (*see p43*); **Four Seasons Hotel Milano** (*see p45*); **Grand Hotel et de Milan** (*see p45*).

For your own swimming pool
Principe di Savoia (*see p43*).

For your own terrace
Hotel Gran Duca di York (*see p41*); **Antica Locanda dei Mercanti** (*see p44*).

For lovers of art nouveau
Ariosto (*see p48*).

For sheer luxury
Bulgari (*see p43*); **Four Seasons Hotel Milano** (*see p45*).

For old-world elegance
Grand Hotel et de Milan (*see p45*).

For minimalist chic
STRAF (*see p41*).

For saving money
London (*see p44*); **Hotel Due Giardini** (*see p47*).

For saving the planet
Ariston (*see p47*).

Principe di Savoia. *See p43.*

When making a reservation, be sure to ask whether the ten per cent VAT (in Italian, IVA, which is pronounced 'ee-va') is included in the quote. For convenience, we have included it in the prices given here, though you may find the hotels haven't done so in their published rates. Also note that many small hotels require payment in advance.

In the listings below, rates include breakfast unless otherwise stated. If you have to pay extra for breakfast, bear in mind that what you get may not be worth the money. In the medium to high brackets, it is generally a buffet with hot and cold food – and sometimes pretty lavish too. Further down the scale, you may just get watery coffee or tea and croissant. If you have a choice in such places, pay for the room without breakfast and go to a local bar instead.

If you arrive at Malpensa or Linate airports with nowhere to stay, avoid the travel agency desks. They will book a hotel for you, but the choice is limited to the places that pay the agency a commission and the cost will be passed on to you. The tourist information centre (via Marconi 1, at piazza Duomo, 02 7252 4301, www.milanoinfotourist.com) can provide a list of hotels, with star ratings and contact details.

Duomo & Centre

Expensive

De La Ville
Via Hoepli 6 (02 879 1311/fax 02 866 609/ www.delavillemilano.com). Metro Duomo/bus 61/ tram 1, 2. **Rates** €335 single; €375 double; €550 junior suite; €803 suite. **Credit** AmEx, DC, MC, V. **Map** p251 E6/p252 E6 **❶**
An elegantly refined atmosphere pervades this traditional hotel near the Duomo and La Scala; while there is no denying that the price reflects the prestigious location, the quality and services are comparable to far more expensive five-star hotels in the area. The well-appointed rooms are very traditional (some have views of the Duomo) and the bathrooms have marble fittings. Perks include a fitness centre with sauna and Turkish bath, plus a rooftop pool with retractable roof for open-air swimming in summer. The adjoining L'Opera restaurant is open until late for post-theatre dining, and the wood-panelled bar is a cosy place to have a drink.
Bar. Concierge. Disabled-adapted rooms. Gym. Internet access (wireless). No-smoking rooms. Parking (€38 per day). Pool (1 indoor, 1 outdoor). Restaurant. Room service. Spa. TV (pay movies).

---

❶ Green numbers given in this chapter correspond to the location of each hotel as marked on the street maps. *See pp248-252.*

The Gray
Via San Raffaele 6 (02 720 8951/fax 02 866 526/ www.hotelthegray.it). Metro Duomo/bus 18, 61/ tram 2, 3, 14, 27. **Rates** €363 single; €528-€990 double. Breakfast €27.50. **Credit** AmEx, DC, MC, V. **Map** p251 E6/p252 E6 **❷**
The Gray, together with the STRAF (*see p41*), represents one of the latest Milanese trends in high-end hostelry. Despite the name (chosen by the architect), there is little half-tone here: the dominant colour scheme is cream, with splashes of bold colour. The clean-lined rooms – three of which look out on to Galleria Vittorio Emanuele II – are sleek, contemporary and equipped with enormous plasma TVs and whirlpool baths. One room has its own Turkish bath, while two have private gyms. The hotel has its own chic restaurant, Le Noir. There's no on-site gym, but guests can use the one at the nearby De La Ville (*see above*).
Bar. Concierge. Disabled-adapted rooms. Internet (dataport/high-speed/wireless). No-smoking rooms. Restaurant. Room service. TV.

Park Hyatt Milan
Via Tommaso Grossi 1 (02 8821 1234/fax 02 8821 1235/http://milan.park.hyatt.com). Metro Duomo/bus 61/tram 2, 3, 14, 27. **Rates** €430-€630 single; €480-€790 double; €630-€790 junior suite; €1,390-€1,550 terrace suite; €3,090-€3,250 diplomatic suite; €3,890-€4,050 presidential suite. **Credit** AmEx, DC, MC, V. **Map** p251 E6/p252 E6 **❸**
Carved out of an old bank building, the Park Hyatt is an exercise in serenity. It's the work of Ed Tuttle, an American architect who has designed resorts in Thailand and Morocco – which perhaps contributed to the elegant simplicity of the space. The courtyard was covered over to create a splendid top-lit lounge. The warm, light-coloured rooms are equipped with generously proportioned bathrooms and modern luxuries such as plasma-screen TVs and complimentary high-speed internet access. Relaxing treatments are available in the small spa, which also has separate steam rooms for men and women. The hotel restaurant (entrance for non-residents in via Silvio Pellico 3) serves contemporary Mediterranean cuisine, while the hotel bar is a favourite spot for fashionable Milanese.
Bar. Concierge. Gym. Internet (high-speed). No-smoking floors. Restaurant. Room service. TV.

Spadari al Duomo
Via Spadari 11 (02 7200 2371/fax 02 861 184/ www.spadarihotel.com). Metro Cordusio or Duomo/ bus 18/tram 2, 3, 14, 24, 27. **Rates** €218-€238 single; €228-€268 double; €294 junior suite; €328 suite. **Credit** AmEx, DC, MC, V. **Map** p250 D7/ p252 D7 **❹**
Specially commissioned artworks and a blue colour scheme throughout set the Spadari apart from other small business hotels, although some may find the deliberate artiness a bit pretentious. Sculptor Gio Pomodoro created a large wall sculpture and fireplace in the hall, and the contemporary bedrooms also come with their own work of art. On the

All in the past

It may boast such funky futuristic hotels such as the Gray and the STRAF, but Milan is also home to some hostelries that are keen to embrace and maximise their past. Walking into the lobby of the **Vecchia Milano** (*see p41*), you cannot fail to be struck, although hopefully not literally, by the Roman column that appears to be the main support for the entire place. This is, impressively, the oldest surviving part of the city. In addition, parts of the city walls dating from the third and fourth centuries can be seen in the restaurant Don Carlos, which is part of the **Grand Hotel et de Milan** (*see p45*).

Perhaps the most impressive example is the top-of-the-line **Four Seasons Hotel Milano** (*see p45*), which was a monastery in the 15th century. Here, the cloister is an integral part of the hotel, with the rooms – don't call them cells – set around what is now a delightful garden. Parts of the original frescoes and columns can still be seen in the library bar.

The splendid **Bulgari** hotel (*see p43*; **photo above**), a newcomer to the Milan hotel scene, having opened in 2004, sits on the site of a former convent. Although most of the edifice (which comprises three façades) dates from the 1950s, part of an 18th-century building remains, and the back wall of the stylish, oval-shaped restaurant follows the line of the old chapel. The grounds (documented as far back as the 13th century) that once preserved the sisters from the distractions of the city are now a relaxing sanctuary for guests.

Another establishment that was formerly a religious house is the **Hotel Palazzo delle Stelline** in corso Magenta (*see p48*),

almost opposite Santa Maria delle Grazie, home of *The Last Supper*. While creating his masterpiece, Leonardo da Vinci was given accommodation in this complex. Today the distinguished former tenant is commemorated in the hotel's restaurant: Gli Orti di Leonardo, which translates as 'Leonardo's vegetable gardens'.

If the devil has all the best tunes, in Milan the church had some of the best rooms. Constructed in the 1890s in Liberty style (the Italian take on art nouveau), the building that is now the **Hotel Gran Duca di York** (*see p41*) was once a place where visiting top-ranking clergy could stay. Although completely refurbished since then, the hotel still bears many of the original features, such as the columns and marble floors in the lobby.

From God to Mammon: the **Sheraton Diana Majestic** (*see p47*) was originally part of a vast pleasure complex known as the Kursaal. Along with a theatre and a restaurant, the hotel was constructed in 1907-8, adjacent to the city's first public swimming pool (*see also p18* **First things first**). The Kursaal became the focus of Milan's leisure activities in the early part of the 20th century. The theatre was later converted to a cinema before its present, more glamorous incarnation as the Gucci showroom, where runway shows are staged during Fashion Week.

The delightfully decadent **Park Hyatt Milan** (*see p39*), meanwhile, was converted from a bank. Look closely from the lovely confines of the circular lounge, and you can see the elegant banking hall, complete with pillars. The customers were clearly very well heeled – as were the people who lived in the apartments on the upper floors, which were subsequently turned into luxurious bedrooms for the hotel.

The origins of the three exquisitely furnished apartments known as **3Rooms** (*see p43*) are much more humble, but no less attractive. The four-storey building that Carla Sozzani chose for her fashion emporium 10 Corso Como – which has since grown to include a restaurant, bar, book and record store, as well as an art gallery – is typical of late 19th-century working-class housing in Milan. Known as a *casa di ringhiera*, it is characterised by apartments leading off railed open walkways that overlook a central courtyard. In the case of 10 Corso Como, the latter is now a tea garden.

seventh floor, Room 74 has floor-to-ceiling windows that offer views of the Duomo, while Room 51 has a small terrace.

Bar. No-smoking rooms. Parking (€21 per day). Restaurant. Room service. TV.

STRAF

Via San Raffaele 3 (02 805 081/fax 02 8909 5294/ www.straf.it). Metro Duomo. **Rates** €257-€514 double. **Credit** AmEx, DC, MC, V. **Map** p251 E6/ p252 E6 **⑤**

Around the corner from the Duomo, the STRAF is an upscale hotel run by the same family that manages the Grand Hotel et de Milan (*see p45*). The sleek, ultra-modern minimalist rooms are equipped with electronic and audio-visual amenities galore, while the utterly central address makes the hotel ideal for downtown shopping. Should the weight of all those bags get you down, every room on the fifth floor is equipped with mini-spas that include electronic Japanese massage chairs and aromatherapy. Other attractions: the excellent breakfast buffet and the cooler-than-thou hotel bar (next door). Despite its chi-chi atmosphere, the STRAF is a remarkably good deal for its category.

Bar. Concierge. Disabled-adapted rooms. Gym. Internet access (dataport, web TV). Internet (high-speed). No-smoking rooms. Restaurant. Room service. TV (free movies).

King. *See p44.*

Moderate

Hotel Gran Duca di York

Via Moneta 1A (02 874 863/fax 02 869 0344/ www.ducadiyork.com). Metro Cordusio/tram 2, 3, 14, 24, 27. **Rates** €98-€118 single; €178-€218 double. **Credit** AmEx, MC, V. **Map** p250 D7/p252 D7 **⑥**

Originally built in the 18th century but given an art nouveau makeover in the 1890s, the Gran Duca di York was most recently refurbished in 2004. Situated within easy walking distance of piazza del Duomo, yet away from the traffic, the hotel offers great value by Milan standards. The peaceful rooms are plain yet comfortable. If you want one of the four that have their own terraces, make your reservations well in advance.

Bar. Concierge. No-smoking rooms. Internet. Room service. TV (pay movies).

Vecchia Milano

Via Borromei 4 (02 875 042/fax 02 8645 4292). Metro Cordusio/bus18/tram 2, 19. **Rates** €55-€85 single; €90-€145 double; €130-€160 triple. **Credit** AmEx, DC, MC, V. **Map** p250 D7/p252 D7 **⑦**

Friendly staff is just one reason guests return again and again to this small, wood-panelled hotel. The central location and reasonable prices are others. The rooms are a bit on the small side and simply furnished, but the building itself is an attractive old palazzo with an inn-like atmosphere. Parking in the very narrow streets around the hotel can be a problem, but fortunately there is a garage nearby.

Bar. Parking (€16.50 per day). Room service. TV.

Airline flights are one of the biggest producers of the global warming gas CO_2. But with **The CarbonNeutral Company** you can make your travel a little greener.

Go to **www.carbonneutral.com** to calculate your flight emissions then 'neutralise' them through international projects which save exactly the same amount of carbon dioxide.

Contact us at **shop@carbonneutral.com** or call into the office on **0870 199 99 88** for more details.

CarbonNeutral®flights

Sforzesco & North

Expensive

Bulgari

*Via Privata Fratelli Gabba 7B (02 805 8051/
www.bulgarihotels.com). Metro Montenapoleone/
tram 1, 2.* **Rates** €560-€750 single/double; €1,500
executive suite; €3,500 Bulgari suite. **Credit** AmEx,
DC, MC, V. **Map** p249 E5/p252 E5 ❽

At the end of a private road behind the Pinacoteca
di Brera's botanic gardens, the Bulgari oozes the
same exclusivity and class as its fine jewellery, with
due attention paid to precious materials. The neu-
tral-toned bedrooms are understated yet luxurious,
with oak flooring and capacious travertine and black
marble bathrooms. Floor-to-ceiling windows open
on to teak balconies overlooking the 4,000sq m
(43,060 sq ft) private gardens surrounding the hotel.
The spa is a study in contemporary calm (*see p139*
Shopping and flopping), and the bar is a magnet
for style-conscious locals as well as hotel guests –
drinks are served on the terrace in summer. The
place to stay if someone else is paying.
*Bar. Concierge. Gym. Internet (dataport). No-
smoking rooms. Parking. Restaurant. Room service.
TV.*

Principe di Savoia

*Piazza della Repubblica 17 (02 62301/fax 02
653 799/www.hotelprincipedisavoia.com). Metro
Repubblica/tram 1, 9, 11, 29, 30.* **Rates** €310-€580
single/double; €310-€920 junior suite; €400-€1,080
elegant suite; €670-€1,200 executive suite; €1,560-
€1,640 deluxe suite; €2,470-€3,850 royal suite;
€13,000 presidential suite. **Credit** AmEx, DC, MC, V.
Map p249 F4 ❾

This historic hotel, parts of which date back to 1927,
prides itself on treating its clientele like royalty
while being in tune with the times – which is to be
expected from a hotel that was the first in Italy to
install phones in all its guest rooms. While most of
the rooms are stately and traditional, complete with
lavish marble bathrooms and Acqua di Parma toi-
letries, there are also 48 for those who prefer a more
contemporary style. Frank Sinatra, Robert de Niro
and Madonna have all stayed in the presidential
suite, which boasts its own pool. Staff are efficient
and down to earth, and the gym is one of the best in
Milan, with panoramic views of the city. OK, so the
location isn't the best (it's slap bang on unwelcom-
ing Piazza della Repubblica), but it's an easy stroll
into the centre. **Photos** *p37.*
*Bar. Concierge. Disabled-adapted rooms. Gym.
Internet (high-speed/wireless). No-smoking rooms.
Parking (€40 per day). Pool (indoor). Restaurant.
Room service. Spa. TV (free movies).*

3Rooms

*Corso Como 10 (02 626 163/fax 02 2900 0760/
www.3rooms-10corsocomo.com). Metro Garibaldi/
tram 11, 29, 30, 33.* **Rates** €250-€310 suite.
Credit AmEx, DC, MC, V. **Map** p248 D4 ❿

You've browsed the boutique, gazed at the gallery
and posed at the bar… now you can even spend the
night at Milan's multi-purpose style emporium, 10
Corso Como (*see p117, p125 and p154*). Describing
itself as as a 'bed and breakfast', 3Rooms is actually three apartments, each consisting of three rooms:
bedroom, bathroom and living room (plus lots of
closet space). Each apartment occupies an entire
floor, overlooking the internal courtyard and tea garden, and is individually decorated, with furnishings
hand-picked from the iconic designers of the last century – Arne Jacobson, Eero Saarinen, Charles and
Ray Eames, Marcel Breuer and Sebastian Matta, to
name but a few. Be warned: there is no lift and the
apartments are on the second, third and fourth floors
of the building. Needless to say, given the limited
accommodation, you will have to book far ahead. 'A
true home away from home', as the press release
says. If your home looks like a room set from
Wallpaper*, that is.
*Bar. Concierge. Internet (high-speed). Restaurant.
Room service. TV.*

UNA Hotel Century

*Via F Filzi 25B (02 675 041/fax 02 6698 0602/
www.unahotels.it). Metro Centrale FS or Gioia/bus
60/tram 2, 9, 33.* **Rates** €133-€476 single suite;
€256-€476 double suite; €266-€476 executive suite.
Credit AmEx, DC, MC, V. **Map** p249 F3 ⓫

Convenient for the central station, this modern
tower-block hotel is popular with business travellers
– which means there are tempting weekend deals
to be had (sometimes the rates are slashed almost
in half). The area around the station is not particularly inviting and can be downright unpleasant at
night, but the hotel itself is set back from the main
road. On the 'executive floor', the hotel's target
customers are well catered for: all the suites have
fax machines, trouser presses and linen bed sheets.
Some rooms also come with fitness equipment. The
patio/garden is a welcome feature in summer.
*Bar. Business centre. Disabled-adapted rooms.
Gym. Internet (high-speed). No-smoking rooms.
Restaurants (2). Room service. TV (pay movies).*

Moderate

Alle Meraviglie

*Via San Tomaso 8 (02 805 1023/fax 178 225 6685/
www.allemeraviglie.it). Metro Cairoli or Cordusio/
tram 1, 3, 4, 12, 14, 24, 27.* **Rates** €118 single;
€145-€225 double. **Credit** AmEx, MC, V. **Map**
p310 A2/p312 A1 ⓬

The *meraviglie* – or wonders – that await the guest
at this lovely B&B, set just off via Dante, are ten
inviting rooms with bright white beds, lavish silk
curtains and fresh cut flowers. (Bathrooms, by contrast, are run-of-the-mill, with basic showers and
large bottles of everyday unctions.) But despite
being set in a converted townhouse, with plenty of
olde-worlde character, there are also up-to-date
touches such as free Wi-Fi connection in each room
(though only some have a TV). If you're planning to

stay in town for a while, you might consider the Milanosuites, also run by Paola Ora and her team. These mini-apartments, complete with cooking facilities, are available by the week or the month.
Bar. Concierge. Internet (wireless). No-smoking rooms. Room service.

Antica Locanda dei Mercanti

Via San Tomaso 6 (02 805 4080/fax 02 805 4090/ www.locanda.it). Metro Cordusio/tram 1, 3, 4, 12, 14, 24, 27. **Rates** €118 single; €130-€355 double. **Credit** AmEx, MC, V. **Map** p250 D6/p252 D6 ⑬
Housed in a 19th-century palazzo just off via Dante, this place feels more like a provincial inn than an urban hotel – although some may find the decor a bit on the twee side. Each room is different, but a light, updated traditional look prevails, with Lloyd Loom chairs, ceiling fans and, in some rooms, original exposed beams and four-poster beds. Fresh flowers and a range of books and magazines replace the usual TV set, but mod cons aren't ignored: there is free wireless internet access in all the rooms. Those on the top floor open on to a plant-filled terrace. Note that before you check in you need to register first at sister establishment, Alle Meraviglie (*see p43*).
Bar. Business centre. Concierge. Internet (wireless). Room service. TV.

Antica Locanda Solferino

Via Castelfidardo 2 (02 657 0129/fax 02 657 1361/ www.anticalocandasolferino.it). Metro Moscova/ bus 41, 43, 94. **Rates** €120-€160 single; €180-€230 double; €260-€300 triple; €180-€250 mini-apartments. **Credit** AmEx, MC, V. **Map** p249 E4 ⑭

This delightful hotel is set in a Napoleonic-era palazzo in the heart of the Brera district. Each of the 11 rooms features floor-to-ceiling windows, antique furniture and Daumier lithographs on the walls, creating the illusion that you've stepped into a corner of 19th-century Milan. Make reservations well in advance and ask for a room at the rear of the building if you're a light sleeper as the street outside gets very noisy. Breakfast can be served in the room.
Concierge. Internet (wireless). Room service. TV (pay movies).

King

Corso Magenta 19 (02 874 432/fax 02 8901 0798/ www.hotelkingmilano.com). Metro Cadorna/bus 18, 50, 58/tram 19, 24. **Rates** €70-€220 single; €80-€300 double; €110-€405 triple. **Credit** AmEx, DC, MC, V. **Map** p250 C6/p252 C6 ⑮
This hotel is centrally located in a picturesque part of town. Travellers with more sophisticated tastes may find the lobby, which matches Venetian stucco effects with baroque chairs, a bit off-putting. But despite the OTT interior design, the welcome is genuine, the rooms are clean, tidy and quiet, and the buffet breakfast is generous. **Photos** *p41.*
Bar. Concierge. Internet (high-speed). No-smoking rooms. Room service. TV.

London

Via Rovello 3 (02 7202 0166/fax 02 805 7037/ www.hotel-london-milan.com). Metro Cairoli/bus 18, 50, 58/tram 1, 3, 4, 7, 12, 14, 27/bus 61. **Rates** €100 single; €150 double. Breakfast €8. **Credit** MC, V. **Map** p250 D6/p252 D6 ⑯

Four Seasons Hotel Milano.

Situated a pretty little side street just round the corner from the Castello Sforzesco, the London offers good value for money. The rooms are simply furnished and a bit small, but the lobby and conversation area around the bar are welcoming and the staff are friendly and easy-going. There's a ten per cent discount if you pay cash.
Bar. Internet (high-speed). Room service. TV.

San Babila & East

Expensive

Four Seasons Hotel Milano
Via Gesù 6-8 (02 770 8167/fax 02 7708 5007/ www.fourseasons.com/milan). Metro Montenapoleone or San Babila/bus 61, 94/tram 1, 2. **Rates** €561-€687.50 single; €638-€797.50 double; €825-€6,050 suite. **Credit** AmEx, DC, MC, V. **Map** p249 E6/ p252 E6 ⓱

It may no longer be the most expensive hotel in Milan, but this deluxe hotel still rakes in the awards, and continues to be a favourite with the fashion and film crowd. No doubt they love the location, slap bang in the middle of the Quadrilatero della Moda. The hotel is housed in a 15th-century convent, although – apart from the idyllic, cloistered courtyard that many of the rooms face on to – you would never know it. Each of the spacious guest rooms is individually designed, with Fortuny fabrics and pear- and sycamore-wood furniture, as well as CD and DVD players. Some suites feature parts of the original frescoes, as do the the library bar and lobby.

The opulent marble bathrooms are kept toasty with underfloor heating and well stocked with oversized towels and plush bathrobes. As well as Il Foyer, the sleek lobby bar (which has Wi-Fi internet access), the hotel also boasts a first-rate formal restaurant, Il Teatro (*see p107*).
Bar. Business centre. Concierge. Disabled-adapted rooms. Gym. Internet access (high-speed). No-smoking rooms. Parking (€51 per day). Restaurants (2). Room service. TV (pay movies).

Grand Hotel et de Milan
Via Manzoni 29 (02 723 141/fax 02 8646 0861/www.grandhoteletdemilan.it). Metro Montenapoleone/bus 61, 94/tram 1, 2. **Rates** €528 single; €583 double; €638-€693 single/ double deluxe; €759 junior suite; €1,089 superior suite; €1,419 deluxe suite. Breakfast €35. **Credit** AmEx, DC, MC, V. **Map** p249 E6/p252 E6 ⓲

In an elegant 19th-century palazzo, the five-star Grand is as sumptuous as it gets, all marble, rich draperies and antiques. The gorgeous suites are named after illustrious past guests, such as Luchino Visconti and Maria Callas and Giuseppe Verdi (the composer called the hotel home when staying in the city, and died here in 1901). The efficient service is as discreet as it is friendly. Though the room prices seem shocking at first glance, it's worth asking about weekend rates: you may be pleasantly surprised. The refurbished Gerry's Bar is a nice place for a drink.
Bar. Concierge. Disabled-adapted rooms. Gym. Internet (high-speed/wireless). No-smoking rooms & floors. Parking (€40 per day). Restaurants (2). Room service. TV (pay movies).

LHR – JFK

The online guide to the world's greatest cities
timeout.com

Hotel Palazzo delle Stelline. *See p48.*

Sheraton Diana Majestic

*Viale Piave 42 (02 20 581/fax 02 2058 2058/
www.starwoodhotels.com/sheraton). Metro Porta
Venezia/tram 9, 29, 30.* **Rates** €214-€418 double
(single occupancy); €435 double; €315-€708 junior
suite; €1,400 suite. **Credit** AmEx, DC, MC, V.
Map p249 G5 ⑲

This five-star art nouveau-style hotel is named after
the first public swimming pool in Milan, which
opened on this site in 1842 (*see p18* **First things
first**). The pool has since been replaced with a garden and the first of many summertime outdoor cocktail bars in the city (*see p118*). The large bedrooms
are elegantly kitted out with antique furniture, while
the bathrooms have attractive marble fittings.
*Bar. Business centre. Concierge. Disabled-adapted
rooms. Gym. Internet (high-speed/wireless). No-
smoking rooms. Restaurant. Room service. TV
(pay movies).*

Moderate

San Francisco

*Viale Lombardia 55 (02 236 1009/fax 02 2668
0377/www.hotel-sanfrancisco.it). Metro Piola/bus 62,
75, 90, 91/tram 33.* **Rates** €52-€75 single; €80-€110
double; €90-€130 triple. **Credit** AmEx, DC, MC, V.

This attractive two-star hotel, with a small garden
and patio, is a find. The rooms are well lit and very
clean, with simple yet adequate furnishings, and
staff are helpful. The downside is that it's off the
beaten track, in a rather run-down area that isn't
very well connected to the centre by public transport.
*Bar. Concierge. Internet (dataport). No-smoking
rooms. Room service. TV.*

Budget

Hotel Due Giardini

*Via Benedetto Marcello 47 (02 2952 1093/fax 02
2951 6933/www.hotelduegiardini.it). Metro Centrale
FS or Lima/bus 60/tram 33.* **Rates** €55-€75 single;
€75-€130 double; €90-€165 triple. **Credit** MC, V.
Map p249 G4 ⑳

If staying in the vicinity of the Stazione Centrale is
imperative, the Hotel Due Giardini is a convenient
and pleasant choice. Housed in a two-storey townhouse in a residential street ten minutes' walk from
the station, it is one of the best-value hotels in town.
Situated on the first and second floors, the rooms are
functional and clean. Although there is no lift, someone is always available to help with luggage. The
place is true to its name, although the 'two gardens'
have been made into one, where breakfast is served
in summer. All rooms have air-conditioning.
*Bar. Concierge. Disabled-adapted rooms. No-smoking
rooms. Room service. TV.*

Nettuno

*Via Tadino 27 (02 2940 4481/fax 02 2952 3819/
www.nettunomilano.it). Metro Lima or Porta
Venezia/bus 60/tram 1, 5, 11, 33.* **Rates** €40-€90
single; €60-€150 double; €75-€180 triple; €90-€200
quad. **Credit** AmEx, DC, MC, V. **Map** p249 G4㉑

This cavernous and rather gloomy one-star hotel is
located between the main station and the centre of
town. A breakfast buffet is included, but there are
also hot and cold drinks dispensers in the lobby and
loads of bars and restaurants nearby. The rooms are
spartan, but spacious and clean, and all now have
air-conditioning and their own bathrooms.
TV.

Porta Romana & South

Moderate

Ariston

*Largo Carrobbio 2 (02 7200 0556/fax 02 7200 0914/
www.aristonhotel.com). Tram 2, 3, 14.* **Rates** €160
single; €180-€230 double; €250 triple. **Credit** AmEx,
DC, MC, V. **Map** p250 C7/p252 C7 ㉒

The Ariston is an extraordinary experiment in bio-
architectural design: the lightbulbs are energy-
efficient; the showers are designed to save water; all
the fittings are made from natural or non-toxic materials. Even the water in your tea is purified, and
organic products are served at breakfast. The location, between the centre of town and the Navigli district, is convenient, and trams stop by the entrance.
*Bar. Business centre. Concierge. Internet (high-
speed). No-smoking rooms. Parking (€25 per day).
Room service. TV.*

Canada

*Via Santa Sofia 16 (02 5830 4844/02 5830 0282/
www.canadahotel.it). Metro Crocetta/bus 94.*
Rates €87-€151 single; €121-€200 double.
Credit AmEx, DC, MC, V. **Map** p251 E8 ㉓

Housed in a mid 20th-century block overlooking a main road, at first glance this hotel doesn't seem to have much going for it. However, the professional staff and warm atmosphere more than make up for the unprepossessing exterior. The rooms are plain, but very tidy and comfortable. All have double-glazing, but it's still advisable to ask for a room overlooking the back. The trump card is the location – a ten-minute walk to the city centre.
Bar. Concierge. Internet (wireless). No-smoking rooms. Room service. TV (pay movies).

Mercure Milano Corso Genova

Via Conca del Naviglio 20 (02 5810 4141/ fax 02 8940 1012/www.mercure.com). Metro Sant' Agostino/tram 2, 14. **Rates** €87-€158 single; €124-€176 double (single occupancy); €149-€194 double; €194-€216 triple/quad.* **Credit** AmEx, DC, MC, V. **Map** p250 C8 ㉔

An excellent choice for both business travellers and families, this comfortable three-star hotel is situated in a quiet and surprisingly green corner of Milan, close to the Navigli district, with its bars and restaurants. The centre of town is just ten minutes' walk away, and you can even borrow a bike to get there.
Bar. Concierge. Internet (high-speed/wireless). No-smoking rooms. TV (pay movies).

Sant'Ambrogio & West

Moderate

Antica Locanda Leonardo

Corso Magenta 78 (02 463 317/4801 4197/fax 02 4801 9012/www.leoloc.com). Metro Cadorna/bus 18, 50, 58/tram 19, 24. **Rates** €95 single; €150-€205 double; €255 triple; €280 quad.* **Credit** AmEx, DC, MC, V. **Map** p250 B6 ㉕

An immaculate little hotel set back from busy corso Magenta, within easy walking distance of Santa Maria delle Grazie and Leonardo's *Last Supper*. The property is in a late 19th-century palazzo, and the rooms are all tastefully decorated with modern or antique wooden furniture (some have a Japanese feel to them, as a nod to one of the owners). There is also a cosy breakfast/bar area where tea and cakes are served. The hotel has been managed by the same courteous and attentive family for more than 40 years, and it shows in the attention to detail. Ask for a room overlooking the flower-filled courtyard.
Bar. Concierge. Internet (wireless). Room service. TV.

Ariosto

Via Ariosto 22 (02 481 7844/fax 02 498 0516/ www.hotelariosto.com). Metro Conciliazione/bus 68/ tram 19, 30. **Rates** €160 single; €180-€230 double; €250 triple.* **Credit** AmEx, DC, MC, V. **Map** p248 A5 ㉖

Via Ariosto is an elegant residential street, handy for both the central sights and the Fiera. The hotel is airy and well lit, with a beautiful art nouveau staircase. All the rooms have double-glazing, parquet flooring, plus marble tiles in the bathrooms; a few

also have walk-in wardrobes. The TVs have a built-in VCR, and videos in different languages are available from reception at no charge. There is also a small, attractive patio garden. The bar and restaurant area resembles a cafeteria – so if you're after ambience, you might want to eat out. There's free internet access in the lobby.
Bar. Business centre. Concierge. Internet (high-speed). No-smoking rooms. Parking (€25 per day). Restaurant. Room service. TV.

Hotel Palazzo delle Stelline

Corso Magenta 61 (02 481 8431/fax 02 4851 9097/ www.hotelpalazzostelline.it). Metro Cadorna/bus 18, 50, 58/tram 19, 24. **Rates** €107 single; €127 single superior; €160 double; €190 suite.* **Credit** AmEx, DC, MC, V. **Map** p250 B6 ㉗

This hotel and conference centre is housed in a beautiful 15th-century palazzo with arched cloisters overlooking a grass courtyard and a huge magnolia tree. The tastefully furnished rooms offer total privacy, cocooned from the hubbub of the city. Leonardo da Vinci is said to have grown vines on this site while painting *The Last Supper* at the Santa Maria delle Grazie monastery across the road. **Photo** *p47.*
Bar. Business centre. Concierge. Disabled-adapted suite. Internet. No-smoking rooms. TV (pay movies).

Zurigo

Corso Italia 11A (02 7202 2260/fax 02 7200 0013/ www.hotelzurigo.com). Metro Missori/tram 15. **Rates** €160 single; €180-€230 double; €250 triple.* **Credit** AmEx, DC, MC, V. **Map** p250 D7 ㉘

This hotel is a bad advertisement for itself. The front door opens off a busy, cobblestone street at a major intersection in downtown Milan, with buses zooming past and trams clanking by every few minutes. Still, no need to worry. None of the rooms overlooks the street. Indeed, the entire place is very quiet and peaceful. The rooms are, without a doubt, on the small side, but they are cosy, with original mosaic floors. Free bike hire is available for those brave enough to pedal about in Milan traffic. For everyone else, it's a ten-minute stroll to piazza del Duomo.
Bar. Business centre. Concierge. Internet (high-speed). No-smoking rooms. Parking (€25 per day). Room service. TV.

Budget

Ostello Piero Rotta

Viale Salmoiraghi 1 (02 3926 7095/fax 02 330 0191/www.ostellionline.org). Metro Lotto or QT8/ bus 48, 68, 78, 90, 91. **Rates** €19 per person. **Credit** MC, V.

The only youth hostel in Milan is out in the suburbs near the San Siro football stadium, though the nearby Lotto metro station makes it easy to reach the centre. The garden provides a welcome escape from city traffic. The staff are not exactly falling over themselves to be helpful and friendly – but that doesn't stop the place being full most of the time, no doubt because of the rates (which include breakfast).

Sightseeing

Introduction

The lie of the land.

A visitor's first impressions of Milan can sit oddly with the traditional notion of 'Bella Italia' – there are no olive groves, or cypress trees; instead, it's usually the dirt, traffic and graffiti that people notice first here. But look closer and you'll find a sophisticated – and fun – place.

Two of Milan's museums stand as metaphors for the city. The **Museo Poldi Pezzoli** (*see p58*) contains just the right amount of well-chosen objects to stimulate your curiosity without being overwhelming. Meanwhile, the **Museo Nazionale della Scienza e della Tecnologia Leonardo da Vinci** (*see p90*) encapsulates the city's winning blend of ancient and modern: housed in a 16th-century monastery, it simultaneously points firmly to the present day and the future by virtue of its collection. (It's worth remembering that 25 per cent of Milan's buildings were

destroyed or became uninhabitable during Allied bombings – this partly explains the striking contrast between old and new.)

As well as culture, there is beauty in Milan, and in surprising abundance. Much of it is hidden behind the imposing granite façades of the numerous *palazzi* – the city is famous for its beautiful courtyards. Once a year, usually on the third weekend of March, the FAI (Fondo per l'Ambiente Italiano) organises a grand 'open courtyard' day across Italy (*see p144*). For one weekend, the courtyards of some of Milan's private *palazzi* are thrown open to the public. If you're lucky enough to be in the city during this celebration, take advantage of it.

MILAN ON FOOT

Large sections of the centre have been given over to pedestrians. In addition to the principal shopping thoroughfares – corso Vittorio Emanuele II and piazza del Duomo – via dei Mercanti and via Dante have been turned into car-free zones, creating a single pedestrian corridor that runs from the Castello Sforzesco all the way to San Babila. Via Garibaldi and corso Como have also been pedestrianised, and similar projects are underway in other areas.

On many Sundays throughout the year, when pollution levels get too high, the council bans cars from the city. There is no way to predict when these *divieti* will take place; they are usually announced by local news services just a few days in advance. But if you happen to catch one of these car-free days, you'll have all of downtown to roam through, accompanied only by taxis and Milanese families.

MILAN BY THE BOOK

Paradoxically, the relative culture gap between Milan and other Italian cities – notably Rome, Florence and Venice – can work in your favour. You can probably visit all of Milan's major sights in well under a week (*see p51* **Must-see Milan**). Many of the city's main attractions are grouped around the central piazza Duomo, home to the city's mammoth Duomo (*see p52*) and its elegant Galleria Vittorio Emanuele II (*see p52*). From here you can reach the other main sights – including the Pinacoteca di Brera (*see p59*), Santa Maria delle Grazie (housing *The Last Supper, see p94* **Supper time**), the Castello Sforzesco (*see p64*) and the Navigli (*see p88*) – in less than 20 minutes on foot.

MILAN'S CHURCHES

More than 100 smaller churches dot the cityscape, providing pleasant surprises. Many of them are all but lost amid the bustle of downtown Milan, and are oases for the harried tourist. Almost without exception, these buildings are first and foremost active houses of worship. This means dress codes (bare shoulders and/or legs are frowned upon) and variable visiting hours. Keep quiet inside churches; a raised voice could get you ejected. Some churches have coin-operated lighting systems, audio-visual aids and computerised displays (usually in Italian, sometimes in English) – bring loose change.

MILAN'S MUSEUMS AND GALLERIES

Milan's major museums and galleries generally stay open throughout the day, and some remain open until 10pm or later one night a week; however, many shut on a Monday.

Admission policy for the city's collections has altered somewhat since our last edition. While many attractions continue to offer free admission, some museums have begun to charge a small fee. Most offer discounts for students and over-60s, especially if you can demonstrate EU citizenship. Bring appropriate ID, though it's worth asking for a *sconto* (discount) even if you have forgotten it. Many galleries and museums stop issuing tickets 30 to 45 minutes before closing time: we've tried to include last entry times where relevant.

TICKETS AND BOOKING

Booking is essential for Leonardo's *Last Supper* (*see p94* **Supper time**), though last-minute cancellations may allow you to get in without a reservation if you're prepared to wait. Many museums and galleries require reservations for groups of seven or more. During the Settimana dei Beni Culturali (Cultural Heritage Week, *see p144*), which is usually held in early spring, all publicly owned museums and sites have extended visiting hours and are free of charge.

GUIDED TOURS

Milan's tourist office (via Marconi 1, 02 7252 4301, www.milanoinfotourist.com; *see also p234*) offers information on tours, as well as tickets for guided bus tours (depart 9.30am Tue-Sun from the tourist office). The APT also runs a three-hour tour with stops at the Castello Sforzesco and Leonardo da Vinci's *Last Supper* (€50 including entry fees).

Fun ways of seeing the city – especially if you have kids in tow – are by tourist tram and open-air tourist bus; both had been suspended before this guide went to press, but there was talk of them being reintroduced in future (ask at the tourist office for further details).

Other guided tour options include:
● Centro Guide Milano (via Marconi 1, 02 8645 0433, www.centroguidemilano.net), a non-profit organisation, offers tours in and around Milan.
● Hello Milano (02 2952 0570, www.friend inmilan.co.uk) offers two-hour personalised tours of the city (€100).
● Sophisticated Italy (02 4819 6675, www. sophisticateditaly.com) has tours for small groups or individuals to experience Lombard food and wine, gardens and golf courses.

Must-see Milan

Thanks to the rising importance of Malpensa airport as an international hub and Milan's prominence as a business and shopping metropolis, an increasing number of tourists hit the city for quick one- and two-day stopovers. Here are a few suggestions for what to do in under 48 hours.
● Check out the **Duomo** (*see p52*). If the weather is fine, pay the surcharge and go up on the roof; you'll enjoy an unbeatable view.
● The **Pinacoteca di Brera** (*see p69*) is a quick five-minute walk from piazza Duomo and boasts the best art collection in the city.
● Walk from piazza Duomo up **via Dante** (*see p64*), a wide pedestrian boulevard packed with shops, bars and cafés. If you're hungry, try something from Garbagnati, a famous Milan bakery located halfway up the boulevard.
● Visit the **Castello Sforzesco** (*see p64*). This Renaissance jewel is the city's centrepiece, housing a number of eclectic museum collections, including rare musical instruments, drawings by Leonardo da Vinci and medieval arms. Entrance to several of the collections is free, so take a gander gratis.
● Visit **Santa Maria delle Grazie** (*see p93*). If you haven't already booked a ticket, your chances of getting in to see Leonardo's *Last Supper* are slim, but they do exist. No luck? Just check out the church and cloister instead.
● Take a break in one of the cafés in **Galleria Vittorio Emanuele II** (*see p52*) for a Milanese classic – the *aperitivo*. Your drinks may be overpriced but will include a few nibbles, as well as some of the best people-watching in the city.

The Duomo & Central Milan

It took 500 years to build – so you can take your time appreciating it.

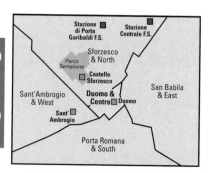

Around the Duomo

Milan, a city so closely associated with the most up-to-date, cutting-edge fashion, and which spearheads the financial growth of Italy today, centres on a building that took half a millennium to construct, the third largest cathedral in the world, the **Duomo** (*see below*) is Milan's jewel, enormous and resplendent, a meeting place and an essential stop on any itinerary. The square in front of it, the **piazza del Duomo**, is the city's beating heart, and you're likely to find yourself walking across it several times a day.

Buildings in the area immediately around the cathedral provide the most striking contrast of this old versus new, with the few medieval buildings that survived heavy World War II bombings tucked in between grey, modern office buildings and parking garages.

Joining the piazza with the other main square in central Milan, **piazza della Scala**, is the magnificent glass-roofed **Galleria Vittorio Emanuele II** (*see p57*), a shopping arcade that has a unique place in the affections of even the most hardened Milanese businessman. The coffee may be pricey, but you'll appreciate the people-watching opportunities.

Back in piazza del Duomo, the tourist office (*see p233*) is located just south of the Duomo steps, though it is likely to move to a temporary site on the square some time in 2006. Staff probably do have the information you want,

you just have to know how to ask for it (try a big smile, it works wonders). From here you can't miss, nor should you, the **Palazzo Reale** (*see p57*), a building whose protracted and fragmented history is almost as interesting as the numerous temporary exhibitions it holds. Part of the Palazzo Reale is also home to the **Museo del Duomo**, although this is closed for refurbishment until at least 2007. When it opens again, you will once more be able to see sculpture, furniture and stained glass that occupied the Duomo between the 14th and 19th centuries, as well as Jacopo Tintoretto's *Christ in the Temple* (1530).

Duomo

Piazza del Duomo (02 8646 3456). Metro Duomo/bus 50, 54/tram 1, 2, 3, 12, 14, 15, 23, 24, 27. **Open** *Church 6.45am-6.45pm daily. Treasury & crypt 9.30am-12.30pm, 2-6pm Mon-Fri; 9.30am-12.30pm, 2-5pm Sat; 1-3.30pm Sun. Baptistery & early Christian excavations 9.30am-5pm daily. Roof Nov-Feb 9am-4.15pm daily. Mar-Oct 9am-5.45pm daily.* **Admission** *Church free. Treasury & crypt €1. Baptistery & early Christian excavations €1.50. Roof €6 by lift; €4 on foot.* **Map** *p251 E7/p252 E7.*

Standing proudly on the piazza del Duomo, the third largest church in Christendom (topped only by St Peter's in Rome and the cathedral in Seville), the Duomo truly is a joy to behold. Although the essential elements were in place by 1391, the Duomo took the best part of 500 years to build. Even now the building work continues: in 2002 a five-year project to clean the façade was undertaken, meaning that visitors won't be able to appreciate the full mind-blowing beauty of the structure again until 2007.

The Duomo was begun in brick, but upgraded to marble as its architects realised the grandiosity of the project on which they were working. It now stands proudly, adorned with Gothic spires and an astonishing wealth of statues, and adored by visiting art and architecture aficionados. As generations of Lombard builders and architects argued with French and German master stone-cutters about the best course to proceed in their mammoth task, an enormous array of styles was unleashed.

Galleria Vittorio Emanuele II. See p57.

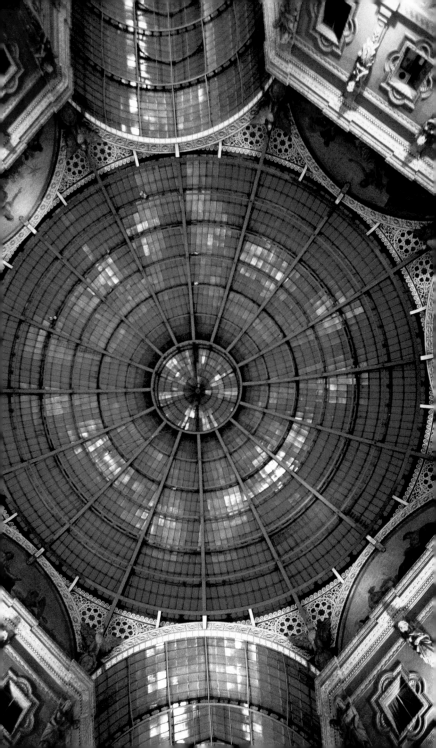

red cell ●◐◯

FITNESS DEPARTMENT

GROUP EXERCISE

PERSONAL TRAINING

DAINAMI®

CYCLING

OASI - WATER SPACE

COMFORT ZONE

GOLF INDOOR

SQUASH

SPA DOWNTOWN

DOWNTOWN HEALTHY FOOD

DOWNTOWN TERRACE

DOWNTOWN MEETING AREA

ACCESSORY SERVICE

GO COPPOLA HAIR STORE

We can't promise everything

DOWN TOWN PALESTRE

TUTTE LE TUE PASSIONI

Construction began in 1386 by order of Bishop Antonio da Saluzzo on a site that had been associated with places of worship since the third century (a Roman temple to the goddess Minerva once stood here). On the orders of Gian Galeazzo Visconti, then ruler of Milan, Lombardian terracotta stone was eschewed in favour of Condoglian marble shipped from Lake Maggiore on the Ticino river, and then along the Navigli, a network of canals in southern Milan built especially for the purpose.

Although consecrated in 1418, the cathedral remained incomplete for centuries. Politics, physical setbacks (a pink granite column sank in Lake Maggiore while in transport), a lack of money and downright indifference kept the project on permanent standby. Finally, early in the 19th century, the façade was put on the church by order of none other than Napoleon Bonaparte; he kick-started the final stages of construction before crowning himself king of Italy here in 1805.

The exterior

A staggering 3,500 statues adorn the Duomo, about two thirds of them on the exterior. The oldest are around the apse end, which was built from 1386 to 1447; those along the sides were added as the building work progressed, between the late 15th and early 18th centuries. The façade is baroque up to the first order of windows and neo-Gothic above. The five bronze doors that provide access to the Duomo were each sculpted by a different artist between 1840 and 1965 according to particular themes.

To appreciate the statues and 135 spires fully, take the lift (near the back of the Duomo, on the left-hand side) to the roof from where, on clear days, you also get breathtaking views of the Alps. A roof visit also brings you closer to the Madonnina (1774) – the gilded copper figure of Mary on the church's highest spire – which is the icon dearest to the hearts of the Milanese (see p56 **Golden girl**).

The interior

The 52 pillars of the five-aisled Duomo correspond to the weeks of the year. On their capitals, imposing statues of saints stretch up into the cross vaults of the ceiling, creating a vertiginous effect. On the floor near the main entrance is a sundial installed in 1768 by astronomers from the Accademia di Brera, placed so that it is struck by a ray of sunlight breaking through a hole in the opposite wall. On the summer solstice (21 June), the ray strikes the tongue of bronze set in the floor; while on the winter solstice (21 December), the ray of light stretches out to reach the meridian. This sundial is so precise that at one time it was used to regulate clocks throughout the city.

In the first chapel on the right is the 11th-century sarcophagus of Bishop Ariberto d'Intimiano and a 17th-century plaque commemorating the founding of the Duomo. With scenes from the life of Christ, the oldest of the stained-glass windows in the next three chapels was made in 1470-75 and is in the fifth bay on the right.

In the crossing of the transept, the presbytery floor is worn by the passage of the many millions of pilgrims who have visited the Duomo over the centuries; Cardinal-saint Carlo Borromeo wanted the Duomo to serve as his model Counter-Reformation church. Flanking the 15th-century high altar are two gilded copper pulpits, both 16th-century works. The organ is also here, its wooden shutters painted with Bible scenes by Giovanni Ambrogio Figino, Camillo Procaccini and Giuseppe Meda.

A nail allegedly from Jesus' cross hangs at the apex of the apse's vaulted roof. Once a year, on the Saturday closest to 14 September (prior to the beginning of vespers), the archbishop ascends to the apex to retrieve the nail, moving slowly and solemnly up through the air in the Duomo's decorated wooden *nivola* – an angel-studded basket first constructed in 1577 under orders by Carlo Borromeo and significantly renovated and redecorated in 1701 (when the *putti*, or angels, were added). The nail is then exhibited at the altar until the following Monday after vespers, when it is once again lifted up to its lofty position below the church ceiling.

In the right transept you'll find a funerary monument to Gian Giacomo Medici that was long attributed to Michelangelo, but is now recognised as the work of sculptor and collector Leone Leoni (1560-63).

On a pedestal in the wall opposite the Medici monument stands an arresting and remarkably lifelike statue of a flayed St Bartholomew. This incredibly accurate study of human anatomy was carved in 1562 by Marco d'Agrate, a student of Leonardo da Vinci. Above and to the right, the splendid stained glass showing St Catherine of Alexandria – who died on the original Catherine wheel – is the work of the Arcimboldo brothers (1556).

Completed in 1614, the sculpture that closes the choir – designed by Pellegrino Tibaldi and carved by Paolo de' Gazzi, Virgilio del Conte and the Taurini brothers – is a masterpiece of its time. The three tiers of the sculpture represent (above) the life of St Ambrose; (centre) the martyred saints venerated by the Milanese church; and (below) Milanese bishops Anatalone and Galdino.

The ambulatory windows blaze with fabulous 19th-century stained glass by the Bertini brothers and depict scenes from both Testaments. From the ambulatory, stairs lead down to the crypt, where Carlo Borromeo is buried. Entrances to the treasury and the choir, with its 16th-century stucco decoration, are also in the ambulatory.

In the left transept the fantastic monsters on the bronze Trivulzio Candelabra, an impressive example of medieval goldsmithing, represent the arts, professions and virtues and were created by the great 12th-century goldsmith Nicolas of Verdun. In the left aisle, the Cappella del Crocifisso (third past the transept) has stunning 16th-century stained glass.

The remains of the earlier churches of Santa Tecla and the Baptistery (where St Ambrose baptised St Augustine in 387) can be reached by descending the stairs just to the left of the entrance.

Golden girl

O mia bella Madonna
Che te brillet de lontan,
Tutta d'òra e piscinina
Ti te dòminet Milan.
Sòtta a ti se viv la vita
Se sta mai coi man in man.
Canten tucc: 'Lontan de Napoli se moeur'
Ma poeu vegnen chì a Milan...

(Oh, my beautiful little Virgin Mary/Shining from afar/All golden and small/You dominate Milan./Under you we live out our lives/We never waste our time./Everyone sings: 'Separated from Naples I die'/But then they move here to Milan.)

Outsiders may find it hard to grasp just what's so special about the golden lady perched almost 110 metres (360 feet) up on the summit of the Duomo, but for most *milanesi* the Madonnina (literally 'little Madonna', though there's nothing petite about this Virgin, which stands at four metres/13 feet tall) is the most heartfelt symbol the metropolis has.

Many songs have been written about her, including the popular paean above. It was penned by Giuseppe D'Anzi in 1934 as a response to the southern Italian immigrants who were coming to Milan to find work and who were soon filling the nightclubs where D'Anzi sang, clamouring to hear their Neapolitan favourites.

In 1754 the directors of the Veneranda Fabbrica del Duomo, the onsite school and stoneworkers' workshop (now a museum, closed for refurbishment; *see p52*), hired sculptor Giuseppe Perego to participate in carving a section of the façade. Ten years later Perego produced the sketches for the Madonnina, and in 1774 the golden Madonna was placed atop the church's highest spire, her arms open and welcoming, her benevolent smile directed down to the industrious Milanese scampering about below.

When Mussolini was in power, he decreed that no other building in Milan should tower over the Madonnina. This rule was flouted in the late 1950s, when the Pirelli skyscraper (127 metres/416 feet) was erected. The outraged cardinal of Milan strongly advised the city to keep the statue as the highest point in the city. An 85cm-tall (33-inch) replica was placed on top of the Pirellone, restoring the Madonnina's lofty position.

At night the statue on top of the Duomo is lit from below, crowning the piazza with a golden glow on Milan's many foggy evenings. In a richer, more ornate city, the high-flying Madonnina might be lost amid the church spires. But for the Milanese she inspires, as the final verse of D'Anzi's song confirms:

...Si, vegnì senza paura
Num ve slongaremm la man
Tutt el mond a l'è paes, a s'emm d'accòrd,
Ma Milan, l'è on gran Milan.

(Yes, come without fear/we'll extend our hands to you/life is the same wherever you go, we agree/but Milan, she's a grand Milan.)

From 4 November until the Epiphany, the great *Quadroni di San Carlo*, a devotional pictorial cycle with scenes from the life of the saint, are displayed in the naves between the pillars. The works are a compendium of 17th-century Lombard painting.

Galleria Vittorio Emanuele II

Between piazza del Duomo & piazza della Scala. Metro Duomo/bus 50, 54, 65/tram 2, 12, 15, 23, 27. **Open** 24hrs daily. **Map** p251 E6/p252 E6.
One of the city's most impressive buildings, the magnificent Galleria Vittorio Emanuele II connects piazza del Duomo with piazza della Scala in grand style, its interior flanked by swanky clothes retailers, enormous media entertainment stores and cafés that'll charge you €10 for a coffee without batting an eye. An impressive cross-shaped glass-roofed arcade, 47m (157ft) long, it's known as 'Milan's living room' ('il salotto di Milano') for good reason: most of the city seems to pass through it at some point during the day, and even if you're only racing through it to get to the other side, you'll notice how it pulsates with life.

The Galleria's designer, Giuseppe Mengoni, pioneered the use of iron and glass in such a complex structure (the Eiffel Tower wasn't built until some 20 years later). The Galleria was officially inaugurated in 1867 by Vittorio Emanuele II, king of a newly united Italy but, in a tragically ironic twist of fate, Mengoni wasn't able to see it open, having fallen to his death from his own creation only a few days earlier.

The ceiling vaults are decorated with mosaics representing Asia, Africa, Europe and America. Beneath you are mosaics representing more local concerns. You will find the coats of arms of Vittorio Emanuele's Savoia family, plus the symbols of Milan (a red cross on a white field), Rome (a she-wolf), Florence (an iris) and Turin (a bull). If you can't see Turin's symbol, look out for the tourists spinning on their heels on the bull's privates – it's said to guarantee good luck. **Photo** *p53*.

Palazzo Reale

Piazza del Duomo 12 (02 875 672). Metro Duomo/ bus 50, 54/tram 1, 2, 3, 12, 14, 15, 23, 24, 27. **Open** for exhibitions only. **Admission** prices vary. **No credit cards. Map** p252 E7/p252 E7.
Constructed in the 1300s on the site of Milan's 11th-century town council office (Palazzo del Broletto Vecchio), the Palazzo Reale was initiated by the Visconti family, then updated in the 16th century as part of the series of architectural reforms under the Sforzas. The city's first theatre company performed at the on-site theatre in 1598, and Mozart played here as a child.

The theatre burned down in 1776 and was replaced by the Teatro alla Scala (*see p59*), whose architect, Giuseppe Piermarini, also gave the palazzo its neo-classical look when he was commissioned to design a residence for Archduke Ferdinand of Austria in the 1770s. Only a fraction of his stuccos and frescoes survived Allied bombing, but

the Sala delle Cariatidi remains in an interesting state of semi-dereliction. Inside the palazzo, the Museo della Reggia shows the splendour of life at court between 1781 and 1860, with rooms devoted to tapestries and lanterns. Some 1,000sq m (10,750sq feet) of exhibition space were recently opened up, including the Appartamento di Riserva (private rooms), frescoed in Late Empire style and decorated with original soft furnishings.

The palazzo also contains, in a nearby building, the Museo del Duomo (closed until at least 2007; *see also p52*), and hosts major exhibitions too – a high-profile Caravaggio retrospective most recently. In the warmer months you may find film screenings or jazz concerts in the palazzo's two courtyards; check local press or the tourist office for details.

Around piazza della Scala

Coming out of the northern end of the Galleria Vittorio Emanuele II, you emerge into **piazza della Scala**, whose name is intimately connected with **Teatro alla Scala** (*see p59*) on its north-western edge, one of the most celebrated opera houses in the world. Partly because its doors are kept closed throughout the day, La Scala may not seem particularly impressive from outside, but buy a ticket to the adjoining **Museo del Teatro** (*see p59*) – or better still, see a performance (*see p165*) – and the magnificence of its lavish auditorium will soon become apparent. On the opposite side of the square, and on the right as you exit the Galleria, sits **Palazzo Marino** (*see p59*), created for a tax-collecting banker. It's now the city hall. Between La Scala and Palazzo Marino, a statue of Leonardo da Vinci presides over the square.

Nearby, in its eponymous piazza, the Jesuits' baroque church of **San Fedele** (*see p59*) faces a statue of the author Alessandro Manzoni – one of Italy's greatest writers. **Casa del Manzoni** (*see p58*), the novelist's perfectly preserved house, is just around the corner, but you will first have to pass the curious **Casa degli Omenoni** (via Omenoni 3; 1565), with its eight stone sentries of Atlas made from solid stone, sculpted by Antonio Abbondio, and **Palazzo Belgioioso** (piazza Belgioioso 2), designed by Giuseppe Piermarini in 1777-81 for Alberico XIII di Belgioioso d'Este; his family's heraldic symbols figure large in the façade's decoration. Adjacent to the palazzo is the classy Boeucc, Milan's oldest restaurant.

West of piazza della Scala, the 18th-century **Palazzo Clerici** (via Clerici 5, 02 863 313 204) has marvellous rococo interiors, and frescoes by Giambattista Tiepolo. The palazzo is open by appointment only. In the other direction, on via Manzoni, you'll find two neo-classical buildings

Teatro alla Scala. *See p59.*

overseen by Luigi Canonica around 1830, **Palazzo Anguissola** (No.10) and **Palazzo Brentani** (No.6), a former headquarters of the Piedmontese government. Nestling between similarly impressive façades along the street is the entrance to the **Museo Poldi Pezzoli** (*see p59*). This late 19th-century Milanese noble domicile holds one of the most prestigious collections of European art, furniture and *objets*.

Casa del Manzoni

Via Morone 1 (02 8646 0403/www.museidelcentro. mi.it). Metro Montenapoleone/bus 61/tram 1, 2. **Open** 9am-noon, 2-4pm Tue-Fri. **Admission** free. **Map** p251 E6/p252 E6.

One of the Casa's friendly attendants will lead you to the perfectly preserved private studies of the great Alessandro Manzoni (1785-1873) and his friend Tommaso Grossi (1791-1853). Second only to Dante in the Italian literature stakes, Manzoni wrote

I promessi sposi (*The Betrothed*), a classic story of frustrated love in the vernacular, in the 1820s. Upstairs is a collection of personal effects, early editions and the room where Manzoni died, after falling on the steps of nearby San Fedele (*see below*) in 1873. The building also houses the Centro Nazionale Studi Manzoniani.

Museo Poldi Pezzoli

Via Manzoni 12 (02 794 889/02 796 334/www. museopoldipezzoli.it). Metro Montenapoleone/ bus 61, 94/tram 1, 2. **Open** 10am-6pm Tue-Sun. **Admission** €7; €5 concessions. **Credit** MC, V. **Map** p251 E6/p252 E6.

A museum that in some sense defines the essence of Milan's attraction, the Museo Poldi Pezzoli is well loved by both locals and visitors, all of whom think of it as something of an underappreciated treat. It is just the right size, with navigable collections of carefully chosen items. Giuseppe and Rosa Poldi Pezzoli, two notable art enthusiasts, left their collections and their strong aesthetic judgement to their son, Gian Giacomo. He expanded the collections, amassing armoured suits and weapons, before graduating to jewellery, tapestries, glasswork, porcelain, paintings, books and statuary. A room upstairs contains a fabulous selection of intricate early timepieces. The paintings are perhaps most widely admired, and include Pollaiuolo's *Portrait of a Young Woman*, Vincenzo Foppa's *Portrait of Francesco Brivio* and Botticelli's *Virgin with Child*.

The building was opened to the public in 1881, to coincide with the National Exhibition, and it exudes the loving care with which the collection was amassed. After Allied bombing in 1943 the Poldi Pezzoli's curators decided to rebuild into a more museum-like space, with labels on pictures. Some consider the Museo Bagatti-Valsecchi (*see p73*) more authentic, retaining as it does the feel of a private collector's house. Ultimately it's a futile debate: it would be a shame to miss either collection.

Palazzo Marino

Piazza della Scala 2 (no phone). Metro Duomo/ bus 61/tram 1, 2. Closed to the public. **Map** p251 E6/p252 E6.

Although you can't enter the Palazzo Marino (it's been the city government HQ since 1861), you can enjoy its interesting history from all four (out)sides. The architect Galeazzo Alessi was commissioned in 1558 by Tommaso Marino, a banker from Genoa who collected taxes in Milan. Marino wanted to impress a noble Venetian lady, and Alessi was instructed: 'When finished, it should be the finest palazzo of Christendom.' The ruse seems to have worked, as Marino married her. However, his financial ostentation irritated the locals, who predicted the palazzo, 'built by stealing, would either burn, fall into disrepair, or be stolen by another thief'. Well, Marino died in financial ruin, and the Austrian army took over the palazzo in 1814, but the building stands unburned for now (though someone did try to plant a bomb there in 1997).

San Fedele

Piazza San Fedele (02 863 521/www.gesuiti.it). Metro Duomo/bus 61/tram 1, 2. **Open** 7.30am-1.15pm, 4-7pm daily. **Admission** free. **Map** p251 E6/p252 E6.

This imposing baroque church is the Milanese headquarters of the Jesuit order. It was designed by Pellegrino Tibaldi in 1569 as an exemplary Counter-Reformation church. Note its single nave, an invention that allowed the priest to keep his eye on the whole congregation. The cupola, crypt and choir were added by Francesco Maria Ricchini between 1633 and 1652. The carved wooden choir stalls in the apse were lifted from Santa Maria della Scala, the church demolished to make way for the Teatro alla Scala.

San Fedele is a veritable *Who's Who* of Milanese baroque and mannerist painting. In the first chapel on the right is Il Cerano's *Vision of St Ignatius* (c1622); in a room leading to the sacristy beyond the second chapel on the right are a *Transfiguration* and *Virgin and Child* by Bernardino Campi (1565). The exuberant carvings on the wooden confessionals and the sacristy (designed by Ricchini and executed by Daniele Ferrari in 1569) help liven up the edifice's Counter-Reformation sobriety. After two years of preparation, restoration work finally began in 2006 on the time-ravaged façade.

Teatro alla Scala & Museo Teatrale alla Scala

Piazza della Scala (02 7200 3744/www.teatro allascala.org). Metro Duomo/bus 61/tram 1, 2. **Open** 9am-12.30pm (last entry noon), 1-5.30pm daily (last entry 5pm). **Admission** Museum €5; €2.50-€4 concessions. **Credit** AmEx, DC, MC, V. **Map** p251 E6/p252 E6.

Cognoscenti travel the world over to pay their respects at La Scala opera house – it attracts stars to both its stage and its audience. When the season begins on 7 December (the feast of Sant'Ambrogio, Milan's much-loved patron saint), paparazzi, gossip TV and even network news descend to catch snaps of the glamorous, fur- and jewel-clad ladies and their suave male companions. But the real stuff happens on the stage, where a consistently excellent line-up of companies regularly raises the roof.

The opera house takes its name from Santa Maria della Scala, the 1381 church that once stood on the same site. It was commissioned by Regina della Scala, wife of Bernabò Visconti, but torn down in 1776, when the Palazzo Reale (*see p57*) was damaged by a fire, leaving the city with no principal theatre. Giuseppe Piermarini was given the task of building a replacement – and what a fine job he did: with its massive stage and seats for 2,015, La Scala is one of Europe's biggest theatres and boasts some of the best acoustics in the world.

It was inaugurated in 1778 with an opera by Antonio Salieri; many of the best-known works of Puccini, Verdi, Bellini and others premièred here. La Scala is also a significant symbol of national pride.

Sightseeing

Palazzo Clerici.
See p57.

Walk on A matter of styles

The Duomo famously took five centuries to build, but rather than appearing to be a mish-mash of styles, it is a harmonious, glorious whole. Equally, the centre of Milan is home to some interesting, lesser-known buildings whose contrasting styles seem to provide a synopsis of the city's history.

A perfect place to begin is **piazza San Sepolcro**. The square itself was part of the forum in Roman times – indeed, Roman remains can be seen in the crypt of the church of **San Sepolcro** (see p63). The façade was renovated in 1717 and then again between 1894 and 1897. More obvious period juxtapositions can be seen opposite the church, on the **Palazzo Castani**, now a police station. The left side is distinctly 1930s, yet slots well into the 18th-century renovation of a late 15th-century façade, the original portal of which remains. This is decorated with medallions featuring portraits of Francesco Sforza as well as, a long way from home, Romulus and Remus.

Next, slip down via Valpetrosa, cross via Torino, and into via della Palla. This leads into **piazza Sant'Alessandro**. If you like baroque, step inside the church of the same name; it's the most OTT example of this style in Milan. The two vast confessionals flanking the altar almost defy description. Marble, inlays, gilt bronze – no expense was spared.

Back to the real world and, heading east, to **piazza Missori**. Look up and to the right and see a high rise in a low-rise city: the **Torre Velasca** (see p82), inaugurated in 1958. The tower takes its name from the

piazza on which it stands, which was created in 1651 by the city's Spanish governor, Juan Fernandez de Velasco. Some 100 metres (330 feet) high, the 26-storey office building has a protruding, cantilevered upper section reminiscent of a medieval tower – although the architects, Studio BBPR, refuted such a claim at the time.

Next, walk up via Mazzini, named after one of the architects of Italian unity. Turn left up via Speronari and into via Falcone for the church of **Santa Maria presso San Satiro** (see p63), with its trompe l'oeil apse.

For a culinary reward after all that pavement pounding, retrace your steps to via Speronari, then cross over via Torino into via Spadari and where you'll find **Peck**, an altogether more modern monument – this time to food and drink (see p107 **The taste maker**).

Destroyed by a night of heavy bombing during World War II, it was swiftly rebuilt after the war's close and reinaugurated in 1946 with an opera conducted by one of Milan's favourites, Arturo Toscanini. Three years of refurbishments were recently completed, although controversy about the directorship continues (see p162 **Melodrama at La Scala**).

The museum, created in 1913, contains a collection of sculpture, autographs, paintings, costumes and other theatrical artefacts. **Photo** p58.

Around piazza Affari

The west end of piazza del Duomo does not just afford striking views of the square, it leads you into the curious via Mercanti, which once formed the epicentre of the city's medieval market. The square is flanked by **Palazzo Affari ai Giureconsulti**, a magnificent building that was once the headquarters of the College of Noble Doctors, which trained Milan's highest-ranking civil servants, and **Palazzo della Ragione** (see p63) – built 1228-33 by Oldrado da Tresseno (then podestà, or city leader) to symbolise and effect the independence Milan had won from its Germanic rulers in the 12th century.

Piazza dei Mercanti was traditionally where Milan's craftsmen and artisans set up shop – a fact reflected in the various street names describing activities that took place there: via Spadari (sword-makers), via Cappellari (milliners) and via Armorari (armourers), to name but a few. Appropriately, the area around

Santa Maria presso San Satiro. *See p63.*

via Orefici (goldsmiths) is still lined with jewellery stores. The coats of arms of patrician families who lived around the piazza are much in evidence (see, for example, the **Loggia degli Osii**, on the south-west side of the square, with Matteo Visconti's shield from 1316), as are portraits of classical scholars and church fathers (for instance the 1645 **Palazzo delle Scuole Palatine**, with statues of St Augustine and the Latin poet Ausonius).

Piazza Cordusio links you to via Dante and the Castello Sforzesco, but if you follow via Meravigli westwards, then take a southerly turn, you will find yourself in 'Milan's Wall Street' – **piazza Affari**, built between 1928 and 1940. Here, the commanding grandeur of the **Palazzo della Borsa**, home to Milan's stock exchange (*borsa*), will remind you that many locals think of their city, the country's financial heavyweight, as the real capital of Italy. The *borsa* was founded in 1808, but only settled in this, its permanent home, in 1931. The Palazzo della Borsa was designed by local boy Paolo Mezzanotte and typifies the rationalist style of the late 1920s and '30s. Stand on the opposite side of piazza Affari and prepare to feel dominated by the muscular façade, all white columns and mythological figures.

Further south, continuing the financial connection, you will pass the Beaux Arts **Banca d'Italia** (piazza Edison), built 1907-12,

which takes up the best part of an entire block. Nearby there's **San Sepolcro** (*see p63*) and the unmissable **Biblioteca e Pinacoteca Ambrosiana** (*see below*), which holds a beautiful collection of art and artefacts. (It is also notable because it was from a balcony on the piazza San Sepolcro side of the Ambrosiana that Mussolini first explained the wonders of fascism to an attentive crowd.)

East of piazza San Sepolcro is **piazza Borromeo**, featuring a baroque statue by Dionigi Bussola of the saint who gave the square its name, and the **Palazzo Borromeo**, with its 15th-century terracotta arches and internal frescoes. Another statue of Borromeo – by Costantino Corti – stands in piazza San Sepolcro. Further south, on and off via Torino, are the churches of **San Sebastiano** and **Santa Maria presso San Satiro** (notable for its architectural optical illusion; for both, *see p63*). If you are feeling peckish after all this walking, then the place for you is most certainly Peck (*see p102 and p107* **The taste maker**), a food-lover's paradise and essential stop even on a sightseeing tour.

Biblioteca & Pinacoteca Ambrosiana

Piazza Pio XI 2 (02 806 921/www.ambrosiana.it). Metro Cordusio or Duomo/bus 50/tram 2, 3, 4, 12, 14, 19, 24, 27. **Open** *Pinacoteca* 10am-5.30pm Tue-Sun. *Library* open only to scholars. **Admission** €7.50; €4.50 concessions. **Credit** AmEx, DC, MC, V. **Map** p250 D7/p252 D7.

Cardinal Federico Borromeo conceived of this library and art gallery as part of a wider cultural project, including an art academy to train aesthetic tastes in conformity with the Counter-Reformation dictates of the Council of Trent. The academy folded in 1776, but the legacy lasts.

The Pinacoteca was founded in 1618, originally based on Borromeo's private art collection of 172 paintings, now located in rooms 1 and 4-7. This includes Titian's *Adoration of the Magi* and a portrait of a man in armour in Room 1; Jacopo Bassano's *Rest on the Flight from Egypt*, Raphael's cartoon for *The School of Athens* and Caravaggio's *Basket of Fruit* in rooms 5 and 6; and works by Flemish masters including Jan Brueghel and Paul Bril in Room 7.

Renaissance masterpieces from outside the cardinal's collection are in rooms 2 and 3, including Sandro Botticelli's *Madonna del Padiglione* and Leonardo da Vinci's *Musician*. The rest of the Pinacoteca contains later works. A lachrymose *Penitent Magdalene* by Guido Reni – darling of the Victorians – is in Room 13 on the upper floor. There are two works by Giandomenico Tiepolo in Room 17. The De Pecis' donation of 19th-century works, including a self-portrait by sculptor Antonio Canova, can be found in rooms 18 and 19. The Galbiati wing houses objects such as a lock of

Lucrezia Borgia's hair (between rooms 8 and 9) and the gloves Napoleon wore when he met his destiny at Waterloo (Room 9), while the Museo Settala is a replica of a 17th-century *Wunderkammer*: a magnificent jumble of scientific instruments, fossils, semi-precious stones, paintings and books.

The Biblioteca's collection includes Leonardo's original *Codex Atlanticus*, a copy of Virgil with marginal notes by Petrarch, an Aristotle with a commentary by Boccaccio, and autograph texts by Aquinas, Machiavelli and Galileo among others. Intriguingly, there's also a book bound in human skin – not that you're likely to see these wondrous objects: the library is open only to bona fide scholars with suitable letters of introduction. *See also p18* **First things first**.

Civico Tempio di San Sebastiano

Via Torino 28 (02 874 263). Metro Duomo/tram 2, 3, 12, 14, 15, 24. **Open** 8am-noon, 3-6.30pm Mon-Sat; 9am-noon, 3.30-6.30pm Sun. **Admission** free. **Map** p250 D7/p252 D7.

When Milan emerged from a bout of the plague in 1576, its residents heaved a sigh of relief and, to express their thanks, constructed this church on the site where the 14th-century church of San Quilino had stood – and dedicated it to the patron saint of those with contagious diseases. Pellegrino Tibaldi designed the building, though he originally planned a much higher dome; if the heavenly vision of the *Evangelists and Church Fathers* (1832) by Agostino Comerio inside the cupola makes your head spin as it is now, just imagine the effect Tibaldi was originally aiming for.

Palazzo della Ragione

Piazza Mercanti (02 7200 3358/www.comune. milano.it). Metro Duomo/bus 50, 60/tram 1, 2, 3, 12, 14, 15, 24, 27. **Open** for exhibitions only. **Admission** prices vary. **No credit cards**. **Map** p250 D6/p252 D6.

The courtyard of the Palazzo della Ragione – also known as Broletto Nuovo (from *brolo*, an old word denoting a place where justice was administered) is one of the few quiet, sheltered corners of central Milan. The palazzo was erected in 1233 by order of Oldrado da Tresseno, the then *podestà* (mayor), to serve as law courts. Oldrado's portrait can be seen in relief on the façade facing piazza del Broletto Nuovo, and he is also the subject of an equestrian statue within the arches of the *broletto*. Markets and public meetings were once held in the ground-floor porticos. People also flocked here to see hangings.

Between the second and third arches on the via Mercanti side of the Palazzo della Ragione is a relief of the *scrofa semi-lanuta* ('semi-woolly sow'), a reference to the legend that the city of Mediolanum was founded on the site where a wild sow with hairy legs (*medio* means 'half', *lanum* is 'wool') was seen running about. (Foundation legends abound, and most are equally unlikely. The theory that brothers Medio and Lano founded the city is too suspiciously

reminiscent of Rome's Romulus and Remus tale, while the idea that its name derives from the German *Mai* – 'May', for a land where it's always spring – is extremely dubious given Milan's weather.)

In 1771 the Holy Roman Empress Maria Theresa decreed the building should become an archive for deeds, and had it enlarged. Today it houses municipal offices and is closed to the public, but as one of the few remaining medieval buildings in the city, retains a sense of history: restoration work carried out in 1988 uncovered 13th-century frescoes.

San Sepolcro

Piazza San Sepolcro (no phone). Metro Cordusio or Duomo/tram 2, 3, 12, 14, 19, 24, 27. **Open** noon-2pm Mon-Fri. **Admission** free. **Map** p250 D7/p252 D7.

The forum of Roman Mediolanum occupied the area between piazza San Sepolcro and piazza Pio XI. It was here that a church dedicated to the Holy Trinity was built in 1030, only to be rebuilt in 1100 and rededicated to the Holy Sepulchre. The church underwent the usual Counter-Reformatory treatment in the early 1600s, and an 18th-century façade was replaced by a neo-Romanesque one in 1894-97. The crypt, which runs the entire length of the church, is all that remains of the original Romanesque structure. A forest of slim columns divides its five aisles, and by the apse is a 14th-century sarcophagus with reliefs of the Resurrection.

Santa Maria presso San Satiro

Via Torino 27-29 (02 874 683). Metro Duomo/ bus 54, 60, 65/tram 2, 3, 12, 14, 15, 24. **Open** 9-11.30am, 3.30-5pm daily. **Admission** free. **Map** p250 D7/p252 D7.

Satiro (or Satirus) was St Ambrose's brother. It was to this lesser-known sibling (who also became a saint) that a certain Archbishop Anspert wanted a church dedicated and he left funds for the job when he died in 876. All that remains of the early basilica is the Greek-cross Cappella della Pietà. In 1478 Renaissance genius Donato Bramante was called in to remodel the whole church in order to provide a fitting home for a 13th-century image of the Virgin that was said to have bled when attacked by a knife-wielding maniac in 1242 – and to accommodate pilgrims flocking to see it. The fresco concerned still sits on the high altar.

Bramante's gift for creating a sense of power and mass – even in a space as limited as the one occupied by this church – emerges in the powerful, barrel-vaulted central nave that ends in a trick-perspective niche that manages to simulate a deep apse within a mere 97cm (38in).

The octagonal baptistery to the right was made by Agostino de' Fondutis in 1483 to Bramante's designs. The Cappella della Pietà contains fragments of early medieval fresco decoration and a terracotta sculptural group of the Pietà from 1482-3, a typically northern Italian devotional work. The church claims the second oldest bell tower in the city, after the one at Sant'Ambrogio. **Photo** *p62*.

Sightseeing

Castello Sforzesco, Brera & Northern Milan

Arty enclaves and a fairy-tale castle.

Every year a new part of Milan claims to be 'the new Brera', but none has yet matched the district's winning combination of chic shops, thronged medieval streets and trendy cafés. The impact of the fairy-tale Castello Sforzesco, which dominates Milan's north-west, shouldn't be downplayed; it lends an air of historical distinction to the slightly less sophisticated aspects of Brera – the drinking holes, the fortune tellers and the touters of contraband designer gear.

It's no wonder that the area lures locals and tourists in equal measure; the Pinacoteca di Brera is a prime art attraction for first-timers to Milan, while the streets around it are crammed with independent contemporary galleries. Beyond the pleasant Parco Sempione, the city extends into its perennially up-and-coming fashion hub, including development-boom zones around the Porta Garibaldi train station and the Isola neighbourhood – once a left-leaning blue-collar stronghold, now a bohemian quarter and struggling artists' paradise.

In this broad area you will find remodelled Romanesque churches, the local version of Chinatown and other ethnic enclaves on via Paolo Sarpi, via Canonica, via Montello and via Bramante, plus museums, galleries, the Piccolo group theatres and more.

Castello Sforzesco & Parco Sempione

The impressive **Castello Sforzesco** (see p65) – a feast of crenellations, machicolations and watchtowers – has adapted over the last seven centuries to fulfil different roles. From ducal residence, defensive rampart and Visconti prison in the 14th and 15th centuries, and army barracks for invading Spanish, French and Austrian armies from the 16th to 19th centuries, it is now in effect a museum of museums, housing no fewer than 12 exhibition spaces.

The castle plays a central role in Milan's urban landscape, presiding over one end of a long pedestrian corridor that runs from the castle down via Dante, through piazza del

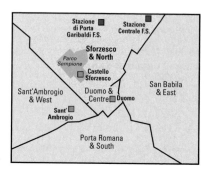

Duomo, and all the way along corso Vittorio Emanuele II to piazza San Babila.

Via Dante is itself notable for several *palazzi*, all begun under Napoleonic rule (1796-1814) and continued in the 19th century. All, that is, except Palazzo Carmagnola (No.2; not open to the public), which, despite its neo-classical façade, dates back to the 14th century and retains its original courtyard. Milanese ruler Ludovico 'il Moro' Sforza used this building to house his most illustrious guests, from da Vinci and artist/architect Donato Bramante to his mistress Cecilia Galleriani. Next door is the original **Piccolo Teatro** (see p176), founded in 1947 and now called Teatro Grassi.

Piazza Castello is cupped by the curved **foro Buonaparte**, which is intersected by the 1895 *Hero of Two Worlds* by Ettore Ximenes. The equestrian statue is dedicated to Giuseppe Garibaldi's involvement in both the Uruguayan civil war and the Italian unification movement. Walking westwards, you will find Cadorna metro and Stazione Ferrovie Nord.

Taking foro Buonaparte north-east will take you past the fascinating exhibitions of the **Museo d'Arte e Scienza** (see p68) to Teatro Strehler (Nuovo Piccolo; see p176).

Beyond Teatro Strehler and the Castello is **Parco Sempione** (see p68), a throwback to Francesco Sforza's predilection for hunting; the park once teemed with deer, hare and pheasants imported from nearby Varese and Como. These days you're much more likely to spot the thousands of Milanese canines that have been crammed into this dog-loving city.

On one side sit the Arena (*see p68*) and the recently refurbished 1906 **Acquario** (viale Gadio 2, Parco Sempione, 02 8846 5750, www.acquariocivico.mi.it), while to the west the Palazzo d'Arte (more commonly known as the **Triennale**; *see p70*) shows art, video and design installations. It's worth making it through to the other side of the park to see the **Arco della Pace** (*see p68*) an unmistakably Napoleonic neo-classical arch, presiding pompously over **corso Sempione**, Milan's answer to the Champs Elysées, strategically located on the road that links Milan and Paris.

Castello Sforzesco/ Civici Musei del Castello

Piazza Castello (02 8846 3700/www.milano castello.it). Metro Cadorna, Cairoli or Lanza/ bus 43, 57, 61, 70, 94/tram 1, 3, 4, 12, 14, 27. **Open** *Grounds* 8am-6pm daily. *Museums* 9.30am-5.30pm Tue-Sun. **Admission** *Grounds* free. *Museums* €3. **Map** p248 C6/p252 C6.

In a hypothetical Milan with no Duomo, the Castello Sforzesco would surely be the main attraction – a 15th-century castle backing on to the city's biggest park, and holding 12 high-quality museums, galleries and archival resources. Begun in 1368 by Galeazzo II Visconti as part of the city's fortifications, the castle continued to expand throughout the 14th century. Filippo Maria Visconti transformed it into a sumptuous ducal residence. Partly demolished during uprisings in 1447, it was restored to its original splendour by Francesco Sforza in the 1450s. The duke's rhetoric suggested that his rebuilding project

was designed to protect the people, but since he had just taken the city by force, it is more likely that it was his own safety he was worried about.

The court gathered here by Francesco's son Ludovico il Moro included Donato Bramante and Leonardo da Vinci, and was regarded as one of Europe's most refined. But when Ludovico was captured by the French in 1499, the castle – like the court – fell into decline.

While Milan was under French rule in the early 19th century, the castle's star-shaped bulwarks were knocked down. In the late 1800s there was talk of demolishing the rest, but luckily for the city, architect Luca Beltrami fought to preserve it, coming up with the idea of headquartering Milan's various art collections here. From 1893 until 1904, Beltrami oversaw the castle's restoration, rearranging and rebuilding unashamedly. His unorthodox efforts saved the edifice from total oblivion. Coming to a spindly point above the façade is an early 20th-century recreation of a tower originally built by the 15th-century architect Antonio Averlino, dubbed Il Filarete (hence the tower's name, Torre del Filarete).

Visitors enter via the enormous piazza d'Armi; gates lead into the Rocchetta (on the left) – the oldest part of the castle – and into the Cortile (courtyard) and Palazzo della Corte Ducale (on the right), in Renaissance style. The entrance to the Civici Musei is here.

The Castello's vast collections cover everything from Renaissance masterpieces to mummies and musical instruments. If you have the time to wander through all the collections – and you'll need most of the day for such an undertaking – you'll find it worth the effort and the entry fee (€3 when we went to press; free on Friday afternoons after 2pm).

Dogs have their day in **Parco Sempione**. *See p68.*

Comprehensive explanations of the works displayed are available (in English) in each room. The Castello also houses historical and photo archives, a print collection and archaeological and art-history libraries, which are not open to the general public. **Photo** *p68*.

Civiche Raccolte d'Arte Antica

The sculpture gallery begins on the ground floor with early Christian and medieval works, including a marble head of the Byzantine Empress Theodora. Dominating Room 2 is an equestrian statue (1363) of Bernabò Visconti by Bonino da Campione. Room 6 contains a bas-relief (1171) from the Porta Romana showing Milanese scenes after one of Barbarossa's rampages. In Room 8, the Sala delle Asse, you'll find heavily restored frescoes attributed to Leonardo. There is a series of portraits of the Sforza family attributed to Bernardino Luini in rooms 9 and 10. The Cappella Ducale (duke's chapel, Room 12) was built by Galeazzo Maria Sforza in 1472 and decorated by the leading painters of the day under the direction of Bonifacio Bembo. Room 14 has a 15th-century portal from the Milan branch of the Medici bank and a collection of arms. Although the swords are forged with fierce inscriptions ('I love peace, but I bring war'), the small size of the suits of armour makes it difficult to believe their Lilliputian wearers constituted a major threat.

In Room 15, Bambaja's masterpiece, the monument to Gaston de Foix, is a tribute to the Lombard classical style of the early 16th century. (De Foix, Louis XII's nephew, was a French military commander who died heroically in Ravenna in 1512.) This journey through Gothic and early Renaissance works of art ends with a sculpture by Michelangelo,

the *Rondanini Pietà*. The piece was first sculpted and subsequently partially destroyed and abandoned in the mid 1550s, but Michelangelo returned to it in the last year of his life, working to perfect it until his death in 1564. Even so, it is unfinished, with the remains of an earlier attempt at the Christ figure clearly visible alongside the incomplete sculpture.

Civiche Raccolte d'Arte Applicata

This section runs the whole gamut of the so-called minor arts: wrought iron (Room 28); ceramics of the world from the 15th to the 19th centuries (rooms 29 and 30; don't miss the eccentric pieces made by architect Giò Ponti (1920s) for Richard Ginori in Room 30); Italian and European porcelain (Room 31); liturgical objects, ivories and scientific instruments (Room 32); leather objects (Room 35); and goldsmith works, enamels, bronzes, textiles and wall coverings. The level of intricacy displayed in some of these objects is truly breathtaking.

Museo di Arte Applicata

Believe us, the Furniture Museum is much more exciting than it sounds, largely because the items on show are particularly precious examples principally from well-off houses, designed for aesthetic pleasure as well as functional purpose. Room reconstructions with paintings help to create a sense of context. Displays range from 16th-century furnishings up to contemporary pieces by Giò Ponti, Carlo Mollino and Ettore Sottsass.

Museo Egizio

The highlight of any Egyptian museum is always the mummy, and the Castello's is no exception, although those who know their ancient Mesopotamian history

Arch enemies: Napoleon's **Arco della Pace** was completed by Ferdinand I. *See p65.*

Grand Centrale

Love it or hate it, Milan's imposing Stazione Centrale is a local landmark on a par with the Duomo – if not quite as internationally renowned. Built between 1912 and 1931, it was designed by Florentine architect Ulisse Stacchini and heavily inspired by Union Station in Washington, DC. World War I slowed progress considerably, and it wasn't until 1925 that construction gathered force – spurred on by Mussolini's desire for a station that would reflect the might of the fascist regime.

The result is an exuberant combination of styles (Liberty dominates) on a grand scale: colossal golem-head fountains flank its imposing 207-metre (679-foot) long façade and, inside, the walls of the vast ticketing hall are embellished with bas-reliefs depicting the signs of the zodiac.

The station has also played a 'central' role in Milanese history. The royal waiting room, which has recently been refurbished for use as an exhibition space, is a reminder of the last days of the monarchy. Platform 21 has a more chilling association. In 1944 it was the starting point for a one-way journey – to Auschwitz.

In more recent times the station was the scene of mass arrivals. From the mid 1950s through to the mid '70s, workers moved from the south to work in the factories in Milan and throughout Lombardy. The city's population grew by an average of several hundred a week over that period. From the station, the new arrivals fanned out to catch trams and buses to addresses written on scraps of paper where a relative or friend waited to help them to make their first moves in the 'big city'.

Today, aside from transport, the station is a valuable resource for the city's population. The pharmacy on the first floor is open 24 hours, as is the supermarket on the ground floor, and the newsstands stay open all day Sunday (most others close at 1pm). Of course, as with any urban station, it's fertile ground for pickpockets, so keep hold of your bag or wallet.

The station is currently undergoing a massive facelift, which is likely to last into 2007. The tourist office is being moved from the first floor, and may well be moved again during the lifetime of this guide. As far as buying train tickets is concerned, however, while it's worth stopping to admire the magnificent hall, canny travellers get theirs from the Doria travel agency around the corner in piazza Luigi di Savoia. There's no extra charge – and no queues.

are likely to get equally excited by the fragments of writing, the statuettes of various grotesque divinities and reconstructed pottery. If you are interested in this period, pay a visit to the Civico Museo Archeologico (see p93).

Museo della Preistoria e Protostoria

Digging deep into Milan's history, this space tells the story of the earliest colonisers of the Lombardy region right from the (neolithic) fourth century BC to the Celts and Gauls who were beginning to be touched by Roman influence. Interesting finds from grave sites and warrior tombs liven the place up, and there is a fascinating section on the prehistoric people who lived in stilt-houses on Lombardy's lakes. One of two collections housed in the basement beneath the Cortile della Rocchetta (the other is the Museo Egizio; see p66).

Museo degli Strumenti Musicali

The castle houses one of the largest collections of musical instruments in Europe (rooms 36-37), brought together by Master Natale Gallini. In all, there are 640 instruments arranged in five sections: string, plucked, keyboard, wind and exotic. The exhibits range from the rare – including violins by Stradivarius – to the bizarre (such as pochette – pocket-sized violins used by dancing instructors).

Pinacoteca di Castello

Reopened in 2005 after a four-year restoration, this is Milan's third major *pinacoteca* (art gallery); the others are the Brera (see p69) and the Ambrosiana (see p62). The gallery proper begins in Room 20, which features a panorama of 15th-century Italian painting, including Mantegna's majestic masterpiece *Madonna and Child with Saints and Angels in Glory* (1497) and Antonello da Messina's *St Benedict* (1470), with his penetrating, suspicious gaze. The Veneto is represented by Giovanni Bellini's innocent *Madonna con Bambino* (1470s). There are also works by the Florentines, including the *Madonna dell'Umiltà* (1430s) by Filippo Lippi.

Room 21 is an extravaganza of Lombard painting from the early to late Renaissance, including Vincenzo Foppa's stoic *St Sebastian* (before 1490) and a *Noli Me Tangere* (c1508) by Bramantino. The 16th-century schools are represented by the languorous male nudes of Cesare da Sesto's San Rocco polyptych (1520s), the melting gaze of Correggio's *Madonna and Child with the Infant St John* (1517) and Moretto da Brescia's *St John the Baptist* (c1520).

Rooms 23-24, meanwhile, are full of the forced elegance and erudition of the Lombard mannerists. The Pinacoteca closes with 17th- to 18th-century

Sightseeing

The imposing **Castello Sforzesco**. See p65.

works: Bernardo Strozzi's fleshy *Berenice* (1630) and the inevitable photo-realistic views of Venice by Canaletto and Guardi. **Photo** *p69*.

Museo d'Arte e Scienza

Via Quintino Sella 4 (02 7202 2488/www.museo delcollezionista.com). Metro Cairoli or Lanza/bus 43, 57, 61, 70, 94/tram 1, 3, 4, 12, 14, 27. **Open** 10am-6pm Mon-Fri; 10am-2pm Sat. Closed 1wk Aug. **Admission** €4-€6. **Credit** MC, V. **Map** p248 D6/p252 D6.

A unique, mature and fascinating museum primarily exposing fraudulent works of art – and revealing the scientific techniques behind such study. Featuring extensive explanations (translated into English, German and French), the underground rooms guide you through fake weapons, icons, paintings and more; the ethnographic collection is superb. Don't miss the secret tunnel to the Castello in Room 14. Upstairs you are invited into the working research labs, established in 1993, which authenticate art internationally. There are also permanent exhibitions devoted to Leonardo's life and work.

Parco Sempione

Metro Cadorna, Cairoli or Lanza/bus 43, 57, 61, 70, 94/tram 1, 3, 4, 12, 14, 27, 29, 30. **Open** *Mar-Apr, Oct* 6.30am-9pm daily. *May* 6.30am-10pm daily. *June-Sept* 6.30am-11.30pm daily. *Nov-Feb* 6.30am-8pm daily. **Admission** free. **Map** p248 C5.

Parks are rare in Milan, but the city's biggest, this 47-hectare (116-acre) expanse that spreads behind Castello Sforzesco, is also its best.

Milan's French rulers began carving the park out of the remains of the ducal gardens – with their orchards, vegetable gardens and hunting reserve – in the early 1800s, but it was only in 1893 that it was landscaped, by Emilio Alemagna. He opted for the then-popular 'English garden' fashion, with winding paths, lawns, copses and a lake.

The Arena Civica, the mini-coliseum designed in 1806 by Luigi Canonica and located at the back of the park, is another addition from the city's Napoleonic period. The rulers of the Roman-inspired French Empire used it for open-air entertainment – chariot races and mock naval battles (for the latter, the arena was flooded with water from nearby canals). Today it is used for international athletic events and occasional concerts.

A handful of museums and galleries nestle in the park, including the Palazzo d'Arte (Triennale, *see p70*); near this palazzo are several abstract sculptures from the 1970s. Be sure to visit Giò Ponti's 1933 Torre Branca, next door to the Triennale, which offers visitors a sweeping, vertiginous 360° view of the entire city. At the base of the tower is designer eaterie Just Cavalli Café (02 311 817).

The Arco della Pace, at the western end of the park, was begun in 1807 to a design by Luigi Cagnola to commemorate Napoleon's victories. Work proceeded too slowly, however, and came to an abrupt halt in 1808 after Napoleon fell from power. Construction resumed in 1826 – with a few essential changes to the faces in the reliefs – and the arch was eventually inaugurated on 10 September 1838 by Austrian Emperor Ferdinand I. Among their decorative sculptures are *Chariot of Peace* by Abbondio Sangiorgio and *Four Victories* by Giovanni Putti. **Photos** *p65 and p66*.

Brera

Brera cries out to be explored. Here, antiques shops, jewellers, boutiques, snazzy bars, traditional cafés, restaurants and minimalist contemporary art galleries alternate along the cobbled streets of this slightly down-at-heel but quietly wealthy area. Formerly the craftmen's quarter, Brera has turned into an edgier extension of the city centre.

At via Brera 15, near the corner of via del Carmine, is the 17th-century **Palazzo Cusani** (not open to the public). An anecdote explains its unusual appearance: the Cusani brothers may have shared the residence in the 18th century, but they did not share taste in architectural aesthetics. It is said that they agreed to disagree, and commissioned architects separately to design their respective entrances, so one façade of the palazzo is in *barocchetto* style, by Giovanni Ruggeri, complete with ornate windows and balcony decorations, while the other is in a more traditional neo-classical style, and was carried out by Giuseppe Piermarini.

Further north along via del Carmine, in the piazza of the same name, is **Santa Maria del Carmine** (*see p71*), one of three (originally) Romanesque churches hidden in this web of roads that sadly fell prey to 19th-century restoration. (The others are **San Marco** – *see p70* – and **San Simpliciano** – *see p71*.) While Santa Maria del Carmine's baroque chapel remains intact, the current façade was added in 1879.

Back on via Brera is the **Palazzo di Brera**, built by Francesco Maria Ricchini in 1651, on the site of a 14th-century Umiliatian convent and Jesuit school. The palazzo houses the **Biblioteca Braidense**, a library with an intriguing collection of volumes as well as richly decorated interiors, an observatory and botanical garden; the Istituto Lombardo Accademia di Scienze e Lettere (Lombard Institute for Science and Art); the Accademia di Belle Arti (Academy of Fine Arts); and the **Pinacoteca di Brera** (*see below*), one of Italy's most prestigious art collections.

The Franciscan church of **Sant'Angelo** (*see p71*) stands north-east of here. From piazza Sant'Angelo, via della Moscova and largo Donegani lead to via Turati and the **Palazzo della Permanente** (via Turati 34, 02 655 1445, www.lapermanente-milano.it), a venue for temporary modern art exhibitions.

Pinacoteca di Brera

Via Brera 28 (02 722 631/reservations 02 8942 1146/www.brera.beniculturali.it). Metro Lanza or Montenapoleone/bus 61/tram 1, 2, 3, 12, 14. **Open** 8.30am-7.30pm Tue-Sun (last entry 6.45pm). **Admission** €5; €2.50 concessions; free under-18s, over-65s. **No credit cards. Map** p248 D5.

If you're only going to visit one museum while in Milan, make it this one. Often considered the supreme art collection in Lombardy, the Pinacoteca began life as a collection of paintings for students of the Accademia di Belle Arti in the same building. Paintings were harvested from churches and monasteries suppressed by the Napoleonic regime.

While it rules out any competition with the Louvre or London's National Gallery, the Pinacoteca's size ensures an accessible, easily navigable visit. The collection is modest in breadth, but exquisite in quality, covering works by major Italian artists from the 13th to the 20th centuries.

The collection includes its share of important works of art, including the exercise in foreshortening that is Andrea Mantegna's *Dead Christ*; a mournful *Pietà* by Giovanni Bellini (both in Room VI); Piero della Francesca's *Virgin and Child with Saints* (Room XXIV); the disturbingly realistic *Christ at the Column* by Donato Bramante, and Caravaggio's atmospheric *Supper at Emmaus* (Room XXIX). Titian, Tintoretto and Veronese are all here, while rooms VIII and IX contain a series of enormous works.

The palazzo was begun in 1651 by Francesco Maria Richini for the Jesuits, who wanted it to house their college, astronomical observatory and botanical garden. In 1776 part of the building was

Pinacoteca di Castello. *See p67.*

Sightseeing

Triennale

The Palazzo d'Arte was constructed in 1932-3 by Giovanni Muzio to provide a permanent home for the Esposizione Internazionale di Arti Decorative. These exhibitions of the decorative and applied arts were originally intended to be held every three years, which is why the building came to be known as the Triennale. But from glorious beginnings and enormously ambitious objectives, which put Milan on the world map as far as promoting design culture was concerned, the Triennale ran out of steam, perhaps never recovering from the shock of the attacks at the 14th fair, in 1968. (This was the year of student and workers' riots Europe-wide, and Milan was not spared.) Indeed, the idea of organising such a huge event every three years has recently been abandoned. Due to become a museum of design, which will put on display the Triennale's extensive collection of furniture, lighting and objects dating from the early 20th century, the space is currently being used as a venue for exhibitions on architecture, urban planning, industrial design, fashion and audiovisual communications. Many of the shows are on loan from other museums, while the exhibitions put on to coincide with the Milan Furniture Fair (mid April) are a highlight of the annual calendar. For the last few years, throughout May and June, the Triennale has held a festival of architecture.

Even the café on the first floor treats patrons to a sit-down tour of 20th-century chair design. The FIAT café in the Triennale gardens is open from April to October. Here, too, the seating consists of reproductions of iconic chairs by the likes of Le Corbusier. The garden also features sculptures by designers Alessandro Mendini, Ettore Sottsass and Gaetano Pesce. The bookshop on the ground floor is excellent.

Palazzo d'Arte (Triennale)

Viale Alemagna 6 (02 724 341/www. triennale.it). Metro Cadorna/bus 61, 94/ tram 1, 19, 27. **Open** 10.30am-8.30pm Tue-Sun. **Admission** varies. **Credit** AmEx, DC, MC, V. **Map** p248 C5.

allocated to the Accademia di Belle Arti, and in 1780 Giuseppe Piermarini completed the main portal. The Pinacoteca was established as a study collection, with plaster casts and drawings for the students at the academy. It was enlarged under Napoleon to house paintings from suppressed religious orders (check out the Canova statue of the notoriously diminutive French emperor in the guise of an ancient Greek athlete in the centre of the courtyard).

Today the 38 rooms are arranged in a circuit that begins and ends with 20th-century Italian painting. Another interesting sight is Gerolamo Savoldo's *Pala di Pesaro*, a 16th-century altarpiece (Room XIV).

If you have time, wander into the Orto Botanico behind the Pinacoteca (open 9am-noon Mon-Fri). Because most of the plants are herbaceous, you won't exactly be dazzled by green foliage (especially in winter), but it's a lovely little spot, and it boasts one of the oldest ginkgo biloba trees in Europe, rising over 30m (98ft) high.

San Marco

Piazza San Marco 2 (02 2900 2598). Metro Lanza/ bus 41, 43, 94/tram 3, 4, 12. **Open** 7.30am-noon, 4-7pm daily. **Admission** free. **Map** p249 E5.
San Marco was built in 1254 by the Augustinian Lanfranco Settala on the site of an earlier church that the Milanese had dedicated to Venice's patron, St Mark. This gesture was to express their thanks to the Venetians for their intervention in the battle against Frederick Barbarossa. Lanfranco's 14th-century sarcophagus still stands here in the south transept. The church's façade was redone by Carlo

Maciachini, a champion of neo-Gothic revival, while inside, nine chapels provide an overview of 16th- and 17th-century Lombard painting.

San Simpliciano

Piazza San Simpliciano 7 (02 862 274). Metro Lanza/ bus 43, 57, 70/tram 3, 4, 12, 14. **Open** 7am-noon, 3-7pm Mon-Sat; 8am-noon, 4-7pm Sun. **Admission** free. **Map** p248 D5.

One of the oldest churches in the city, San Simpliciano was founded in the fourth century by St Ambrose (and dedicated to his successor) and finished in 401. The original church was called the Basilica Virginum and had a porticoed structure where penitent parishioners and neophytes attended mass. The present façade was added in 1870 by Carlo Maciachini in the neo-Gothic style he favoured, while the central entrance was reconstructed in the 11th-12th centuries. The apse decoration, *The Coronation of the Virgin*, is by Leonardo da Vinci's follower, Il Bergognone.

Santa Maria del Carmine

Piazza del Carmine 2 (02 8646 3365). Bus 61/ tram 1, 3, 4, 12, 14, 27. **Open** 7.15am-noon, 4-7.15pm daily. **Admission** free. **Map** p248 D5.

Little remains of the original Romanesque church built in 1250 and rebuilt in 1400. The current façade is the work of Carlo Maciachini (1880). However, the structure contains much Milanese history: the tomb (1472) of ducal councillor Angelo Simonetta stands in the right transept, while the body of finance minister Giuseppe Prina was brought to the sacristy after he had been killed by the populace for raising the tax on salt in 1814. The wooden choir (1579-85) houses the plaster models that were used by the artists working in the Duomo in the 19th century.

Sant'Angelo

Piazza Sant'Angelo 2 (02 632 481). Metro Moscova/ bus 41, 43, 94. **Open** 8am-7.30pm Mon-Fri; 8am-1pm, 3.30-7.15pm Sat, Sun. **Admission** free. **Map** p249 E5.

Built in 1552 to a design by Domenico Giunti, and intended to take the place of a Franciscan church the Spanish had destroyed to build defences, Sant'Angelo is a highly significant example of 16th-century Milanese architecture. The interior is full of paintings by noteworthy Milanese and Lombard artists from the 16th and 17th centuries, including Antonio Campi, Il Morazzone and Camillo Procaccini.

Porta Garibaldi, Isola & beyond

From western Brera, the most interesting and direct link to the north is **corso Garibaldi**. An array of speciality stores and one-off boutiques will satisfy your window-shopping needs until you reach **Santa Maria Incoronata** (*see p72*) – a rare example of a double-fronted temple. It's not just the outside that's interesting; the 15th-century Biblioteca

Umanistica (Humanities Library) inside ranks highest among many artistic treasures.

The neo-classical arch of **Porta Garibaldi** dominates this end of the street. Built in 1826, the arch was known as Porta Comasina until 1860, when it was renamed in honour of Giuseppe Garibaldi. The unemployed from Como and Brianza would pass under the arch to seek work in Milan's factories – so many, in fact, that the residential districts of Garibaldi and Isola were created to accommodate them. With the continued decline of Milan's industrial sector, the areas north of viale Crispi are now beginning to form the nexus for a finance-cum-fashion-cum-convention area, although several years after planning began, nothing has yet come of the project.

Linking Porta Garibaldi to the train station of the same name is **corso Como**, a short, entirely pedestrianised boulevard with a host of excellent restaurants, popular bars and trendy boutiques, including Carla Sozzani's 10 Corso Como (*see p117, p125 and p154*). To the west is viale Montello, which forms the border of Milan's **Chinatown**, harbouring an assortment of interesting food shops and restaurants. North up the bleak via Ceresio is the **Cimitero Monumentale** (*see p72*), a temple to Milanese art nouveau, aka the Liberty style.

To the east of Porta Garibaldi, on a 1,000 square-metre (10,753 square-foot) site that was once occupied by Pirelli's tyre factory, rises the **Grattacielo Pirelli**, or Pirellone (Big Pirelli), as the locals call it. Erected between 1955 and 1960, the Pirellone is a tribute to post-World War II reconstruction, designed by a team of architects that included Giò Ponti, Pier Luigi Nervi and Arturo Danusso. The sides of the building are tapered, a feat that required great architectural skill. The Pirellone has notched up a handful of records in its 50-year life: it was the first building in Milan to dare rise higher than the Madonnina on top of the Duomo (*see p56* **Golden girl**); and until the end of the 1960s, it was also the world's highest skyscraper in reinforced cement. On 18 April 2002 the Pirellone made the headlines again when a small plane flew into it, in a chilling, though apparently unintentional, repeat of 9/11.

Just to the right of the Pirellone is the massive bulk of Ulisse Stacchini's **Stazione Centrale** (*see p67* **Grand Centrale**), an overwhelming example of the heavy end of the Milanese Liberty style, built between 1912 and 1931. The front aspect is entirely covered in Aurisina stone, while the roof was constructed from five huge iron and glass panels. On the façade, Anno IX refers to 1931, the ninth year of Mussolini's fascist regime, when the station was opened.

Brera. *See p68.*

The *quartiere* of **Isola** (Island) is so named because of its isolation – it lies across the via Farini bridge along the east side of the cemetery, on what used to be the 'wrong' side of the railroad tracks. In the 19th century, this area was a gathering place for drunkards and petty criminals. However, carpenters, blacksmiths, artists and the like have taken up the opportunities offered by low property prices, and now the area is filled with artisan workshops: jewellery makers, painters and sculptors have all opened pretty ateliers here. While Isola does not have the cool appeal of Brera, its fans point to its lower prices and more 'authentic' atmosphere. It's best avoided at night, though.

From piazza Segrino in the heart of this area, via Thaon di Revel leads to the church of **Santa Maria alla Fontana** (*see below*), which has a sanctuary previously attributed to both Leonardo da Vinci and Donato Bramante.

West of here, the run-down industrial zone of Bovisa had been poised to undergo a minor renaissance linked to the creation of a university campus and the Museo del Presente in its decommissioned gasworks, which would house art from the 1970s onwards. However, several years after being given the go-ahead, both projects remain politicians' dreams; instead, young architects are leading the way forward, buying up flats and renovating them. To the north-east, a university hub and the Teatro degli Arcimboldi (*see p165*) are injecting fresh cultural life into the neighbourhood of Bicocca.

Cimitero Monumentale

Piazzale Cimitero Monumentale (02 8846 5600/02 659 9938). Bus 41, 43, 51, 70/tram 3, 4, 11, 12, 14, 29, 30, 33. **Open** 8am-6pm Tue-Sun. Closed some afternoons. **Admission** free. **Map** p248 C3.

The Egyptians had their pyramids, the Milanese have the Cimitero Monumentale, last resting place of the perpetually ostentatious. The cemetery was begun in 1866 by Carlo Maciachini, the result being 250,000sq m (2,688,000sq ft) of pure eclecticism. It's virtually an open-air museum of art nouveau, though later Italian artists – including Giacomo Manzù, Adolfo Wildt and Lucio Fontana – were also commissioned to produce monuments.

The whole complex centres on the 'Temple of Fame' (Famedio), where celebrated *milanesi* and other illustrious bodies are buried, including Luca Beltrami (restorer of the Castello Sforzesco and champion of the neo-Gothic movement); conductor Arturo Toscanini; poet Salvatore Quasimodo and entertainer Giorgio Gaber. The most famous resident is novelist Alessandro Manzoni, whose tomb is located right in the middle of the Famedio.

Non-Catholics are buried in separate sectors; the Jewish sector, to the south, is notable for its comparative restraint. A free map of the cemetery indicating the most noteworthy monuments is available at the entrance.

Santa Maria alla Fontana

Piazza Santa Maria alla Fontana 11 (02 688 7059). Metro Garibaldi or Zara/bus 82, 83/tram 4, 11. **Open** *Church* 8am-noon, 3-7pm Mon-Fri; 8am-1pm, 4-7pm Sat, Sun. *Sanctuary* 3-5pm Sat; 9.30am-12.30pm Sun. **Admission** free. **Map** p248 D2.

This church is essentially a modern structure in the neo-Renaissance style, with various nondescript additions. The presbytery, however, rests on a much older sanctuary, open at weekends. According to local lore, French governor Charles d'Amboise was miraculously cured at a spring here, and so had an oratory built on the spot in 1506. The design for the building has variously been attributed to Leonardo da Vinci and Donato Bramante, but more rigorous scholarship has it as the work of Giovanni Antonio Amedeo. The original font is still inside the church.

Santa Maria Incoronata

Corso Garibaldi 116 (02 654 855). Metro Garibaldi or Moscova/bus 41, 43, 94. **Open** 7.30am-1.30pm, 4-7.30pm Mon-Fri; 7.30am-noon, 4-7.30pm Sat; 8am-12.30pm, 4-7.30pm Sun. **Admission** free. **Map** p248 D4.

This basically Romanesque church is, in fact, made up of two buildings erected by Guiniforte Solari and united in 1468. The one on the left went up in 1451, coinciding with the arrival in Milan of Duke Francesco Sforza. As a result, the Augustinian fathers dedicated it to the new duke. Nine years later, Francesco's wife Bianca Maria Visconti decided that another church be erected next to and adjoining the first. She intended to show publicly the strength of their marital union. In the apse are frescoes from the 15th to 17th centuries. Frescoes in the chapels of the left nave are attributed variously to the Leonardo-esque painter Bernardo Zenale and da Vinci's *pupillo*, Il Bergognone. Guided tours held on Saturdays can be arranged by appointment.

San Babila & Eastern Milan

From designer heaven to peaceful havens.

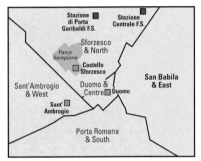

If you divide Milan down the middle through the centre of Galleria Vittorio Emanuele II, the Castello Sforzesco would be mirrored by an equally impressive, though entirely different rectangle – the fashion district known as the Quadrilatero della Moda. It is a glittering gateway into an area dominated by shopping all the way up to corso Buenos Aires – a wide boulevard that boasts the single highest density of shops per square metre in Europe. It's not all clothes-for-cash though; there is also room for relaxation and some culture in the Giardini Pubblici, as well as a clutch of interesting museums and *palazzi*.

Via Manzoni & the Quadrilatero della Moda

Via Manzoni is named after the 19th-century author whose house stands just off the La Scala end of the street (*see p165*). Before his death in 1873 the thoroughfare was known as corsia del Giardino because it was lined with lush-gardened villas, and because it led to the public green space, the Giardini Pubblici (*see p74*). The park remains, but because of the road's elite status, its private gardens have gradually been replaced by people-dense real estate.

Heading north-east, via Manzoni culminates at **Porta Nuova**, a gate that was once part of the fortifications built to protect the city from the attacks of Frederick Barbarossa. Though

the gate was first erected in 1171, it was heavily restored in 1861, using white and black marble, and the more friable sandstone. The arches were then decorated with Roman funerary stones found in the area. Beyond the gate is **piazza Cavour** (*see p74*).

The style and wealth of Milan's fashion quarter, the **Quadrilatero della Moda**, is awe-inspiring – little wonder it is also known as the Quadrilatero d'Oro ('Golden Rectangle'). This designer heaven is delineated by via Montenapoleone, via Sant'Andrea, via Manzoni and pedestrianised via della Spiga. If you think €750 is a reasonable price for a pair of shoes or your dog just wouldn't be comfortable without a Christian Dior coat, then this is the place for you.

But even the visitor without a gold card will find this area worth a look, on both an anthropological level (as an insight into how the other half lives) and a cultural one: two eccentric but rewarding museums, the **Museo Bagatti Valsecchi** (*see below*) and the **Museo di Milano e Storia Contemporanea** (*see p74*), are located here, as is one of Milan's prettiest (and least-visited) churches, **San Francesco di Paola** (*see p74*). Because of the fashion feeding frenzy nearby, you may be lucky enough to have these all to yourself for an hour or two.

Museo Bagatti Valsecchi

Via Gesù 5 (02 7600 6132/www.museobagatti valsecchi.org). Metro Montenapoleone/bus 34, 61/tram 1, 2. **Open** 1-5.45pm Tue-Sun. Closed Aug. **Admission** €6; €3 Wed. **Credit** MC, V. **Map** p249 E6/p252 E6.
Opened in 1994, this late 19th-century neo-Renaissance *palazzo* – residence of the Bagatti Valsecchi brothers, Fausto and Giuseppe – is now a homage to the extraordinary tastes of these collectors. Inside are numerous works of Renaissance art – however, paintings are not the real reason to visit. The brothers shared a cultivated taste for all things Renaissance, and strove to reproduce 15th-century *palazzo* life in their own home, down to the toys their children played with. Artworks are not labelled, in order to preserve the feel of a private home. Instead, informative English-language sheets are available in each room.

Museo di Milano e Storia Contemporanea

*Palazzo Morando Attendolo Bolognini, via Sant'
Andrea 6 (02 7600 6245). Metro Montenapoleone/
bus 94/tram 1, 2.* **Open** *Museum* 2-5.30pm Tue-Sun.
Closed Aug. *Exhibitions* 9.30am-1pm, 2-5.30pm Tue-
Sun. **Admission** *Museum* free. *Exhibitions* free-€4.
No credit cards. Map p249 F6/p252 F6.

Fully renovated in 2002, the 18th-century Palazzo
Morando Attendolo Bolognini is both a living
museum exhibiting the former private apartments
of the Countess Bolognini (including her collection
of porcelain, sculptures and other objects), and
home to a section of the city's civic art collections.
The bulk of the artwork exhibited here consists of
Luigi Beretta's collection, donated in 1935. These
paintings have helped historians create a thorough
picture of the city as it was during the Napoleonic
era and under Austrian rule, as well as chart its
urban development over the years. Also of interest
are the exhibits showing how the city has expanded over the centuries. The ground floor has been
remodelled as a space for travelling exhibitions.

San Francesco di Paola

*Via Manzoni 3 (no phone). Metro Montenapoleone/
tram 1, 2.* **Open** 9am-noon, 4-6.30pm daily.
Admission free. **Map** p249 E5/p252 E5.

Displaying an almost divine sense of irony, this
charming baroque church constructed by the
Minimi fathers (a particularly ascetic Franciscan
order founded in 1506) lies right in the heart of the
wealthiest and most ostentatious part of Milan. Its
attractive baroque façade (completed in 1891) plays
with concave and convex forms. Inside, in addition
to the classic marble altars, gilded woodwork
and detailed stucco, you'll find a painting in the
vault by Carlo Maria Giudici figuring the glory of
San Francesco di Paola, the church's patron saint.

Piazza Cavour to Giardini Pubblici

At the north-eastern end of via Manzoni is
piazza Cavour, an attractive square dedicated
to Camillo Benso, Conte di Cavour, the 19th-
century statesman credited with bringing
about the unification of Italy. His statue stands
in the north-east corner of the square. The
massive grey neo-classical hulk on the square's
east side is the **Palazzo dell'Informazione**
(No.2), designed in 1942 as the headquarters
for the fascist newspaper *Il Popolo d'Italia*.
Mussolini's daily only survived until July
1943, but thanks to its relative proximity to
the most newsworthy area of the city (the
finance capital of piazza Affari; *see p61*), the
building has become the Milanese headquarters
for many Italian and international press
agencies, among them Reuters and the
Associated Press.

If the designer excesses of the Quadrilatero
della Moda leave you in need of some breathing
space, cross over piazza Cavour to the **Giardini
Pubblici** (*see below*). In addition to providing
a welcome swathe of greenery, the gardens
include the **Civico Museo di Storia
Naturale** (*see below*), the **Museo del
Cinema** (*see p76*) and the **Planetario
Ulrico Hoepli** (*see p76*). The **PAC** gallery
(*see p156*) has hosted a series of interesting
installations, while its larger neighbour, the
Museo dell'Ottocento (formerly the Galleria
d'Arte Moderna; *see p76*) in the (also renamed)
Villa Belgiojoso Bonaparte, reopened in March
2006 after three years of restoration. South
of the park, on corso Venezia, is Giuseppe
Sommaruga's art nouveau **Palazzo
Castiglioni** (No.47; 1900-03), which
was occupied by the German army during
World War II.

Civico Museo di Storia Naturale

*Corso Venezia 55 (02 8846 3280/guided tours
02 783 528). Metro Palestro.* **Open** 9am-5.30pm
Tue-Fri; 9am-6pm Sat, Sun. **Admission** €3; free
under-18s. **No credit cards. Map** p249 F5.

Giovanni Ceruti's neo-classical building was put up
in 1838 to house the collections left to the city by aris-
tocrat Giuseppe de Cristoforis, and became Milan's
first civic museum (now the Natural History
Museum). Its displays cover palaeontology, botany,
mineralogy, geology and zoology. Highlights include
the lifesize reconstructions of a triceratops and
allosaurus in the paleontology rooms, and the old-
fashioned dioramas on the upstairs floor. There is a
stunning insect section too, and the minerology area
near the entrance is particularly fine, displaying the
largest sulphur crystal ever found, as well as some
spectacular Brazilian specimens. English explanations are scattered seemingly at random throughout
the museum.

Giardini Pubblici

*Metro Palestro, Porta Venezia, Repubblica or Turati/
bus 94/tram 1, 9, 11, 29, 30.* **Open** 6.30am-dusk
daily. **Map** p249 F5.

As corso Venezia takes you away from the built-up
areas of the city centre towards the built-up areas of
its outskirts, you'll notice the expansive green lungs
of the Giardini Pubblici on your left. The gardens
were designed in the English style by Giuseppe
Piermarini in 1786, and enlarged in 1857 to include
the Villa Reale (recently renamed Villa Belgiojoso
Bonaparte) and the Palazzo Dugnani. The park's
present arrangement – complete with natural
elements, such as waterfalls and rocky outcrops –
was the work of Emilio Alemagna for the 1871
International Expo. In addition to the galleries and
museums on its outer edges, the park has a bar with
outdoor tables (open 8am-7pm daily) and a small
children's train (€1.50 a ride). There are also more
dogs than you could throw a stick at.

Museo del Cinema

Via Manin 2B (02 655 4977/www.cinetecamilano.it).
Metro Turati/bus 41, 43, 94/tram 1, 2. **Open**
3-6pm Fri-Sun. Closed July, Aug. **Admission** €3;
€2 concessions. **No credit cards. Map** p249 F5.
Accessed through a little gate at the side of the
newly restored late 17th-century Palazzo Dugnani,
Milan's cinema museum may be small, but it report-
edly had such illustrious fans as Alfred Hitchcock
and Frank Capra. Highlights of the collection include
early Italian forays into moving pictures, such as the
17th-century Venetian contraption *mondo novo*,
which allowed one to see images on perforated
coloured prints by candlelight, the Lumière brothers' efforts and original sketches by Luchino
Visconti for his film *Senso*. For information on film
showings, *see p151*.

Museo dell'Ottocento

Villa Belgiojoso Bonaparte, via Palestro 16 (02
7600 2819/www.villabelgiojosobonaparte.it). Metro
Palestro/bus 94. **Open** 9am-1pm, 2-5.30pm Tue-Sun.
Admission free. **Map** p249 F5.
Reopened in spring 2006, this freshly restored neo-
classical villa, built by the Austrian architect
Leopold Pollack in 1790 for Count Ludovico
Barbiano di Belgiojoso, was formerly known as Villa
Reale. Napoleon lived here in 1802 and, after him,
Austrian field marshal Count Joseph Radetzky.
After unification, ownership passed to the Italian
royal family, who gave it to the city of Milan in 1921.
Today it is the home of the Museo dell'Ottocento
(Museum of the 19th Century; formerly the Galleria
d'Arte Moderna).
The collection, made up of bequests by leading
Milanese families, is spread over 35 rooms in the central body and on the first and second floors of the
west wing of this U-shaped building. The ground
floor is given over to neo-classical paintings, sculpture and bas-reliefs. On the first floor are paintings
from the Romantic period, the mostly Milan-based
Scapigliatura movement, and the branch of post-
Impressionism known as Divisionism, as well as
some Futurist works. Look out for Giuseppe Pellizza
da Volpedo's fine example of the socialist arte nuova
movement, *The Fourth Estate*. The second floor
showcases the Grassi and Vismara collections, the
latter including works by modern Italian and international masters such as Giorgio Morandi, van
Gogh, Gauguin, Cézanne, Matisse and Picasso. Fine
views of the restored, English-style garden are
afforded from the second-floor windows.

Planetario Ulrico Hoepli

Corso Venezia 57 (02 8846 3341/www.comune.
milano.it/planetario). Metro Palestro. **Open** *Shows*
9pm Tue, Thur; 3pm, 4.30pm Sat, Sun. Closed July,
Aug. **Admission** €3; €1.50 concessions. **No credit**
cards. Map p249 F5.
A gift to the city from publisher Ulrico Hoepli, the
building was constructed in 1930 by Pietro
Portaluppi in faux-classical style. Projections take
place in a great domed room, last renovated in 1955.

From piazza San Babila to Porta Venezia

Corso Vittorio Emanuele II, one of Milan's
main commercial arteries, links piazza del
Duomo (*see p52*) with piazza San Babila.
Formerly known as corsia dei Servi (after a
church erected by the fathers of the Serviti
order), this wide pedestrianised thoroughfare
gets a special mention in Alessandro Manzoni's
I promessi sposi, as the scene of the 1628 bread
riots. These days, quality, affordable clothing
stores and one of Milan's few department
stores, La Rinascente (*see p123*), are found on
this porticoed street.
Under the arcades near the late neo-classical
church of **San Carlo al Corso** (No.13; *see p78*)
is a third-century statue representing a Roman
magistrate. With typical Milanese pragmatism,
the sculpture has become known as the *omm de*
preja (man of stone). During the Austrian
occupation, the hard-done-by Milanese would
vent their spleen against their foreign rulers by
attaching satirical notes to the statue late at
night. Unfortunately, since the statue was
moved to a higher position, it's covered
in graffiti instead.
The *corso* is capped at its far end by **piazza**
San Babila, an unattractive post-war revamp.
The brick faux-Romanesque façade of the
church of **San Babila** (*see p78*) stands meekly
in the north-east corner of the square, dwarfed
by the surrounding abundance of steel, stone
and racing traffic.
Corso Venezia shoots straight out of piazza
San Babila and north-east to Porta Venezia. The
street is notable for a string of elegant noble
residences. Almost as soon as you leave piazza
San Babila you'll see the yellow walls of the late
15th-century **Casa Fontana Silvestri** (No.10)
on your right. It is one of the few remaining
examples of a Renaissance residence in the
city; the terracotta decoration on the façade
is typically Lombard. Across the street, at
No.11, is the **Seminario Arcivescovile**,
commissioned by Carlo Borromeo in 1565 to
implement the Council of Trent's regulations
concerning the education of the clergy. The
monumental doorway, decorated with
allegorical representations of Hope and
Charity, was added in 1652.
The neo-classical **Palazzo Serbelloni**
(No.16), at the intersection with via San
Damiano, was finished in 1793; it hosted
Napoleon in 1796, Metternich in 1838, and King
Vittorio Emanuele II and Napoleon III in 1859.
It is now home to the journalists' club, the
Circolo della Stampa. Across the road is via
Senato, which will lead you to **Palazzo del**

Walk on Taking Liberty

At the end of the 19th century, as adventurous European gentry were founding coffee plantations in South America and directing new-fangled flying dirigibles around Paris, belle époque artistry reigned supreme. The art nouveau, or Liberty style, as the Italians call it, was quickly adopted by the Milanese, and nowhere is their love affair with its architectural expression more evident than in the network of streets (Cappuccini, Barozzi, Vivaio, Mozart) around piazza Duse.

From Palestro metro station, walk south on corso Venezia and turn left into via Serbelloni and left again into via dei Cappuccini. In the space of just a few streets are three *palazzi* designed by the architect Giulio Ulisse Arata for the Berri Meregalli family. Take a right into via Barozzi, where you'll find the first (No.1), its solid 1910 façade decorated with animal heads. Turn left into Mozart for the second (No.21). Its elaborate embellishments – floral capitals and grotesque masks – also have a practical purpose: to hide unsightly gutters. Two nudes frescoed around the central balcony on the first floor heighten the grandiose ornamentation. Take a left up via Vivaio and another left on via dei Cappuccini for the third (No.8). Built

between 1911 and 1914, it unites a curious combination of architectural styles, from Gothic to Renaissance to Liberty.

Retrace your steps back to via Vivaio, turning left up via Cossa and passing through piazza Duse before making a left into via Salvini. Emerging on corso Venezia, turn right, skirting the green expanse of the Giardini Pubblici. You may want to take a detour for a picnic here or duck into one of the museums in its grounds. Just beyond Porta Venezia is another Liberty enclave. Cross traffic-choked piazza Oberdan to via Malpighi, which sprouts from the square's north-east corner, for two gems of art nouveau architecture by Giovanni Battista Bossi. Casa Galimberti (1905) is at No.3 and Casa Guazzoni (1903-06; **photo** *below*) at No.12; both flaunt colourful, exuberantly decorated façades. Retrace your steps to the square; south on viale Piave, the Liberty-style Sheraton Diana Majestic (*see p47*) was once part of a pleasure complex that included a theatre and Milan's first public pool.

Senato (built 1608-30). Since 1872 the palazzo has housed the Archivio di Stato. With courtyards by Fabio Mangone and a concave façade by Francesco Maria Richini, the building was initially designed for the College Elvetico, a Counter-Reformation stronghold, and was later used as government offices under Austro-Hungarian Emperor Joseph II and, even later, Napoleon.

Back on corso Venezia, **Palazzo Rocca Saporiti** (No.40) was built to a plan by La Scala's stage designer Giovanni Perego in 1812; its imposing Ionic columns and cornice surmounted by statues of gods make it a perfect example of neo-Palladian architectural canons. The façade is decorated with a frieze displaying scenes from the history of Milan and was equipped with a loggia on the first floor from which its residents could watch parades. At No.47 is **Palazzo Castiglioni**, with its bronze and wrought-iron art nouveau decoration; the façade once contained statues of female nudes, which earned it the nickname Ca' di Ciapp, or 'House of Buns'.

Corso Venezia ends in **piazza Oberdan**, where deafening, lung-challenging traffic screams across **Porta Venezia**. Originally known as Porta Orientale, this was one of the eight main entrances in the 16th-century Spanish fortifications. It was the first to be redesigned by Giuseppe Piermarini (architect of La Scala) in 1782, when the city's Spanish walls were torn down to make way for tree-lined avenues. In 1828 Piermarini's original neo-classical gate, which he left unfinished, was replaced by the two triumphal arches still standing today; bas-reliefs of Milanese history decorate the two buildings. Designed by Rodolfo Vantini, both elements have triple vantage points: towards the city, towards the country and towards the main thoroughfare, viale Luigi Májno/bastioni di Porta Venezia. To the north-west of the piazza is the minimalist exhibition space **Spazio Oberdan** (*see below*).

Continuing north-east from Porta Venezia, corso Buenos Aires extends all the way up to **piazzale Loreto**. The historically minded visitor might be tempted to visit this square, as it marks the spot where Mussolini and his lover Clara Petacci were publicly displayed, hanged by their feet, after a joint execution in 1945. Only come if you are extremely dedicated to your political geography, though – it's a grim square, and the largely mainstream stores of corso Buenos Aires will make you question your faith in Milan's fashion pre-eminence. Instead, take a slight detour to the small but interesting **Casa Museo Boschi-di Stefano** (*see below*).

Casa Museo Boschi-di Stefano

2nd Floor, Via Giorgio Jan 15 (02 2024 0568). Metro Lima/bus 60/tram 9, 11, 29, 30. **Open** 2-6pm Wed-Sun. Closed Aug. **Admission** free. **Map** p249 G4.
Husband-and-wife partnership Antonio Boschi and Marieda di Stefano took their modern art collection seriously: they once sold their car to buy more paintings, and even hid part of their collection behind a false wall in their country home during the war. So it is no surprise that they left their life's work to the people of Milan. The foundation opened in February 2003, with ten rooms, filled with 250 works of 20th-century art up to the '70s. The collection itself numbers 2,200 pieces, but only a selection is on show at present, including an entire room of Mario Sironi.

San Babila

Corso Monforte 1 (02 7600 2877). Metro San Babila/bus 54, 60, 61, 65, 73. **Open** 8am-noon, 3.30-6pm daily. **Admission** free. **Map** p249 F6/p252 F6.

Standing out like a sore thumb in the midst of the post-war architecture and hectic traffic of piazza San Babila is the church that gives the square its name. The original fourth-century basilica was rebuilt in the 11th century and further modified in the 16th, only to have its Romanesque façade badly 'restored' in 1906 by Paolo Cesa Bianchi, who also did the main altar. It's not the most inspiring church in Milan, but remains notable if only because Alessandro Manzoni was christened here in March 1785.

San Carlo al Corso

Piazza San Carlo, off corso Vittorio Emanuele II (02 773 302). Metro Duomo or San Babila/bus 54, 60 61, 65, 73. **Open** 7am-12.20pm, 4-8pm Mon-Sat; 9am-1pm, 4-10pm Sun. **Admission** free. **Map** p251 F6/p252 F6.
Considered the final work of the neo-classical movement in the whole of Italy, this church was begun in 1839 and completed in 1847; it stands on the site of Santa Maria de' Servi, built in 1317, which was demolished in order to create corso Vittorio Emanuele II. The present structure is essentially a cylinder covered with a dome, recalling the pantheons in Rome and Paris, and boasts the highest bell tower in the city (84m/276ft).

Spazio Oberdan

Viale Vittorio Veneto 2 (02 7740 6302/www. provincia.milano.it/oberdan). Metro Porta Venezia/ tram 1, 9, 11, 29, 30. **Open** times vary. **Admission** prices vary. **No credit cards. Map** p249 G5.
Just off the traffic-ridden nightmare of piazza Oberdan lies this calm, white, multi-purpose exhibition space. Designed by Gae Aulenti and Carlo Lamperti and completed in 1999, it hosts temporary shows and also has a cinema and bookshop.

Corso Monforte & south

Via del Conservatorio connects busy corso Monforte to the Porta Vittoria zone and the city's law courts (*see p79*). Just past the political science department of the Università di Milano, located in the late baroque Palazzo Resta-Pallavicino at No.7, is a little piazza whose south-east corner is enclosed by Milan's second-largest church, **Santa Maria della Passione** (*see p79*).

Directly opposite is **via della Passione**, opened up in 1540 to create a panoramic view of the church and allow access to the canals that once ran through the area. Continue south on via del Conservatorio to corso di Porta Vittoria. Once on this thoroughfare, go west for the church of **San Pietro in Gessate** (*see p79*), or east for the **piazza V Giornate**, with its 1895 monument by Giuseppe Grandi, devoted to the five days in March 1848 when the Milanese ended Austrian rule in the city (*see p16* **Five days that shook Milan**).

Crossing corso di Porta Vittoria brings you to a heavy, travertine-clad building, the **Palazzo di Giustizia** (law courts). This monstrous monument to justice was built between 1932 and 1940 by Marcello Piacentini in the then-popular fascist style as a replacement for the old Palazzo dei Tribunali in piazza Beccaria. It boasts well over 1,000 rooms and covers an area equivalent to more than three city blocks. Hopefully you won't have any reason to visit the building's interior (though its enormous atrium is decorated with mosaics by 20th-century artists, including Mario Sironi), but a long walk around the outside will give you an idea of its monolithic proportions.

Just to the west, at corso di Porta Vittoria 6, the city's library (*see p228*) is housed in the splendid 17th-century **Palazzo Sormani**. East along via San Barnaba, meanwhile, is the elegant **Rotonda della Besana**. This circular, porticoed structure was built at the end of the 17th century as a graveyard for the Ca' Granda hospital (*see p82*); the little church in the centre occasionally serves as an exhibition space.

San Pietro in Gessate

Piazza San Pietro in Gessate, at corso di Porta Vittoria (02 5410 7424). Bus 60, 73, 77, 84/ tram 12, 23, 27. **Open** 7.30am-6pm Mon-Fri; 8.30am-noon, 4-8pm Sat; 8.30am-1pm, 4.30-8pm Sun. **Admission** free. **Map** p251 F7/p252 F7.
This church was commissioned by Florentine banker Pigello Portinari and built between 1447 and 1475 to a design by Pietro Antonio and Guiniforte Solari. In 1862, frescoes were discovered under a layer of plaster. During the 16th and 17th centuries, even artwork was affected by the mass paranoia at the time of the plague – these frescoes were covered with fresh lime-based plaster in order to disinfect them. By all accounts, the frescoes have remained healthy, and today, although heavily damaged during World War II, large parts of the decoration are still in place. The church's eight-stall choir is a reconstruction based on what was left of the one built in 1640 by Carlo Garavaglia: the original was used as firewood during World War II. While the façade was attached in 1912 by Diego Brioschi, the 17th-century entrance has been preserved. Note that the church is sometimes closed in the afternoon in summer.

Santa Maria della Passione

Via Bellini 2 (02 7602 1370). Metro San Babila/ bus 54, 61. **Open** 7am-noon, 3.30-6.15pm Mon-Fri; 9am-12.30pm, 3.30-6.30pm Sat, Sun. **Admission** free. **Map** p251 F6/p252 F6.
Construction of the church of Santa Maria della Passione began in 1486 following a design by Giovanni Battagio. It was originally a Greek-cross church, but one arm was lengthened to form a nave and six semicircular side chapels were added in 1573, making it the second-largest church in Milan after the Duomo. The façade and the adjacent monastery –

now the seat of the Conservatorio di Musica Giuseppe Verdi (*see p165*)– were added in 1692 by Giuseppe Rusnati, who kept the building low so as not to distract attention from the massive octagonal lantern of the dome (designed by Cristoforo Lombardo in 1530).

The barrel vault of the church abounds with frescoes of the Evangelists, St Ambrose, St Augustine, angels and allegories of the virtues by Giuseppe Galbesio da Brescia (1583); more intriguing are the paintings lower down in the church's three-aisled interior, a veritable picture gallery of works by many of the leading 16th- and 17th-century Lombard artists, including Crespi, Procaccini and Bramantino; Crespi's masterpiece *San Carlo Borromeo Fasting* is perhaps the most impressive. The 16th-century wooden choir stalls are inlaid with mother-of-pearl. In the niches of the choir are two fabulous organs, both of which are still used for concerts; the shutters were painted by Crespi with scenes from the Passion.

Santa Maria della Passione.

Porta Romana, the Navigli & Southern Milan

Archaic canals and basilicas offer a link to the past.

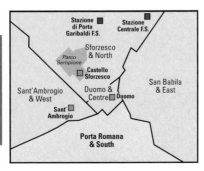

Southern Milan's Navigli area constitutes a living museum to the city of old, when a complex series of canals (*navigli*) created a network of trade routes and helped establish the city not only as an important economic hub, but also a major port. Not bad for a land-locked metropolis. The waterways now operate as cultural arteries, lined with restaurants and bars – reliable bets even on a Sunday – and leading to inviting side streets packed with a wealth of reliquaries, necropolises and exquisite stained glass. Because most visitors tend to stay close to the centre of town, you will often find yourself enjoying these attractions in welcome solitude.

The area around Porta Romana is also famous for its small shops and craftsmen's studios, and is building a reputation as a restaurant and bar quarter. Expect to see more attractions on the map over the next few years.

From piazza Fontana to Porta Romana

The area stretching from via Larga to Porta Romana is largely student territory, which is reflected in its shops, bars and cafés. This means eclectic shopping and, in general, more modest prices than in other central locations.

Piazza Fontana initially appears to be notable only for its small fountain, a surprisingly unusual sight in Milan. Look

a little closer and you'll see the former location of the Milanese court, the **Palazzo del Capitano di Giustizia**, built in 1578 by Piero Antonio Barca, and, on the west side of the square, the **Palazzo Arcivescovile** (No.2). This archbishop's palace dates from 1174, when a previous structure was rebuilt after Barbarossa sacked the city; its rectory courtyard was designed in 1565 by Pellegrino Tibaldi.

Since 12 December 1969 the piazza has been most closely associated with a terrorist bomb that killed 16 people; a plaque on the exterior of the Banca Nazionale dell'Agricoltura commemorates the blast that went off inside. On the grass opposite the bank a smaller plaque recalls 'Giuseppe Pinelli, anarchist railwayman. An innocent killed in the grounds of the police headquarters, 16.12.1969'. Pinelli was reported by local police to have jumped from a window while being questioned about the bombing, thus confirming his guilt, but several enquiries have cast this view into serious doubt. Most people now agree that he was thrown out, already dead. The events were made literary by Dario Fo in his play *Accidental Death of an Anarchist* (1970); the Nobel Prize-winning author (unsuccessfully) stood as a candidate for mayor of Milan in early 2006.

Across via Larga in **piazza Santo Stefano** you'll find the churches of **San Bernardino alle Ossa** and **Santo Stefano Maggiore** (for both, *see p83*). The former is a sanctuary dating back to the 13th century that was originally erected to handle the burial of corpses for the nearby Ospedale del Brolo, Milan's most important hospital prior to the construction of the Ospedale Maggiore (now the Cà Granda). This way station for the dead is rendered even more macabre by its ossuary, a sanctum decorated with human bones that dates back to an 18th-century reconstruction – the ossuary had been all but destroyed in 1642 when the tower of nearby Santo Stefano collapsed on it.

Via Larga takes you south-west past Milan's largest theatre, the Lirico (No.14; currently closed for refurbishment), designed in 1778 by Giuseppe Piermarini and given an internal

Sant'Eustorgio.
See p86.

overhaul in 1939 by Renzo Gerla and Antonio Cassi Ramelli. Continuing down via Larga you eventually arrive at the 26-storey skyscraper **Torre Velasca**, inaugurated in 1958. The tower's top-heavy structure, which looks almost medieval in its design, was the architects' ingenious response to the need for more office space than the available ground space allowed. The tower takes its name from the square on which it stands, itself named after 17th-century Spanish governor Juan Fernandez de Velasco. It was designed by the architectural firm Studio BBPR (Lodovico Belgiojoso, Enrico Peressutti and Ernesto Nathan Rogers). The other B, Gianluigi Banfi, died in a German concentration camp in 1945. (See also BBPR's monument to the victims of nazism in the Cimitero Monumentale; *see p71.*)

Via Chiaravalle, on your left as you walk down via Larga, leads to the church of **Sant'Antonio Abate**, originally built in the 1300s, but remodelled in both the 15th and 16th centuries. It contains several interesting paintings, including a St Cajetan by Cerano. From here you can't miss the magnificent **Ca' Granda** ('big house'; *see p83*) originally conceived in the 15th century to bring the city's 30-plus minor hospitals under one roof. The building now houses the arts faculties of the Università degli Studi di Milano.

Piazza San Nazaro leads south-east down to **Porta Romana**, a 1598 monumental gate designed by Aurelio Trezzi. It was a customs point for those arriving from or leaving for the south (every major Italian city has a Porta Romana leading in the direction of the capital). To the south, the Porta Romana area – roughly delineated by the viale Filippetti, corso Lodi and viale Isonzo, and as far as via Bocconi – is slowly but surely turning into a nightlife centre. Locals describe it as up and coming, although it hasn't quite come yet.

Basilica dei Santi Apostoli e Nazaro Maggiore

Piazza San Nazaro in Brolo 5 (02 5830 7719). Metro Missori/bus 94/tram 4, 24. **Open** 7.30am-noon, 3.30-6.30pm daily. **Admission** free. **Map** p251 E8.

Situated on what was the ancient colonnaded corso di Porta Romana, San Nazaro was one of the four basilicas built during St Ambrose's evangelisation drive, between 382 and 386. Constructed to accommodate relics of the apostles Andrew, John and Thomas, the church was given the name Basilica Apostolorum. When Ambrose brought the remains of local martyr St Nazarus (who died in 396) here, the church was rededicated. You can see the saintly remains in the two altars of the choir, but the silver vessel holding them is a copy; the one St Ambrose commissioned is in the treasury of the Duomo.

When it was built, the basilica stood outside the city walls in a Christian burial area established by Ambrose when still a bishop, hence the sarcophagi behind the church. The church was destroyed by fire in 1075 and rebuilt using material from the original structure, including the pilasters holding up the central dome. The *basilichetta* of San Lino, to the right of the altar, dates from the tenth century. The octagonal Cappella Trivulzio, designed by Bramantino –

All roads lead to Rome – and every Italian city has a **Porta Romana**.

his only known architectural foray – was added to the church in 1512 as a mausoleum for the powerful Trivulzio family.

Reworked in the late 16th century and given a neo-classical interior in the 1830s, the basilica suffered considerable damage during World War II. Between 1946 and 1963 it was stripped of many of its post-fourth-century trappings to restore a sense of its early Christian austerity.

Ca' Granda (Università degli Studi di Milano)

Via Festa del Perdono 7 (02 503 111/freephone 800 188 128). Metro Duomo or Missori/bus 54, 60, 77/tram 12, 23, 24, 27. **Open** 8am-6pm Mon-Fri; 8am-12.30pm Sat. Closed Aug. **Admission** free. **Map** p251 E7/p252 E7.

Now home to the arts faculties of Milan university, Ca' Granda began its life as a hospital and hospice. It was Francesco Sforza who set out to consolidate Milan's 30 hospitals into one Casa Granda or Ospedale Maggiore (main hospital) in 1456. The Ca' Granda was also a place to protect the poor and sick (and by doing so ensure the spiritual salvation of its sponsors) – and also to confine beggars, the mad and the otherwise socially embarrassing in order to create a more attractive city.

Francesco's favourite architect, Antonio 'Il Filarete' Averlino, incorporated the idea into his grandiose plan to transform Milan into an ideal Renaissance city. The building has one wing for men and another for women, each subdivided into four inner courts and separated by the Cortile Maggiore (Great Court). Communications between Filarete and Francesco during the building of the hospital took on a bizarre pseudo-familial tenor, with Sforza depicted as the patron-father, the architect as mother and the building as child. In the end, relations between the two soured: Filarete felt that Sforza could have done more to promote his architectural career.

Work continued on the project after Filarete's death (c1469), but ground to a halt with the fall of Ludovico il Moro, picking up again from time to time through the 17th and 18th centuries. In 1939 the hospital was moved to its new headquarters at Niguarda, in the northern suburbs. The university took up residence here in 1958.

The façade, with its typically Lombard terracotta decoration, is one of the few in the city to have been completed in the 1400s. The courtyards, also from the 15th century, contained the women's baths. The Cortile Maggiore, with its Renaissance portico and baroque loggia, is decorated with busts sculpted from the yellow, rose and grey stone from Angera on Lake Maggiore. It was reconstructed after sustaining heavy damage during World War II. The neo-classical Macchio wing – now home to university offices – once contained an art gallery. There's a canvas by Guercino (1639) in the 17th-century church of the Annunciata (02 5830 7465, 02 5503 8389, open 7.30am-1.30pm Mon-Fri during university term) inside the courtyard.

San Bernardino alle Ossa

Piazza Santo Stefano (02 7602 3735). Metro Duomo or Missori/bus 54, 60, 73/tram 12, 23, 27. **Open** 7.30am-6.30pm Mon-Fri; 7.30am-noon Sat, Sun. **Admission** free. **Map** p251 E7/p252 E7.

One of Milan's bizarrest attractions, the San Bernardino alle Ossa's ossuary chapel manages to create beauty from a rather macabre template. The chapel, on the right as you enter, is decorated in delightfully disturbing fashion with pictures and patterns picked out in human bones supplied by the nearby Ospedale del Brolo, and the occasional skull from decapitated criminals. Other, more colourful theories, suggest that these are the bones of the illegitimate children of Milanese noblewomen, or martyrs from Arian massacres. The interior gloom is enlivened by the bright colours of the vault painting by Sebastiano Ricci (1659-1734), *Triumph of the Soul Among the Angels*. The chapel itself was built in 1695 on the site of a structure dating back to 1210.

San Calimero

Via San Calimero 9-11 (02 5831 4028). Metro Crocetta/bus 94/tram 4, 24. **Open** 8am-noon, 4-6pm daily. **Admission** free. **Map** p251 E8.

Thought to have been built in the fifth century over the remains of a pre-existing pagan temple to Apollo, this church is dedicated to Saint Calimero, the fourth bishop of Milan, whose body it houses. The chapel was rebuilt in Romanesque style in the 12th century, and then again in 1609 by Francesco Maria Ricchini. Disastrous restoration work by Angelo Colla in 1882 wiped out most traces of earlier architecture. The terracotta façade, with its porch resting on two stately lion bases, dates from Colla's renovation. San Calimero is notable for its rare, double-arched portal affording access to the courtyard leading to the *canonica*, or priest's house – one of the few examples in the Romanesque style left in Milan.

Santo Stefano Maggiore

Piazza Santo Stefano (no phone). Metro Duomo or Missori/bus 54, 60, 73/tram 12, 23, 27. **Map** p251 E7/p252 E7.

Santo Stefano was originally built in the fifth century, but what you see today is a 1584 reconstruction by Giuseppe Meda and Aurelio Trezzi, with a baroque bell tower added between 1643 and 1674 by Carlo Buzzi. The fragmentary pilaster just in front of the façade on the right is the only remnant of the medieval atrium where Galeazzo Maria Sforza was assassinated on 26 December 1476.

From via Torino to Porta Ticinese

If the area north of the Duomo carries a sense of 'rich older folk', then via Torino and corso di Porta Ticinese are where the rich younger folk hang out; consequently, the pavements and trendy shops can become as packed as a rock concert. Narrow and heavily trafficked,

Sightseeing

The remains of a once-thriving artisan community survives in the **Navigli**. *See p88.*

via Torino runs down from the south-west corner of piazza Duomo to largo Carrobbio (a name derived from the Latin *quadrivium*, a place where four roads meet), providing the intrepid pedestrian with a host of bargain shops, harried-looking *milanesi* and inviting side streets.

South of via Torino, down via Palla is the often-overlooked church of **Sant'Alessandro**. Begun in 1601 and worked on by various architects including Francesco Maria Richini, it was finally given a rococo façade in the 18th century. Inside are numerous interesting works, including Daniele Crespi's *Beheading of John the Baptist*.

Returning to via Torino and again digressing south, via Soncino leads to the **Palazzo Stampa**, a beautiful Renaissance building once home to a traitor. At the beginning of the 16th century, the building's owner Massimiliano Stampa was on excellent terms with the city's rulers, the Sforza family. But as the Sforzas' star began to wane, Stampa sold his allegiance to Holy Roman Emperor Charles V. In return, he obtained the title of Count of the Soncino. Stampa was suddenly elevated to Renaissance star status, and his palazzo was soon considered the most important salon in the city, attracting A-list nobility from across the region. Alas, Stampa's time in the sun was relatively brief, and the palazzo passed to the Casati

family within the century. The new owners effected various changes to the building, opening, for example, a new entrance on to via Soncino. But they kept the count's 15th-century tower, crowned with the golden globe, eagle, crown and cross escutcheon (still visible today) used by Charles V to express royal ownership. Opposite the Palazzo Stampa is the church of **San Giorgio al Palazzo** (*see p86*).

Corso di Porta Ticinese shoots south out of largo Carrobbio, passing by via Gian Giacomo Mora on the right; the name of this street commemorates a man falsely accused of spreading plague in 1636, and tortured for his sins. His house was demolished and in its place a pillar was erected, which gets a mention in Manzoni's *Storia della colonna infame* (1842).

Further down corso di Porta Ticinese, on the left, is the church of **San Lorenzo Maggiore** (*see p86*). Facing the church are 16 massive Roman columns. They were recovered some time after the third century, most likely from a Roman spa or temple, and erected here in commemoration of St Lawrence, who was martyred in 258.

At the junction of corso di Porta Ticinese with via de Amicis and via Molino delle Armi is the **Antica Porta Ticinese**, which dates from the 12th century. It marks what in ancient times was the entry point into the city for travellers coming from Ticinum (modern-day Pavia, south

Sightseeing

of Milan), before the city walls were demolished and rebuilt further out to encompass the growing community. Via de Amicis leads west from here to the site of the **Roman Amphitheatre** (No.17, 02 8940 0555, closed Sat afternoons & all Sun). First uncovered in 1936 but only brought fully to light in the 1980s, the structure has suffered not so much the ravages of time as those of church-builders: much of it was dismantled and used to build San Lorenzo. A small, free museum of antiquities has recently opened on the site (closed Wed, Fri & Sat afternoons & all of Mon & Sun). North-west of here, across corso Genova, the little church of **San Vincenzo in Prato** (*see p88*) stands in what was a pre-Christian necropolis.

Behind San Lorenzo is **piazza della Vetra**, a name that probably derives from *castra vetera* (old barracks), an allusion to the fact that Roman soldiers defending the imperial palace camped here. During the Middle Ages, the piazza was often used as a point from which to defend the city; the Seveso and Nirone rivers converged here and were redirected to feed defensive waterworks around the city walls. All these military associations may have prepared piazza della Vetra for an even bloodier vocation: as an execution ground. For a period of nearly 800 years, from 1045 to 1840, the square was the place where commoners condemned to death were decapitated. (The nobility met their

gruesome end in the more central, slightly more attractive, piazza Broletto.)

From here you can cut south across via Molino delle Armi to the pretty **Parco delle Basiliche** and along corso di Porta Ticinese to the impressive **Museo Diocesano** (*see below*), a splendid collection of religious art and artefacts. To the south, the church of **Sant'Eustorgio** (*see p86*) stands on the spot where the first Milanese Christians are reputed to have been baptised by the apostle Barnabus. Alternatively, leave the park heading east along via Banfi and into via Cosimo del Fante to corso Italia, where you'll find the church of **Santa Maria dei Miracoli** (*see p88*).

Museo Diocesano

Corso di Porta Ticinese 95 (02 8940 4714/ bookings 02 8942 0019/www.museodiocesano.it). Metro Sant'Ambrogio/bus 94/tram 3. **Open** 10am-6pm Tue-Sun. **Admission** €8.50; €6 concessions. *Combined ticket with Cappella Portinari at Sant'Eustorgio & Cappella di Sant'Aquilino at San Lorenzo* €12. **No credit cards**. **Map** p250 C8. The Museo Diocesano contains a wonderful collection of religious art treasures culled from churches and private collections throughout Lombardy. The museum, which opened in 2001, is a streamlined operation distributed over three floors of the former Dominican convent of Sant'Eustorgio. A slick entrance leads into a great hall; from here visitors can follow colour-coded ground plans on pamphlets, or simply read the explanatory placards and computer points scattered around (in Italian).

On the ground floor are select pieces from St Ambrose's time (coloured ochre on the plan), followed by the first part of a (blue-green) itinerary that works from the 14th to 19th centuries, a multimedia room and a collection of 17th- and 18th-century Italian paintings; there are also some works from the currently closed museum at Santa Maria della Passione (*see p78*). Liturgical furniture (reliquaries, crucifixes, chalices and the like) is housed in the basement.

The first floor contains a space for the bulk of the collections as well as temporary exhibitions. The blue-green itinerary that began on ground level ends here with the museum's most recent pieces. This floor also houses the collections of several cardinals: Federico Visconti's (1617-93) is contained in one small room, with copies of famous drawings, including portraits of Raphael and Titian by an anonymous Lombard painter of the 17th century; Giuseppe Pozzobonelli's collection (1696-1783) has 17th-century Italian landscapes; Cesare Monti's (1593-1650) has Lombard and Venetian works of the 16th and 17th centuries (don't miss Tintoretto's *Christ and the Adulteress*, 1545-7).

There is also a collection of 14th- and 15th-century altarpiece paintings with gold backgrounds, accompanied by a video (in Italian) explaining the gold-leafing process.

San Giorgio al Palazzo

Piazza San Giorgio 2 (02 860 831). Tram 2, 3, 14.
Open 8.30am-noon, 3.30-7pm daily. **Admission**
free. **Map** p250 D7/p252 D7.

Founded in 750, San Giorgio was rebuilt in 1129 and
heavily reworked in the 17th and early 19th centuries.
Amid the neo-classical trappings are a baptismal font
fashioned out of a Romanesque capital and a couple
of pilasters at the far end of the central nave from the
original church. Don't miss the striking cycle of
Scenes from the Passion of Christ by Bernardino Luini
(1516) in the third chapel on the right. Commissioned
to fresco the whole church, he fled Milan after killing
a clergyman critical of his work.

San Lorenzo Maggiore

*Corso di Porta Ticinese 39 (02 8940 4129). Metro
Sant'Ambrogio/bus 94/tram 3.* **Open** *Church &
Cappella di Sant'Aquilino* 7.30am-12.30pm, 2.30-
6.30pm Mon-Sat; 7.30am-6pm Sun. **Admission**
€2; €1 concessions. *Combined ticket with Museo
Diocesano & Cappella Portinari at Sant'Eustorgio*
€12. **No credit cards. Map** p250 D8.

Built at the end of the fourth century, San Lorenzo
may have been the chapel of the imperial Roman
palace. It is certainly one of the oldest centrally
planned churches anywhere. A survivor from the
days when Milan represented the stronghold of the
Roman Empire in the West, it shows all the signs of
repeated remodelling. Fires all but destroyed it in
the 11th and 12th centuries, but it was rebuilt to the
original Roman model. When the cupola collapsed
in 1573, the new dome – the tallest in Milan and a
far cry from the original – outraged the local populace. Some traces of the original portals can be seen
in the façade, heavily reworked in 1894.

On the backs of the two great arches that flank the
main altar, columns were placed upside down to
symbolise the Christian religion rising up from the
ruins of paganism. To the right, the octagonal
fourth-century Cappella di Sant'Aquilino may have
been an imperial mausoleum. Legend has it that a
group of porters discovered St Aquiline's corpse in
a ditch; taking it to the Duomo, they got lost in the
fog and ended up in San Lorenzo. Thus his remains
are here, and he became the patron saint of porters.
On the walls of the *cappella* are fragments of the late
fourth-century mosaics that once covered the entire
chapel. Behind the altar, a passage leads under the
church, where stones from pre-existing Roman
structures used in the construction of San Lorenzo
can be seen, as well as a Byzantine sarcophagus.

Outside the church stand 16 Corinthian columns
from the second and third centuries. They were
moved here from an unidentified temple in the fourth
century, and topped with pieces of architrave, only
some of which date from the same period. The 17th-
century wings flanking the entrance to San Lorenzo
were designed to link the columns to the church in a
sort of pseudo-ancient atrium. In the centre, a bronze
statue of Emperor Constantine is a copy of one in
Rome; a reminder of his Edict of Milan (313), which
put an end to the persecution of Christians.

Sant'Eustorgio

*Piazza Sant'Eustorgio 1 (02 5810 1583/Cappella
Portinari 02 8940 2671). Bus 59/tram 3, 9, 14,
15, 29, 30.* **Open** *Church* 7.30am-noon, 3.30-
6.30pm daily. *Cappella Portinari* 10am-6pm daily.
Admission *Church* free. *Cappella Portinari* €6; €3
concessions. *Combined ticket with Museo Diocesano
& Cappella di Sant'Aquilino at San Lorenzo* €12.
No credit cards. Map p250 D8.

The origins of this church are shrouded in legend.
One story has it that Sant'Eustorgio, when he was
still a bishop in the fourth century, had the place
built to house relics of the Three Kings – the site was
chosen when animals pulling the relic-laden cart
reached this spot and refused to budge. Frederick
Barbarossa supposedly absconded with the relics
in 1164, but they were returned in 1903 and are
venerated each Epiphany (6 January). The ceremony
takes place at the end of a mass timed to coincide
with the arrival of a procession from piazza del
Duomo led by the 'Three Kings' (played by a trio
of local residents).

Whatever its origins, the building has traces of
seventh-century work, was rebuilt by the Dominican
order in 1190 after being razed by Barbarossa, was
restored and revamped on several occasions up to
the 15th century, and had a new faux-Romanesque
façade stuck on it in 1865. (The little pulpit on the
façade is a 16th-century substitution of the original
wooden one from which Dominican Inquisitor St
Peter Martyr preached.) Sant'Eustorgio was the first
of Milan's churches to have a clock put in its bell
tower, in 1306. The former convent is now home to
the Museo Diocesano (*see p85*).

Inside, the church is filled with works by Milanese
and Lombard artists from the 13th to the 15th
centuries: Giovannino di Grassi, Giovanni da
Milano, Giovanni di Balduccio (see his Gothic funeral monument to Stefano Visconti, 1327, in the fourth
chapel on the right), Bernardino Luini and the
maestri campionesi all feature. The fourth chapel
on the right contains the 14th-century painted wood-
en crucifix that was supposed to cure pregnant
women of fever attacks.

The main attraction, however, is the Cappella
Portinari, built between 1462 and 1466 by Florentine
banker Pigello Portinari for his own tomb, and as a
repository for the body of St Peter Martyr, murdered
when heretics sunk a knife into his skull 200 years
earlier (in their defence, he had been a particularly
zealous Inquisition torturer). Perhaps the earliest
truly Renaissance work in the city, the chapel unites
the classical forms championed by Brunelleschi in
Tuscany with typical Lombard fresco decoration by
Vincenzo Foppa. Foppa's scenes from the life of the
Virgin and St Peter Martyr's miracles (1466-8) are
perhaps the painter's greatest masterpieces. In the
centre of the chapel, the Ark of St Peter Martyr, containing most of the saint's remains, is by Giovanni
di Balduccio (1336-9). The rest of him (his skull) is
in a silver urn in the little chapel to the left of the
Cappella Portinari. **Photo** *p81*.

Messing about on the *navigli*

Crucial to Milan's communications and commercial development from the 12th century onwards, the *navigli* (or what remains of the once-extensive network of canals anyway) had been much neglected since the late 1970s. The dark waters can prove all too tempting to those who need to get rid of an old washing machine or fridge – revealed each winter when the canals are drained for cleaning.

In recent years, as the canal banks have become lively evening destinations, the traditional crafts community that once thrived on the lower floors of the area's *case di ringhiera* (typical Milanese working-class apartment buildings) has suffered; many bar owners and restaurateurs are happy to pay the sort of rents that art restorers, bookbinders or violin makers simply can't.

Helping to preserve the past and create a new cultural heritage for the Naviglio Grande, the **Associazione del Naviglio Grande** (02 8940 9971, www.navigliogrande.mi.it) is responsible for numerous seasonal activities. For the last 22 years, this 100-strong association has organised a monthly antiques market along the canal's banks (*see p141*). Local bars and restaurants stay open all day, creating a fun atmosphere. Another of the association's initiatives takes place on the third Sunday in May, when the canal is transformed by over 200 stalls of blooms at the annual flower festival. At Christmastime, the association organises an impressive display of 20,000-plus lights along the Naviglio Grande; the reflections dancing on the water create a magical effect.

If you want to explore the canals by water, **Incoming Partners** (02 6702 0280, www.incomingpartners.it) runs daily tours from April to mid September. A 24-seater boat departs at 9.30am and 4pm for a two-hour cruise, up the Naviglio Grande, through the Darsena and down the Naviglio Pavese, as far as the Conca Fallata (two locks will be negotiated during the trip). Rates start at €18 per person (€10 concessions) and advance reservations are essential. Trips depart from the dock at Alzaia del Naviglio Grande 66, which is five minutes' walk from Porta Genova metro station.

If you fancy getting your hands dirty, the association **Navigli Lombardi** (02 667 9131, or www.naviglilombardi.it) musters volunteers for an annual clean-up of the canal banks (the last one was in spring 2006).

Sightseeing

Santa Maria dei Miracoli presso San Celso

Corso Italia 37 (02 5831 3187). Metro Missori/ bus 94/tram 15. **Open** 7am-noon, 4-6.30pm daily. **Admission** free. **Map** p250 D8.

Two little chapels once stood on this site where, according to legend, St Ambrose was led by a vision to the bodies of martyrs Nazaro and Celso. The chapel of San Nazaro fell down long ago, but so great was the flow of pilgrims to the remaining chapel of San Celso – where, in the 15th century, the Virgin was said to be working miracles galore – that in 1493 construction began on something bigger: Santa Maria dei Miracoli. Preceded by a fine early 16th-century *quadriportico*, this church has a lively façade from the same era, animated by sculptures by Stoldo Lorenzi and Annibale Fontana. The interior was decorated by the usual cast of Lombard Renaissance, mannerist and baroque artists.

A separate entrance through a gate and across a garden will take you to what remains of San Celso. Founded in the ninth century and rebuilt in the 11th, this little Romanesque church is decorated with frescoes from the 11th to 15th centuries. It is now also a venue for art exhibitions, theatrical performances and concerts. Although restoration work was still taking place as this guide went to press, the church remains open.

San Vincenzo in Prato

Via Daniele Crespi 6 (02 5810 4586). Metro Sant'Agostino/bus 94/tram 2, 14. **Open** 7.45-11.45am, 4.30-7pm daily. **Admission** free. **Map** p250 B8.

Once an expanse of *prati* (fields), the area around this small church was used first as a pagan, and subsequently Christian, necropolis. Benedictine monks occupied the adjacent monastery in the ninth century and remained there until 1520; it's uncertain whether the present church dates from the ninth or 11th century. French occupiers turned it into a storehouse and then barracks in 1798. Later it became a chemical factory, belching fumes that earned it the nickname the Casa del Mago (Magician's House). It was restored and reconsecrated in the 1880s.

The Navigli

North-west of piazza Sant'Eustorgio is the **Darsena**, the confluence of the two canals that connect Milan with the Ticino and Po rivers (the Olona river still flows in underground). Built in 1603, the Darsena was Milan's main port, a hotbed of commercial activity for goods flowing in and out of the city. Today the waters have stilled, but every Saturday people continue to congregate at the nearby Papiniano open-air market (*see p141*) for great bargains, luscious foods and fresh produce.

The *navigli* (canals), which extend south and west from the Darsena between Porta Ticinese and Porta Genova, are all that remain of a once-vital network of arteries. The canals themselves may seem a bit of a let-down (especially if you visit in winter, when they are drained and cleaned), but their significance in the city's development makes them a powerful draw. First of all, they are partly the result of Leonardo da Vinci's engineering nous, and are thus intimately connected to the highest cultural point of Milan's history. Furthermore, the waterways provided an essential link to the rest of Italy, and enabled Milan to become a thriving port by the late 19th century. Today boutiques, artists' studios, antiques restorers, bookshops and, increasingly, nightspots, line the canal banks and side streets.

Excavations for the Naviglio Grande – which carries the waters of the diverted Ticino river from Lake Maggiore to the Darsena – were begun in 1177. Canals for Bereguardo, the Martesana and Paderno followed, boosting Milan's already considerable commercial clout. Barges floated in, carrying coal and salt (not to mention marble from Candoglia on Lake Maggiore used in the construction of the Duomo); they left laden with iron, grain, fabric and other goods manufactured in the city.

In 1359 a project was initiated to build the Naviglio Pavese. The waterway was initially conceived merely to irrigate Gian Galeazzo Visconti's hunting reserve near Pavia, but in the 15th century Ludovico il Moro called in Leonardo da Vinci to improve the system and create a canal network that extended into the heart of the city. Funding issues hampered a 1597 scheme to extend the *navigli* yet further, leaving the Conca Fallato ('failed sluice') in the southern suburbs until the French applied themselves to the task in the 19th century. Not long after its inauguration in 1819, its traffic rates were outstripping those on the Naviglio Grande. Although much of the historic network had been filled in by the 1930s (the ring road known as the *cerchia dei navigli,* which includes via Senato and via San Damiano, follows the line of a former canal), after World War II, materials for reconstructing the badly bombed city were transported by water. However, the last working boat moored on 30 March 1979.

San Cristoforo

Strada Alzaia Naviglio Grande (no phone). **Open** 7.30am-noon, 4-7pm daily. **Admission** free.

The unassuming San Cristoforo is, in fact, two churches sandwiched together: the one on the left is the older of the two and probably dates from the late 12th century. It was enlarged in 1398 when the adjacent Cappella Ducale was built to celebrate the end of a long famine; the portal and rose window were added at this time. The façade has traces of 15th-century fresco decoration and the bell tower also dates from this period. Inside are frescoes by 15th- and 16th-century Lombard painters.

Sant'Ambrogio & Western Milan

The Last Supper and other local flavours.

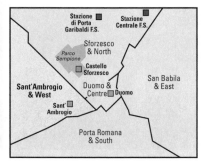

Via Meravigli and corso Magenta are not Milan's most attractive thoroughfares, to say the least, but they do provide access to some interesting attractions that are less frequented by tourists (*The Last Supper* aside, of course). The area strikes a pleasant balance between active, bustling streets (thanks to the nearby Università Cattolica) and shops that exude a more olde-worlde vibe, such as antiques merchants and rare-book dealers. Take a wander around the backstreets and you'll be pleasantly surprised.

Sant'Ambrogio & around

The Duomo may be more beautiful to look at, but there's a church in Milan that is arguably more important to locals. **Sant'Ambrogio** (*see p91*), named after the city's patron saint, dates back to Roman times and has more of a claim to being the city's 'true' church. Sant'Ambrogio was built outside the Roman city walls in an area of early Christian cemeteries and imperial buildings. Nine Italian kings were crowned at its altar between the ninth and 15th centuries (four of them are buried here). Even Napoleon (1805) and Ferdinand of Austria (1838) chose to respect this tradition, paying a visit immediately after their coronations in the Duomo.

Once a year the square outside the church hosts the Oh Bej! Oh Bej! festival (*see p146*); the rest of the time you'll find it filled with students from the nearby **Università Cattolica del Sacro Cuore** (*see p92*), an ex-monastic complex that now houses Milan's Catholic university.

South-west across the square, the **Pusterla di Sant'Ambrogio** is a 1939 imitation of the medieval gate that once stood here, part of the 1171 defences built after Barbarossa's attacks. Some older materials, including a 14th-century

Casa di Riposo per Musicisti. See *p96*.

Sant'Ambrogio rivals the Duomo as Milan's most important church. *See p91.*

relief showing saints Ambrose, Gervasius and Protasius, have been incorporated into it. West of the basilica is the Roman *colonna del diavolo*, a column scarred by two holes said to have been made by the Devil's horns: the Dark One apparently suffered a fit of pique at Ambrose's purity and incorruptibility.

To the south, in via de Amicis, is the crypt of **Santa Maria della Vittoria** (*see p92*), which houses artefacts from recent archaeological digs around Lombardy. North-west, beyond the Pusterla, the **Museo Nazionale della Scienza e della Tecnologia Leonardo da Vinci** (*see below*) is a magic box of technological wonders from across the ages.

Next door, the church of **San Vittore al Corpo** (*see p92*) stands on via degli Olivetani, where the prison of San Vittore – the temporary home of many of the businessmen and politicians caught up in the *Tangentopoli* scandal (*see p20*) and subsequent Mani Pulite investigations of the 1990s – has loomed threateningly since its construction in the 1860s and '70s. It's a colourless neighbourhood around the prison, so instead, take a leisurely walk south-west from Sant'Agostino metro station down via Modestino, which merges into via Andrea Solari. Passing the church of Santa Maria del Rosario on the right, you come to the **Fondazione Arnaldo Pomodoro** (on the left; *see below*), a sculpture gallery that opened in 2005 in the former industrial area of Ansaldo, now filling with smart housing complexes.

Fondazione Arnaldo Pomodoro

Via Andrea Solari 35 (02 8907 5394/www. fondazionearnaldopomodoro.it). Metro Sant'Agostino/ tram 14, 29, 30. **Open** 11am-6pm Wed, Fri-Sun (last entry 5pm); 11am-10pm (last entry 9pm) Thur. Closed Aug. **Admission** €7; €4 concessions. **No credit cards**. **Map** p250 A8.

As he approached his 80th birthday, the celebrated sculptor Arnaldo Pomodoro finally realised his dream of setting up a centre dedicated to promoting his art. The building looks like a metallic warehouse, and its size – 3,500sq m (37,670sq ft) and 15m (49ft) high – allows it to accommodate large installations. The foundation has also launched an international competition to discover young sculpting talent.

Museo Nazionale della Scienza e della Tecnologia Leonardo da Vinci

Via San Vittore 21 (02 485 551/www.museoscienza. org). Metro Sant'Ambrogio/bus 50, 54, 58, 94. **Open** 9.30am-5pm Tue-Fri; 9.30am-6.30pm Sat, Sun. **Admission** €8; €3-€6 concessions. **No credit cards**. **Map** p250 B7.

This impressive science and technology museum is a fitting tribute to Milan's revered temporary resident. One of the most fascinating halls here showcases replica models based on da Vinci's doodlings – military theory, ballistics and aeronautics are all covered. But it is just one section of a 10,000-item collection with an all-encompassing remit.

The museum is housed in the 16th-century Edificio Monumentale, a monastery converted into a barracks by Napoleon. A section of the foundations of the Roman San Vittore fort can be found in one of the museum's courtyards, as can an octago-nal imperial mausoleum thought to be the resting place of Emperor Valentinian II.

The current museum was established after World War II, during which the buildings were badly dam-aged by Allied bombs, and it has expanded to become one of the most important museums of its kind in Italy. It's hard to think of any aspect of indus-try or technology that has been left out, with dis-plays dedicated to printing, metallurgy, bell-casting, minting, engines, horology and time-keeping, as well as the sciences of physics, optics, acoustics and astronomy. An exhaustive computing section shows the evolution of calculating techniques from Pascal's abacus of 1642 to the first IBM processor. Exhibits are laid out so you can see the evolution of a cart-wheel into a Vespa, or a Morse code transmitter to a state-of-the-art mobile phone with MP3 player.

On the mezzanine, the Civico Museo Navale Didattico has a vast collection of model boats and ships from all over the world. Its recently donated Mursia Collection includes figureheads, decorated shells, models of ships, compasses and whales' teeth, as well as an extensive library.

The museum's series of interactive labs was expanded in 2005 to include Robotics, and Genetics and Biotechnology. The 16 so-called 'i.labs' are areas where children can learn hands-on about the back-ground and application of cutting-edge advance-ments in science and technology.

One of the major draws over the coming years is expected to be the *Enrico Toti*, the first submarine constructed in Italy after World War II. It was launched on 12 March 1967 as an SSK (hunter-killer submarine), primarily as a deterrent against the nuclear-propelled torpedo-launchers of the Soviet Army. It was discharged from service in 1999, and the following year the Italian Navy donated the ves-sel to the museum. After extensive preparation and transportation, it opened to view in December 2005. Groups of six people can enter at a time.

Sant'Ambrogio

Piazza Sant'Ambrogio 15 (02 8645 0895). Metro Sant'Ambrogio/bus 50, 54, 94. **Open** *Church* 7.15am-noon, 2.30-7pm Mon-Sat; 7.15am-1.15pm, 3-7.45pm Sun. *San Vittore chapel* 7.30am-noon, 3.30-7pm daily. **Admission** free. **Map** p250 C7.
The charismatic Bishop Ambrose (Ambrogio) – who defended orthodox Christianity against Arianism and later became Milan's patron saint – had this Basilica Martyrum built between 379 and 386. The remains of local martyr-saints Gervasius and Protasius still lie in the crypt.

The church was enlarged in the eighth century, when the Benedictines erected the Campanile dei Monaci (monks' bell tower) to the right of the façade. In the ninth century, under Archbishop Anspert, the atrium preceding the façade was added; it was here that the populace sought sanctuary in times of trou-ble. The church's Romanesque appearance stems from ninth- and tenth-century redesigns. Anspert's

atrium was remodelled in the 11th century, when a complete reconstruction of the church got under way. Its capitals feature carved scenes from Bible stories and mythical beasts symbolising the strug-gle between Good and Evil.

The Torre dei Canonici (canons' tower) to the left of the façade was built between 1128 and 1144. Further changes to the interior of the church were made in 1196 after the dome collapsed.

In 1492 Ludovico 'il Moro' Sforza called on Donato Bramante to remodel the eighth-century Benedictine monastery. The fall of il Moro in 1499 put an end to Bramante's makeover, which as a result was limit-ed to one side of the old cloister (the Portico della Canonica, accessible from the left of the nave). The church had a lucky escape from a planned remodel-ling job in the 17th century, but suffered severe air-raid damage in 1943. The bombing destroyed Bramante's work, which was subsequently recon-structed using salvaged original materials.

Saintly vision

In a near-contemporary mosaic portrait in the church of Sant'Ambrogio, Milan's patron saint, Ambrose (c334-97), looks simple and humble. It's a misleading picture: this patrician Roman was a man of vast learning, a musician, a writer and an uncompromising weeder-out of heretics. And if his famously charitable works make his saintly status well deserved, his equally famous refusal to buckle under temporal authority gives some measure of the man who set the model for centuries of strong Church control in northern Italy.

Ambrose came to Milan as a public official but was proclaimed bishop by the locals in 374, then hastily ordained afterwards. He was an avid student of the (pagan) ancients, as is obvious from the quotations and influences on his writings. It was he who imposed his Christian-Neoplatonic ideas on a doubting African convert called Augustine, who would go on to become one of the Church's greatest teachers and a saint.

With a crystal-clear vision of the need for the Church to emerge as a guiding beacon as the Roman Empire declined, Ambrose stood up to even the highest powers. Not only did he refuse to allow Empress Justina to build an Arian chapel in Milan, but he also bundled Emperor Theodosius unceremoniously out of his church after news reached him of a massacre perpetrated under the emperor's orders.

The interior has the sober proportions of the austere Lombard Romanesque style, its three aisles covered with ribbed cross-vaults and false galleries holding up the massive walls. Beneath the pre-Romanesque pulpit, reconstructed from the original pieces after the dome collapsed on it in 1196, lies what is known as the Stilicone Sarcophagus. This fourth-century masterpiece was traditionally believed to have been the burial place of the Roman general of that name who served the Emperor Honorius and died in 408. Later research disproved this legend. The 12th-century golden altar, illustrated with scenes from the life of Christ on the front and of St Ambrose on the back, once covered the porphyry casket commissioned to house the remains of Ambrose, Protasius and Gervasius when they were dug up in the ninth century. The three saints now share an ornate glass coffin-for-three in the crypt. Suspended protectively above the altar, the tenth-century *ciborium* (canopy) is in the form of a little temple; its four porphyry columns decorated in stucco are recycled Roman artefacts. Chapels on the right of the church house the remains of Satiro and Marcellina, Ambrose's brother and sister.

To the right of the main altar, a series of chapels leads to the Sacello di San Vittore in Ciel d'Oro. Part of the church's original fourth-century structure, this chapel was clinically reworked in the 1930s, so that only its glorious, glowing golden fifth-century mosaics in the dome remain to remind us of its antique glory. They portray St Ambrose standing between Gervasius and Protasius, with a sprinkling of other minor local martyrs looking on. This section of the church has been converted into a small museum (access is through the 18th-century Cappella di Sant'Ambrogio Morente) consisting of the mosaics and precious church furnishings, including the silver and gold cross that was carried by Cardinal-saint Carlo Borromeo in 1576 in a procession giving thanks for the end of the plague.

There are more mosaics, from between the fourth and eighth centuries (though restored after extensive damage in 1943) in the apse of the main church. Christ sits enthroned between Gervasius and Protasius, while Ambrose performs miracles all around – including an interesting act of bi-location, where he's in Milan and at the funeral of St Martin in France at the same time.

The museum that was once housed in the cloisters has been split up and the exhibits moved to the Museo Diocesano (*see p85*) and the San Vittore in Ciel d'Oro chapel here. The other remnant of the museum is an exhibition space in the Antico Oratorio della Passione (piazza Sant'Ambrogio 23A, opening times vary with exhibition, admission free). **Photo** *p90*.

Santa Maria della Vittoria

Via de Amicis 11 (mobile 329 966 5460). Metro Sant'Ambrogio/bus 94/tram 2, 14. **Open** 10am-5pm Mon-Fri. **Admission** free. **Map** p250 C7.
This Romanian Orthodox church is most notable for its crypt built by Cardinal Luigi Omodeo in 1669 as a family mausoleum. The crypt now houses exhibits on recent archaeological research on prehistoric and Roman Lombardy.

San Vittore al Corpo

Via San Vittore 25 (02 4800 5351). Metro Sant'Ambrogio/bus 50, 54, 58, 94. **Open** 7.30am-noon, 3.30-7pm daily. **Admission** free. **Map** p250 B7.
The church and former monastery of San Vittore al Corpo grew up around the mausoleum of Emperor Valentinian II, who died in 392; parts of this ancient structure are now beneath the Museo Nazionale della Scienza e della Tecnologia Leonardo da Vinci (*see p90*). The complex was taken over in 1010 by Benedictine monks, who got down to some serious rebuilding. It was given another overhaul in 1560, when it became one of Milan's most sumptuously decorated churches. Works by many local names of the late 16th and 17th centuries – Girolamo Quadrio, Camillo Procaccini, Giovanni Ambrogio Figino, Daniele Crespi – are still here. There are also choir stalls with wood-inlay intarsia work from the 1580s.

Università Cattolica del Sacro Cuore

Largo Gemelli 1 (02 72 341). Metro Sant'Ambrogio/bus 50, 58, 94. **Open** 8am-9.30pm Mon-Fri; 8am-4.30pm Sat. Closed Aug. **Admission** free. **Map** p250 C7.
In 1497 Ludovico il Moro called upon Donato Bramante to expand what had been– before it was turned over to the Cistercian order in the late

Civico Museo Archeologico. *See p94*.

The rococo façade of the **Palazzo Arese Litta** is almost as dramatic as the theatre within.

15th century – the most powerful and influential Benedictine monastery in northern Italy during the Middle Ages. Although Bramante was hired to add four grandiose cloisters, only two were completed (an Ionic one in 1513 and a Doric one in 1630). As a result of an agreement between the Catholic Church and the Fascist government, in 1921 the ex-monastery became home to the Catholic university. Throughout the 1930s and '40s architect Giovanni Muzio overhauled the complex in his trademark dry, straightforward style. The student life has proved more colourful than the architecture: the 1968 protests kicked off here.

Santa Maria delle Grazie & around

Corso Magenta links a number of important sights. With its dazzling frescoes by Bernardino Luini, the church of **San Maurizio** is chief among them, but unfortunately it is closed for long-term renovation. Next door is the **Civico Museo Archeologico** (*see p94*), a less glitzy though no less interesting sight; the two share architectural remains (seen from the back) dating from the time when Milan was one of the Roman army's most influential strongholds.

Across the road at No.24, the Palazzo Arese Litta, now home to the **Teatro Litta** (*see p175*), has a rococo façade with two giant masks and two colossal telamons flanking the entrance. It was designed in 1645 by Francesco Maria Ricchini, while the rococo façade by

Bartolomeo Bolli was added in the mid 18th century. A monumental staircase leads to the Sala Rossa, with its red brocaded walls, where a pearl embedded in the floor recalls a tear shed by the awestruck Duchess Litta when she met Napoleon.

Heading west along corso Magenta, there are two other *palazzi* of note. The one at No.29 was given to Lorenzo de' Medici in 1486 by the Sforzas (though today there's nothing more remarkable about the edifice than that odd fact). At No.12 you'll find the **Casa Rossi**, a notable building designed by Giuseppe Pestagalli around 1860 to simulate the superimposed logge of Renaissance *palazzi*. The building boasts a peculiar octagonal courtyard that's worth a gander.

Continuing westwards along corso Magenta, you come to **Santa Maria delle Grazie** (*see p95*) and the refectory housing Milan's most precious work of art, *The Last Supper* (*see p94* **Supper time**). While you're here, pay a visit to the church itself – a welcome break from the timetabled tourism surrounding Leonardo's masterpiece. Nearby, on via Carducci, stop for a drink in Bar Magenta (*see p119*), a mainstay of the Milanese bar scene.

Still on corso Magenta, the **Palazzo delle Stelline**, at No.61, has now been rather brutally remodelled but continues to house the charitable foundation named after the palazzo, as well as a hotel (*see p48*). Built on the site of the original Santa Maria della Stella convent after the latter burned to the ground, the palazzo was designated by Carlo Borromeo as an orphanage – and continued to function as such until the 1970s. The present Fondazione Stelline works to promote the cultural, social and economic development of the city.

Civico Museo Archeologico

Corso Magenta 15 (02 8645 0011). Metro Cadorna/bus 18, 50, 58/tram 19, 24, 27. **Open** 9am-1pm, 2-5.30pm (last entry 5pm) Tue-Sun. **Admission** €3; €1 concessions. **No credit cards. Map** p250 C6/p252 C6. The origins of the Archeological Museum are almost as interesting as the collections within. The entrance

courtyard once formed a section of the Monastero Maggiore, a Benedictine convent that housed the city's most influential order of nuns (currently closed for renovation along with its church, San Maurizio).

Downstairs you'll find a stretch of Roman city walls (built under Emperor Maximian in the third century), and in the rear cloister the remains of a first-century Roman house and two towers. Indeed almost the whole ground floor is dedicated to arte-facts from the important settlement Mediolanum, including the unique Coppa Trivulzio from the late fourth century, a cup created from a single piece of glass, and the wonderful stone Zeus head from the first or second century.

Supper time

Milan's relationship with Leonardo da Vinci is on the up – it's almost as if the city has rediscovered its greatest ever artist-in-residence. Galleries and museums all over town have installed or refurbished their own Leonardo sections. But it is *Il Cenacolo* (1495-7) or *The Last Supper* that remains the biggest art tourist draw in Milan, and deservedly so.

Da Vinci was invited to the city by Ludovico 'il Moro' Sforza to become 'pictor et ingenarius ducalis' – the duke's painter and engineer. In fact, he produced fewer than ten works of art during his two periods of residency here (17 years from 1482, then seven years beginning in 1506), spending most of his time engaged in engineering matters (for more on this, see the Leonardo exhibitions at the Museo Nazionale della Scienza e della Tecnologia, *see p90*, and Museo d'Arte e Scienza, *see p64*).

Between 1495 and 1497 Leonardo worked on *The Last Supper*, arguably the greatest painting of the Renaissance. The work captures the dramatic moment immediately

after Jesus has revealed that one of his disciples will betray him. The artist portrays their expressions of shock, amazement and hostility with an acute psychological probity. Leonardo's compositional technique has also drawn much comment – the disciples are divided into four groups of three, and three doorways form the background behind Jesus (the arch of the central door also doubles as a halo for the serene Christ).

It won't take you long to realise that the painting is in a seriously deteriorated condition. Leonardo experimented with a new technique for *The Last Supper*, painting on to dry plaster, rather than mixing his paints with the substance while it was still wet. This enabled him to retain control over tone and nuance, but prevented the paints from impregnating the plaster base.

The work has a history of dereliction. Paint began to peel off even within Leonardo's lifetime, resulting in what critics would come to call 'the most famous wreck in the history of art'. By the beginning of the 16th century *The Last Supper* was fading fast, and artists

The Egyptian collection was principally created from 19th-century findings, as well as donations from the Milanese Egyptologist Luigi Vassalli. One of the most significant materials is the 'Book of the Dead', a kind of Egyptian guidebook to burial and voyage into the afterlife. The impressive prehistoric section covers the Milanese environs from the Neolithic period to Roman times.

Plans to enlarge the museum and create a new early medieval section are in the pipeline, and Greek, Etruscan and Gandhara materials will move to the Archeological Museum in Ansaldo, between via Bergognone and via Tortona, once it is completed (though this could take a few years yet). **Photo** *p92.*

Santa Maria delle Grazie

Piazza Santa Maria delle Grazie (02 4801 4248). Metro Cadorna or Conciliazione/bus 18/tram 24. **Open** 7.30am-noon, 3-7pm daily. **Admission** free. **Map** p250 B6.

The church of Santa Maria delle Grazie was begun in 1463 to a plan by Guiniforte Solari. Just two years after it was finished in the 1480s, Ludovico 'il Moro' Sforza commissioned architect Donato Bramante to turn the church into a family mausoleum reflecting the new Renaissance style. (Some experts reject this theory, doubting Bramante's involvement in the project at all, or ascribing a minor, preliminary planning role to him.) So down came Solari's apse and up went

were frequently called in to touch sections up. In the early 19th century, invading French soldiers used the monastery refectory as a stable, and the Renaissance masterpiece was used for target practice during their drunken binges.

World War II air raids came close to blowing up parts of the church, including three walls of the refectory where *The Last Supper* is located, leaving the fresco standing on its own under the open sky (a divine act of salvation, perhaps?). Ironically, despite surviving all this, the work still suffers from a philistinic wound inflicted early in its life – the entrance door that has been carved into the bottom centre, chopping off Jesus' feet.

Though the mural has been more or less *in restauro* since it was first painted, the biggest, most definitive restoration got under way in 1977. This removed layers of paint and detritus accumulated over the centuries, and, when the fresco was finally unveiled again in 1995, allowed some of the original luminous colours to re-emerge.

It has been necessary to reserve your (timed, 15-minute) visit to see the painting for some years now (do try to book one of the informative guided tours; otherwise you can hire an audio set for an extra €2.50). Not surprisingly, visitor numbers have increased even more since the publication of Dan Brown's bestselling *The Da Vinci Code* in 2003, and are likely to surge again when the film adaptation is released in 2006. Brown's novel claims that da Vinci hid secret messages in his paintings and, specifically, that there is no Holy Grail in the painting, that the disciple immediately to Jesus' right ('with flowing red hair, delicate folded

hands, and the hint of a bosom') is actually Mary Magdalene, and that 'an enormous, flawlessly formed letter M' is traced by Jesus and the group to his right (signifying Mary, of course). The book has captured the imagination of millions, but it is worth remembering that it's a work of fiction. John the Baptist was commonly painted with a feminine aspect in Leonardo's time, and, Cenacolo staff point out, da Vinci's early sketches for the painting identify the figure as the Baptist.

On the opposite wall, Donato da Montorfano painted his *Crucifixion* in 1495. Leonardo added the portraits of Ludovico il Moro, his wife Beatrice and their children, but these too have faded beyond recognition.

Other must-see sites for Leonardo-hunters include the Navigli (*see p88*), the Museo Poldi Pezzoli (*see p58*) and Gli Orti di Leonardo restaurant in the Palazzo delle Stelline hotel (*see p48*), not to mention the reconstruction of Leonardo's horse (at the Ippodromo, piazzale dello Sport 15, in the San Siro district, *see p96*, www.leonardoshorse.org), gifted to the city in 1999 by an impassioned American who managed to find the funding to construct Leonardo's never-completed equestrian tribute to Ludovico Sforza.

The Last Supper (Il Cenacolo)

Santa Maria delle Grazie, piazza Santa Maria delle Grazie 2 (02 498 7588/reservations obligatory 02 8942 1146/www.cenacolo vinciano.it). Metro Cadorna or Conciliazione/ bus 18/tram 24. **Open** 8.15am-6.45pm Tue-Sun. *Guided tours in English* 9.30am, 3.30pm. **Admission** €8; €3.25 concessions; free under-18s, over-65s. *Guided tour* €3.25. **Credit** AmEx, DC, MC, V. **Map** p250 B6.

a Renaissance tribune in its place. At the same time, the adjoining Dominican monastery was given the *chiostrino* (small cloister) and a new sacristy. The monks ran an active branch of the Inquisition in their monastery from 1553 to 1778, and continued to endow their church with decorative elements. The complex escaped meddling restoration until the late 19th century, when some faux-Renaissance elements were added. World War II bombing in 1943 destroyed the great cloister of the monastery but spared the *chiostrino* and the refectory with Leonardo's *Last Supper* on its wall (*see p94* **Supper time**).

The terracotta façade of the church is in the best Lombard tradition; the portal is attributed to Bramante. Inside, Solari's Gothic leanings in the three-aisled nave clash with the fresco-covered arches and Bramante's more muscular, massive style. Standing out amid works by leading local artists from the 15th to 17th centuries is an altarpiece (in the sixth chapel on the left) showing the Holy Family with St Catherine by the 16th-century Venetian painter Paris Bordone. The carved wooden choir stalls in the apse date from 1470.

Entrance to the Bramantesque *chiostrino* is just before the main altar, where a door on the left takes you through the Cappella di Santa Maria delle Grazie e del Santissimo Sacramento and the old sacristy/bookstore, with 15th-century frescoes (sometimes erroneously attributed to Leonardo) and huge cabinets with wooden inlay and painted Bible scenes. One cabinet used to hide a secret passage to the Castello Sforzesco, used by Il Moro. A door leads out into the *chiostrino*, also known as the frog cloister after the four bronze amphibians continually spurting water from their mouths in the centre of the pool. Its gardens provide a welcome, relaxing atmosphere after the bustle and crowd in the piazza outside the church. During mass the cloisters can be accessed through a door in via Caradosso 1 (same opening times as the church).

Fiera MilanoCity & San Siro

It's entirely possible that you have come to Milan to attend one of the many trade fairs held in the **Fiera MilanoCity** (*see below*); if not, it's unlikely you'll be drawn to the area, although it is full of beautiful, tree-lined neighbourhoods. The Fiera is one of the largest trade-fair grounds in Europe, stretching all the way from the post-war construction around largo Domodossola to piazzale Giulio Cesare and viale Scarampo, the thoroughfare that leads to the *autostrada* for Turin and the lakes. For years discussions about municipal development were monopolised by various proposals for moving the complex somewhere further away from downtown. And in 2005 an even bigger Fiera Milano site opened in Rho, in the northwestern outskirts of the city. Now the debate rages as to what to do with the 'old' complex;

in the meantime it continues to host trade events, although the famous Furniture Fair is held at the Rho site (*see p145*).

The **Casa di Riposo per Musicisti** (*see below*), final resting place of composer Giuseppe Verdi, is a short walk down leafy via Buonarroti from the piazzale Giulio Cesare side of the Fiera. Further south, posh shopping strip corso Vercelli heads east from piazza Piemonte.

West of the Fiera is the neighbourhood of **San Siro**, a verdant area characterised by modern apartment buildings, luxury cars and rooftop swimming pools. It is the site of the city's world-famous San Siro soccer stadium, or, to give it its proper name, Stadio Giuseppe Meazza (*see p170*). It's also home to several parks: Monte Stella (via Cimabue or via Terzaghi), an artificial hill created from World War II rubble; the Parco del Trenno (via Novara or via Cascina Bellaria); and nearby Boscoincittà (via Cascina Bellaria or SS11).

Casa di Riposo per Musicisti – Fondazione Giuseppe Verdi

Piazza Buonarroti 29 (02 4996 0001/02 499 6009). Metro Buonarroti/bus 61, 67. **Open** *Crypt* 10am-noon, 2.30-6pm daily. **Admission** free.
A statue of composer Giuseppe Verdi presides over piazza Buonarroti, where a neo-Romanesque palazzo, designed in 1899 by architect Camillo Boito (the top floor is a post-war addition), houses a retirement home for musicians. Across the courtyard – often filled with the sound of retired tenors or sopranos running through a few scales – stairs lead down to the crypt where Verdi and his wife Giuseppina Strepponi are buried. **Photo** *p89*.

Fiera MilanoCity

Piazzale Giulio Cesare (freephone 800 820 029/02 499 71/information desk 02 4997 7703/www.fiera milano.it). Metro Amendola-Fiera/bus 48, 68/tram 19, 27/787 shuttle from Linate. **Open** times vary. **Admission** prices vary.
Milan's original trade fair was set up near Porta Venezia in 1920 in an effort to kick-start an economy that was proving slow to recover from World War I. As fair events grew, the structure was moved to its current location, expanding as permanent pavilions were added over the years. Of the original buildings, only the Palazzo dello Sport (1925) and a few art nouveau edifices near the beginning of via Domodossola survived wartime bombing. But reconstruction work was swift in the post-war period, and the Fiera is now among the largest trade structures in Europe. Its 375,000sq m (4 million sq ft) area hosts 26 exhibition pavilions and each year it plays host to tens of thousands of exhibitors and millions of visitors – although the new site in Rho is even more massive. Two internal pavilions are more architecturally notable than the others: the Padiglione dell'Agricoltura (1957-61) and the Padiglione della Meccanica (1968-9).

Eat, Drink, Shop

Restaurants

Finding food 'like *mamma* used to make' may be getting harder in Milan, but culinary variety – and even serious gastronomy – is on the rise.

Eat, Drink, Shop

You can't eat like you used to in Milan. And at restaurant tables across town, the locals are asking themselves why. One reason seems to be demographics. As the city adjusts to a post-industrial economy, the old regional restaurants, which once catered to labourers from the south pining for some home cooking, have given way to ethnic restaurants catering to Italians who have been abroad. This has been a mixed blessing for the Milanese. On the one hand it has become harder to find a simple (and simply priced) plate of mozzarella; on the other it's now possible to get good ethnic food.

The second reason is economic. Despite government assurances to the contrary, most Milanese diners have noticed that the meal that used to cost them 45,000 lire now costs them €40. Have they been shortchanged? This is one of the great debates in Milan (and Italian politics), and one of the prime topics of conversation at dinner. (For the record, the official lire to euro exchange rate was 1,936.27, which means that that the price is only up 73 per cent).

The third reason is the Slow Food-isation of Italy. The Slow Food movement (*see p32* **In the slow lane**) has done much to make the country more aware of its gastronomic heritage. It has also been at the forefront of the push to make Italy take its gastronomy more seriously – particularly in restaurants. For many years, there was not much difference between dishes served within and outside the home. The restaurant was simply the place to go when *mamma* was too tired to cook or there were too many people to feed. The food at most restaurants, then, was home-style, and the cook was – more likely than not – a surrogate *mamma*, who made sure the family was well fed and content.

Once food became serious, though, the rules of the game changed. The chefs are largely trained, and male, and the sense of satisfying abundance has given way to the challenge of boutique quality. The good old plate of mozzarella has become a plate of mozzarella di bufala DOC, and has been priced accordingly. Is this good or bad? For those looking for pristine ingredients, carefully prepared, the answer is 'good'. For those who look for hidden pleasures and the thrill of the hunt, things are more ambiguous. Yes, there is more choice these

days, but wasn't part of the charm of that little trattoria the fact that the salami was cured by *zio* Tommaso, and a big plate would cost 3,000 lire? Now Uncle Tommaso has opened up an *azienda agricola*, and the same (albeit smaller) plate of salami costs €8.

For the visitor, all this means that tracking down the stereotypical trattoria with red checked tablecloths and straw-wrapped flasks of Chianti is harder than ever, though they do exist, if you know where to look (we've included the best below). And, also on the plus side, dining in Milan still offers value, despite the switch to euros.

MAKING A MEAL OF IT

Do Italians still eat an *antipasto* (starter), followed by a *primo* (usually pasta, risotto or soup) and *secondo* (meat or fish course), accompanied by a *contorno* (vegetable side dish) and finally dessert, cheese, fruit, coffee… and perhaps a *digestivo/amaro* or a grappa?

 The best **Restaurants**

For traditional Milanese cuisine
Masuelli San Marco (*see p106*); Trattoria Madonnina (*see p112*); Da Abele (*see p106*).

For a romantic evening
Innocenti Evasioni (*see p105*); Osteria delle Vigne (*see p111*).

For something ethnic
Tara (*see p106*); Warsa (*see p109*).

For regional Italian cuisine
Dongiò (Calabrian, *see p111*); Al Merluzzo Felice (Sicilian, *see p111*); Giulio Pane e Ojo (Roman, *see p111*).

For seeing and being seen
Da Giacomo (*see p106*); Armani/Nobu (*see p105*).

For top-flight Italian cuisine
Osteria Grand Hotel (*see p111*); Cracco-Peck (*see p102*), Joia (*see p106*).

Old-school food and old-school diners at **Da Giannino L'Angolo d'Abruzzo**. *See p106.*

On paper, yes, but in practice few Milanese care to spend the two or three hours necessary to do such a meal justice. Most prefer to choose two out of the three main courses (*antipasto*, *primo* and *secondo*), complementing the meal with a *contorno* here and a slice of cheese there. (Many will still, however, finish with the grappa or *digestivo*). The full Italian meal is a luxury, not a diner's obligation, so don't feel pressured into eating more than you want.

Fixed-price meals are still seen as something for the tourists (indeed, you might want to steer clear of anywhere that has a *menu turistico* written in several languages). Some of the more upscale/creative restaurants will offer a tasting menu (*menù degustazione*). This can be a good way of sampling a bit of everything if you're not going to be in town long enough to eat your way through the Milanese repertoire.

WHAT TO EAT

For years Milan acted as a magnet for southern Italians looking for work. The result was that pasta became as common as Lombard rice and polenta. Nevertheless, most Milanese still have a soft touch for well-prepared risotto: thick kernels of arborio or carnaroli rice, slowly simmered in broth, supplemented with vegetables, seafood or meat, butter and sometimes cheese. The result is divinely decadent. True Lombard pasta dishes tend to be based on fresh pasta. *Tortelli di zucca*, pumpkin-stuffed pasta, and *pizzoccheri*

(buckwheat pasta with cheese, cabbage and potato) are both Lombard specialities.

Unlike other Italian soups, Lombard versions are so thick they easily constitute a main course. *Zuppa pavese* (broth with bread and eggs) and *zuppa di porri e bietole* (with leeks and Swiss chard) are found in rural eateries. *Casoeúla* is a soupy cabbage stew with polenta, pork and sausage. Polenta, topped with mushrooms or meat, is a common feature of Lombardy, especially in winter.

When it comes to *secondi*, land-locked Lombardy is a surprisingly good place to eat both freshwater fish and seafood. Milan is Italy's biggest sea-fish distribution centre: the morning catch is flown in so quickly that it's as fresh here as on the coast. Lakes and rivers yield sturgeon and grey caviar in late November. Perch, trout, carp, salmon and eel are also used in the cuisine of the lake regions.

Succulent cuts of meat – veal in particular – are transformed into namesake specialities: *ossobuco alla milanese* (braised veal shanks) and *cotoletta alla milanese* (breaded and fried veal chop). Lombardy also produces some excellent cured meats.

> ❶ Purple numbers given in this chapter correspond to the location of each restaurant as marked on the street maps. *See pp248-252.*

MILAN•
VIA PIOPPETTE
(Colonne di S.Lorenz
TEL.++39 02.8940867
www.exploitmilano.co

EXPLOIT
DRINKS&DINNER

Living

liqueurs & delights

MILANO
PIAZZA SEMPIONE 2
(Arco della Pace
TEL.++39 02.3310082∢
www.livingmilano.com

The region is a cheese-lover's heaven too, its offerings ranging from sharp gorgonzola to oozing *taleggio* and spreadable *stracchino*. In most traditional Lombard dishes, olive oil is replaced by butter, and heavy cream is common.

For more on local cuisine, *see pp30-34 and p108* **On the menu**.

WHERE TO EAT

Traditionally, an *osteria* was something like a social club, a place where the working class could get a glass of wine and some nibbles; a trattoria was a cheap eaterie serving basic home cooking (*cucina casalinga*); and a *ristorante* was a more refined venue. These distinctions are best left to students of historical linguistics, though, particularly since '*osteria*' has become a trendy addition to a restaurant name; many creative chefs eschew the '*ristorante*' title, and many *trattorie* charge restaurant prices. Their decor might be all exposed brick and plain wood floors, but the owners probably paid top dollar for that distressed look.

GLASS CONSCIOUSNESS

Food is not the only thing being taken more seriously these days. Italian wines, particularly regional ones, have finally moved out of the shadows cast by Barolo, Barbaresco and Chianti. Italian wine lists tend to include a dazzling range of national wines, from local Nebbiolo to Nero d'Avola from Sicily. The DOC (*denominazione di origine controllata*) seal of quality on the bottle is a reliable pointer to a good wine, but there are some equally wonderful wines sold under the humble guise of *vini da tavola* (table wines) because they do not conform to stringent DOC regulations.

Lombardy is more wine consumer than wine maker. That said, the Franciacorta area between Bergamo and Brescia produces champagne-quality sparkling wines and the Oltrepò wines from the hills on the far side of the Po river provide a variety of good-value reds and whites.

Most *trattorie* and *osterie* (and some restaurants) also serve *vino sfuso*, which can be ordered in quarter-, half- or one-litre carafes. While the quality varies greatly, if you're lucky you'll get a young, quaffable wine, particularly at the better *trattorie*. The traditional accompaniment to pizza is beer or soft drinks.

If you've ordered a full meal, you might be invited to a *digestivo* or a grappa on the house. The choice of *digestivi* is endless; Ramazzotti – a dark, syrupy liqueur made from herbs and spices – is a distinctly Milanese variant.

UP IN SMOKE

In January 2005 Italy joined the no-smoking revolution. Initially a law was passed that made it compulsory for restaurants to have designated smoking sections, provided they had the right hardware (extractor fans and so on). When this proved too expensive and impracticable, most places went completely no-smoking. So be prepared to stand outside if you want a puff.

Eat, Drink, Shop

Good to go

For the typical Milan worker, a lunch hour means exactly that, and most restaurants in town are adept at getting people back to work before the boss gets angry. Bars, too, are attuned to the city's prandial needs: even the humblest will have a decent selection of sandwiches. The menu at better-stocked bars can seem quite baroque, and many also offer a *tavola calda*, which means that you can find hot pastas or simple main courses (usually made earlier that day, and reheated in the microwave).

In addition, Milan has shops selling pizza by the slice (*al trancio*), slabs of focaccia and *panzerotti* (fried or baked turnover similar to a calzone). Many bakeries (*panificio*) also provide quick bites to go.

Just behind the Rinascente department store by the Duomo is **Panzerotti Luini** (via Santa Radegonda 16, 02 8646 1917, closed Mon afternoon, Sun), a Milan institution that has been selling *panzerotti* and focaccia since 1940. Another local favourite is **Princi**, a well-stocked chain of bakeries offering mouth-watering slabs of focaccia and pizza. It has several central locations, including via Speronari 6 (Centre, 02 874 797, closed Sun) and via Ponte Vetero 10 (North, 02 7201 6067, closed Sun), which also dishes up hot food in the afternoon. Its branch at piazza XXV Aprile (North, 02 2906 0832) is open round the clock, making it a favourite meeting spot for clubbers. At via Solferino 5 (North, 02 805 3096, closed Sun), **Pattini Marinoni** is one of the better *panifici* in town, serving salads and hot dishes alongside pizza and focaccia.

If you want something more substantial, but still quick, check out **La Cotoletteria** (corso Garibaldi 11, North, 02 874 809, closed Mon), a showcase for that most Milanese (or is it Austrian?) dish: breaded veal escalope, with various toppings, all at around €13.

PRACTICALITIES

Most eating establishments charge *coperto* (cover charge) for providing a tablecloth and bread. This should never be more than €4.

Italians are not big on tips and only tend to leave one if they feel the food or service was outstanding. Tourists, however, are generally expected to be more generous: anything between five and ten per cent will put a smile on your waiter's face, but bear in mind that you're under no obligation to leave anything, especially if you're dissatisfied with the service.

Italy is still predominantly a cash society and many establishments will try to dissuade you from using plastic. However, all but the smallest *trattorie* and *pizzerie* accept credit cards. By law you must be given an official receipt (*scontrino fiscale*) upon paying the bill. Hold on to this: in the unlikely event that a policeman catches you leaving a restaurant without one, you (and the restaurateur) could receive a nasty fine.

Italians like to eat at regular times and opening hours are fairly standard. The times listed here refer to those when hot meals can be ordered, though the establishment may stay open much later. Normal eating hours are 12.30-2.30pm and 8-10pm.

CLOSE TO THE VEG

Exclusively vegetarian restaurants are few and far between in Milan; **Joia** (*see p106*), a temple to vegetarian haute cuisine, is an honourable exception, as is its cheaper outpost, **Joia Leggero** (*see p111*). However, non-meat-eaters are by no means limited to salads and pizzas. Most Milanese restaurants offer a range of delicious vegetable dishes and pasta sauces; main courses can often be replaced by a *contorno* or a vegetable *antipasto*. Life will be harder for vegans (Lombard cuisine is heavily dairy-based), but again, there is never any shortage of fresh fruit and vegetables.

Average restaurant prices given in the listings below are per person and are based on three courses (two for *pizzerie*) and do not include drinks. They should be used as a guideline only.

Duomo & Centre

Italian

Cracco-Peck

Via Victor Hugo 4 (02 876 774/www.peck.it). Metro Duomo/bus 54, 60, 65/tram 2, 3, 14, 27. **Meals served** 12.30-2pm, 7.30-10pm Mon-Fri; 7.30-10pm Sat (winter only). Closed 3wks Dec-Jan, 3wks Aug. **Average** €100. **Credit** AmEx, DC, MC, V. **Map** p250 D7/p252 D7 **❶**

Cracco-Peck's creative, modern menu is custom-made for Milan's expense account-laden power brokers. The two Michelin stars and consistently high ratings in the Italian Gambero Rosso and Veronelli fine dining guides are guarantees that food is taken seriously here. But even the Milanese are Italian enough not to confuse dining well with eating well. And they are Italian enough to know that it is eating well that matters. Do you eat well at Cracco-Peck? If you choose a *primo* of cocoa-flavoured pasta and sea urchins, do you find the addition of the cocoa pretentious, or do you applaud the chef for using an ingredient that needs to be pristinely fresh? When a waiter walks by with a tennis ball-sized white truffle, do you shake your head at the extravagance, or ask to take a look at the truffle tasting menu? (Two or three tasting menus are available.) Certainly, Cracco-Peck is a beacon of Italy's serious dining movement, and it would raise nary an eyebrow in New York, Paris or London. Indeed, it would be considered good value, with its relatively full portions and a wine list that doesn't require a banker's approval. The debate it raises has as much to do with Italian traditionalism as it does with odd ingredients in the pasta. For more on Peck, *see p107* **The taste maker**.

Peck Italian Bar

Via Cesare Cantù 3 (02 869 3017/www.peck.it). Metro Duomo/bus 54, 60, 65/tram 2, 3, 14, 27. **Meals served** 11.30am-8pm daily. **Average** €40. **Credit** AmEx, DC, MC, V. **Map** p250 D7/p252 D7 **❷**

In addition to its food hall and restaurant, the Peck empire also includes a casual café. The mood is one of upscale bustle, with stockbrokers from the nearby Borsa rubbing elbows with Milanese *signore* in for a morning's shopping at La Rinascente. The menu features a brief selection of *primi* and *secondi*, along with a variety of pastries from the cases near the entrance. In a land where it is next to impossible to sit down for a meal outside fixed lunch and dinner times, Peck Italian Bar serves food all day long.

Le Terrazze

La Rinascente, via Radegonda 3 (02 877 159). Metro Duomo/bus 54, 60/tram 2, 3, 13. **Meals served** 7-10pm Mon; noon-2.30pm, 7-10pm Tue-Sat. **Average** €40. **Credit** AmEx, DC, MC, V. **Map** p250 E6/p252 E6 **❸**

The café/restaurant on the seventh floor of the Rinascente department store offers brilliant views of the Duomo's rooftop statuary. In the summer the conservatory roof is taken off, and you can enjoy the stonework while sitting outside on the terrace. But it's the view, not the food, that is the main draw here: while there's nothing wrong with the somewhat limited menu, you can easily get better fare elsewhere.

Trattoria Milanese

Via Santa Marta 11 (02 8645 1991). Metro Cordusio/tram 2, 3, 14. **Meals served** noon-2.30pm, 7.15-10.30pm Wed-Mon. Closed mid July-Aug. **Average** €45. **Credit** AmEx, DC, MC, V. **Map** p250 D7/p252 D7 **❹**

Centro Ittico – Raw Fish Café.
See p105.

American Bar
Cucina & Grill

LAPIROGUE

&opening
june'06
coffee&more

The crisp, white tablecloths at this friendly trattoria are a clue as to the quality of the place: this is traditional but upmarket fare, at prices to match. Pasta,
rice, meat and fish dishes are all simple yet assured:
even a plate of vegetables cooked in chilli and garlic manages to impress. To finish, it has to be the
warm *zabaglione* – perfect on a cold winter's night.
The cheap Italian beer goes well with everything.

Sforzesco & North

Italian

L'Altra Pharmacia
*Via Rosmini 3 (02 345 1300/www.laltrapharmacia.it).
Bus 43, 57/tram 12, 14.* **Meals served** noon-
2.30pm, 7.30-11.30am Mon-Sat. Closed 1wk Jan,
2wks Aug. **Average** €35. **Credit** AmEx, DC,
MC, V. **Map** p248 C4 ❺
This cosily rustic eaterie in Milan's Chinatown, with
simple paper place mats and modern art copies on
bare brick walls, attracts a varied clientele, from the
regulars to the odd celeb. If you're dining with a
crowd, try the delicious *risotto milanese mantecato
in forma di grana* – risotto with saffron served in
the hollowed-out rind of a parmesan cheese. Those
with a strong stomach might want to tuck into a
plate of tripe and beans.

Anema e Cozze
*Via Palermo 15 (02 8646 1646). Metro Moscova/
bus 41, 94.* **Meals served** 12.30-3pm, 7.30pm-
midnight daily. **Average** €15 (lunch €10).
Credit AmEx, MC, V. **Map** p248 D5 ❻
Franchised pizza has come to Italy, with mixed
results. This Neapolitan-style chain of *pizzerie*, however, gets high marks from connoisseurs. In addition to the full menu of pizzas, you can find a good
assortment of fresh fish (or put the two together and
order a *pizza frutti di mare*).
Other locations: Strada Alzaia Naviglio Grande 70,
at via Casale, South (02 837 5459).

Centro Ittico – Raw Fish Café
*Via Martiri Oscuri 19, North (02 2804 0396/
www.rawfishcafe.it). Metro Pasteur/bus 199/tram 1.*
Meals served 12.30-2pm, 8-11pm Mon-Sat. Closed
Aug. **Average** €50-€55. **Credit** AmEx, DC, MC, V.
Map p249 H1 ❼
This fish specialist has moved from its old space
under the railway arches of Stazione Centrale to a
new location just up the road. Quite frankly, it's not
an improvement: today it awkwardly occupies the
far end of what is obviously a night-time venue (the
feeling at lunchtime is distinctly 'morning after').
However, the fish and seafood are good and jumping fresh, and prices are not excessive. Before you
sit down, have an ogle at the fabulous display laid
out on ice and pick out your victim. The place is popular with crowds tucking into great platters of oysters, giant prawns, steaming mounds of spaghetti
with clams, lobster or baby squid, and hunks of
seared tuna and swordfish. **Photos** *p103.*

Emporio Armani Café
*Via dei Giardini 2 (02 7231 8680/www.giorgio
armani.it). Metro Montenapoleone/bus 61, 94/tram
1, 2.* **Meals served** noon-3pm, 8-11pm Mon-Fri;
noon-4pm, 8-11pm Sat; noon-4pm Sun. **Average**
€40. **Credit** AmEx, DC, MC, V. **Map** p249 E5 ❽
A bit more relaxed than its neighbour in the Armani
superstore, Nobu (*see p105*), this is a perfect place
for a revitalising lunch after a hard morning shopping on via Montenapoleone and the surrounding
streets. In the evening you can buy an exclusively
priced dinner to round off your designer purchases.
The menu covers salads, pasta and meat dishes, and
an excellent club sandwich.

Innocenti Evasioni
*Via Privata della Bindellina (02 3300 1882/www.
innocentievasioni.com). Bus 57/tram 1, 14.* **Meals
served** 8-10pm Mon-Sat. Closed Aug. **Average** €30.
Credit AmEx, DC, MC, V.
Well worth the trek to its unlikely location (tucked
away down a narrow and uninviting-looking private
road near piazzale Accursio), this delightful restaurant offers superb food and excellent value. Two
softly lit dining rooms look on to a pretty garden and
nice little details make it feel special: a basket of
freshly baked breads, complimentary nibbles before
the *antipasto*, and the use of silver covers (in spite
of it not being a formal sort of place). There is also
a comprehensive wine list. The menu, featuring
meat, fish and vegetarian choices, is based on fresh,
seasonal ingredients prepared with imagination and
flair without being fussy. Desserts, such as the hot
nougat soufflé with whisky sauce, are spectacular.

La Latteria
*Via San Marco 24 (02 659 7653). Metro Moscova/
bus 41, 94.* **Meals served** 12.30-2.30pm, 7.30-
10pm Mon-Fri. Closed Aug, 1wk Dec. **Average**
€25. **No credit cards**. **Map** p249 E4 ❾
This small trattoria in the Brera district is one of the
better examples of the new Italian emphasis on good
food. It offers clean, creative takes on the standards,
as well as a chance to eavesdrop on the local fashion designers talking business over a plate of pasta.
No reservations are taken, and there aren't many
tables, so be prepared to get there early, or wait.

Bar/restaurants

Armani/Nobu
*Via Pisoni 1 (02 6231 2645/www.giorgioarmani.it).
Metro Montenapoleone/tram 1, 2.* **Meals served**
noon-2.30pm, 7-11.30pm Mon-Sat. **Average** €75.
Credit AmEx, DC, MC, V. **Map** p249 E5 ❿
Raw fish just doesn't get any more fashionable
than the sushi at the Milan outpost of Nobuyuki
Matsuhisa's restaurant empire. Purists will say that
the food isn't at the same level as his New York or
London flagships. People-watchers, however, will
tell you that Nobu's happy hour is *the* place to be if
you want to nibble on sushi and see Milan's fashion
world unwind.

Ethnic

Serendib

*Via Pontida 2 (02 659 2139). Metro Moscova/
bus 41, 94.* **Meals served** 7.30pm-midnight daily.
Closed 10 days Aug. **Average** €25. **Credit** MC, V.
Map p248 D4 ⓫

A Sri Lankan restaurant quietly providing some of
the best-value food in Milan's growing ethnic scene.
It's pleasantly low-lit, with standard eastern decor;
there's a choice of set menus based on vegetable,
meat or fish main dishes. Wash that curry down
with Three Coins lager, and finish off with ginger
tea. At weekends it's especially popular, so it's a
good idea to book.

Tara

*Via Cirillo 16 (02 345 1635/www.ristorante
tara.com). Metro Cadorna/bus 57/tram 1, 29, 30.*
Meals served noon-2.30pm, 7-11.30pm Tue-Sun.
Average €25. **Credit** AmEx, DC, MC, V. **Map**
p248 B4 ⓬

When this thriving Indian restaurant just north of
Parco Sempione opened up a few years ago, its manager proclaimed that it would be more than just a
curry house. Although the menu is quite straightforward (tandoori and curry dishes), the quality of
the ingredients – and the cooking – means the
flavours ring true. It also does Sunday brunch.

San Babila & East

Italian

Bottiglieria Da Pino

*Via Cerva 14 (02 7600 0532). Metro Duomo or
San Babila/bus 54, 60, 73/tram 15, 23, 27.*
Meals served noon-3pm Mon-Sat (bar open
8am-8pm Mon-Sat). Closed Aug, 1wk Dec/Jan.
Average €15-€20. **No credit cards**. **Map**
p251 F6/p252 F6 ⓭

Out front, this trattoria on a side street near largo
Augusto looks like any of the other bars in the neighbourhood. In the dining room behind the bar, though,
you'll find all the hustle, bustle and perpetual motion
of an old-style workers' trat. You'll also find impeccably prepared food and plates of artisan cheese.

Da Abele

*Via Temperanza 5 (02 261 3855). Metro Pasteur/
bus 56.* **Meals served** 8pm-midnight Tue-Sun.
Closed Aug, 2wks Dec-Jan. **Average** €30.
Credit AmEx, DC, MC, V.

This ultra-friendly place specialises in risotto, and a
damn good job it does of it too: hot, steaming mounds
of the stuff come in various forms (with fennel, speck
and onion, for example, or with aubergine and
smoked ricotta). Meat dishes are also available if rice
isn't your thing. Save room for desserts such as white
and dark chocolate cake. Service is friendly and informal, and reservations are made on a same-day basis,
so if you haven't booked, get there early.

Da Giacomo

*Via P Sottocorno 6 (02 7602 3313/www.dagiacomo
cena.it). Tram 29, 30.* **Meals served** 7.30-11pm
Tue; 12.30-2.30pm, 7.30-11pm Wed-Sun. Closed 3wks
Aug; 2wks Dec-Jan. **Average** €50. **Credit** AmEx,
DC, MC, V. **Map** p249 G6 ⓮

It looks like nothing on the outside: an anonymous
trattoria with frosted windows in an anonymous
street. But Da Giacomo is one of Milan's most exclusive (though by no means most expensive) restaurants. In a series of bright and chatty rooms
decorated by the late Renzo Mongiardino (interior
designer to the rich and famous), major players from
Milan's fashion and business worlds jostle for elbow
room. Service can be uncertain, and the competent
Mediterranean cuisine, with the emphasis on fish,
might not win any prizes. But this is just what the
city's captains of industry want: colour and comfort
food in a 'trattoria' that is as difficult to infiltrate as
the Ivy in London. Go with Miuccia or Giorgio – or
book well ahead.

Da Giannino L'Angolo d'Abruzzo

*Via Rosolino Pilo 20 (02 2940 6526). Metro Porta
Venezia/tram 5, 11.* **Meals served** 12.20-2.30pm,
7.30-11pm Tue-Sun. **Average** €25. **Credit** DC, MC,
V. **Map** p249 H5 ⓯

L'Angolo is a throwback to the days when Italian
restaurants really did have red checked tablecloths.
The tables may wobble, but the sense of abundance
is rare for Milan. Meals start with grilled bruschetta and may finish with an own-made *digestivo*. In
between, you'll get a mountain of pasta and down-
home *secondi* such as grilled lamb and sausages.
Photo *p99*.

Joia

*Via P Castaldi 18 (02 2952 2124/www.joia.it).
Metro Porta Venezia or Repubblica/tram 29, 30.*
Meals served 12.30-2.30pm, 7.30-11pm Mon-
Fri; 7.30-11pm Sat. Closed Aug, 2wks Dec-Jan.
Average €60. **Credit** AmEx, DC, MC, V.
Map p249 F4 ⓰

This calm, minimalist but woody-warm space near
the Giardini Pubblici is the domain of Swiss chef
Pietro Leemann, whose often inspired and always
creative cooking has earned him a Michelin star –
an unusual achievement for a vegetarian chef. His
oriental-influenced menus (which also include a few
fish and vegan dishes) feature whimsically named
concoctions such as 'Towards the Core of the Green
Planet' and 'Purple Sphere on a Light Background',
which are characterised by contrasting colours, tex-
tures, shapes and flavours. There are several set
menus (€50-€90), including the lunchtime *'piatto
quadro'*, a snip at €15. There's now also a second
(cheaper) restaurant, Joia Leggero (*see p111*).

Masuelli San Marco

*Viale Umbria 80 (02 5518 4138/www.masuelli-
trattoria.com). Bus 84, 90, 91, 92.* **Meals served**
8-10.30pm Mon; 12.30-2.30pm, 8-10.30pm Tue-Sat.
Closed 3wks Aug, 2wks Dec-Jan. **Average** €40.
Credit AmEx, DC, MC, V. **Map** p251 H8 ⓱

The taste maker

Like many an empire, **Peck** combines humble beginnings with determined expansion. Started as a delicatessen in 1883 by an émigré from Prague, Peck has grown into a three-storied mecca for serious Italian foodies, a Michelin-rated restaurant, and a dowager-endowed café, all in the heart of Milan.

As is also the case with many empires, Peck sometimes tips into self-aggrandizement. At Cracco-Peck (*see p102*), Carlo Cracco's 'creative genius' is as heavily emphasised as the quality of his ingredients. Many of those same ingredients can be found at the Peck food hall around the corner (*see p135; pictured*), along with the hand-candied chestnuts and the €2,000 bottle of wine.

The coffee bar on the first floor of the food hall is also home to the €5 cup of luwak-excreted espresso. For the uninitiated, the luwak is a small nocturnal animal that lives in Indonesia and eats ripe coffee berries for their flesh; the beans come out the other end relatively intact, though enzymes in the luwak's digestive tract have added a touch of fermentation. The result is one of the rarest coffees in the world, valued for its spicy flavour and floral notes. (Think of it as €1 for the espresso and €4 for the stories you can tell.)

Even the relatively casual Peck Italian Bar (*see p102*) is not without pretension, though, in all fairness, the clientele is as responsible for this as Peck.

Beyond the tendency towards extravagance, high standards and a typically Italian delight in so much *abbondanza* permeate Peck. The food is displayed joyously, whether it be the majestic Parma hams in the food hall, or Carlo Cracco's latest creation at the restaurant. And while Peck's prices may not be for the faint-hearted, they are not out of line for the quality of the offerings.

A Milanese institution that never fails to live up to its reputation. The atmosphere is warm, the service attentive, and the cuisine stretches from Piedmont to Lombardy. Some of the dishes may not be to everyone's taste – such as the *filetti di aringhe* (herring fillets in milk), *bollito misto* (mixed boiled meats) or even tripe – but you won't find better versions of these classics in Milan. Start with the excellent choice of cured hams and salami, and order a good bottle of barbera.

Il Teatro

Four Seasons Hotel, via Gesù 6-8 (02 7708 1435/ www.fourseasons.com). Metro Montenapoleone or San Babila/bus 61, 94/tram 1, 2. **Meals served** 7.30-11pm Mon-Sat. Closed Aug. **Average** €100. **Credit** AmEx, DC, MC, V. **Map** p249 E6/p252 E6 ⓭ The flagship restaurant of one of Milan's flagship hotels doesn't disappoint. Overlooking a beautiful courtyard, Il Teatro has a formal atmosphere (crisp tablecloths, immaculate table settings and lots of

Eat, Drink, Shop

On the menu

Antipasti

Antipasto di mare: assorted fish. Common selections include *alici marinate* (marinated anchovies); *carpaccio* (very thin slices of raw fish, usually salmon/*salmone*, swordfish/*pesce spada*, or tuna/*tonno*); *insalata di mare* (seafood salad, usually served at room temperature).

Affettati: cold cuts (often just called *antipasto misto*). Common selections include *bresaola* (cured, air-dried beef); *coppa* (cured pork meat from the neck and shoulder); *culatello* (similar to Parma ham); *lardo* (bacon fat, but delicious when prepared well and placed on warm bread); *pancetta* (the same cut as bacon, cured, not smoked); *prosciutto cotto* (boiled ham); *prosciutto crudo* (Parma ham); *salame* (salami); *salame di cinghiale* (wild boar); *salame d'asino* (donkey); *salame d'oca* (goose).

Nervetti: salad of calf's foot, often served with beans and onions at room temperature.

Sott'aceti: pickles. The most common types are *cipolle* (onions) and *cetrioli* (cucumbers).

Verdure ripiene: vegetables stuffed with breadcrumbs, and sometimes cheese. Common selections include: *carciofi* (artichokes); *melanzane* (aubergines); *peperoni* (green, red, or yellow bell peppers); *zucchine* (courgette).

Pasta

All'arrabbiata: with a spicy tomato sauce.
Al pomodoro: with a simple tomato sauce.
Al ragù: with a meat sauce.
Alle vongole: with a clam sauce.
Casoncelli: meat-stuffed ravioli, often served with *burro sfuso* (brown butter with sage leaves) and *pancetta*.
Pizzoccheri: buckwheat noodles from the Valtellina area, cooked with potatoes, cabbage, and cheese.
Tortelli alla zucca: ravioli stuffed with pumpkin, a speciality of Mantova.

Risotto

Alla certosina: prepared with frogs' legs and snails, a speciality of Pavia.
Alla milanese: prepared with saffron and, traditionally in the pre-BSE world, bone marrow.
Con radicchio: made with red *radicchio trevigiano* (other vegetables can also be used, most notably pumpkin).
Con valcalepio: made with red wine, sometimes served with beans or sausages.

Carne (meat)

Al forno: roast meat or poultry. Common selections include *agnello* (lamb); *coniglio* (rabbit); *faraona* (guinea hen); *pollo* (chicken); *tacchino* (turkey).
Alla griglia: grilled meat or poultry.
Arrosto: roast meat, most often beef (simply *arrosto*), pork (*maiale*) or veal (*vitello*).
Busecca: a stew of tripe, lard, butter, beef, tomatoes and beans.
Cotoletta milanese: breaded veal chop, served on the bone.
Cotechino: pork sausage.
Casoeûla: a stew made from of pork cuts, sausage and cabbage.
Involtini: small rolls of beef or aubergine (*melanzane*) stuffed with ham and cheese.
Ossobuco: braised veal shanks.
Polpette: meatballs.
Polpettone: meat loaf.
Salsicce: sausages, often roasted or grilled.
Stufato: braised meat.

Pesce & frutti di mare (fish & seafood)

Fritto misto: mixed fried seafood, most often *calamari* (squid), *pesciolini* (sprats) and sometimes *gamberi* (prawns).
Lavarello: a freshwater fish from Lake Como.
Persico: a freshwater fish from Lake Como.
Seppie in umido: cuttlefish in a tomato casserole.

Vegetables/contorni (side dishes)

Asparagi: asparagus.
Carciofi: artichokes.
Fagioli: haricot or borlotti beans.
Fagiolini: cooked green beans with garlic and lemon.
Funghi: mushrooms, often sautéed with olive oil, garlic and parsley.
Insalata: salad, either *mista* (mixed) or *verde* (green). Usually served with olive oil and vinegar.
Melanzane: aubergines.
Mostarda: mustard; also candied fruit flavoured with mustard oil, often served with roasts.
Polenta: ubiquitous cornmeal mush, often served with roasts and *stufati* (stews). *See also p34 and p188* **Corn star**.
Pomodori: tomatoes.
Spinaci: spinach.
Zucchine: courgettes.

Trattoria Madonnina – laid-back food and quirky decor. *See p112.*

fawning by waiters), but at least it's an excuse to dress up and enjoy. In any case, Sergio Mei Tomasi's award-winning food is undoubtedly the star. The dishes make proper use of the freshest of regional Italian ingredients (Tuscan lamb, Sicilian ham, for instance), and though they can sound over-fussy on paper, they rarely fail to impress. And well they shouldn't, given the prices (the cheapest appetiser is €22, though the tasting menu is a comparative bargain at €76). Try to save room for the cheese plate (you get to choose from a trolley) or a seductive dessert (such as pannacotta, Valrhona chocolate tart or blackcurrant soufflé).

La Terrazza di via Palestro

4th Floor, via Palestro 2 (02 7600 2277/www.esperia ristorazione.it). Metro Palestro or Turati/bus 61, 94. **Meals served** noon-2.30pm, 7-10pm Mon-Fri. Closed 3wks Aug, 2wks Dec-Jan. **Average** €45. **Credit** AmEx, DC, MC, V. **Map** p249 F5 ⑲

On the top floor of an office block just outside Porta Nuova, this panoramic restaurant with summer terrace is one of the few with a sense of design to match Milan's reputation. The look is *Wallpaper** 1950s retro, with cherry-wood consoles and chrome globe lights. Light, modern seafood dishes dominate the menu, beginning with the house speciality, 'Mediterranean sushi': a surprisingly successful attempt to use Italian fish, rice and pasta to recreate the spirit of Japan's top food export.

Ethnic

Warsa

Via Melzo 16 (02 201 673/www.ristorantewarsa.it). Metro Porta Venezia/tram 5, 9, 11, 30. **Meals served** noon-3pm, 7-10.30pm Mon, Tue, Thur-Sun. **Average** €15. **Credit** MC, V. **Map** p249 G5 ⑳

Eritrean cooking was one of the first ethnic foods to establish itself in Milan, with many of the restaurants setting up shop in the Porta Venezia area, home to much of Milan's large African community. Warsa's menu includes dishes with veal, beef and chicken, plus plenty of vegetarian options – all eaten with your fingers. Try the *miès*, an aromatic wine.

Pizza & snacks

Pizzeria 40

Via P Castaldi 40 (02 2940 0061). Metro Porta Venezia or Repubblica/tram 29, 30. **Meals served** noon-3pm, 6-11pm Mon, Thur-Sun; noon-3pm Tue. **Average** €10. **Credit** AmEx, MC, V. **Map** p249 F4 ㉑

If you've been shopping in corso Buenos Aires, this is an ideal place to stop for a quick lunch or snack. Although there are some pasta dishes on the menu, the house speciality is *pizza al trancio* – deep-pan pizza served in whopping big slices (real men ask for it *abbondante* – in an extra-large portion).

Eat, Drink, Shop

Il **Teatro**. *See p107.*

Porta Romana & South

Italian

Al Merluzzo Felice
Via Lazzaro Papi 6 (02 545 4711). Metro Lodi or Porta Romana/bus 62, 77/tram 9, 29, 30.
Meals served 8-11pm Mon; 12.30-2pm, 8-11pm Tue-Sat. **Average** €40. **Credit** AmEx, DC, MC, V. **Map** p251 G9 🄢
The 'Happy Cod' is always packed to the gills, so book ahead. Sicilian favourites like *arancini* (huge fried rice balls) make for tasty first courses, but the speciality is swordfish, prepared in a variety of ways. Other temptations include smoked tuna, octopus and deep-fried breaded sardines. The atmosphere is warm and welcoming, the service friendly and attentive, and the cellar chock-full of good Sicilian wines.

L'Ape Piera
Via Lodovico il Moro 11 (02 8912 6060/www.ape piera.com). Bus 47/tram 2. **Meals served** noon-3pm, 8pm-midnight Mon-Fri; 8pm-midnight Sat. Closed 3wks Aug, 1wk Jan. **Average** €45. **Credit** AmEx, MC, V.
A trad-looking Naviglio *osteria*, complete with original beams and cobbled paving. Interesting specialities include *zuppetta di pomodorini con gamberi* (cherry tomato and shrimp soup), *risotto con mirtilli e coniglio* (with blackcurrants and rabbit) and *filetto con asparagi* (fillet steak with asparagus). Finish off with *millefoglie con zabaione all'arancia* (a puff pastry dessert with orange-flavoured zabaglione sauce).

Da Teresa
Via Pavia 3 (02 5811 1126/www.cucinapugliese dateresa.it). Bus 50, 91/tram 3, 15. **Meals served** noon-2.30pm, 8-11pm Mon-Sat. **Average** €20. **Credit** AmEx, MC, V. **Map** p250 C9 🄣
Half social club, half ambassador for Pugliese cooking, this simple trattoria, with its formica tables and accents from the south, is just a step or two above going to your Italian aunt's house for dinner. There are no frills, and the waiter may well ask you why you haven't cleaned your plate.

Dongiò
Via Corio 3 (02 551 1372). Metro Porta Romana/ bus 62, 77/tram 9, 29, 30. **Meals served** 12.30-2.30pm, 7.30-10.30pm Mon-Fri; 7.30-10.30pm Sat. Closed 3wks Aug. **Average** €25. **Credit** AmEx, DC, MC, V. **Map** p251 G9 🄤
A favourite stand-by for locals craving solid homely cooking. This Calabrian trat serves up well-spiced *primi* such as *fusilli con 'nduja* (Calabrian sausage) and some of the best steaks in town.

Giulio Pane e Ojo
Via L Muratori 10 (02 545 6189/www.giulio paneojo.com). Metro Porta Romana/bus 62, 77/ tram 9, 29, 30. **Meals served** 12.30-2.30pm, 8pm-12.30am Mon-Sat. Closed 2wks Aug. **Average** €25. **Credit** AmEx, MC, V. **Map** p251 G9 🄥
A comfortable *osteria* offering a taste of Rome. Favourites include the Roman classic *spaghetti cacio e pepe* (with crumbled salty sheep's cheese and black pepper) and *abbacchio scottadito*, perhaps the most tender lamb chops you'll ever have.

Joia Leggero
Corso di Porta Ticinese 106 (02 8940 4134/www. joia.it). Metro Porta Genova/bus 47, 74/tram 2. **Meals served** 7.30-11pm Mon; 12.30-2.30pm, 7.30-11pm Tue-Sat. Closed 2wks Aug. **Average** €35. **Credit** AmEx, MC, V. **Map** p250 C8 🄦
Translated as 'Joia Light', this is the newer, more casual (and cheaper) outpost of the renowned haute cuisine veggie restaurant (*see p106*). In the evening it serves tasting plates of Joia creations, while during the day there is a fixed lunch with creative vegetarian and piscine options.

Osteria delle Vigne
Ripa di Porta Ticinese 61 (02 837 5617). Metro Porta Genova/bus 47, 74/tram 2. **Meals served** noon-3pm, 8-11.30pm daily. Closed 1wk Aug. **Average** €30 (lunch €10). **Credit** AmEx, MC, V. **Map** p250 B9 🄧
This cosy *osteria* is a prime example of the Slow Food movement's influence on Italian dining. It's not as inexpensive as it used to be, but there is still a wonderfully varied wine list and an eclectic menu. If that's not enough to tempt you, the ambience is decidedly laid-back – a plus in a district where the eating places tend to be noisy and overcrowded. The *caramelle di ricotta e spinaci* (sweet-shaped ravioli stuffed with spinach and ricotta cheese) is a delight. The tables are spacious, and it's a good place to relax and chat.

Osteria Grand Hotel
Via Ascanio Sforza 75 (02 8951 6153). Bus 59, 91. **Meals served** 8-10.30pm Tue-Sat; noon-2pm, 8-10.30pm Sun. Closed 3wks Aug, 1wk Dec-Jan. **Average** €30. **Credit** AmEx, DC, MC, V. **Map** p250 C10 🄨
The emphasis at this upscale eaterie is on Slow Food – fine cold cuts and cheeses, solid *primi*, such as ravioli or risotto, followed by lamb or steak. Unusually for Italy, the extensive wine list has labels from around the world. The shady area outside is a welcome attraction in warm weather.

La Topaia
Via F Argelati 40 (02 837 3469). Metro Porta Genova or Romolo/bus 47, 90, 91. **Meals served** noon-2.30pm, 8-11.30pm Mon-Fri; 8-11.30pm Sat. Closed 3wks Aug. **Average** €25. **Credit** AmEx, DC, MC, V. **Map** p250 B9 🄩
This delightful old-style restaurant, complete with candlelight and guitar-strumming crooners, is a short distance from the packed bars of the Naviglio Grande. The menu is solidly traditional, with hearty dishes such as *minestrone d'orzo* (barley soup) and *stinco arrosto* (roast shin of pork). The desserts are lovingly made, and the friendly atmosphere more than makes up for the indifferent wine list.

Eat, Drink, Shop

Shambala.

Trattoria Madonnina

Via Gentilino 6 (02 8940 9089). Metro Porta Genova/bus 59/tram 3, 15. **Meals served** noon-2.30pm Mon-Wed; noon-2.30pm, 8-11.30pm Thur-Sat. Closed Aug, 1wk Dec/Jan. **Average** €25 (lunch €15). **Credit** MC, V. **Map** p250 C9 **30**

Ten minutes' walk from Porta Genova metro station, this is a great down-to-earth place with an appealingly rustic vibe, thanks to the wooden tables, red and white checked tablecloths, and old road signs and posters on the wall. The food couldn't be more traditional, either: simple pastas with tomato or meat sauces, cuts of meat with veg, and cheese plates, all at cheap-as-chips prices (at lunchtime, from €3.20 for a simple *pasta al pomodoro*). **Photo** *p109.*

Ethnic

Shambala

Via Ripamonti 337 (02 552 0194). Tram 24. **Meals served** 8pm-1am daily. Closed 3wks Aug, 2wks Dec-Jan. **Average** €45. **Credit** AmEx, DC, MC, V. **Map** p251 F11 **31**

Although Shambala is in the boondocks, the Milanese flock to it for its cool vibe, good southern Asian cuisine and gorgeous summer garden. In winter you can eat in a long, glassed-in veranda. The food ranges from old favourites such as pad thai and sashimi to more unusual dishes like chicken breast with pink grapefruit in a green curry sauce. The decor takes its cue from Indonesia, while a background of flickering candlelight and chill-out music makes for a mellow ambience. Romantics should book a table laid in one of several antique carved beds.

Sushi-Kòboo

Viale Col di Lana 1 (02 837 2608). Tram 9, 15, 29, 30. **Meals served** 12.30-2.30pm, 7.30-11.30pm Tue-Sun. Closed 2wks Aug. **Average** €30. **Credit** AmEx, DC, MC, V. **Map** p250 D9 **32**

A Japanese restaurant with a wide choice of fresh sushi and surprisingly reasonable prices. In the bright, clean interior you can eat seated around the conveyor belt or at a table.

Pizza & snacks

Be Bop

Viale Col di Lana 4 (02 837 6972). Bus 65, 79/tram 9, 15, 29, 30. **Meals served** 12.30-2.30pm, 7.30-11pm daily. **Average** €25. **Credit** AmEx, MC, V. **Map** p250 D9 **33**

A short walk from the Darsena, this art deco-ish pizzeria serves up large, thin-crusted pizzas and a delightful assortment of *primi*.

Premiata Pizzeria

Via Alzaia Naviglio Grande 2 (02 8940 0648). Metro Porta Genova/bus 47/tram 2, 9, 29, 30. **Meals served** 12.30-2.30pm, 7.30pm-1am daily. **Average** €25. **Credit** AmEx, MC, V. **Map** p250 C9 **34**

When Milanese argue about the best pizza in town, this place – at the beginning of the Naviglio Grande – invariably pops up. With chewy, Neapolitan-style pizzas (cooked in a wood-fired oven, of course), a satisfying roster of *primi* and *secondi*, and comfortable dining rooms (and outside garden), it's a great place to come after a stroll along the canals.

Sant'Ambrogio & West

Italian

Da Leo

Via Trivulzio 26 (02 4007 1445). Metro De Angeli or Gambara/bus 18, 63, 72, 80. **Meals served** 12.30-2.30pm, 7.30-10.30pm Tue-Sat; 12.30-2.30pm Sun. Closed 3wks Aug, 2wks Dec. **Average** €40. **No credit cards.**

Giuseppe Leo has been going to Milan's fish market at the crack of dawn for the past 30 years to select the freshest produce for his fish-only restaurant. The dishes served here are simple and wholesome: spaghetti (no other pasta is served) *in bianco* (without tomatoes) with tuna, clams, king prawns or calamari; and main course fish dishes. The interior is unpretentious, the service friendly and efficient, the wine list extensive. It's best to book ahead for dinner.

Cafés, Bars & *Gelaterie*

Knock back a quick caffeine shot or linger over cocktails.

A few years ago the average Milanese 'bar' was essentially a standard European café: open 7am to 7pm, shut on a Sunday, serving morning coffee, lunchtime sandwiches, early-evening *aperitivi*, then more coffee until closing time. But an influx of flashy cocktail bars – some offering DJs, live music, art exhibitions, elaborate happy hour buffets (*see p119* **Get happy**) and later opening hours – has shaken up the scene in recent times. Courting ultra-fashionable custom, many of these new (or revamped) establishments take their design cues from glossy style magazines, while their decor seems to change as frequently as the city's catwalk collections.

That's not to say traditional bars have been usurped. As the new watering holes are frequented by a young, trend-conscious crowd, many Milanese stick to their favourite, tried-and-tested locals. Indeed, the majority of bars still conform to the old-school model, fulfilling a variety of functions. This is where to go for a quick caffeine fix. *Il caffè* (by which Italians mean espresso) is usually consumed while standing at the bar. Just don't expect to accompany it with a cigarette – the smoking ban, which was introduced in 2005, has put paid to that (*see p101*).

COFFEE TALK

Whether neighbourhood bar or smart café, the etiquette is the same: non-regulars are expected to pay at the *cassa* (cash desk) before consuming. If you prefer to sit down and be served, be prepared to pay at least double. Identify what you want, then pay (place your *scontrino* (receipt) on the bar to grab the bartender's attention).

A few tips for the uninitiated: in Milan, cappuccino is called *cappuccio*, while a latte is *cappuccino senza schiuma* (without froth). A *cappuccio* is rarely consumed after 11am – and never after a meal. To get a short, thick espresso ask for *un caffè*. If you want more than a dribble that barely covers the bottom of the cup, ask for a *lungo* (about double the height of an espresso, and thus weaker) or a *caffè americano* (a big cup half full of diluted espresso). If you want milk in your espresso, order a *caffè macchiato caldo* or *freddo* (with a spoon of hot froth or a dash of cold milk from a jug on the bar). True caffeine hounds could attempt a *ristretto*, an even more concentrated espresso (to go the other way, ask for a *caffè decaffeinato*). For something of the moment, try a *marocchino*, the latest coffee trend – a mixture of coffee, chocolate and frothed milk served in a glass.

WHERE TO GO

If you're on a brief visit, try to spend an evening in the Navigli and Porta Ticinese area (south-west of the centre). You can't go wrong here, as the waterways and backstreets are dotted with cafés and jazz bars (just watch out for the mosquitoes in summer). For a quieter evening, the Brera district, a short walk north of the Duomo, is a good bet, though it can get packed in summer as people come to sit at the outside tables on the cobbled streets. If, on the other hand, you're tempted by the trendier new locations, then the area north of Castello Sforzesco is the place to be. Just go to the Arco della Pace and start walking north.

For our favourite *pasticcerie* (cake shops), *see p134*.

The best Cafés

For chocoholics
Chocolat (*see p120*); **Biffi** (*see p120*).

For oenophiles
Dynamo (*see p114*); **Cantine Isola** (*see p114*).

Celeb spotting
10 Corso Como (*see p117*); **Diana Garden** (*see p118*).

Art lovers
Luminal (*see p115*); **Fitzcarraldo** (*see p118*); **Lounge Paradise** (*see p120*).

Killer cocktails
Caffè Verdi (*see p114*); **Honky Tonks** (*see p115*); **Bar Basso** (*see p117*).

> ❶ Pink numbers given in this chapter correspond to the location of each café, bar and *gelateria* as marked on the street maps. See pp248-252.

Duomo & Centre

Cafés & bars

Caffè Miani (aka Zucca)
*Galleria Vittorio Emanuele II (02 8646 4435/www.
caffemiani.it). Metro Duomo/bus 54, 60, 65/tram 12,
23, 27.* **Open** 7.30am-8.30pm Tue-Sun. Closed Aug.
Credit AmEx, DC, MC, V. **Map** p249 E5/p252 E6 **1**
Most bars in the Galleria are tourist traps, but this
place, which has been in the arcade since it opened
in 1867, is an institution, once frequented by Verdi
and Toscanini. The interior is spectacular, with an
inlaid bar and mosaics by Angelo d'Andrea. Many
people who come here order that most Milanese
of aperitifs, the rhubarb-based Zucca. You might
want to stand and drink at the bar – prices increase
dramatically once you sit down and have a waiter
come to your table.

Caffè Verdi
*Via Giuseppe Verdi 6 (02 863 880). Metro Cordusio
or Duomo/bus 61/tram 1, 2.* **Open** *Mar-Oct* 7am-
8pm Mon-Sat. *Nov-Feb* 7am-8pm daily. Closed mid
July-Aug. **Credit** AmEx, DC, MC, V. **Map** p249 E6/
p252 E6 **2**
This quietly dignified *caffè* is a must for opera fans.
Situated across the road from La Scala, it's a convenient coffee-break spot for company members. But
even if you don't run into Placido Domingo, you can
soak up the atmosphere, surrounded by busts and
photos of composers, while unobtrusive classical
music plays in the background. Cocktails have
names like Callas, Verdiano and Mozart, and the
Martinis, in particular, are excellent. It also serves
food, and is popular with bankers at lunchtime.

Victoria Café
*Via Clerici 1 (02 805 3598/02 8646 2088/www.
victoriacafe.it). Metro Cordusio or Duomo/bus 61/
tram 1, 3, 4, 12, 14.* **Open** 7.30am-2am Mon-Fri;
5pm-2am Sat. Closed 3wks Aug. **Credit** AmEx,
MC, V. **Map** p248 D6/p252 D6 **3**
Named after a coffee machine, not the British queen,
this is one of the few decent watering holes within
walking distance of the Duomo. Housed in a former
bank building tucked away behind La Scala and
done out in art nouveau style, it caters to business
types during the day and bright young things at
night. It is also popular with expats, attracted to its
on-tap Guinness, Kilkenny and Tennents and cocktails (€5 during happy hour, 6-8.30pm). **Photo** *p115.*

Sforzesco & North

Cafés & bars

Bhangrabar
*Corso Sempione 1 (02 3493 4469/www.bhangra
barmilano.com). Tram 1, 29, 30.* **Open** noon-3pm,
6.30pm-2am Mon-Fri, Sun; 6.30pm-2am Sat. Closed
2wks Aug. **Credit** MC, V. **Map** p248 B5 **4**

If you go for a drink at this lounge bar and restaurant, you could feasibly skip dinner, since the cocktails (€6 during happy hour, which runs from
6.30-9.30pm) include as many trips as you like to
the substantial Indian buffet. Handmade screens
imported from India are used to create intimate
alcoves, and a DJ keeps the warm and friendly atmosphere buzzing with soul, jazz, fusion and rare groove
sounds. Highly recommended.

Caffè Letterario
*Via Solferino 27 (02 2901 5119). Metro Moscova/
bus 41, 43, 94.* **Open** 8am-2am Tue-Sat. Closed
2wks Aug. **Credit** AmEx, DC, MC, V. **Map** p248
D4 **5**
This small but charming restaurant, bar and gallery
changed management in November 2005 and underwent extensive renovation. A programme was quick
to emerge – on Thursdays, Fridays and Saturdays
there are art gallery openings, poetry readings and
music – making it a popular meeting place for culture buffs. Entrance to these events costs €8-€10
and includes your first drink. It's also a great place
to hang out during the day.

Cantine Isola
*Via Paolo Sarpi 30 (02 331 5249). Metro Moscova/
bus 51, 57/tram 3, 12, 14.* **Open** 10am-10pm Tue-
Sat; 10am-2pm, 4-8pm Sun. **Credit** DC, MC, V.
Map p248 C4 **6**
The minute you enter this tiny place you're hit by a
heady cellar aroma and a floor-to-ceiling display of
dusty bottles. Established in 1896, Isola still draws
a cosmopolitan crowd of all ages for its huge variety of fine wines and distillates.

Deseo
Corso Sempione 2 (02 315 164). Tram 1, 29, 30.
Open 6pm-2am daily. Closed Aug. **Credit** AmEx,
DC, MC, V. **Map** p248 B4 **7**
'Design' is the byword at this new cocktail bar in the
Arco della Pace area, which is especially popular
among the thirtysomething crowd. White pouffes
and sofas, dark furniture, mirrors and big columns:
you get the idea. Linger for cocktails while you tuck
into the big free buffet at happy hour (little pizzas,
pasta, rice, vegetables, salami).

Dynamo
*Piazza Greco 5 (02 670 4353/02 669 2124/www.
dynamo.it). Bus 43, 81.* **Open** 6pm-2am Tue-Sun.
Closed 2-3wks Aug. **Credit** AmEx, DC, MC, V.
Away from the super-trendy (not to mention super-
crowded) watering holes in the city centre is this
stylish cocktail bar built over three floors. There's
a lounge bar-cum-restaurant on the ground floor;
a raised chill-out area and an impressive selection
of fine wines from all over Italy (tastings are available). The basement has a dancefloor and comfy
seating. Events such as art exhibitions and themed
music nights are hosted on a regular basis, and
there's a jazz club every Wednesday. The popular
Sunday brunch (11.30am-4pm) is yet another reason
to pay a visit.

Happy hour at **Victoria Café**.
See p114.

Honky Tonks

Via Fratelli Induno 10 (02 345 2562). Bus 57, 78/ tram 1, 14, 19, 33. **Open** 6pm-2am daily. Closed 2wks Aug. **Credit** AmEx, DC, MC, V. **Map** p248 B3 ❾

A combination of duff lounge furniture and shabby antiques gives this jazz bar a welcoming, laid-back feel. Bartenders mix a mean cocktail, while the Tex-Mex dishes keep hunger at bay. There is live music on Mondays, Thursdays and Saturdays. Too loud for a romantic evening or an intimate chat, it's much better as a place to get revved up before moving on to a club.

Jamaica

Via Brera 32 (02 876 723/www.jamaicabar.it). Metro Lanza or Montenapoleone/bus 61, 94/tram 3, 4, 12. **Open** *June-Sept* 9am-2am Mon-Sat. *Oct-May* 9am-2am Mon-Sat; 10am-11pm Sun. Closed 1wk Aug. **Credit** AmEx, DC, MC, V. **Map** p248 D5 ❾

According to local lore, Mussolini had an unpaid tab here when he became prime minister in 1922. This venerable bar, established 1921, changed its name to Jamaica after World War II (it was inspired by the 1939 Hitchcock film *Jamaica Inn*, which was based on the Daphne du Maurier novel). In the 1950s Jamaica became a favoured hangout of artists and writers, and started hosting art and photography exhibitions long before everybody else. A Milan institution through and through.

Luminal

Via Monte Grappa 14 (02 6269 4675/www.luminal-milano.it). Metro Garibaldi/tram 11, 25, 29, 30, 33. **Open** 6pm-midnight Mon; 6.30pm-4am Tue-Sun.

Closed Aug. **Admission** €10-€20 Thur-Sun. **Credit** AmEx, DC, MC, V. **Map** p249 E4 ❿

Enormous chandeliers dominate the ground floor of this elegant nightspot, which also hosts art and design exhibitions during the day. The cocktails are not the cheapest (€8-€10), but the well-heeled clientele (including VIPs from the fashion world) don't mind shelling out. The upstairs dancefloor is presided over by international DJs.

Milano

Via Procaccini 37 (02 3653 6060). Tram 12, 14, 29, 30, 33. **Open** 6pm-2am Tue-Sat. **Credit** AmEx, DC, MC, V. Closed Aug. **Map** p248 B3 ⓫

The fountain at the entrance to this bar is just a hint of what is to come. A huge open fireplace stands in one corner of the vast space, filled with original artworks and deep 1960s sofas that give it the feel of a penthouse from a James Bond movie. The creative, fresh fruit cocktails cost €8 all day, but at happy hour (6-9.30pm) the bar is loaded with top-notch nibbles, including smoked salmon and, in season, fresh oysters. Cool background music completes the atmosphere of what is one of the hippest spots in Milan.

Nordest Caffè

Via Borsieri 35 (02 6900 1910/www.nordestcaffe.it). Metro Garibaldi or Zara/bus 82, 83/tram 4, 11. **Open** 8am-1am Mon-Fri; 8.30am-8.30pm Sat, Sun. Closed 1wk Aug. **No credit cards.** **Map** p249 E2 ⓬

The 'North-East Café' is one of several lively bars in the Isola neighbourhood. The high-tech interior is a bit on the cold side, but live jazz sessions in the evening warm things up. It's a good place to kick off before heading to the Blue Note Jazz Club (*see p164*).

Bitter pleasures

Few cities have a drink so closely associated with them as Milan does with Campari. The name is emblazoned in neon advertising; its distinctive red colour is splashed across billboards, and the liquid is poured, shaken and served in cocktails all over town.

The Campari clan is Milanese through and through. The family tomb in the Monumental Cemetery (see p71) is a life-sized sculpted rendition of the city's most famous artwork, Leonardo's Last Supper, though they showed some restraint by not having a bottle of the family's famous concoction on the table.

Gaspare Campari invented his herbal brew in 1860 in nearby Novara, and it was first poured in his namesake bar in Milan's Galleria Vittorio Emanuele II (see p114). Although the bar – with its time-worn zinc inlaid counter and art nouveau decor – is now named after a competing aperitif, the vermouth Zucca, it's still a good place to sip a Negroni, a boozy blend of Campari, gin and vermouth.

Campari's bittersweet flavour is difficult to define, and most of the ingredients are a well-guarded secret. The usual components – alcohol, distilled water, sugar – are mixed with oranges and dozens of herbs. Maybe ginseng, maybe rhubarb. Just two people keep the recipe, and one of them is the Campari factory director. The other is a secret. The radiant tint comes from squished

bugs. Desiccated cochineal corpses are a traditional colourant and are imported from South America.

Detractors say the drink tastes like a boozy cough syrup. The makers acknowledge it is an acquired taste: Campari is rarely taken by itself. The most popular mixer is soda water – never mineral water. You can buy pre-mixed Campari Soda in tiny triangular bottles designed by Fortunato Depero, the Futurist artist also responsible for many advertising posters for Campari in the 1920s (now collectors' items). Other artists who have crafted provocative campaigns for the drink include Federico Fellini, Bruno Munari and Milton Glaser.

The large bottle is called Campari Bitter and is a bartender's best friend in busy Milan hotspots, where other popular pours of the red elixir include a Shakerato, made from crushed ice and Campari; Campari e bianco, with spumante; and the Americano, equal parts Campari and red vermouth, with a splash of soda water and a sliver of orange peel.

A century of Campari production in Milan came to an end in late 2005, when the factory relocated to Piedmont, home to that other aperitif that blends so often with Campari, vermouth. But that will do little to dent its local popularity: in fact, there's even drink that combines the two: a Milano-Torino.

Radetzky

Corso Garibaldi 105 (02 657 2645). Metro Moscova/ bus 41, 43, 94. **Open** 8am-1.30am daily. Closed 2wks Aug. **Credit** AmEx, DC, MC, V. **Map** p248 D4 ⑬
Named after the despised Austrian field marshal who suppressed the 1848 uprising, this is a hip hang-out throughout the week, but it is particularly useful on Sundays, when Milan is pretty lifeless. Famous for its brunches, Radetzky caters to a rather snobby crowd from the fashion and advertising industries. It also prides itself on its *cotoletta alla milanese* (Wiener Schnitzel), served at all hours.

Roialto

Via Piero della Francesca 55 (02 3493 6616). Bus 43, 57, 78/tram 1, 29, 33. **Open** 6pm-2am Tue-Sun. **Credit** AmEx, DC, MC, V. **Map** p248 A3 ⑭
Not much to look at from the outside, the Roialto has been a hit since it took over a spacious warehouse in 1999 (now there's an increasing number of clubs and bars opening up in the area). With its vintage armchairs, overhead fans and Cuban rum and cigars displayed behind the enormous bar, you almost expect Humphrey Bogart to walk in. Try the piña colada, served in a fresh coconut.

10 Corso Como

Corso Como 10 (02 2901 3581/www.10corsocomo. com). Metro Garibaldi/tram 11, 25, 29, 30, 33. **Open** 4pm-2am Mon; noon-3pm, 6pm-2am Tue-Sun. Closed 1wk Aug. **Credit** AmEx, DC, MC, V. **Map** p248 D4 ⑮
Designed by American artist Kris Ruhs, this court-yard café is part of Carla Sozzani's multifunctional arts complex, which includes a photography gallery (*see* p154), shop (*see* p125) and restaurant. A favourite with fashion folk and celebs (Giorgio Armani is said to be a regular, while the whole place was sealed off when Madonna paid a visit), it occupies an old *casa a ringhiera* (working-class apartment building). Try the excellent No.1 cocktail.

35

Via P Castaldi 35 (02 2953 3350). Metro Porta Venezia/tram 5, 9, 11, 29, 30. **Open** 6.30pm-2am Mon-Sat. Closed Aug. **Credit** AmEx, DC, MC, V. **Map** p249 G5 ⑯
This small and trendy American bar is near Porta Venezia. The atmosphere is intimate and fashionable, and the vibe, provided by a mix of Milanese habitués of the happy hour and tourists, is easy-going and friendly. The 35 cocktails aren't bad either (try the Bloody Mary or the caipirinha with fresh fruit), and during happy hour (6.30-9pm) they come with decent free snacks.

Gelaterie

Toldo

Via Ponte Vetero 9A (02 8646 0863). Metro Cairoli or Lanza/bus 18, 50, 58, 61/tram 1, 3, 4, 12, 27. **Open** *Apr-Sept* 7am-midnight Mon-Sat. *Oct-Mar*

7am-8pm Mon-Sat. Closed 1wk Jan, 1wk Aug. **No credit cards. Map** p248 D6/p252 D6 ⑰
This *gelateria* has been famous for its ice-cream since the 1960s. From noon onwards it offers a 'happy coffee' deal: for the price of an espresso (80c) you get a little crunchy hazelnut cup filled with ice-cream. If this whets your appetite, you can buy a cone of the stuff for less than €2.

San Babila & East

Cafés & bars

Art Deco Café

Via Lambro 7 (02 2952 4760/www.artdecocafe.it). Metro Porta Venezia/tram 5, 9, 11, 29, 30. **Open** 6pm-2am daily. Closed 3wks Aug. **No credit cards. Map** p249 G5 ⑱
This place is worth a visit for its Miami Beach interior, with revolving lights that create hundreds of different pastel colours, and the massive TV screen that broadcasts the Fashion TV channel – quite a change for a location that used to house a snooker hall. Some people find it a bit too cool, but, hey, this is Milan after all.

Art Factory Café

Via Andrea Doria 17 (02 669 4578/www.art factory.it). Metro Caiazzo or Loreto/bus 92. **Open** 7am-2pm Mon-Sat; 6-9.30pm Sun. Closed 2wks Aug. **Credit** AmEx, DC, MC, V. **Map** p249 H3 ⑲
A lively hotspot on three levels, the Art Factory Café offers a delicious buffet during happy hour (6-9.30pm). With the in-house DJ stoking up the atmosphere, it caters to a younger crowd.

Atomic Bar

Via Felice Casati 24 (mobile 334 147 7164/www. atomicbar.it). Metro Porta Venezia or Repubblica/ tram 1, 5, 11. **Open** 9pm-2am Tue-Sun. Closed Aug. **No credit cards. Map** p249 F4 ⑳
Although it opened about a decade ago, this small nightspot is still popular. It doesn't go in for happy hour, as it tends to liven up later on, but it's a great place to come after dinner – perhaps at one of the Indian restaurants nearby. The dinky dancefloor is usually heaving at the weekends, but during the week you can have a drink and a boogie without feeling overwhelmed.

Bar Basso

Via Plinio 39 (02 2940 0580/www.barbasso.com). Metro Lima or Piola/bus 60. **Open** 9am-1.15am Mon, Wed-Sun. Closed 3wks Aug. **Credit** AmEx, MC, V. **Map** p249 H4 ㉑
Mirko Stocchetti, Bar Basso's owner since 1967, is credited with introducing cocktails to bars in Milan (before then they were available only in hotels). Stocchetti and his son Maurizio still enjoy coming up with interesting concoctions. The house special is called Negroni Sbagliato ('Incorrect Negroni'), and it's made with spumante (sparkling white wine) instead of gin.

Eat, Drink, Shop

La Belle Aurore

Via Abamonti 1, at via Castel Morrone (02 2940 6212). Bus 60/tram 11, 23, 33. **Open** 8am-2pm Mon-Sat. Closed 2wks Aug. **No credit cards.** **Map** p249 H5 ㉒

This Parisian-style bar has been a favourite haunt of local writers and artists for over 15 years. Students and intellectuals come at all times of the day to sip coffee or a dry Martini, read the newspapers or add to their *oeuvre*.

Diana Garden

Sheraton Diana Majestic Hotel, viale Piave 42 (02 205 8081/www.starwoodhotels.com). Metro Porta Venezia/tram 9, 29, 30. **Open** *June-Sept* 10am-1am daily. *Oct-May* 10am-midnight daily. Closed 3wks Aug. **Credit** AmEx, DC, MC, V. **Map** p249 G5 ㉓

The legendary bar of the Sheraton Diana Majestic (*see p47*) has been a happening place since it opened in 2000. It's something of a hotspot for the Milanese fashion elite, who get to sip aperitifs while gazing at the catwalk shows that are staged inside during Fashion Week. In summer you can sit in the fabulous garden (its themed decor changes each season), but the place is also lively in the winter. Once you've tired of staring at the impeccably attired clientele, feast your eyes on the decadent, semi-circular interior. Cocktails aren't the cheapest, at €8-€12.

Lelephant

Via Melzo 22, East (02 2951 8768/www.lelephant.it). Metro Porta Venezia/tram 9, 29, 30. **Open** 6pm-2am Tue-Sun. Closed 3wks Aug. **No credit cards.** **Map** p249 G5 ㉔

Although first and foremost a gay and lesbian bar (*see p158*), this establishment caters to all. Cocktail prices drop to €5 during happy hour (6.30-9.30pm). Lelephant is across the road from the Art Deco (*see p117*), and within walking distance of the Diana Garden (*see above*), should you want to bar-hop.

Gelaterie

La Bottega del Gelato

Via Pergolesi 3 (02 2940 0076). Metro Caiazzo or Loreto/bus 92. **Open** 9am-10pm Mon, Tue, Thur-Sun. Closed 3wks Aug. **No credit cards.** **Map** p249 H3 ㉕

On an insalubrious street between corso Buenos Aires and Stazione Centrale, this slightly scruffy place serves some of the tastiest ice-cream in Milan. Flavours include pink grapefruit, almond and creamy pine nut (not to be missed).

Porta Romana & South

Cafés & bars

Le Biciclette

Via Torti, at via Conca del Naviglio (02 839 4177/ 02 5810 43259/www.lebiciclette.com). Metro Sant'Ambrogio/bus 94/tram 3, 14. **Open** 6pm-2am Mon-Sat; 12.30-4pm, 6pm-2am Sun. Closed 3wks Aug. **Credit** AmEx, DC, MC, V. **Map** p250 C8 ㉖

This vibrant bar and restaurant, which opened in a former bike shop in 1998, is part of a growing nightlife hub in the area. Le Biciclette prides itself on its art shows and its Sunday brunch. It also has an imaginative approach to its happy hour buffet (6-9.30pm), which is sometimes themed (recently, for instance, everything included orange).

Caffè della Pusterla

Via E de Amicis 22 (02 8940 2146). Metro Sant'Ambrogio/bus 94/tram 2, 3, 14. **Open** 7am-2am Mon-Sat; 9am-2am Sun. **Credit** AmEx, MC, V. **Map** p250 C8 ㉗

Wine cocktails (such as red wine with lemon sorbet) are the thing here. This establishment caters to an assorted clientele throughout the day, with families and locals giving way to a younger crowd at happy hour (6-9pm).

Cuore

Via G Mora 3 (02 5810 5126/www.cuore.it). Metro Sant'Ambrogio/bus 94/tram 2, 3, 14. **Open** 6pm-2am daily. Closed 2wks Aug. **No credit cards.** **Map** p250 C7 ㉘

Tucked away in a quiet little street near San Lorenzo alle Colonne, this place is hard to find (look out for the letter 'C'), but well worth the effort. Cuore (heart) features ever-changing decor and an entertainment programme including DJs and bands. The atmosphere is fun and friendly: it's a popular spot with everyone, including the local gay crowd.

Fitzcarraldo

Via Filippetti 41 (02 5843 0665). Metro Porta Romana/bus 62, 77/tram 9, 29, 30. **Open** 6pm-2am Tue-Sun (gallery from 10.30am). Closed Aug. **Credit** MC, V. **Map** p251 F9 ㉙

One of the new trendy spots in Milan, Fitzcarraldo is housed in an old furniture shop, and some colonial-style pieces and accessories are still for sale. Most of the stock seems to have found its way into the bar; the huge space is full of comfortable sofas and low wooden tables. Cocktails are on the steep side (€8), but the gallery is worth a look.

Fresco Art

Viale Monte Nero 23 (02 5412 4675). Metro Porta Romana/bus 62, 77/tram 9, 29, 30. **Open** 7.30am-2am Tue-Sun. Closed 1wk Aug. **Credit** MC, V. **Map** p251 G8 ㉚

Run by the same organisation that owns the popular ATM bar at bastioni di Porta Volta 15 (which is currently closed for renovation), Fresco Art is situated near the Palazzo di Giustizia, so, not surprisingly, it's the favourite haunt of the lawyers and solicitors. It's a good place for a sedate coffee in the morning, though it can get very busy at lunchtime. The evening is a nicer time to visit, when it's a calm place to unwind – a sophisticated clientele comes to enjoy the happy hour buffet (6-9pm) and soft music in the pleasantly neutral interior.

Get happy

While the 'happy hour' most of us are familiar with is about downing as many two-for-one drinks in the space of 60 minutes, in Milan it has become a considerably more drawn-out and luxurious affair. The hard-working Milanese aren't big boozers, but after a day at the office they like to see and be seen in elegant surroundings, sip a cocktail and chat with friends. And although the Milanese happy hour includes a token drop in drinks prices (usually about €1), cheap alcohol isn't its main focus – it's a slower, gentler affair, normally with good free nibbles to boot. We're not talking crisps and nuts here: a growing number of establishments lay on generous and imaginative buffets, with salads, pasta dishes and much more. **Bhangrabar** (*see p114*) offers a spread of Indian specialities, while **Milano** (*see p115*) ups the stakes further with smoked salmon and oysters.

Comfort is also paramount: the new breed of bar is furnished with sofas and comfy armchairs. The keyword these days is '*spazio multifunzione*' (multifunctional space), with every effort being made to keep customers within that space as long as possible once they've been lured through the door for happy hour. Your aperitif may even be accompanied by an art exhibition – try **Le Biciclette** (*see p118*) or **Fitzcarraldo** (*see p118*). Other venues provide a backdrop of cool lounge music or smooth jazz – some bars, such as **Art Factory Café** (*see p117*), **Bhangrabar** (*see p114*) and **Luminal** (*see p115*) specifically employ early-evening DJs. And if you're enjoying yourself too much to move on, many bars have restaurants and dancefloors, so you can segue seamlessly from cocktails to dinner and dancing without having to step outside.

Eat, Drink, Shop

Sant'Ambrogio & West

Cafés & bars

Baci & Abbracci
Via E de Amicis 44 (02 8901 3605/www.bacie abbracci.it). Metro Sant'Ambrogio/bus 94/tram 2, 3, 14. **Open** 12.30-2.30pm, 6.30pm-2am Mon-Fri; 6.30pm-2am Sat, Sun. Closed Aug. **Credit** AmEx, DC, MC, V. **Map** p250 C7 ③
'Kisses and Cuddles' is frequented by soccer players – and the girls who decorate their arms. It prides

itself on the quality of its cocktail ingredients, as well as its happy hour buffet spread (6.30-9pm). Food – including award-winning pizza – is served at lunchtime and in the evenings.

Bar Magenta
Via Carducci 13 (02 805 3808/www.barmagenta.it). Metro Cadorna/bus 18, 58, 70, 94/tram 1, 19, 24, 27. **Open** 8am-2am Mon-Fri; 9am-2am Sat, Sun. **Credit** MC, V. **Map** p250 C6 ③
Not the most stylish of places (the wooden interior is more Edwardian London than modern Milan), this is nevertheless an institution, and one much loved

Chocolat – no dieters allowed.

by the expat community. It comes into its own in the summer months, when the young customers sit at outdoor tables and generally crowd the pavement.

Biffi
Corso Magenta 87, at piazza Baracco (02 4800 6702). Metro Conciliazione/bus 18/tram 24, 29, 30. **Open** 6.30am-8.30pm daily. Closed 1wk Aug. **Credit** MC, V. **Map** p250 C6 ⊕
One of Milan's historic cafés, Biffi is located on the edge of one of the city's most affluent neighbourhoods. The counter is cosy but never overcrowded, and the tearoom has a handful of tables for chatting and resting. The tri-chocolate, tri-layered cake will impress even the most seasoned chocoholic.

Chocolat
Via Boccaccio 9 (02 4810 0597). Metro Cadorna or Conciliazione/bus 199/tram 1, 19, 27, 199. **Open** 7.30am-1am daily. **Credit** AmEx, DC, MC, V. **Map** p250 C6 ⊕
Not far from *The Last Supper*, this gorgeous café excels in all things chocolate. From the huge, sensual mounds of luscious ice-cream in sinful flavours (believe us, they taste as good as they look) to the tarts, brownies, biscotti and slabs of posh chocolate

at the bar, everything is tempting. Should you want to linger, there are a few tables and leather pouffes both downstairs and up.

Lounge Paradise
Via Montevideo 20 (no phone). Metro Sant'Agostino/ bus 50/tram 29, 30, 33. **Open** 6pm-midnight daily. Closed mid Aug-mid Apr. **No credit cards.** **Map** p250 A8 ⊕
Next to one of the city's public pools, this bar is the ultimate destination in summer. Run by the people behind Cuore (*see p118*), it's a surprisingly successful combination of South Pacific style and 1930s Chicago. The bar hosts regular art installations.

Mama Café Restaurant
Via Caminadella 7 (02 8699 5682/www.mama cafe.it). Metro Sant'Agostino/bus 50/tram 29, 30. **Open** 8am-1am Mon-Sat. Closed 2wks Aug, 1wk Dec. **Credit** AmEx, DC, MC, V. **Map** p250 C7 ⊕
A warm and welcoming wine bar in the heart of the Sant'Ambrogio district. Here the happy hour is called 'happy wine'; from 7 to 8.30pm you can enjoy a reduced-price glass of red grignolino from Piedmont or white vermentino from Liguria accompanied by regional nibbles. Meals are also served, and there's live music on most Fridays and Saturdays.

Morgan's
Via Novati 2 (02 867 694). Metro Sant'Ambrogio/ bus 50, 58, 94/tram 2, 14. **Open** 6pm-2am Mon-Sat. Closed Aug. **Credit** AmEx, DC, MC, V. **Map** p250 C7 ⊕
This is a small, friendly bar popular with a laid-back thirtysomething crowd for its warm, pub-on-a-winter's-evening interior and general lack of pretence. Morgan's is located in one of the more agreeable areas of the city: the quiet, residential (and very affluent) backstreets south of piazza Sant'Ambrogio.

San Vittore
Viale Papiniano 2 (02 3705 9178/www.sanvittore milano.it). Metro Conciliazione/bus 58, 68/tram 29, 30. **Open** 6pm-2am daily. Closed Aug. **Credit** AmEx, DC, MC, V. **Map** p250 A7 ⊕
The name, San Vittore, is the same as Milan's central prison across the road. There's something for everyone here: in addition to the cocktails and wines, the shop doubles as a deli, with a great choice of salami and cheeses from across Europe. There's good music too, including live jazz from time to time.

Gelaterie

Gelateria Marghera
Via Marghera 33 (02 468 641). Metro De Angeli/ tram 24, 63. **Open** Oct-Feb 10am-midnight Mon-Thur, Sun; 10am-1am Fri, Sat. *Mar-Sept* 10am-1am daily. **No credit cards.**
One of Milan's best ice-cream parlours, Marghera offers a mind-boggling array of flavours (the rum chocolate is to die for). The high quality of the product on sale ensures there are always queues – and that the staff are too harassed for friendliness.

Shops & Services

Ostentatious designer flagships jostle for attention in Italy's capital of conspicuous consumption, but it's also a rich terrain for bargain hunters.

Luxe out: **Prada** is among the exclusive brands born in Milan. *See p127.*

Art and history lovers are drawn to Venice, Florence and Rome, but for retail riches, there's nowhere like Milan – Italy's undisputed capital for fashion and furniture.

The city's bid for shopping supremacy began as far back as the Middle Ages, when silk merchants set up their stalls in the streets around via del Carmine in the Brera district; meanwhile, traders hawked their wares in the covered market on piazza Mercanti, and milliners (which get their name from the city, although at that time they were general haberdashers as opposed to hatters), sword-makers, armourers and goldsmiths spilled into the streets beyond.

But as the demand for swords and armour dwindled, the city's mercantile pulse moved to the Quadrilatero della Moda, or 'Fashion Rectangle' (sometimes referred to as the 'Golden Rectangle'), between via Montenapoleone and via della Spiga. The area first came into its own in the early 19th century when Milan's aristocrats moved in, creating a market for shops selling luxury goods such as antiques, jewellery and fabric.

FAMOUS NAMES

Today these streets are mostly lined with big-league fashion boutiques. Among others, you'll find such home-grown labels as Armani, Prada, Versace, Dolce & Gabbana, Krizia and Gianfranco Ferré. While residents complain that globalisation has rendered the area bland, the designers have made efforts to ensure that their Milan flagships are memorable: Armani's superstore in via Manzoni (with its café and Nobu restaurant) is the largest in the world; Gianfranco Ferré's boutique on via Sant'Andrea boasts a spa; and the Dolce & Gabbana men's boutique on corso Venezia has a barber, women's health spa and Martini bar.

Another historic shopping spot is the Galleria Vittorio Emanuele II, the glass-roofed arcade near the Duomo. It opened in 1867, which makes it one of the world's oldest shopping malls. In 2004 Louis Vuitton and Gucci joined one of the arcade's oldest residents: Prada's original shop, which started selling leather goods here in 1913 (**photo** *p121*).

There's plenty of scope for bagging a bargain. Shops selling end-of-season returns, catwalk cast-offs and seconds abound, as do second-hand and vintage clothes boutiques. You'll also find heart-stopping bargains in the markets, from Gucci shoes to cashmere sweaters. (*See p132* **Chic at half the price**.)

Anyone allergic to big brands should head to the smaller, more alternative stores on corso di Porta Ticinese or in Brera. Other zones worth a trawl are corso Vercelli (the western continuation of corso Magenta) and the Isola area, behind Stazione Garibaldi. For the Italian version of high-street shopping, try corso Buenos Aires, via Torino or corso Vittorio Emanuele. Though most of the shoppers on these lesser streets still look intimidatingly smart, head-to-toe Prada is not obligatory here.

OPENING HOURS

Traditionally, Tuesday to Saturday retail hours are 9.30am-12.30pm and 3.30-7.30pm, with a half day on Monday (3.30-7.30pm), although most clothing boutiques in the Quadrilatero della Moda now open on Monday mornings as well. The majority of shops still close on Sundays, though fashion stores stay open during the major fairs, and, in these cash-starved times, increasingly throughout the year. Few shops in downtown Milan still close for lunch. However, much of the city shuts down in August for the summer holidays. Sales take place in January and July.

TAX REFUNDS

Non-EU residents can claim back the value added tax (IVA in Italian) on purchases totalling over €154.94 from a single store that displays a 'Tax-Free Shopping' sign. To do so, ask for a 'VAT back' form at the moment of purchase, keep your receipts, and pack your unworn, newly acquired stuff at the top of your suitcase (you may have to show it). Then have the receipts for your goods stamped at customs when you leave Italy and submit your 'VAT back' paperwork. Next, head for a refund centre (those at Malpensa and Linate airports are open 7am-11pm daily) or send in your paperwork when you get back home. There's also a tax-free centre on the seventh floor of La Rinascente department store (*see p123*), where you can get your cash back before leaving the country. However, you'll still have to queue to clear documents at the airport. For more information, visit www.globalrefund.com.

Antiques

Via Pisacane (metro Porta Venezia) is home to more than 30 antiques shops, selling everything from ceramics to timepieces. Otherwise, shops dealing in furnishings from the 16th to the 19th centuries are located in several ancient streets west of the Duomo: via Lanzone, via Caminadella, via San Giovanni sul Muro and via Santa Marta. The most prestigious (and expensive) antiques dealers have stores in the centre (try via Manzoni) and in the Brera area. For bargains (as well as the occasional rip-off), check out the canal-side antiques market along the Naviglio Grande (*see p141*).

Books & stationery

Fabriano

Via Verri 3, East (02 7631 8754). Metro Montenapoleone or San Babila/bus 54, 64, 91. **Open** 10am-7.30pm Mon-Sat. Closed 3wks Aug. **Credit** AmEx, DC, MC, V. **Map** p249 E6/p252 E6.
This quality paper-maker dates back to 1264, and Italy's currency has always been printed on its sheets. Despite the company's long history, its products are thoroughly up to date, and include writing paper in contemporary colours as well as artists' pads and watermarked paper.

La Feltrinelli

Via Ugo Foscolo 1-3 (enter from piazza Duomo, through Autogrill), Centre (02 8699 6903/ www.lafeltrinelli.it). Metro Duomo/bus 54, 60, 65/tram 12, 23, 27. **Open** 10am-11pm Mon-Sat; 10am-8pm Sun. **Credit** AmEx, DC, MC, V. **Map** p251 E6/p252 E6.
This central outpost of one of Italy's leading book chains has lots of titles in English, including an excellent selection of travel books. The international branch at piazza Cavour 1, North (02 6595 644), stocks books in English, Spanish, French, German, Portuguese and Russian, plus a large range of international magazines and DVDs.
Other locations: throughout the city.

Libreria Babele

Via San Nicolao 10, West (02 8691 5597/ www.libreriababele.it). Metro Cadorna/bus 50, 58, 94/tram 1, 19, 24. **Open** 2-7pm Mon; 10am-7pm Tue-Sun. Closed 2wks Aug. **Credit** AmEx, MC, V. **Map** p250 C6.
Milan's leading gay and lesbian bookshop stocks thousands of titles, plus magazines, postcards and DVDs/videos in Italian and English. It also hosts exhibitions and cultural events.

Mastri Cartai e Dintorni

Corso Garibaldi 26-34, North (02 805 2311/ www.mastricartai.com). Metro Lanza/bus 57, 70/ tram 3, 4. **Open** 3.30-7.30pm Mon; 11am-7.30pm Tue-Sat. Closed 3wks Aug. **Credit** AmEx, DC, MC, V. **Map** p248 D4.

The texturally rich paper sold here begs the question of where paper stops and art begins. Products run the gamut from thick, brightly coloured card to handmade book-binding paper. You'll be hard-pushed to leave without one of the shop's delightful signature *sculture luminose* (paper lampshades).

Messaggerie Musicali

Corso Vittorio Emanuele, at Galleria del Corso 2, Centre (02 760 551/www.messaggeriemusicali.it). Metro Duomo/bus 54, 60, 65/tram 12, 23, 27. **Open** 1-8.30pm Mon; 10am-11pm Tue-Sun. **Credit** AmEx, DC, MC, V. **Map** p251 E6/p252 E6.
This large, four-level book and music store has a vast selection of English-language volumes on the first floor, plus CDs and DVDs. There's also a ticket counter for concerts and other events.

Panton's English Bookshop

Via Mascheroni 12 (entrance in via Ariosto), West (02 469 4468/4549 7568/www.englishbookshop.it). Metro Conciliazione/bus 68/tram 29. **Open** 9.30am-7.30pm Mon-Sat. Closed 10 days Aug. **Credit** AmEx, DC, MC, V. **Map** p248 A5.
Founded in 1979, this shop boasts the most varied and comprehensive English-language selection of both fiction and non-fiction in the city. There are also English-language DVDs, audio books, rare antiquarian history and travel books, and an extensive children's section, plus a noticeboard with expat community postings.

Department stores

Coin

Piazza V Giornate 1A, East (02 5519 2083/www.coin.it). Bus 60/tram 12, 23, 27. **Open** 10am-8pm Mon-Fri; 10am-8.30pm Sat; 11am-8pm Sun. **Credit** AmEx, DC, MC, V. **Map** p251 G7.
A retail focal point on the mid-priced shopping street of corso di Porta Vittoria, this eight-storey department store caters to the refined Milanese taste for classic, reasonable-quality, good-value clothing and accessories for men, women and children. It also sells homewares, cosmetics and shoes, and there's a restaurant and two bars if you start to flag. **Other locations**: corso Vercelli 30-32, West (02 4399 0001); piazzale Cantore 12, South (02 8940 9550).

La Rinascente

Piazza Duomo, Centre (02 88 521/www.rinascente.it). Metro Duomo/bus 54, 60, 65/tram 12, 23, 27. **Open** 9am-10pm Mon-Sat; 10am-8pm Sun. **Credit** AmEx, DC, MC, V. **Map** p251 E7/p252 E7
This eight-floor colossus (part of a nationwide chain) sells just about everything you can think of, from lingerie to colourful ceramics. On the top floor there is a tax-free shopping information point, a branch of chic hairdresser's Aldo Coppola (*see p137*), an Estée Lauder spa, plus an indoor and outdoor café where you can sip hot chocolate while admiring the gargoyles on the Duomo's roof. There's a linked passageway on the first floor to La Rinascente's trendy teenage store, Jam.

Dry-cleaning/laundry

Ondablu

Via Savona, opposite No 1, South (no phone/www.ondablu.com). Metro Porta Genova/tram 14, 29, 30. **Open** 8am-10pm daily. **No credit cards**. **Map** p250 A8.
Coin-operated launderette with washers and dryers. **Other locations**: throughout the city.

Tintoria Alberti

Piazza Castello 2, Centre (02 8901 7677). Metro Cairoli or Lanza/bus 57, 27/tram 1, 4, 7. **Open** 8am-12.30pm, 3-7pm Mon-Fri; 8am-12.30pm Sat. Closed 3wks Aug. **No credit cards**. **Map** p250 C6/p252 C6.
Big-name designers and well-dressed Milanese alike rely on this reputable dry-cleaner.

Fashion

Bags & leather goods

Coccinelle

Via Bigli 28, at via Manzoni, Centre (02 7602 8161 /www.coccinelle.it). Metro Montenapoleone/tram 12. **Open** 10am-7pm Mon-Sat; 11am-2pm, 3-7pm Sun. Closed 1wk Aug. **Credit** AmEx, DC, MC, V. **Map** p251 E6/p252 E6.
This outpost of the Parma-based leather goods chain is one of the best stocked in Milan. Dive in for everything from classic wallets in pretty pastels to handbags with fringes, studs and whatever bits and bobs the fashion crowd are demanding this season – all at prices that won't make you swoon with shock. **Other locations**: corso Buenos Aires 16, East (02 2040 4755); corso Genova 6, South (02 8942 1347); via Statuto 11, North (02 6552 851).

Cut

Corso di Porta Ticinese 58, South (02 839 4135). Metro Porta Genova/tram 2, 3, 14. **Open** 3-7.30pm Mon; 10.30am-1.30pm, 3-7.30pm Tue-Sat. Closed Aug. **Credit** AmEx, DC, MC, V. **Map** p250 C8.
You won't find any tacky leather blazers here. Cut sells a range of high-quality artisan-made leather garments for men and women; you can also have items made to measure.

Valextra Outlet

Via Cerva 11, Centre (02 7600 3459/www.valextra.it). Metro San Babila/bus 54, 60, 65/tram 12, 27. **Open** 10am-7pm Tue-Sat. Closed 3wks Aug. **Credit** AmEx, DC, MC, V. **Map** p251 F7/p252 F7.
This is the kind of shop that makes a trip to Milan worthwhile. Tucked behind piazza San Babila, it stocks mouth-watering end-of-line wallets, handbags and luggage from the legendary leather brand for 40% less than the usually stratospheric prices. Although these bags are beloved of the jet set, their sleek lines aren't subject to the whims of fashion, making them a great investment. Not convinced you've got a deal? Visit the full-price boutique, at via Manzoni 3, Centre (02 9978 6060), and compare.

Eat, Drink, Shop

VERSACE

Pianegonda. *See p129.*

Boutiques

Antonioli
Via Pasquale Paoli 1, at Porta Ticinese, South (02 3656 6494/www.antoniolishop.com). Metro Porta Genova/bus 47, 74/tram 2, 9. **Open** 3-7.30pm Mon; 11am-7.30pm Tue-Sun. Closed 3wks Aug. **Credit** AmEx, DC, MC, V. **Map** p250 B9.
This place is a hit with the international fashion crowd that regularly descends on the city. Most of the clothes for men and women are dark and deconstructed – and the decor in this former cinema (featuring a distressed steel skateboard ramp and scraped-down walls) has been designed to match. Labels include Dries Van Noten, Dsquared2, Rick Owens and Ring.

Biffi
Corso Genova 6, South (02 831 1601/www.biffi. com). Metro Sant'Ambrogio/bus 94/tram 2, 14. **Open** 3-7.30pm Mon; 9.30am-1.30pm, 3-7.30pm Tue-Sat. Closed 2wks Aug. **Credit** AmEx, DC, MC, V. **Map** p250 C8.
A Milanese institution for men's and women's classic designer labels, Biffi also stocks the mildly wild trend pieces of the season. Among the designers showcased here are Gucci, Fendi, Yohji Yamamoto, Marc Jacobs and John Galliano.

No Season
Corso di Porta Ticinese 77, South (02 8942 3332/ www.noseason.com). Metro Porta Genova/tram 3, 2, 14. **Open** 3.30-7.30pm Mon; 10.30am-1.30pm, 3.30-7.30pm Tue-Sat. Closed 2wks Aug. **Credit** AmEx, DC, MC, V. **Map** p250 C8.

An oasis of cool and calm in this chaotic shopping street, No Season sells men's, women's and children's fashions and shoes, along with all the necessary music, books and gadgets to fill the spaces of modern urban living. Labels include Costume National, Givenchy and Viktor & Rolf.

10 Corso Como
Corso Como 10, North (02 2900 2674/www. 10corsocomo.it). Metro Garibaldi/tram 11, 29, 30, 33. **Open** 3-7.30pm Mon; 10.30am-7.30pm Tue, Fri-Sun; 10.30am-9pm Wed, Thur. **Credit** AmEx, DC, MC, V. **Map** p248 D3.
This emporium is owned by former Italian *Vogue* editor Carla Sozzani. Prices are not for the faint-hearted, but this place is a must-see for neophyte and seasoned fashionistas alike. The merchandise mix includes men's and women's fashions, accessories, shoes, bags, housewares, books and CDs. Also on site are a café/restaurant (*see p117*), a photography gallery (*see p154*) and a posh B&B (*see p43*). Those on a budget take note: there's an outlet selling previous season's stock at reduced prices, open weekends only (*see p132* **Chic at half the price**).

Zap!
Galleria Passarella 2, Centre (02 7606 7501). Metro San Babila/bus 54, 60, 65/tram 12, 27. **Open** 10am-7pm Mon-Sat. Closed 2wks Aug. **Credit** AmEx, DC, MC, V. **Map** p251 F6/p252 F6.
Taking up where the old Fiorucci store left off (*see p129* for its surviving, smaller incarnation, Love Therapy), this pink-walled mini department store stocks around 40 labels for women – including Blumarine, Red by Valentino, Moschino lingerie

Label gazing

Viktor & Rolf.

Just Cavalli.

If seeking out the latest catwalk looks is your idea of paradise, there is no happier hunting ground than the famed Quadrilatero della Moda ('Fashion Rectangle'), between via della Spiga, via Montenapoleone, via Manzoni and via Sant'Andrea (Map p252 E/F 5/6). You'll find more designer stores per square inch here than just about anywhere else in the world, and even if the price tags are beyond your budget, you can spend many a happy hour admiring the constantly updated store interiors and cutting-edge window displays.

The area is best reached from metro Montenapoleone or San Babila, by bus 61, 94 or 200, or by tram 2. Below is a list of the principal big-league designer shops. All will accept any kind of plastic you flash at them.

Giorgio Armani

Via Sant'Andrea 9 (02 7600 3234). **Open** 10.30am-7.30pm Mon-Sat.
Armani Collezioni *Via Montenapoleone 2 (02 7639 0068).* **Open** 10.30am-7.30pm Mon-Sat; 2.30-7.30pm Sun.
Superstore *Via Manzoni 31 (02 6231 2605).* **Open** 10.30am-7.30pm Mon-Sat; 2.30-7.30pm Sun.
Accessories *Via della Spiga 19 (02 783 511).* **Open** 10am-7pm Mon-Sat; 10am-2pm, 3-7pm Sun.

Armani Junior *Via Montenapoleone 10 (in arcade; 02 783 196).* **Open** 3-7pm Mon; 10am-7pm Tue-Sun.
Armani Casa *See p138.*

Cacharel

Via San Paolo 1 (02 8901 1127). **Open** 3.30-7.30pm Mon; 10am-7.30pm Tue-Sat.

Roberto Cavalli

Via della Spiga 42 (02 7602 0900).
Just Cavalli *Via della Spiga 30 (02 7631 6566).* **Open** (both shops) 10am-7pm Mon-Sat.

Chanel

Via Sant'Andrea 10A (02 782 514).
Open 10am-7pm Mon-Sat.

Dolce & Gabbana

Womenswear *Via della Spiga 26 (02 7600 1155/02 799 950).*
Menswear *Corso Venezia 15 (02 7602 8485).*
D&G *Corso Venezia 7 (02 7600 4091).*
Accessories *Via della Spiga 2 (02 795 747).*
Open (all shops) 10am-7pm Mon-Sat.

Etro

Via Montenapoleone 5 (02 7600 5049).
Open 10am-7pm daily.

Eat, Drink, Shop

Made-to-measure *Via Montenapoleone 5 (02 7639 4216).* **Open** 10am-1.30pm, 2.30-7pm Mon-Sat.
Perfumes *Via Verri, at via Bigli 2 (02 7600 5450).* **Open** 3-7pm Mon; 10am-1.30pm, 2.30-7pm Tue-Sat.

Exté
Via della Spiga 6 (02 783 050). **Open** 3-7pm Mon; 10am-7pm Tue-Sat.

Fendi
Via Sant'Andrea 16 (02 7602 1617). **Open** 10am-1.30pm, 2.30-7pm Mon-Sat.

Gianfranco Ferré
Via Sant'Andrea 15 (02 794 864). **Open** 10am-7pm Mon-Sat.

Alberta Ferretti
Via Montenapoleone 21A (02 7602 2780). **Open** 10am-7pm Mon-Sat.
Philosophy by Alberta Ferretti *Via Montenapoleone 19 (02 796 034).* **Open** 10am-7pm Mon-Sat.

Gucci
Via Montenapoleone 5-7 (02 771 271). **Open** 10am-7pm Mon-Sat.
Galleria Vittorio Emanuele II (02 859 7991). **Open** 10am-7pm Mon-Sat; 2-7pm Sun.

Hermès
Via Sant'Andrea 21 (02 7600 3495). **Open** 3-7pm Mon; 10am-7pm Tue-Sat.

MaxMara
Piazza del Liberty 4 (02 7600 8849). **Open** 10am-7.30pm Mon-Sat; 10.30am-2pm, 3-7.30pm Sun.
Via Cuneo 3 (02 4800 4728). **Open** 10am-7.30pm Mon-Sat.
Via Orefici, at via Hugo 1 (02 8901 3509). **Open** 10am-7.30pm Mon-Sat.
Corso Genova 16 (02 837 5665). **Open** 3-7.30pm Mon; 10am-1.30pm, 3-7.30pm Tue-Sat.
Sportmax *Via della Spiga 30 (02 7601 1944).* **Open** 10am-7.30pm Mon-Sat.

Miu Miu
Corso Venezia 3 (02 7600 1799). **Open** 10am-7.30pm Mon-Sat.

Moschino
Via della Spiga 30 (02 7600 4320).
Via Sant'Andrea 12 (02 7600 0832). **Open** (both shops) 10am-7.30pm Mon-Sat.

Prada
Womenswear, menswear, sportswear, shoes, bags, eyewear *Galleria Vittorio Emanuele II 63-65 (02 876 979).* **Open** 10am-7.30pm daily.
Menswear, men's accessories *Via Montenapoleone 6 (02 7602 0273).* **Open** 10am-7.30pm Mon-Sat; 11am-7pm Sun.
Womenswear, women's accessories, women's footwear *Via Montenapoleone 8 (02 777 1771).* **Open** 10am-7.30pm Mon-Sat; 10am-7pm Sun.
Men's & women's sportswear *Via Sant'Andrea 21 (02 7600 1426).* **Open** 10am-7.30pm daily.
Accessories *Via della Spiga 18 (02 780 465).* **Open** (all above shops) 10am-7.30pm daily.
Lingerie *Via della Spiga 5 (02 7601 4448).* **Open** 10am-2pm, 3-7.30pm Mon-Sat.

Trussardi
Accessories *Piazza della Scala 5 (02 806 8821).*
Womenswear, menswear *Via Sant'Andrea 3-5 (02 7602 0380).* **Open** (both above shops) 10am-7pm Mon-Sat.
T-Store (casualwear) *Galleria San Carlo 6 at Corso Europa (02 783 909).* **Open** 3-7.30pm Mon; 10am-7.30pm Tue-Sat; 3-7.30pm Sun.

Valentino
Menswear *Via Montenapoleone 20 (02 7602 0285).* **Open** 10am-7pm Mon-Sat.
Womenswear *Via Santo Spirito 3 (02 7600 6478).* **Open** 10am-7pm Mon-Sat; 10am-2pm, 3-7pm Sun.

Gianni Versace
Via Montenapoleone 11 (02 7600 8528). **Open** 10am-7pm daily.

Viktor & Rolf
Via Sant'Andrea 14 (02 796 091). **Open** 10am-2pm, 3-7pm Mon-Sat.

Louis Vuitton
Womenswear, menswear & accessories *Via Montenapoleone 2 (02 777 1711).* **Open** 9.30am-7.30pm Mon-Sat; 11am-7.30pm Sun.
Accessories, footwear *Galleria Vittorio Emanuele II (02 7214 7011).* **Open** 10am-8pm Mon-Sat; 11am-7.30pm Sun.

Ermenegildo Zegna
Via Pietro Verri 3 (02 7600 6437). **Open** 10am-7pm Mon-Sat.

Eat, Drink, Shop

In with the old

Cappelleria Mutinelli

Milan may be known as the capital of change-with-the-wind design – but it's also a treasure trove of historic, artisan-based shops and workshops. While many of these stores are located in out-of-the-way streets in obscure neighbourhoods, others in the centre of town are sandwiched between the blazing windows of the attention-grabbing designers, so they're easy to miss.

Among the latter is cutlery and shaving specialist **Lorenzi** (via Montenapoleone 9, Centre, 02 7602 2848, www.glorenzi.com), which has the honour of being the street's oldest shop (established 1929). This is where smart *signore* come to buy wedding gifts such as cutlery sets with mother-of-pearl handles. There is also a vast assortment of razors and boar-bristle shaving brushes. Lorenzi also has a private museum nearby displaying 4,000 shaving implements; to see it, make an appointment at the shop.

Another must-visit store in the centre (around the corner from the opera house) is dance boutique **Porselli** (piazza Ferrari 6, Centre, 02 805 3759, www.porselli.it), which is where La Scala's ballerinas buy their pointe shoes and tutus. With its red velvet sofas, gilt-edged mirrors and chatty assistants (of a certain age), it feels more like a private parlour frozen in the 1950s than a place where you might actually part with cash. But the leather-soled ballet shoes designed for street wear, in a rainbow of colours, provide temptation to do so.

It's hard to believe that anything more than five years old has managed to survive on bustling corso Buenos Aires, where mainstream chains appear to be the order of the day. But inside milliner's shop **Cappelleria Mutinelli** (corso Buenos Aires 5, East, 02 2952 3594), the chequerboard marble floor, polished wood fittings and antique pillars transport you back at least a century. It certainly hasn't lost any of its appeal; the shop is always packed with Milanese customers of all ages, trying on everything from felt trilbies to knitted ski caps.

Equally nostalgic is glove retailer **Sacchi** (corso Magenta 15A, North, 02 869 3314), not far from piazza Cordusio. This is the kind of shop where assistants ask you to prop your elbow on a little velvet cushion, before helping you to slip on one of the exquisite, hand-finished gloves. Tiny wooden drawers and boxes line the walls – each filled with gloves in such luxurious materials as kid skin and silk.

Porselli.

and Milano je t'adore. Other fabulous finds include glittery jewellery by Tarina Tarantino, fur-trimmed baskets and diamanté tiaras by Hello Kitty.

Independent designers

Anybody who is anybody in fashion has an outlet in Milan (*see p126* **Label gazing**). Global names aside, the Milan-based designers below maintain their own following.

Anna Fabiano
Corso di Porta Ticinese 40, South (02 5811 2348). Metro Porta Genova/bus 47, 74/tram 2, 9. **Open** 3-7.30pm Mon; 10.30am-2pm, 3-7.30pm Tue-Sat. Closed 3wks Aug. **Credit** AmEx, MC, V. **Map** p250 C8.
This is the sole outlet for clothes and accessories by Fabiano, whose quirky styles include hand-painted, full 1950s-style skirts and beautifully tailored jackets with patchwork inserts on the collar turn-ups. Step out in something by Fabiano, and you'll be amazed by how many people comment on it.

Apolide by Stephan Janson
Via Goldoni 21, East (02 752 6171/www.stephan janson.com). Metro Porta Venezia/bus 54, 60, 61, 62/tram 12, 27. **Open** 10am-7pm Mon-Fri. Closed 1wk Aug. **Credit** AmEx, DC, MC, V. **Map** p249 H6.
Flowing evening dresses, swirling capes, tailored suits with knee-length skirts or culottes are sold in this out-of-the-way location set in a garden. Well worth the hike.

Co-Co
Via Pietro Giannone 4, North (02 3360 6356). Metro Moscova/bus 41, 43, 94/tram 3, 4, 12, 14. **Open** 10am-7pm Mon-Fri; 11am-5pm Sat. Closed Aug. **No credit cards. Map** p248 C4.
Tucked in a courtyard in Milan's downbeat Chinatown, this hard-to-find shop is an Aladdin's cave of classic skirts, jackets, coats, shoes and bags – all with a funky twist. Designers Nicoletta Ceccolini, Maretta Toschi and Serenella Brunetti pride themselves on producing stylish looks at contained prices; their beautifully cut trousers alone are worth the trip.

Isabella Tonchi
Via Maroncelli 5, North (02 2900 8589/www.isabella tonchi.com). Metro Garibaldi/tram 11, 29, 30, 33. **Open** 10am-7pm Mon-Sat. Closed Aug. **Credit** AmEx, DC, MC, V. **Map** p248 D3.
A former designer for Fiorucci and Miu Miu, Tonchi opened this elegant white shop a couple of years ago to showcase her linear, elegant – but never dull – pieces (knee-length pleated skirts; quilted dresses).

Love Therapy by Elio Fiorucci
Largo Toscanini 1, at corso Europa, East (02 7609 1237/www.lovetherapy.it). Metro San Babila/bus 54, 60, 65/tram 12, 27. **Open** 10am-7pm Mon-Sat; 1-8pm Sun. **Credit** AmEx, DC, MC, V. **Map** p251 F6/p252 F6.

When Milan's famed Fiorucci store closed down in 2003 (its premises taken over by the city's first H&M), it seemed like the end of the line for the label immortalised with Halston and Gucci in the Sister Sledge song. But the disco era fave lives on in this small store. The shop's kitschy-cool pieces – T-shirts scattered with Fiorucci's famous angel motifs, dwarf-themed snow globes, fluorescent litter-bins, fuchsia feather handcuffs – will remind you why Fiorucci was a hit in the first place.

Jewellery

Bliss
Piazza Duomo 25, Centre (02 805 4565/www. bliss.it). Metro Duomo/bus 54, 60, 65/tram 12, 27. **Open** 10am-7pm daily. **Credit** AmEx, DC, MC, V. **Map** p251 E7/p252 E7.
Bliss is fine jeweller Damiani's lower-priced line. Pieces for both men and women range from subtle classics to fashion-led items like bicep bracelets with flower and star charms. The sparklers here may be chips rather than rocks – but there's no doubting they're the real thing.

DoDo
Corso Venezia 8, Centre (02 7631 7581/www. parlacondodo.com). Metro San Babila/bus 54, 60, 65/tram 12, 27. **Open** 3-7pm Mon; 10am-7pm Tue-Sat. Closed 2wks Aug. **Credit** AmEx, DC, MC, V. **Map** p251 F6/p252 F6.
In 1995, Milan-based jeweller Pomellato launched DoDo, a range of whimsical yellow-gold charms shaped like animals, birds and flowers. Today half a million customers flock to DoDo's Italian outlets every year. As well as this stand-alone shop, the range is sold in other jewellery and department stores, including Coin and La Rinascente.

Donatella Pellini
Via Manzoni 20, Centre (02 7600 8084). Metro Montenapoleone/tram 12. **Open** 3.30-7.30pm Mon; 9.30am-7.30pm Tue-Sat. Closed Aug. **Credit** AmEx, DC, MC, V. **Map** p249 E6/p252 E6.
Jewellery designer Donatella Pellini augments her signature bold synthetic-resin pieces with striking baubles and bangles that she has collected on her worldwide travels.

Pianegonda
Via Montenapoleone 6, Centre (02 7600 3038). Metro Montenapoleone or San Babila/bus 54, 64, 91. **Open** 3-7pm Mon; 10am-7pm Tue-Sat. Closed 1wk Aug. **Credit** AmEx, DC, MC, V. **Map** p251 E6/p252 E6.
These silver and yellow-gold baubles – for both men and women – by Vicenza-based designer Franco Pianegonda are out to make a statement. Creations include outsized silver crosses, rings with giant slabs of quartz or aquamarine, and chunky silver chains. Pianegonda's fans include Britney Spears and Jennifer Lopez – which gives some idea of the look. It may not be cheap, but fortunately you don't have to be J Lo to afford this stuff. **Photo** *p125.*

CA-DO

E S S E N T I A L   L I V I N G

LINEAR, MINIMAL, ESSENTIAL
The beds manufactured by URUSH
mingle together your wish to sleep
naturally with the need to decorate
your private spaces with first-class furniture
URUSHI's style talks to your soul
whispering to it. URUSHI's style.

FU-CI

SHIMA

Fashion-conscious Milanese women hot-foot it to **Mauro**. *See p134.*

Lingerie

Kristina Ti
*Via Solferino 18, North (02 653 379/www.
kristinati.com). Metro Moscova/bus 41, 43, 94/
tram 3, 4, 12, 14.* **Open** 3-7pm Mon; 10am-7pm
Tue-Sat. Closed 3wks Aug. **Credit** AmEx, DC, MC,
V. **Map** p248 D5.
The best thing to come out of Turin since the Fiat
Cinquecento, Kristina Ti's lingerie is delicate almost
to the point of fragility. There's also a super-femi-
nine ready-to-wear clothing line.

La Perla
*Via Montenapoleone 1, East (02 7600 0460/
www.laperla.com). Metro Montenapoleone or San
Babila/bus 54, 61/tram 1, 12.* **Open** 3-7pm Mon;
10am-7pm Tue-Sat. Closed 2wks Aug. **Credit**
AmEx, DC, MC, V. **Map** p249 E6/p252 E6.
How can something so small cost so much? Well, La
Perla's sophisticated lingerie, manufactured in
Bologna using only the finest fabrics, is of out-
standing quality – which goes some way towards an
explanation anyway. The label also encompasses
glamorous swimwear and ready-to-wear pieces. A
men's only La Perla store recently opened at via
Manzoni 17, Centre (02 8053 092).

Mid-range clothing

Apart from branches of Euro giants such as
H&M and Zara throughout the city, these
Italian brands are worth checking out.

L'Altramoda
*Corso Venezia 5, Centre (02 7602 1117/www.
laltramoda.it). Metro San Babila/bus 54, 61.* **Open**
10am-7pm Mon-Sat. Closed 1wk Aug. **Credit** AmEx,
DC, MC, V. **Map** p249 F6/p252 F6.
This Roman womenswear chain is the place to head
when you're looking for a glam outfit at an affordable price. The label hasn't expanded much beyond
Italy yet, so you can show off your nous back home.
Other locations: corso Vercelli 20, West (02 4699
248); via Solferino 2, North (02 653 362).

Ethic
*Corso di Porta Ticinese 50, South (02 5810 5669/
www.ethic.it). Bus 3, 94.* **Open** 3.30-7.30pm Mon;
10.30am-2pm, 3-7.30pm Tue-Sat. Closed Aug.
Credit AmEx, DC, MC, V. **Map** p250 C8.
Ethic's hip looks and low prices are targeted at a
trendy young customer base. The stuff won't last
forever, but it oozes sexy Italian style.
Other locations: corso Garibaldi 34, North
(02 805 2284).

Eat, Drink, Shop

Chic at half the price

Il Salvagente.

When in Milan, do as many of the chicest Milanese do and seek out cut-price clothes – to mix with the latest (full-price) catwalk looks. Below is a selection of some of the best discount boutiques and bargain basements in the city.

Stock houses

Many stock houses are treasure troves of designer goods, with racks of end-of-season shop and warehouse returns, stock from boutiques that have closed down, and some factory seconds – though even at discounts of 50-70 per cent, prices tags can still cause the occasional 'ouch!'

Among the best known and longest established is **Il Salvagente**, which garners large piles of the top stuff, simply because it's been around for ever. Pick through an ever-changing kaleidoscope of designer goods for men and women; for children there's a separate location called **Salvagente Bimbi**.

But Il Salvagente ('The Lifebelt') is no longer the only hope for impoverished fashionistas who fear that their bank manager is about to throw them overboard. Increasingly, determined shoppers find equally worthwhile bargains at discount outlets with more convenient, central locations. Some – like **Dmagazine Outlet** – are wedged between the full-priced stores on the smartest shopping drags; come here for serious discounts on clothes by Miu Miu, Marc Jacobs, Marni... and much, much more.

Next, head for **Basement** – located (as the name suggests) in a cellar on via Senato – for price slashes of 50-70 per cent on brands including Dolce & Gabbana, Prada and YSL.

Serious bargainistas should also make a pitstop at **Outlet Matia's**, in yet another basement, this time in Brera, for dramatic discounts on classy labels such as Aspesi, Ermenegildo Zegna and MaxMara. Affordable cashmere knits in a rainbow of colours sometimes fill a boardroom-sized table here.

Down an alley off corso Vittorio Emanuele, **DT Intrend** deals in the MaxMara brands, including Sportmax and Marella.

For last season's (unworn) women's shoes by such sought-after designers as René Caovilla, Gianni Barbato and Alessandro dell'Acqua, head to **Le Vintage**, in the increasingly trendy Isola area, behind Garibaldi Station. There's also a small but well-chosen selection of 1960s and '70s vintage clothes.

Finally, fashion slaves on a budget shouldn't miss the **10 Corso Como Outlet**, a slightly shabbier version of the über-cool original store (*see p125*), with endless racks of (mostly black) clothes by Helmut Lang, Chloé, Comme des Garçons et al. Don't gasp when you check the price tags; though unmarked, most have been slashed by a further 50-70 per cent.

Basement
Via Senato 15, Centre (02 7631 7913). Metro Palestro/bus 61, 94, 200. **Open** 3-7pm Mon; 10am-7pm Tue-Sat. Closed Aug. **Credit** AmEx, DC, MC, V. **Map** p249 F5.

Dmagazine Outlet
Via Montenapoleone 26, Centre (02 7600 6027/www.dmagazine.it). Metro Montenapoleone/tram 12. **Open** 9.30am-7.45pm daily. **Credit** AmEx, DC, MC, V. **Map** p249 E6/p252 E6.

DT Intrend
Galleria San Carlo 6, Centre (02 7600 0829). Metro Duomo/bus 54, 60, 61, 65/tram 12, 23, 27. **Open** 3.30-7.30pm Mon; 10am-7.30pm Tue-Sat. **Credit** AmEx, DC, MC, V. **Map** p251 E6/p252 E6.

Outlet Matia's
Piazza Mirabello 4, North (02 6269 4535). Metro Moscova/bus 41, 43, 94/tram 3, 4, 12, 14. **Open** 10am-2pm, 3.30-7pm Mon-Sat; 10am-1.30pm, 3.30-7pm Sun. Closed Aug. **Credit** MC, V. **Map** p249 E5.

Eat, Drink, Shop

Il Salvagente

*Via Fratelli Bronzetti 16, East (02 7611
0328/www.salvagentemilano.it). Metro Porta
Venezia/bus 54, 60, 61, 62/tram 12, 27.*
Open 3-7pm Mon; 10am-12.30pm, 3-7pm
Tue, Thur, Fri; 10am-7pm Wed, Sat. Closed
Aug. **No credit cards**. **Map** p251 H6.

Salvagente Bimbi

*Via Balzaretti 28, East (02 2668 0764/
www.salvagentemilano.it). Metro Piola/bus
62, 90, 91/tram 11, 23.* **Open** 3-7pm Mon;
10am-1pm, 3-7pm Tue, Thur, Fri; 10am-7pm
Wed, Sat. Closed Aug. **No credit cards**.

10 Corso Como Outlet

*Via Tazzoli 3, North (02 2901 5130).
Metro Garibaldi/bus 52, 70/tram 3, 4, 7,
11, 29.* **Open** 1-7pm Fri; 11am-7pm Sat, Sun.
Closed 2wks Aug. **Credit** AmEx, DC, MC, V.
Map p248 D3.

Le Vintage

*Via Garigliano 4, North (02 6931 1885).
Metro Garibaldi or Zara/bus 23, 43, 82/
tram 2, 4, 11.* **Open** 3-8pm Mon; 11am-2pm,
3-8pm Tue-Fri; 11am-1pm, 2-6pm Sat; 1-7pm
Sun. Closed 3wks Aug. **Credit** AmEx, DC, MC,
V. **Map** p249 E2.

Second-hand & vintage

Not surprisingly in this image-obsessed city,
many Milanese women (and men) have
wardrobes that are full to bursting point.
The canniest offload last season's clothes
to help fund, as well as make room for, the
latest designer looks – which all adds up
to a rich terrain for bargain hunters.

Il Nuovo Guardaroba has well-organised
racks of classic women's pre-worn clothing
and accessories, with a small selection of
men's items too; a separate shop nearby,
Il Guardarobino, caters for children, offering
clothing and baby hardware, such as strollers
and highchairs.

At **L'Armadio di Laura** there's good reason
for the sign reading 'Please don't ask for
further discounts' – the prices in this
thriftstore-like shop are low enough already.

For vintage clothing from old hands in the
business, try **Cavalli e Nastri**. Each piece in
this tidy collection is in mint condition and
selected with a razor-sharp eye; obvious and
dowdy 'period' pieces have been weeded out,
leaving only the crème de la crème of vintage

chic. If you're looking for a Victorian gown or
a 19th-century smoking jacket, try its other,
larger location, at via de Amicis.

Passionate vintage fans should head
straight for **Franco Jacassi**, a treasure trove of
antique clothing, bags, shoes, hats, buttons,
trimmings and rare fashion publications. This
is where Milan's big-name designers come
when they need inspiration.

For fabulous '50s looks, make for **Miss
Ghinting**, run by two stylish Milanese 'misses'
in the Isola district; their stock is a well-edited
mix of tailored pieces from that era, plus
some from the '60s and '70s.

L'Armadio di Laura

*Via Voghera 25, South (02 836 0606).
Metro Porta Genova/bus 68/tram 11, 29,
30.* **Open** Spring, summer 10am-6pm
Tue-Sat. Autumn, winter 10am-6pm Mon-Sat.
Closed late July-early Sept. **Credit** MC, V.
Map p250 A8.

Cavalli e Nastri

*Via Brera 2, North (02 7200 0449). Metro
Cairoli or Lanza/bus 61/tram 3, 4, 12.*
Open 3.30-7pm Mon; 10.30am-7pm
Tue-Sat. Closed Aug. **Credit** AmEx, DC,
MC, V. **Map** p248 D5.
Other locations: via de Amicis 9 (entrance in
via Arena), South (02 8940 9452).

Franco Jacassi

*Via Sacchi 3, North (02 8646 2076/
www.vintagedelirium.com). Metro Lanza/
bus 61/tram 1, 3, 4, 12, 27.* **Open** 9.30am-
1pm, 2-6.30pm Mon-Fri. Closed Aug. **Credit**
AmEx, MC, V. **Map** p248 D6/p252 D6.

Il Guardarobino

*Via Senofonte 9, West (02 4801 5802).
Metro Amendola Fiera/bus 68/tram 19, 27.*
Open 10am-1pm, 3-7pm Tue-Sat. Closed
2wks July, Aug. **No credit cards**.

Miss Ghinting

*Via Borsieri, opposite No.16, North (02 668
7112/www.missghinting.com). Metro
Garibaldi/bus 82, 83/tram 4, 7, 11.* **Open**
10am-1pm, 3-7.30pm Tue-Sat. Closed Aug.
Credit AmEx, DC, MC, V. **Map** p249 E3.

Il Nuovo Guardaroba

*Via Privata Asti 5A, West (02 4800 1678).
Metro Wagner/bus 61, 67/tram 24.* **Open**
10am-1.30pm, 3-6pm Tue-Fri; 10am-6pm Sat.
Closed 2wks July, 4wks Aug. **No credit cards**.

Eat, Drink, Shop

Shoes

Les Chaussures Mon Amour
*Via Cherubini 3, North (02 4800 0535/www.
leschaussures.it). Bus 61/tram 16, 18.* **Open** 3-8pm
Mon; 10.30am-8pm Tue-Sat. Closed 3wks Aug.
Credit AmEx, MC, V. **Map** p248 A6.
This colourful store off corso Vercelli sells up-to-the-
minute women's shoes by offbeat brands like
Fornarina and Irregular Choice. But the best bargains are the shop's own-label shoes, made in the
nearby footwear-manufacturing town of Vigevano,
ranging from suede pixie boots to ballerina pumps.

Mauro
*Corso di Porta Ticinese 60, South (02 8942 9167).
Metro Porta Genova/bus 47, 74/tram 2, 9.* **Open**
3-7.30pm Mon; 10am-7.30pm Tue-Sat; 2-7pm Sun.
No credit cards. Map p250 C8.
This tiny store is always packed with Milanese
signoras and fashionistas fighting over the latest
own-brand styles, which are made in Italy. You'll
find everything here from suede courts in purple and
turquoise to basic black knee-high boots – all at
good prices. **Photo** *p131*.

Le Solferine
*Via Solferino 2, North (02 655 5352). Metro
Moscova/bus 41, 43, 94/tram 3, 4, 12, 14.*
Open 3-7.30pm Mon; 10am-7.30pm Tue-Sat.
Credit AmEx, DC, MC, V. **Map** p248 D5.
Le Solferine has a choice selection of non-ubiquitous
designer footwear for men and women by the likes
of René Caovilla, Ungaro and Emilio Pucci. A good
source of special-occasion shoes.

Food & drink

See also p141 **Markets**.

Confectionery & cakes

L'Antica Arte del Dolce
*Via Anfossi 10, East (02 5519 4448/www.
ernstknam.it). Bus 84/tram 9, 29, 30.* **Open** 10am-
1pm, 4-8pm Tue-Sat; 10am-1pm Sun. Closed 2wks
Aug. **Credit** AmEx, MC, V. **Map** p251 H7.
A stone's throw from the Prada offices, this is where
the fashion crowd comes for a sweet fix. Gourmet
cakes, desserts, biscuits, jams and cakes are whisked
up in the kitchens by pastry chef Ernst Knam – who
trained under renowned restaurateur Gualtiero
Marchesi – and his able team. Among the more
palate-testing selections are apple and rosemary tart
and aubergine and chocolate mousse. Sweet tooths
beware: many an addiction has started here.

Giovanni Galli Pasticceria
*Corso di Porta Romana 2, South (02 8645 3112/
www.giovannigalli.com). Metro Porta Romana/bus
54, 199, 200/tram 12, 15, 16, 24, 27.* **Open** 8.30am-
1pm, 2-8pm Mon-Sat; 9am-1pm Sun. Closed 3wks
Aug. **Credit** AmEx, DC, MC, V. **Map** p251 E7.

Giovanni Galli Pasticceria.

Milan's best address for *marrons glacés*, made daily
from fresh chestnuts in Galli's own kitchens. The
alchechengi (Cape gooseberries dipped in chocolate),
not to mention the pralines filled with mint, nougat
or orange, are just as good.
Other locations: via Victor Hugo 2, Centre
(02 8646 4833).

Pasticceria Marchesi
*Via Santa Maria alla Porta 11A, North (02 876
730). Metro Cairoli or Cordusio/bus 18/tram 12, 19,
24.* **Open** 7.30am-8pm Tue-Sat; 7.30am-1pm Sun.
Closed Aug. **Credit** MC, V. **Map** p250 D6/p252 D6.
In one of Milan's most beautiful buildings (with a
gorgeously patterned exterior), this historic *pasticceria* and bar serves up wonderful old-fashioned
cakes filled with chocolate and custard cream. It also
sells prettily packaged own-brand chocolates.

Delicatessens

Peck
*Via Spadari 9, Centre (02 802 3161/www.peck.it).
Metro Duomo/bus 54, 60, 65/tram 12, 27.*
Open 3-7.30pm Mon; 8.45am-7.30pm Tue-Sat,
last 2 Suns of Dec. **Credit** AmEx, DC, MC, V.
Map p250 D7/p252 D7.

Eat, Drink, Shop

A temple of fine food and wine for more than 120 years, Peck was founded in 1883 by a humble pork butcher from Prague, Franz Peck. These days, the main action is in the three-floor flagship shop on via Spadari, which has a butcher's, bakery, delicatessen, a vast selection of wines from all over the world, prepared foods, oils and bottled sauces, plus a delightful tearoom (upstairs). There are also a sit-down gourmet restaurant, Cracco-Peck, and a café, Peck Italian Bar (for both, *see p102*), at separate locations. For more about the Peck empire, *see p107* **The taste maker**.

Il Salumaio di Montenapoleone

Via Montenapoleone 12, Centre (02 7600 1123/ www.ilsalumaiodimontenapoleone.it). Metro Montenapoleone/tram 12. **Open** 3.30-7pm Mon; 8.30am-1pm, 3.30-7pm Tue-Sat. Closed 3wks Aug. **Credit** AmEx, DC, MC, V. **Map** p249 E6/p252 E6.

Wedged in an inner courtyard between Dior and Lorenz (watches), this temple to all things edible is one of the last non-clothing stores to hold out in the centre of Milan. Wander in for tempting arrays of freshly made pasta and biscuits, cured meats, 100 varieties of cheese, and bottles stuffed with olives, artichokes, peppers, porcini mushrooms and just about anything else you can fit in a jar. There's also a café-cum-restaurant (open 12.30-6pm), a great place to take a shopping break.

Health food

Centro Botanico

Piazza San Marco 1, North (02 2901 3254/www. centrobotanico.it). Metro Lanza/bus 57, 61, 70. **Open** 10am-2.30pm, 3.30-8pm Mon-Fri; 10am-8pm Sat; 3-7.30pm Sun. Closed 3wks Aug. **Credit** AmEx, DC, MC, V. **Map** p248 D5.

A major centre for health and natural products, stocking organically grown produce, groceries and baked goods, vitamin supplements, pure-fibre clothing and more. There's also a juice bar and lunchtime café on site.
Other locations: via Vincenzo Monti 32, North (02 463 807).

Wine

Fine food emporium **Peck** (*see p134*) has an extensive wine selection.

L'Altro Vino

Viale Piave 9, East (02 780 147). Metro Porta Venezia/bus 54, 61/tram 9, 29, 30. **Open** 11.30am-7.45pm Tue-Sat. Closed Aug. **Credit** AmEx, DC, MC, V. **Map** p249 G6.

Thanks to the knowledgeable and approachable proprietors, this pleasant shop, where you can wander around without feeling intimidated. L'Altro Vino offers a vast selection of Italian and international bottles, and holds regular tastings on the first and third Thursdays of the month.

Enoteca Cotti

Via Solferino 42, North (02 2900 1096/www. enotecacotti.it). Metro Moscova/bus 41, 43, 94/tram 3, 4, 12, 14. **Open** 8.30am-1pm, 3-7.30pm Tue-Sat. Closed Aug. **Credit** MC, V. **Map** p248 D5.

The overflowing shelves of Milan's oldest *enoteca* contain more than 1,000 wines, plus grappas, whiskies, rums, cognacs, and such gourmet delights as pâté de foie gras.

N'Ombra de Vin

Via San Marco 2, North (02 659 9650/www. nombradevin.it). Metro Moscova/bus 41, 43, 94/ tram 3, 4, 12, 14. **Open** 3.30pm-midnight Mon; 8.30am-midnight Tue-Sat. Closed 3wks Aug. **Credit** AmEx, DC, MC, V. **Map** p248 D5.

The vaulted cellars of this 15th-century former monk's refectory provide an atmospheric shopping experience. Owner and wine expert Cristian Corà will help you choose from among the 3,000 bottles. At the entrance there's a small wine bar, offering soups, cold cuts, cheese and pan-fried risotto, as well as wines by the glass. **Photo** *p137*.

Health & beauty

State-of-the-art gym Downtown Palestre (*see p172*) offers beauty treatments for men and women. For designer spas, *see p139* **Shopping and flopping**.

Cosmetics & perfumes

Calé Fragranze d'Autore

Via Santa Maria alla Porta 5, North (02 8050 9449/www.cale.it). Metro Cairoli or Cordusio/bus 18/tram 12, 19, 24. **Open** 3-7pm Mon; 10am-7pm Tue-Fri; 10am-7.30pm Sat. Closed Aug. **Credit** AmEx, DC, MC, V. **Map** p250 D6/p252 D6.

Silvio Levi, grandson of the founder, sniffs out rare, artisan-made perfumes (and shaving creams and hair products) for this family-run company. Finds include Acqua di Biella's No.1, created in 1871, with hints of bergamot, mint and white musk. The wood-beamed room upstairs houses a collection of historic bottles and packaging – not to be missed.

Madina

Via Meravigli 17, Centre (02 8691 5438/www. madina.it). Metro Cairoli or Cordusio/bus 18/tram 12, 19, 24. **Open** 3.30-7.30pm Mon; 10am-7.30pm Tue-Sat. Closed 3wks Aug. **Credit** AmEx, DC, MC, V. **Map** p248 D6/p252 D6.

Products that carry the name Madina Milano become coveted souvenirs not only for their high quality, but also for their international cachet. The make-up line has a strong following in the beauty trade, no doubt attracted partly by the sheer number of shades: 120 lipsticks, 50 lip glosses, 250 eye-shadows and 300 tones of foundation, blusher, bronzer and face powder.
Other locations: via Tivoli 8, North (02 860 746); corso Venezia 23, East (02 7601 1692).

OUR CLIMATE NEEDS
A HELPING HAND TODAY

Be a smart traveller. Help to offset your carbon emissions from your trip by pledging Carbon Trees with Trees for Cities.

All the Carbon Trees that you donate through Trees for Cities are genuinely planted as additional trees in our projects.

Trees for Cities is an independent charity working with local communities on tree planting projects.

www.treesforcities.org   Tel 020 7587 1320

Trees for Cities
Charity registration number 1032216

Sample the wares at **N'Ombra de Vin**'s on-site wine bar. *See p135.*

Profumo

Via Brera 6, North (02 7202 3334). Metro Lanza/ bus 61/tram 1, 3, 4, 12, 27. **Open** 10am-7pm Mon-Sat. Closed 2wks Aug. **Credit** AmEx, DC, MC, V. **Map** p248 D5.

Set in the 16th-century Palazzo Beccaria, this enticing, pale pink store stocks a selection of rare Italian and international candles and perfumes, including delicate (and not-so-delicate) scents by Carthusia of Capri, Acampora of Naples and Frédéric Malle of Paris. Among the bestsellers are Lorenzo Villoresi's powdery Teint de Neige with notes of rose, jasmine, musk and heliotrope.

Hairdressers

Aldo Coppola

8th Floor, La Rinascente, piazza Duomo, Centre (02 8905 9712/www.aldocoppola.it). Metro Duomo/ bus 54, 60, 61, 65/tram 12, 23, 27. **Open** 10am-9pm Mon-Sat; 10am-7pm Sun. **Credit** MC, V. **Map** p251 E7/p252 E7

Coppola, who opened his first salon in Milan in 1965, now has nine across town, including this funky outpost on the top floor of La Rinascente department store, which affords views of the Duomo's roof. It's not cheap, but a safe bet if you feel like a splurge. The salon is overseen by Coppola's right-hand man Roberto Castelli, and the master shearer himself puts in an appearance on Saturdays.
Other locations: throughout the city.

Antica Barbieria Colla

Via Gerolamo Morone 3, Centre (02 874 312). Metro Montenapoleone/tram 1, 2. **Open** 8.30am-12.30pm, 2.30-7pm Tue-Sat. Closed 3wks Aug. **No credit cards**. **Map** p249 E6/p252 E6.

Going for that groovy Puccini look? The barbers in this shop have been shearing since 1904 and proudly display the brush that was used to keep the composer's locks coiffed. Call for an appointment.

Marchina Hair Stylist

2nd Floor, corso Venezia 3, East (02 799 636). Metro San Babila/bus 54, 60, 65/tram 12, 27. **Open** 9am-6.30pm (later by appointment) Mon-Wed, Fri, Sat; 9am-10pm Thur. **Credit** DC, MC, V. **Map** p249 F6/p252 F6.

Expert snipper Pino Marchina leads a team of cutters, colourists and beauticians in this clean, modern salon near San Babila. There's a full menu of grooming and pampering services for men and women, prices are reasonable and the staff efficient and friendly.

Herbalists

For pharmacies, *see p228.*

Erboristeria Officinale Mediolanum

Via Volta 7, North (02 6572 882/www.erboristeria mediulanum.it). Metro Moscova/bus 41, 43, 94/tram 3, 4, 12, 14. **Open** 3.30-7.30pm Mon; 9.30am-1pm, 3.30-7.30pm Tue-Sat. Closed Aug. **Credit** AmEx, MC, V. **Map** p248 D4.

Eat, Drink, Shop

In bed with Giorgio – understated designer style at **Armani Casa**.

Expert Gabriella Fiumani presides over this intriguing herbalist's, mixing tisanes, cosmetic remedies and medicinal concoctions from more than 400 herbs stored in drawers and cupboards at the back of the shop. Other products include organic herbal cosmetics, as well as spices and seasonings – from myrrh granules to blue poppy seeds – displayed in huge glass jars.

Officina Profumo Farmaceutica di Santa Maria Novella

Corso Magenta 22, North (02 805 3695).
Metro Conciliazione/bus 18, 58/tram 24, 29, 30.
Open 10am-1pm, 3.30-7.30pm Tue-Fri; 10am-1pm, 3.30-6pm Sat. Closed 3wks Aug, 2wks Dec/Jan.
Credit AmEx, DC, MC, V. **Map** p250 B6.
This small outpost of the legendary herbalist and apothecary may not have the history of the original 16th-century Florentine store – but it does have most of the products, from skin-whitening cream to almond paste hand-softener and hand-moulded milk, mint and olive oil soaps. In their old-fashioned packaging, they make charming gifts.

Home design & accessories

As the host city of Europe's largest furniture fair, the Salone Internazionale del Mobile (*see p144*) each April, it's hardly surprising that Milan is an excellent place to shop for designer furniture and household goods. The best place to start is via Durini (home to B&B Italia, Gervasoni and Cassina, among others). From there, head up via Manzoni, for several more design stores. There is also a growing number of interesting design shop/gallery crossovers in the area between Brera and corso Como – *see also p154* **Intelligent design**.

Alessi

Corso Matteotti 9, Centre (02 795 726/www.
alessi.com). Metro San Babila/bus 54, 60, 65/tram 12, 27. **Open** 3-7pm Mon; 10am-7pm Tue-Sat.
Closed 2-3wks Aug. **Credit** AmEx, DC, MC, V.
Map p249 E6/p252 E6.
Alessi's Milan flagship store – not far from the main household designer drag Via Durini – has everything the company has ever done in bright plastic and polished steel, from toothpick holders to the famous Merdolino loo brush. For the outlet store in Crusinallo, *see p191* **Alessi's cave**.

Armani Casa

Via Manzoni 37, East (02 657 2401). Metro
Montenapoleone or Turati/tram 12. **Open** 10.30am-7.30pm Mon-Sat. **Credit** AmEx, DC, MC, V.
Map p249 E5/p252 E6.
Oozing the same understated sophistication as the designer's clothes, this black lacquer-and-red store showcases furniture and cushions in Giorgio's favourite tones of grey, beige, cream and black. Portable purchases include streamlined hip flasks, leather-bound notebooks, and candles on metal stands shaped like Armani table lamps.

Shopping and flopping

E'Spa at Gianfranco Ferré.

Shopped till you can shop no more? If your aching body needs some post-retail therapy, the designers have thought of everything. Several have opened spas in the very heart of the city's premier shopping district. So you can relax, revitalise – and start all over again.

Gianfranco Ferré has a small but perfectly formed spa within its boutique. The black-and-gold tiled pool overlooks the lawn of a walled garden. Jacuzzi, steam bath, mud treatments and facials are available. If you've been lugging around too many shopping bags, consider the Life-Saving Back Massage. Don't want to waste valuable shopping time? No problem – the spa stays open late. After 7pm, when the store is closed, just ring the bell. But do book well in advance as this place is deservedly popular.

Not to be outdone, **Dolce & Gabbana** have both a barber's for the boys and a 'Beauty Farm' for women in their menswear store (for the unlikely scenario of waiting while a dandified partner browses, perhaps?). Partner or not, you may be tempted to book in for the day. For €280 you get a sea-salt body scrub, followed by a de-stressing massage, facial, manicure and pedicure. Or if it's just your feet that are aching, opt for the pedicure alone – at €20, it's surprisingly cheap.

Although it's billed as a 'tribute from the Italian jeweller to the world of luxury', there's nothing flashy about the cool, contemporary **Bulgari Hotel**. The spa, featuring subdued lighting effects and a stone and gold-mosaic

swimming pool, is an understated and serene sanctuary. As you might expect, it has prices to match the exquisite setting: a half-day 'ritual' (€220) starts with a 25-minute 'ceremonial' foot massage as you sip herbal tea and includes a choice of detoxifying, hydrating, muscle-relaxing, energising or nourishing massage. A full-day package, which includes lunch and use of pool and spa facilities, costs from €275. Or opt for an individual treatment such as a facial (€110), manicure (€40) or pedicure (€50).

Bulgari Hotel Spa

Via Privata Fratelli Gabba 7B, Centre (02 805 8051/www.bulgarihotels.com). Metro Montenapoleone/tram 1, 2. **Open** 9am-9pm daily. **Credit** AmEx, DC, MC, V. **Map** p249 E5.

Dolce & Gabbana Beauty Farm

Corso Venezia 15, Centre (02 7640 8888/ www.dolcegabbana.it). Metro San Babila/ bus 54, 61, 94/tram 2. **Open** 2-9pm Mon; 10am-9pm Tue, Fri; 10am-7pm Wed, Thur, Sat. Closed 3wks Aug. **Credit** AmEx, DC, MC, V. **Map** p249 F6/p252 F6.

E'Spa at Gianfranco Ferré

Via Sant'Andrea 15, Centre (02 7601 7526/www.gianfrancoferre.com). Metro Montenapoleone or San Babila/tram 12. **Open** 10am-10pm Tue-Fri; 10am-9pm Sat; 11am-8pm Sun. Closed 2wks Aug. **Credit** AmEx, DC, MC, V. **Map** p249 F6/p252 F6.

Church chic

Franco Manenti.

The pope may be based in Rome, but his numerous clerical minions in Milan have to shop somewhere. Seeking (divine) inspiration for gifts? The city's religious stores also welcome ordinary mortals, who come here to snap up cut-priced clerical garments, surprisingly affordable hand-embroidered trimmings and kitschy religious souvenirs.

Priests and nuns have been buying their wardrobe essentials at **Confexclero di Mario**

Baldrighi (via Larga 6, Centre, 02 8646 3750, www.baldrighi.it) since time immemorial, but more recently Milan's trendiest teenagers have also started to come here to stock up on black or white turtle-neck sweaters in pure virgin wool, zip-up convent cardies and long strings of rosary beads, in pink or blue crystal, silver or black. Also popular are nuns' smoky-grey nylon slips (€13); worn as outerwear, they could almost pass for D&G.

If you've always dreamed of owning a bishop's mitre, **Franco Manenti** (via Larga 11, Centre, 02 5830 0322, www.manenti.it) is the shop for you. Recently revamped to resemble the inside of a stylish church (all dark wood, pale stone and antique furnishings), it's a treasure trove of hand-embroidered trimmings and ribbons, fabrics in rich hues of red, gold and purple and lavishly decorated clerical headgear. Also on offer are all manner of priestly accessories, from chalices to bishop's capes. Alhough it may be hard to believe, there's not a kitschy item in the place. Prices (especially for trimmings) are a snip.

Tucked in a side street behind the Duomo, **Agenzia Ecclesiastica Arcivescovile Tricella** (largo Schuster 1, Centre, 02 805 2331) is the place where the Milanese come when the head breaks off one of the Three Wise Men statues in their Christmas Nativity display. The shop is packed with artisan-made religious statuettes of all shapes and sizes – from Mary, Joseph and Baby Jesus to the donkey and the ox. But it's not just for Christmas: there's a wealth of camp stock, from lute-playing, trumpet-blowing angels to lamps made from statuettes of the Madonna (complete with Day-Glo halos). It even sells glass altar ampullae – which make excellent cruet sets, don't you know.

B&B Italia

Via Durini 14, Centre (02 764 441/www.bebitalia.it). *Metro San Babila/bus 54, 60, 65/tram 12, 27.* **Open** 3-7pm Mon; 10am-7pm Tue-Sat. Closed Aug. **Credit** AmEx, MC, V. **Map** p251 F7/p252 F7.
The list of doyens who have designed for minimalist kings B&B Italia is like a *Who's Who* of international design. Expect to find geometric vases by Ettore Sottsass, salad bowls by Arne Jacobsen and kitchen utensils by Milanese design hero Antonio Citterio, all displayed on museum-like plinths in this massive store.

High-Tech

Piazza XXV Aprile 12, North (02 624 1101/www. *high-techmilano.com). Metro Garibaldi or Moscova/* *tram 11, 30, 33.* **Open** 10.30am-7.30pm Tue-Sun. **Credit** AmEx, DC, MC, V. **Map** p248 D4.
A labyrinth packed to the rafters with everything for the design-conscious home-owner, from office accessories to bath products. Hours can evaporate wandering from room to room – or simply trying to locate the exit. Cargo High-Tech (via Meucci 39, East, 02 2722 1306), the offshoot, sells cut-price merchandise; it also has a bar and bakery on site.

Eat, Drink, Shop

Markets

Note that credit cards are not accepted at most of the stalls on the markets listed below.

Antiquariato sul Naviglio Grande

Strada Alzaia Naviglio Grande/Ripa di Porta Ticinese, South (02 8940 9971/www.naviglio grande.mi.it). Metro Porta Genova/bus 59/tram 3, 9, 15, 29, 30. **Open** *Jan-June, Aug-Nov* 9am-5pm last Sun of mth. *Dec* 9am-5pm Sun before Christmas. **Map** p250 C9.

Around 400 antiques dealers display their wares at this picturesque market alongside the canal. Goods range from furniture and silverware to vintage watches and old prints and postcards. The local bars and restaurants stay open all day when the market is in full swing, creating a buzzy atmosphere.

Fauché

Via Fauché, North. Bus 43, 57/tram 1, 12, 14, 19, 33. **Open** 8.30am-1pm Tue; 8.30am-5pm Sat. **Map** p248 A3.

The fashionistas' favourite market for cut-price designer shoes. Alongside discounted footwear by big names such as Gucci and Prada you can find smaller, more interesting labels like Alessandro dell'Acqua and Les Tropeziennes.

Isola

Piazzale Lagosta/via Garigliano, North. Metro Garibaldi or Zara/bus 43, 82, 83/tram 2, 4, 11. **Open** 8.30am-1pm Tue; 8.30am-5pm Sat. **Map** p249 E2.

This underrated market is a bargain hunter's delight. Look out for cut-price Tuscan ceramics, end-of-season clothes by Miss Sixty and other labels, offcuts of brightly coloured printed Como silks. It's also good for food products and ultra-cheap, wear-once-then-chuck-'em clothes.

Mercato Comunale

Piazza Wagner, West. Metro Wagner/bus 18, 61, 67/tram 24. **Open** 8.30am-1pm Mon; 8.30am-1pm, 4-7.30pm Tue-Sat.

Disaster struck this smart covered market when subsidence was discovered beneath the building in 2003. The Mercato Comunale has now reopened after a major overhaul and remains one of the best places to shop for gourmet food. The cornucopia includes fruit, fish, meat, cheese and flowers.

Papiniano

Viale Papiniano, West. Metro Sant'Agostino/ bus 50/tram 29, 30. **Open** 8.30am-1pm Tue; 8.30am-5pm Sat. **Map** p250 B8.

The city's most popular open-air market starts at piazzale Cantore and goes up as far as Sant'Agostino metro station. The melange of goods includes food, plants, clothing, shoes, homewares and textiles. Walk past the junk and keep your eyes peeled for designer bargains on the prettier-looking stalls – and also beware of pickpockets.

Music

See also p123 **Messaggerie Musicali**.

La Bottega Discantica

Via Nirone 5, North (02 862 966/www.discantica.it). Metro Cairoli or Cordusio/bus 18/tram 12, 19, 24. **Open** 3-7pm Mon; 9.30am-1pm, 3-7pm Tue-Sat. Closed Aug. **Credit** MC, V. **Map** p250 C6/p252 C6.

A meeting point for classical music lovers and musicians in Milan, selling everything from the latest recordings on CD to rare LPs. La Bottega also has its own recording label, specialising in antique and modern Italian classical music. There's an extensive section of folk and ethnic music too.

La Feltrinelli – Ricordi Media Store

Galleria Vittorio Emanuele II, Centre (02 8646 0272/www.lafeltrinelli.it). Metro Duomo/bus 54, 60, 65/tram 12, 23, 27. **Open** 10am-11pm Mon-Sat; 10am-8pm Sun. **Credit** AmEx, DC, MC, V. **Map** p251 E6/p252 E6.

A subterranean media emporium beneath the glass-covered Galleria, Ricordi stocks a varied selection of CDs of all genres, plus instruments, sheet music, games and concert/theatre tickets. La Feltrinelli bookstore (*see p122*) is connected from inside.

Opticians

Salmoiraghi & Viganò

Corso Matteotti 22, East (02 7600 0100/www. salmoraighievigano.it). Metro San Babila/bus 54, 60, 65/tram 12, 27. **Open** 3-7pm Mon; 10am-7pm Tue-Sat. **Credit** AmEx, DC, MC, V. **Map** p249 E6/p252 E6.

A solid optician that's well known throughout Italy for its professionalism and selection of frames. **Other locations**: throughout the city.

Photocopy/fax/ photo developers

Almost any stationery store (*cartoleria*) will offer a fax and photocopy service; just ask. Esselunga supermarket (viale Papiniano 27, West, 02 498 7674, www.esselunga.it, branches throughout the city) does traditional one-day photo processing, and its rates are cheaper than the 30-minute specialist photo places. It will also print digital photos in 24-48 hours.

Mail Boxes Etc

Via del Torchio 4, South (02 7200 2932/www. mbe.it). Metro Duomo/bus 54, 60, 65/tram 2, 3, 14, 27. **Open** 9am-6.30pm Mon-Fri. Closed 3wks Aug. **Credit** AmEx, DC, MC, V. **Map** p250 C7/p252 C7.

Provides photocopying and fax facilities, UPS courier pick-up, business card printing, Western Union point, internet access, document laminating, postbox rental, packaging and office supplies sales. **Other locations**: throughout the city.

Eat, Drink, Shop

THE ITALIAN JOB

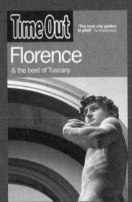

Time Out
'The best city guides in print' The Independent
Florence
& the best of Tuscany

Time Out
'The best city guides in print' The Independent
Milan

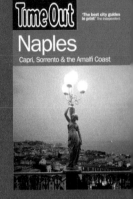

Time Out
'The best city guides in print' The Independent
Naples
Capri, Sorrento & the Amalfi Coast

Time Out
'The best city guides in print' The Independent
Rome

Time Out
'The best city guides in print' The Independent
Turin

Time Out
'The best city guides in print' The Independent
Venice
Verona, Treviso & the Veneto

Arts & Entertainment

Features

Festivals & Events

Religious ceremonies contrast with commercial affairs to fun-filled effect.

Milan's calendar of events may not be bursting at the seams, but what it lacks in quantity it makes up for in atmosphere. The usually reserved Milanese take to the streets in a riot of noise and colour for their traditional celebrations, including Oh Bej! Oh Bej! and Carnevale, both festivals with religious origins. Just as colourful in their own way are the less historic events, such as the (various) Fashion Weeks and the Furniture Fair, both of which highlight the slick, commercial face of the city.

The traditional festivals tend to be located around the city's prominent churches, particularly the Duomo, or in residential neighbourhoods, while the more explicitly commercial events take place mainly at the Fiera MilanoCity exhibition centre, one of the largest trade-fair grounds in Europe, and the newer, bigger Fiera Milano site in Rho, in the north-western outskirts of the city (for both, *see p96*). Built in record time according to plans by Italian architect Massimiliano Fuksas, the Rho complex is an avant-garde glass and steel affair, and – for students of architecture – well worth a visit in its own right. Call 02 49 971 (freephone 800 820 029) or take a look at the Fiera's website (www.fieramilano.com) for a list of events.

Before visiting Milan it's worth checking out what's going on here during your stay. The buzz generated by international events can be exciting, but on the downside, hotels are booked up months in advance and taxis are harder to find than usual, so it pays to plan ahead.

Don't miss
Events

Giornata FAI di Primavera
See right.

Stramilano
See right.

La Notte Bianca
See p146.

Oh Bej! Oh Bej!
See p146.

Milano Marathon
See p146.

For further information about what's on, contact the tourist information office (02 7252 4301, www.milanoinfotourist.com, *see also p233*). The office publishes *Milano Mese*, a monthly guide to events throughout the city, which is also on the site (click on the 'Tourism' page).

Spring

Settimana dei Beni Culturali
Various locations throughout the city (information freephone 800 991 199/www.beniculturali.it). **Date** early spring.
During Cultural Heritage Week, all of Italy's publicly owned museums and galleries are free, along with some privately owned sites. Events include special openings, guided visits, concerts, shows and wine/food tasting sessions. Guided tours are also organised for the disabled.

Giornata FAI di Primavera
Various locations throughout the city (information 02 467 6151/www.fondoambiente.it). **Date** 3rd weekend of Mar.
During this weekend many of Milan's historic *palazzi* and monuments that are closed for the rest of the year open up to the public, thanks to the sponsorship of the Fondo Ambiente Italiano, Italy's version of the National Trust. About half the structures taking part are accessible to the disabled.

Mercato dei Fiori
Along the Naviglio Grande, South (02 8940 9971/www.navigliogrande.mi.it). Metro Porta Genova/bus 47, 59, 71, 74/tram 3, 4, 9, 15, 29, 30. **Map** p250 B9. **Date** Apr.
This flower fair creates a spectacular splash of colour and fragrance along the canal. Nurseries and horticultural schools from all around Italy take part.

Stramilano
www.stramilano.it. **Date** 1st or 2nd Sun of Apr.
Central Milan is closed to traffic as locals and athletes from all over the world take to the streets and battle it out over two main distances: the Stramilano itself (15 km/9.3 miles) or the more serious half-marathon distance race (21.097 km/13 miles), in which runners of international acclaim sometimes take part. The Stramilano sets off from piazza Duomo and goes through some of the main arteries in the city, including corso Vittorio Emanuele, corso Venezia and corso Buenos Aires, to finish at the Arena Civica in Parco Sempione.

Salone Internazionale del Mobile (Furniture Fair)

Fiera Milano, Rho (information freephone 800 820 029/02 499 71/02 725 941/www.fieramilano.com). Metro Rho. **Date** mid Apr.

Milan goes into party mode for one of the world's largest exhibitions of furniture and fittings from cutting-edge designers worldwide. As of 2006 the five-day event is being held at the fair premises in Rho, but collections over recent years have also increasingly been shown at smaller venues around the city, including the furniture companies' own showrooms in the centre of town. On the Sunday the event is open to the public: pick up a copy of *Interni* magazine for a list of what's on where (or visit www.internimagazine.it).

Pittori del Naviglio Grande

Along the Naviglio Grande, South (02 8940 9971/ www.navigliogrande.mi.it). Metro Porta Genova/ bus 47, 59, 71, 74/tram 2, 3, 9, 15, 29, 30. **Map** p250 B9. **Date** 2nd weekend of May.

This open-air art exhibition along the Naviglio Grande showcases work by more than 300 artists from all over Italy.

Orticola ai Giardini Pubblici

Giardini Pubblici, East (02 7600 1496/www.orticola. org). Metro Palestro or Turati/bus 61, 94. **Map** p249 F5. **Date** mid May.

OK, it's not the Chelsea Flower Show, but this is still a charming little exhibition-cum-market, organised by the Associazione Orticola di Lombardia, one of the first Italian institutions to encourage public interest in gardens and plants.

Cortili Aperti

Various locations throughout the city (02 7631 8634/ www.italiamultimedia.com/cortiliaperti). **Date** late May.

Private residences open their splendid courtyards to the public for one Sunday for this initiative. In previous years many of the art nouveau buildings along corso Venezia (*see p77* **Walk on**), including Casa Fontana Silvestri, Palazzo Serbelloni and Palazzo Castiglioni, have taken part.

Summer at Idroscalo

Idropark Fila, Circonvallazione Idroscalo Est 51, Segrate (02 7020 0902/www.provincia.milano.it/ droparkfila). **Date** late May-Sept.

The summer season of sporting events, concerts and nightlife (as well as picnics) gets underway at the Idroscalo Park, on the eastern outskirts of town.

Summer

Milano Moda Uomo Primavera/Estate

Information www.cameramoda.it. **Date** June.

Men's Fashion Week for spring and summer might not be the most important event in Milan's fashion calendar, but it is responsible for bringing some of

February's **Fashion Week**. *See p146.*

the world's best-looking men to the city for a couple of weeks. Shows, events, special presentations and catwalks take place all over town, with some events going on at Fiera MilanoCity too.

Milano d'Estate

Castello Sforzesco, North (information 02 7252 4301/ www.milanoinfotourist.com). Metro Cadorna, Cairoli or Lanza/bus 43, 57, 61, 70, 94/tram 1, 3, 4, 12, 14, 27. **Map** p248 C6/p252 C6. **Date** June-Aug.

Open-air concerts and performances are organised to entertain those unfortunate *milanesi* who can't leave the city in the heat of the summer. The action takes place in and around the grounds of the Castello Sforzesco. Be sure to wear insect repellent.

Navigli Summer Jamboree

Navigli area, South. Metro Porta Genova/bus 47, 59, 71, 74/tram 2, 3, 9, 15, 29, 30. **Map** p250 B9. **Date** June-Sept.

The usually traffic-choked streets around the Navigli take a breather for an annual summer jamboree, allowing bars and restaurants to spill out into the pavements between 8pm and 2am every day for several months.

Festa del Naviglio

Along the Navigli, South. Metro Porta Genova/
bus 47, 59, 71, 74/tram 2, 3, 9, 15, 29, 30.
Map p250 B9. **Date** 1st 2wks of June.

An eventful fortnight in the canal area, with street artists, concerts, sporting events, antiques markets, cooking demonstrations and more.

La Notte Bianca

Information www.comune.milano.it. **Date** mid June.

A 'white night' in Italian means a sleepless night, which should give you a clue as to how much fun there is to be had at this event. Once a year the *milanesi* dance, eat and shop the night away from early evening right the way through to 6am as bars, restaurants, shops, cinemas et al stay open into the wee small hours. Great stuff.

Notturni in Villa

Information 02 8912 2383/www.amicidella
musicamilano.it. **Date** mid June-Aug.

A series of jazz and classical music concerts is held in patrician villas around the city, such as Villa Simonetta, at the end of corso Sempione. The performances start at 10pm and entry is free.

Sagra di San Cristoforo

In front of San Cristoforo, Navigli, South
(information 02 7252 4301/www.milanoinfo
tourist.com). Metro Porta Genova/bus 47, 59, 71,
74/tram 2, 3, 9, 15, 29, 30. **Date** 3rd Sun of June.

The feast of the patron saint of travellers takes place in the square in front of the little church of San Cristoforo. Decorated boats float down the Naviglio and vehicles are duly blessed.

Festival Latino Americando

Forum di Assago, via D Vittorio 6, Assago (03 224
7679/www.latinoamericando.it). Metro Famagosta
then bus to Assago. **Date** late June-early Aug.

Milan celebrates all things Latino during the summer months with this festival in Assago, on the outskirts of the city. Over 60 concerts, events and exhibitions celebrate aspects of the continent's culture, including music, arts, dance, food, handicrafts and cinema. Many top-name Latin musicians fly in to give performances.

Autumn

Milano Moda Donna Primavera/Estate

Information www.cameramoda.it. **Date** late Sept-early Oct.

Yet another Fashion Week. On this occasion leading Italian designers present their womenswear collections for spring/summer. Events galore are held in and around the city and at Fiera MilanoCity.

Milano Marathon

www.milanocitymarathon.it. **Date** early Oct.

Nearly 5,000 competitors take part in Milan's annual marathon, held on a Sunday. It starts at Stazione Centrale and finishes in piazza del Duomo.

Winter

Oh Bej! Oh Bej!

Piazza Sant'Ambrogio, West. Metro Sant'Ambrogio/
bus 50, 58, 94. **Map** p250 C7. **Date** 7 Dec.

This street market is one of Milan's most important festivals and is held on the feast of the city's patron saint Sant'Ambrogio. The streets around piazza Sant'Ambrogio throng with crowds sampling traditional food, including pancakes, pastries, roasted meats, chestnuts and mulled wine. Stalls sell everything from handicrafts and antiques to CDs and African sculptures. Be warned, though: it can get pretty crowded. Goldsmiths made a gift to the city of a chiselled silver statue of Sant'Ambrogio, which is exhibited to the public on this day in the Duomo cathedral, although lovers of solemn religious ceremonies might do better to go along to the special morning service in the Sant'Ambrogio basilica itself.

Epiphany

Various locations throughout the city. **Date** 6 Jan.

Epiphany is also known as La Befana, after a kind-hearted witch who is said to bring presents to well-behaved children and coal to the naughty ones Crowds turn out for the morning procession of the Three Wise Men from the Duomo to the church of Sant'Eustorgio, where their relics are said to be kept

Milano Moda Uomo Autunno/Inverno

Information www.cameramoda.it. **Date** mid Jan.

Men's Fashion Week for autumn and winter is a bit of a sideshow to the women's event (*see below*). Still the talent it attracts is first rate.

Carnevale

Various locations throughout the city. **Date** Feb/early Mar.

Milan's Carnevale takes place in the days following Shrove Tuesday, later than in the rest of Italy. The celebrations are essentially for children, who roam the streets in fancy dress chucking handfuls of confetti and spraying foam at people. A fancy dress parade takes place around the Duomo on the first Saturday of Lent: take your camera. Various events also take place in the evening, so check local listings.

Milano Moda Donna Autunno/Inverno (Fashion Week)

Information www.cameramoda.it. **Date** late Feb.

Milan's moment in the fashion spotlight, as 80-odd designers unveil their autumn/winter collections. Catwalks are assembled at venues around the city, though entry to the shows is by invitation only. Some of the smaller houses show at the Fiera, but a growing number are setting up in the former industrial sites in the south and east of the city. Prada's renovated warehouse puts on art displays outside of Fashion Week (02 546 70515, www.fondazione prada.org; *see p153*), while Armani holds his shows at the former Nestlé factory that he has transformed into a theatre (via Bergognone 59). **Photo** *p145.*

Children

Bambini on board.

Puppets for your poppets at **Teatro del Buratto al Pime**. *See p149.*

Italy is famous for being a child-friendly society – even if, somewhat bizarrely, it has the world's lowest birth rate. Being an only child is so common here that it's said that aunts and uncles are becoming endangered species. What's true is that there's no need to worry about taking the kids to pizzerias and restaurants, as the waiters are likely to make a fuss over them.

That said, Milan does present more than its fair share of challenges for parents: the city has a seriously bad pollution problem, and it is the youngest and oldest members of the population who are the worst affected. In addition to being polluted, Milan also has an acute shortage of green space (the two factors are doubtless connected). Thankfully, the lack of decent outdoor places to take the kids is compensated for by a relatively good selection of indoor activities. There are some great play centres and museums, and these, along with the friendly eateries and ice-cream parlours, should guarantee an enjoyable trip for all the family.

GETTING AROUND
Although public transport is one of the many things that the Milanese complain about, it can actually be enjoyable if you are in no particular hurry. The subway is quick but crowded (while buses are slow and crowded), and, at €1 per person per journey (valid for 75

minutes, or €3 for a 24-hour pass), tickets are refreshingly cheap. The city's trams (also €1) can be a nice way to travel too. Found all over the centre of town (in particular near the Duomo), there are three types: the small vintage orange ones, which have period piece interior decor (complete with wooden benches and cute little lampshades), the large modern orange ones and the even larger futuristic green ones. There is also a special *tram turistico* (tourist tram); this was out of service at the time of writing, on account of a change in management, but was due to be relaunched later in 2006. Look out too for the open-air tourist bus tour that was due to begin service.

On the downside, a few words of caution: in Italy people park anywhere and everywhere, so it can be hard to negotiate the kerbs with a pushchair. Also, the two older metro lines (red and green) do not have lifts, so you will have to manhandle your buggy down the stairs or escalators. Line 3 (yellow) and the Passante are fitted with lifts, but there's no guarantee they'll be working at all times.

INFORMATION
Children's events are listed in the *Vivi-Milano* supplement (Wednesday) of the *Corriere della Sera* and in the *Tutto Milano* supplement (Thursday) of *La Repubblica*.

Arts & Entertainment

Sightseeing

Around the Duomo

One of the advantages of Milan's Duomo-centric, compact geography is that many of the must-see attractions are within walking distance of each other. A safe bet is to head to the **Duomo** (*see p52*). It's on most tram routes (but take the subway if you're pressed for time), and, in addition to offering lots to see and do, it is in the middle of a large (mostly) pedestrianised route that runs from piazza San Babila right up to the Castello Sforzesco.

Piazza del Duomo and the nearby **Galleria Vittorio Emanuele II** (for both, *see p52*) are good places for watching the world go by, but the best attraction for families is the cathedral roof. It's a 150-step climb (the kids should sleep well that night) to the top, but there's also a lift. When you're up there, you get a wonderful view of the city and (on a good day) the surrounding countryside, including the Alps.

Rather less well known are the intriguing acoustics of the colonnades in nearby **piazza dei Mercanti** (*see p62*), which is next to via dei Mercanti, a medieval-style street with a number of buskers, clowns and other interesting characters, particularly on weekends. If you climb the steps and head to the covered courtyard furthest from the Duomo, stand in one of the corners and get your child to stand in the opposite one. Communicate with each other by whispering into the corner, just as crafty merchants did (presumably with a view to ripping off customers) in days of old. Don't feel embarrassed: if people stare at you, they are merely admiring your insider knowledge of local history.

Museums & attractions

In terms of child-friendly museums, pride of place goes to the **Museo Nazionale della Scienza e della Tecnologia Leonardo da Vinci** (*see p90*), which is close to *The Last Supper* (*see p93*). The museum's large collection of fossils and models of da Vinci's inventions might not be every child's idea of a blast, but its 'railway pavilion' (*padiglione ferroviario*) is outstanding. This large shed contains real trains and trams dating back to the 19th century that can be clambered on. The area outside the pavilion has a science park where kids can run around and let off steam (no pun intended), as well as a couple of cool fighter planes, while the next building houses an impressive collection of boats (both models and the real thing), plus the cross-section of a passenger cruiser. The museum's main section also contains vintage

Carnevale capers. *See p149.*

cars, bikes and motorbikes. The museum also has a submarine, the *Enrico Toti*, although guided tours need to be booked at least a week in advance and cost an additional €8.

A trip to the **Civico Museo di Storia Naturale** (*see p74*) can also be a worthwhile experience for young visitors, thanks to its model dinosaurs and other goodies. The museum is situated in the **Giardini Pubblici** (*see p73*), which also contains the **Planetario Ulrico Hoepli**, a small but interesting planetarium (*see p74*) that holds occasional presentations in Italian.

Another fun place to take children is the **Castello Sforzesco** (*see p64*), which is walkable from the Duomo. Of particular interest here is the armoury hall (Room 14), which features a knight on horseback and some vicious-looking swords.

Milan also has its own toy museum, the **Museo del Giocattolo e del Bambino**, though it's quite a hike from the centre. This features antique toys as well as a mock-up of a 19th-century classroom. The museum forms part of the city's old orphanage.

Football fans, meanwhile, might like to take a trip to **San Siro** (*see p96*), for a walk around this decidedly impressive stadium. Inside there's a small museum that documents the history of the city's two teams, Milan and Inter, but we would advise against taking small children to the games themselves, unless you have pricey seats. If British soccer grounds have cleaned up their act in the post-Hillsborough era, then Italy seems to have gone the other way: the atmosphere at San Siro (and at other grounds) can be pretty nasty these days, with right-wing thugs making their presence felt.

Museo del Giocattolo e del Bambino

Via Pitteri 56, East (02 2641 1585/www.museodel giocattolo.it). Bus 54. **Open** 9.30am-4pm Mon-Fri; 9.30am-12.30pm, 3-6pm Sat, Sun. Closed Aug. **Admission** €5; €3 concessions; free under-14s Sun. **No credit cards.**

Babysitting

Il Nano Gigante
Via Lambrate 18, East (02 2682 6650/www.ilnano gigante.it). Metro Loreto or Pasteur/bus 55, 62/tram 33. **Open** noon-7pm Mon-Fri; 10am-7pm Sat, Sun. Closed Aug. **Admission** €5-€10, plus €15 joining fee. **Credit** MC, V.
In addition to being a good place for kids to play, the centre also runs a 'baby parking' system, which enables you to leave your child here for €8 per hour (book at least two days in advance).

ProntoBaby
Via Lario 16, North (02 6900 2201/www.infanzia. com). Metro Zara/bus 82, 83/tram 4, 90, 91. **Open Office** 9am-5pm Mon-Fri. Closed Aug. **Rates** from €7.50 per hr. **No credit cards**. **Map** p249 E2.
This school for childcare professionals runs a babysitting service (they come to you). The sitters are students from the school and most speak some English.

Fun & games

See also above Il Nano Gigante.

Fun & Fun
Via Beroldo 2, East (02 2851 0671/0687/www. fun-and-fun.com). Metro Loreto or Pasteur/bus 55, 62/tram 33. **Open** 3-7.30pm Mon-Fri; 10am-8pm Sat, Sun. Closed Aug. **Admission** €7.50 Mon-Sat; €10.90 Sun. **No credit cards**. **Map** p249 H2.
Many local kids have their birthday parties at this indoor play centre, which has a giant climbing frame.

Play Planet
Via Veglia 59, North (02 668 8838/www.play planet.it). Metro Maciachini/bus 51, 200. **Open** 3.30-7.30pm Mon-Fri; 10am-8pm Sat; 10am-7.30pm Sun. Closed Aug. **Admission** €7 Mon-Wed, Fri; €4 Thur; €9 Sat, Sun. **Credit** MC, V.
Another good indoor play centre.

Pottery Café
Via Solferino 3, North (02 8901 3660). Metro Lanza/bus 41, 43, 61. **Open** 11am-7pm Mon; 9am-7pm Tue-Fri; 10am-8pm Sat, Sun. Closed 1-2wks Aug. **Credit** MC, V. **Map** p248 D5.
Kids aged four and over can create colourful and cheerful ceramics in this café-cum-art lab while mum and dad relax over a cappuccino.

Teatro del Buratto al Pime
Via Mosè Bianchi 94, West (02 2700 2476/ www.teatrodelburatto.it). Metro Amendola-Fiera or Lotto/bus 67, 68/tram 16. **Open** times vary. **Admission** €6. **No credit cards**.
The season at this puppet theatre runs from October to March. Shows are in Italian. **Photo** p147.

Shopping

It may not have a Hamleys, but Milan has some fine toy shops on a smaller scale. If you're in the Duomo area (and the chances are you will be),

then **La Città del Sole** in via Orefici (No.13, 02 8646 1683, closed Sun & 2wks Aug) is worth a visit. It has a wooden display Brio trainset, on which kids are welcome to play, as well as a large selection of puzzles. And, if you happen to have included *The Last Supper* in your itinerary, then **Tofy Toys** in nearby via Ruffini (No.9, 02 469 4776, closed Sun & Aug) is a small but well-stocked shop run by a friendly couple.

Milan's larger book/media stores, such as **La Feltrinelli** (*see p122*), are also good places to go with the kids in tow. In the west of town, the branch at piazza Piemonte 2 (02 433 541) is an open space, which means that you could even leave junior in the kiddies' books section while you browse in books (there are a few in English), music or movies. In addition, **Libreria dei Ragazzi** (via Tadino 53, East, 02 2953 3555, closed Sun) is a children's bookstore with a good range of Italian books, some in English.

If it's kids' clothes you're after, then Milan has plenty to offer. **Salvagente Bimbi** (*see p132* **Chic at half the price**) has designer returns by top labels, while there's also a selection of children's shops in the centre. Via Dante, which runs from piazza Cordusio (near the Duomo) to piazza Cairoli (near the Castello Sforzesco), has at least three, among them **Petit Bateau** (No.12, 02 8699 8098), **L'Angelo** (No. 18, 02 866 151, closed Sun) and **Du Pareil Au Même** (No.5, 02 7209 4971, closed Sun & 1wk Aug).

When to go

Milan is at its best in spring and early summer, although early autumn can also be agreeable. In July it starts to get unbearably hot, while everything grinds to a halt in August, when most families flee to the seaside. There is, however, some consolation for those left behind. In recent years the city council has organised a summer beach in this most land-locked of cities. This has a swimming pool and sand (with beach volley courts) located under and around the Arco della Pace, at the northern end of Parco Sempione (*see p64*). It's not a patch on the Paris version, but if you're stuck in Milan in the summer months, it's worth bearing in mind, as are the city's pools (*see p172*).

One of the best times for small kids in Milan is Carnevale, the traditional end-of-winter festival that takes place at the start of Lent. Youngsters are encouraged to dress up, and you will often see toddlers in their Zorro outfits out walking with their parents (or grandparents). Piazza Duomo is a highly entertaining place on the Carnevale weekend but, if you get squirted with shaving foam by merry pranksters, don't say we didn't warn you.

Film

Cinema paradiso – as long as you speak the lingo.

If you're a fan of first-run Italian movies, you'll be in your element in Milan. Most Italian films are not distributed outside Italy, but being in the city with the highest number of screens in the country (over 100 at last count) increases your chances of seeing them. At any one time there will be two or three films showing across the city; the rest of the programming tends to be made up of US or UK productions, with perhaps a couple of French ones thrown in for good measure.

In nearly all cases, though, you will have to be able to understand Italian, since the Italian movies shown won't come with subtitles or dubbing (the non-Italian ones are dubbed). The only variant on that theme is the one English-language movie a week, showing Monday, Tuesday and Thursday at a different cinema each time.

But while the number of new films screened in Milan is impressive compared with other major European cities (it's on a par with London, a city ten times its size), what is singularly missing here is any second-run or repertory. So if you were hoping to catch up with some old Fellini, Visconti or Pasolini flicks, or even one of the recently revived Italian B-movies of the 1970s, you're out of luck.

As an alternative, however, you may be successful in getting DVD copies of your favourite Italian movies. Try the bookshops attached to the Anteo cinema, and the Cineteca Italiana, as well book and record stores, such as Messaggerie Musicali (*see p123*). Another source is the newsstand. Several newspapers and magazines offer a different film each week for about €9, so you may be in luck.

Milan is also the venue for a number of excellent film festivals (*see p152*), and has three open-air cinemas – these are atmospheric and great fun, even if you don't speak the language (*see p151*).

TICKETS AND INFORMATION

For information about which flicks are playing where and when, consult the local listings in the Milan pages of daily newspapers *Corriere della Sera* or *La Repubblica*. Movies shown in their original language are advertised as *film* (or *versione*) in *lingua originale* (sometimes simply abbreviated to *lingua orig*).

At most cinemas, tickets cost between €4 and €5.75 for the early afternoon shows, and

from €6 to €7.50 for evening performances. Wednesday nights cost less, but it is a good idea to book in advance if the film is on its first run. Show times vary considerably, although in most cinemas the last show begins at around 10.30pm.

First-run cinemas

Arcobaleno Film Center

Viale Tunisia 11, East (02 2940 6054/reservations 199 199 166/information 02 2953 7621/www. cinenauta.it). Metro Porta Venezia/tram 1, 5, 11, 29, 30. **Tickets** €4-€6; €4.50 concessions. *Ten films* €35; €30 non-Italian students. **Credit** (only for phone or web reservations) AmEx, DC, MC, V. **Map** p249 G4.

Arcobaleno Film Centre takes part in the popular Sound & Motion scheme, which brings the best foreign-language titles to the city. The cinema shows recent releases in their original languages on Tuesday afternoon and evening (mostly without intrusive subtitles).

Odeon

Via Santa Radegonda 8, Centre (199 757 757). Metro Duomo/bus 50, 54, 60/tram 1, 2, 12, 14, 27. **Tickets** €4.50-€7.50. **Credit** MC, V. **Map** p251 E6/p252 E6.

Once a bustling production house, the Odeon is now a cineplex with ten screens. It often shows mainstream films in the original language, occasionally dedicating an entire week to a screening, but there is no set schedule.

Art-house cinemas

Anteospazio Cinema

Via Milazzo 9, North (02 659 7732/www.anteo spaziocinema.com). Metro Moscova/bus 41, 43, 94/ tram 11, 29, 30, 33. **Tickets** €4-€6 (shop & restaurants only) MC, V. **Map** p248 D4.

With its restaurant, bookshop, exhibition space, film courses and conferences – not to mention three screens showing everything from classics to avant-garde films to independent contemporary flicks – the Anteo offers something for just about everyone. (as long as you speak Italian, that is). Original-language films are shown on Monday as part of the Sound & Motion scheme.

Ariosto

Via L Ariosto 16, West (02 4800 3901). Metro Conciliazione/bus 61, 66, 67/tram 24, 29, 30. **Tickets** €6; €4 concessions. **No credit cards**. **Map** p248 A6.

This is the place to catch first- or second-run Spanish and French films. Recent international and independent films are screened in Italian at 5pm, 7.30pm and 10pm Tuesday to Sunday, and in *lingua originale* on Monday.

Il Cineforum Mr Arkadin

Auditorium San Carlo, corso Matteotti 14, Centre (mobile 348 756 8859/www.cinearkadin.org). Metro San Babila/bus 54, 60, 61, 65. **Tickets** €4, plus a one-off annual membership fee (€4). **No credit cards. Map** p249 F6/p252 F6.

An 'alternative space' that screens movies and also hosts film-related talks and events. The non-profit Cineforum Mr Arkadin is the place to catch avant-garde films or those that aren't often shown. Productions aren't daily, so call or check the website before turning up.

Cinema Gnomo

Via Lanzone 30A, South (02 804 125/www.comune. milano.it). Metro Sant'Ambrogio/bus 50, 58, 94. **Tickets** €4.10, plus a one-off membership fee (€2.60). **No credit cards. Map** p250 C7.

Film buffs would do well to check out weekly listings at the Cinema Gnomo. The cinema is run in close collaboration with the Comune di Milano and offers a varied, off-the-beaten-track selection of films chosen with great care. Experts often pop along to help with deconstruction.

Cinema Mexico (The Rocky Horror House)

Via Savona 57, South (02 4895 1802/www. cinemamexico.it). Metro Porta Genova or Sant'Agostino/bus 61, 68, 90, 91/tram 14. **Tickets** €4-€6. **No credit cards. Map** p250 A8.

An interesting choice of recently released original-language films is shown here all day on a Thursday as part of the Sound & Motion scheme. The Jim Sharman cult favourite that gave the cinema its nickname is shown here every Friday at 10pm, much to the delight of locals who just love dressing up for the occasion. Cinema Mexico also runs workshops on a variety of film-related subjects.

Cineteatro San Lorenzo alle Colonne

Corso di Porta Ticinese 45, South (02 5811 3161/ www.teatroallecolonne.it). Bus 94/tram 3. **Tickets** €4. **No credit cards. Map** p250 C8.

This art-house cinema-cum-theatre shows a limited but well-chosen selection of independent films.

Cineteca Italiana

Spazio Oberdan, viale Vittorio Veneto 2, East (02 7740 6300/www.cinetecamilano.it). Metro Porta Venezia/tram 29, 30. **Tickets** €5, plus a one-off annual membership fee (€3). *Eight shows* €32. **No credit cards. Map** p249 F5.

Spazio Oberdan's rich and varied cinema programme (Wednesday to Sunday) includes seminars, debates and screenings on themes as far ranging as the origins of pornography in film and cinematic

Museo del Cinema.

shorts. Special attention is dedicated to forgotten old favourites and silent cinema. There are details of events on the website.

Museo del Cinema

Palazzo Dugnani, via D Manin 2B, East (office 02 2900 5659/information 02 655 4977/www. cinetecamilano.it). Metro Turati/bus 43, 94/tram 1, 2. **Tickets** *Museum* (incl film ticket) €3; €2 concessions. **No credit cards. Map** p249 F5.

As well as cabinets full of cinematographic curios and film-related displays, the Museo del Cinema offers screenings of mainly obscure Italian and foreign titles on Friday afternoons. Weekends are given over to children's films and cartoons, a celluloid world in its own right. *See also p74.*

Open-air cinemas

Various locations

Conservatorio di Musica Giuseppe Verdi *Via Conservatorio 12, East (02 762 1101/www.consmilano.it). Metro San Babila/bus 56, 61, 84/tram 12.* **Map** p251 F6.

Teatro Litta *Corso Magenta 24, West (02 8645 4546/www.teatrolitta.it). Metro Cadorna/bus 18, 50, 54/tram 19, 24.* **Map** p250 C6/p252 C6.

Umanitaria *Via Daverio 7, Centre (02 579 6831/www.umanitaria.it). Metro Crocetta/bus 60, 79/tram 4, 12, 27.* **Map** p251 F7.

One of the best things about mid-summer in Milan is the open-air cinema. Films are almost always dubbed into Italian, but, even if you don't understand all the dialogue, the experience – just once in your life – is worth it. Summer sanctuaries include the three splendid cinema locations listed above, which together offer a good choice of new releases. Keep an eye out in local listings in daily newspapers *Corriere della Sera* and *La Repubblica* under the heading '*Cinema all'aperto*'.

Festivals

Festival del Cinema Africano a Milano

Via G Lazzaroni 8, North (02 6671 2077/ 02 669 6258/www.festivalcinemaafricano.org). Metro Centrale FS/bus 42, 60, 81, 82/tram 2, 5, 9. **Date** late Mar. **Tickets** prices vary. **No credit cards.** Map p249 F3.

This seven-day festival of works by African filmmakers, which now also includes movies from Asia and Latin America, celebrated its 16th edition in 2006. The competing films and videos, including non-fiction titles, are screened in six cinemas around the city. Meetings with directors and festival participants are organised at varies venues, such as FNAC (via Torino, at via della Palla 2, Centre, 02 869 541).

Film Festival Internazionale di Milano

Various locations throughout the city (02 8918 1179/www.miff.it). **Date** late Mar-early Apr. **Tickets** prices vary. **No credit cards.** This festival was established in 2000 and has already been hailed by the national press as a European Sundance. As Como resident George Clooney states on the festival homepage, it is dedicated to 'bringing to light the excellence in independent cinema and the filmmakers behind it'. A tall order, perhaps, but the festival does make a good job of promoting film as art and provides an international platform for experimental and indie filmmakers to strut their celluloid stuff. Statuettes of Leonardo's horse (*see p94* **Supper time**) go to prize-winners.

Festival Internazionale di Cinema Gaylesbico e Queer Culture

Cinema Manzoni, via Manzoni 40, Centre (02 7602 0650/www.cinemagaylesbico.com). Metro Montenapoleone/tram 2. **Date** late May-early June. **Tickets** prices vary. **No credit cards.** Map p249 E5.

It would be fair to say that this gay film festival – set up in 1986 – has become an established part of the annual cinematic calendar. The programme features films by directors from countries as diverse as Canada, Israel, Haiti and Ghana, and there are plenty of British flicks too. Shorts, documentaries and TV shows also get a look-in. Check the website for details of sideline events.

Milano Film Festival (MFF)

Teatro Strehler (Nuovo Piccolo), largo Greppi, North (02 7233 3222/www.milanofilmfestival.it). Metro Lanza/bus 43, 57, 70/tram 3, 4, 12, 14. **Date** mid-late Sept. **Tickets** *Daily pass* €6. *Weekly pass* €20. **No credit cards.** Map p248 D5.

Now in its 11th year (2006), the Milano Film Festival started off as a showcase for shorts by young local filmmakers, and was only opened to international contributors and feature films in 2000. It's a good chance to witness the latest developments in international cinematography, and to see what folk outside the world of cinema can come up with. The festival is a superbly organised interdisciplinary affair that also covers art exhibitions, live music, performances and workshops. Take your pillow along for the movie marathon, in which some 300 Italian short films are screened. Some shows also take place at Castello Sforzesco.

Sport Movies & TV International Festival

Via E de Amicis 17, South (02 8940 9076/ www.ficts.com or www.sportmoviestv.com). Metro Sant'Ambrogio/bus 94/tram 3. **Date** late Oct-early Nov. Map p250 C8.

Celebrating 25 years in 2007, this important festival is dedicated to sports films, documentaries and television programmes. Featuring more than 200 films and videos, it's a must-visit for sports enthusiasts and cinema fans alike.

Invideo

Spazio Oberdan, viale Vittorio Veneto 2, East (02 7740 6300/www.mostrainvideo.com). Metro Porta Venezia/tram 1, 9, 11, 29, 30. **Date** early-mid Nov. Map p249 F5.

Established in 1990, the International Exhibition of Video Art & Cinema Beyond is dedicated to experimental non-fiction cinematic and video works, and is Italy's most important festival dedicated to the world of electronic arts and new technologies. So if it's non-mainstream cinema, video documentaries, art and animation you're after, this one's for you.

Festivals of Festivals

Various locations throughout the city (www. lombardiaspettacolo.com). **Tickets** prices vary. Several non-Milan-based festivals get to showcase their films in cinemas around the city shortly after the prize-winning ceremonies. Among those to watch out for is 'Cannes e dintorni' (June), an opportunity to see what caught on on the Côte d'Azur. Also worth catching are 'Panoramica – I Film di Venezia' and 'Frontiere – I Pardi del Festival di Locarno' (both early-mid September), where you can feast your eyes on the pick of the crop from the Venice and Locarno international film festivals. All the films – more than 70 in all – are original language with Italian subtitles. A weekly pass costs €40, while a discounted pass (*abbonamento ridotto*) is only €25, although you won't be able to attend prime-time evening showings.

Galleries

Avant-garde views and design stars.

Tancredi's *Untitled*, **Galleria Blu**. *See p154*.

For a country as rich in art as Italy, and especially in a city as avant-garde as Milan, it is odd that there is no modern art museum on a par with, say, Tate Modern in London or the MoMA in New York. Instead of revolving around a central exhibition space, or being held in orbit by a single movement, Milan's contemporary art scene comprises a galaxy of private spaces.

It has long been noted that Milanese gallery proprietors, owing either to their own tastes or the success of artists at foreign auctions, tend to gravitate towards non-Italian names. This is slowly changing as more and more galleries are opening around the city, many of them pushing home-grown talent – a generation that has benefited from global exposure.

There is a high concentration of long-established galleries in the chic neighbourhood of Brera, but newer ones are popping up all over the city, especially around Porta Romana and Porta Garibaldi, and in the unlikely industrial area around Lambrate train station.

Except in August, when much of the city shuts down for holidays, there are plenty of shows to attend. For a list, pick up a copy of the *Artshow* booklet (www.artshow.it) from the tourist information centre near the Duomo or from any of the galleries listed here. Note that some are housed in apartment buildings: ring the bell and you'll be buzzed in.

Antonio Colombo Arte Contemporanea

Via Solferino 44, North (02 2906 0171/www.colombo arte.com). Metro Moscova/bus 4, 43, 94/tram 11, 29, 30, 33. **Open** 4-7.30pm Tue-Sat. Closed Aug, 2wks Dec-Jan. **Map** p248 D5.
Established in 1996, Antonio Colombo's gallery focuses on young Italian artists. The emphasis is on figurative art and media, including painting, sculpture, photography and installations.

B&D Renoldi Arte Contemporanea

Via Calvi 18, East (02 5412 2563/www.bnd.it). Bus 60, 73/tram 12, 27. **Open** 10.30am-7.30pm Tue-Sat. Closed Aug, 2wks Dec-Jan. **Map** p251 G7.
This very cool space provides a backdrop for works in a variety of technological media, including digital photography, video and light.

Ca' di Fra'

Via Farini 2, North (02 2900 2108). Metro Garibaldi/tram 3, 4, 11, 29, 30, 33. **Open** *Sept-June* 10am-1pm, 3-7pm Mon-Sat. *July* By appointment only. Closed Aug, 2wks Dec-Jan. **Map** p248 D3.
Discover the work of young Italian and international artists in this charming, cosy space. Recent exhibitions have featured Gian Paolo Tommasi and Mimmo Iacopino.

C/O (Care Of)

Fabbrica del Vapore, via Luigi Nono 7, North (02 331 5800/www.careof.org). Bus 41, 43/tram 12, 14, 29, 30, 33. **Open** 3-7pm Tue-Sat. Closed Aug, 2wks Dec-Jan. **Map** p248 C3.
Run by Viafarini (*see p156*), this non-profit gallery, which aims to increase public knowledge of contemporary art, features monthly exhibitions, conferences, workshops and external projects.

Fondazione Prada

Via Fogazzaro 36, at via Cadore, East (02 5467 0515/www.fondazioneprada.org). Bus 62, 84/tram 3, 4, 9. **Open** 10am-7pm Tue-Sun. Closed Aug. **Map** p251 H8.
Situated in a former bank archive, this massive space is worth seeing in its own right. The majority of artists showing here are non-Italian and have included Thomas Friedman, Anish Kapoor, Marc Quinn and Carsten Höller.

Intelligent design

Few cities can compete with Milan in the international design stakes. Some of the world's sexiest cars, sleekest kitchenware and coolest furniture have taken shape here, and it's no coincidence that the city hosts the Salone Internazionale del Mobile – the largest modern furniture fair in Europe (*see p144*).

Although the curves of such iconic sports cars as Alfa Romeo were first sketched in the city (note the Visconti serpent and red cross on its logo) decades earlier, it was in the 1980s that Milan truly began to define itself as a design leader. This period – remembered as '*Milano da bere*' (loosely translated, 'Milan in a glass', a reference to the free-flowing cash splashed in bars and restaurants) – was an exciting time in the city. The economy was booming, AC Milan was the best football team in Europe, and one of the world's leading artist-cum-designers, Austrian-born Ettore Sottsass, started his Memphis group here. He brought together the brightest stars in contemporary art and architecture and turned them on to such everyday items as office chairs, lampshades and can openers.

The group split up in the late '80s, but its showroom, **Galleria Post Design** – renamed after the company was purchased by Alberto Bianchi Albrici in 1996 – remains at via della Moscova 27 (North, 02 655 4731, www.memphis-milano.it, closed Sun & Aug). The gallery hosts frequent themed design exhibitions (for example, at time of writing, a series of carpets by Nathalie Du Pasquier). All around it, in the area between Brera and corso Como, a number of similar 'design galleries' have sprung up. It's hard to put your finger on what constitutes a store and what constitutes a gallery in this city, as the fields of art and commerce have become inseparably fused.

Arguably the neighbourhood's design-gallery hub, **Dilmos** (piazza San Marco 1, North, 02 2900 2437, www.dilmos.com, closed Mon morning, Sun, all of Aug & 2wks Dec-Jan) is party central during the furniture fair. Stock such as sculptural, cubist-inspired bookcases and a hand-painted cabinet featuring a detail from the Sistine Chapel truly crosses the line between design and visual art.

Clio Calvi/Rudy Volpi (via Pontaccio 17, North, 02 8691 5009, www.cliocalvirudy volpi.com, closed Mon & Aug) is much like any other gallery – except that mirrors and desks are on display instead of paintings and sculptures. Featuring pieces by Sottsass and Andrea Branzi, the duo have assembled an intimate collection of limited-edition shelving, tables, chairs and knick-knacks.

Italhome Sedie Collezioni (largo Treves 2, North, 02 655 1787, www.pianetasedia.com, closed Sun, Mon morning & all of Aug) houses a collection of classic designs by such luminaries as Giò Ponti (architect of Milan's Pirelli tower) and Le Corbusier. Browsing at Brescia-based lighting company **Luceplan**'s store (via San Damiano 5, East, 02 7601 5760, www.luceplan.it, closed Mon & 3wks Aug) is like taking a tour through the best in lighting design, including works by Luciano Baldessarri and Luciano Balestrini.

Not strictly a design gallery, but certainly providing plenty of visual stimuli, **Crazy Art** (via Madonnina 11, Centre, 02 875 212, www.crazyart-milano.com, closed Sun, Mon & Aug) displays an eclectic mix of furniture, coats of arms, paintings and toy boats spanning the centuries from the 1500s to the 1950s. You'll never know how much you always wanted a chair constructed entirely of deer antlers until you set eyes on it.

Galleria Blu

Via Senato 18, East (02 7602 2404/www. galleriablu.com). Metro Montenapoleone or Turati/bus 61, 94. **Open** 10am-12.30pm, 3.30-7pm Mon-Fri; 3.30-7.30pm Sat. Closed Aug, 2wks Dec-Jan. **Map** p249 F5.

Milan's oldest – and arguably most prestigious – venue was founded in 1957 to promote post-war avant-garde artists. This was the first gallery in the world to showcase Lucio Fontana, Alberto Burri and Emilio Vedova. The roll call of prominent names whose work is or has been exhibited here includes Braque, Basquiat, Chagall, Giacometti, Kandinsky, Klee, Matisse, Tancredi and Warhol. **Photo** *p153*.

Galleria Carla Sozzani

Corso Como 10, North (02 653 531/www. galleriacarlasozzani.org). Metro Garibaldi/ tram 11, 29, 30, 33. **Open** 3.30-7.30pm Mon; 10.30am-7.30pm Tue, Fri-Sun; 10.30am-9pm Wed, Thur. **Map** p248 D3.

Part of Carla Sozzani's 10 Corso Como style/culture/ café complex (*see p117 and p125*), this gallery specialises in photography. The artists on show are mostly non-Italians and include the likes of Bruce Weber, Edward S Curtis, Rodman Wanamaker, Herb Ritts and Mary Ellen Mark. During Milan Fashion Week and the Milan Furniture Fair, the gallery is also open Monday mornings. **Photo** *p155*.

Galleria Emi Fontana

Viale Bligny 42, South (02 5832 2237). Metro Porta Romana, then tram 9, 29, 30/bus 79. **Open** 11am-7.30pm Tue-Sat. **Map** p251 E9.

Galleria Emi Fontana has been showing the hottest international contemporary artists working in all media – including Turner Prize-winner Gillian Wearing – since 1992.

Galleria Formentini

Via Formentini 10, North (02 8646 5075). Metro Cairoli or Lanza/tram 3, 4, 12. **Open** 10am-5pm Mon-Fri. Closed Aug. **Map** p248 D5.

Located on the second floor of a palazzo, this space is curated by art students from the Accademia di Brera; the deconsecrated church next door serves as classroom space. Recent exhibitions, backed by corporate sponsors, have focused on interpretations of Milan, especially by young foreigners.

Galleria L'Affiche

Via Unione 6, Centre (02 8645 0124/www.affiche.it). Metro Duomo or Missori/tram 2, 3, 4, 12, 14, 15, 24, 27. **Open** 4-7pm Tue-Sat. Closed Jan, July, Aug. **Map** p250 D7/p252 D7.

As well as exhibitions at the gallery in via Unione, L'Affiche has a store that sells posters from the early 20th century to the present at via Nirone 11.

Galleria Pack

Foro Buonaparte 60, North (02 8699 6395/ www.galleriapack.com). Metro Cairoli or Lanza/bus 18, 50, 58, 94/tram 1, 3, 4, 12, 27. **Open** 1pm-7.30pm Tue-Sat; mornings by appointment. Closed Aug, 2wks Dec-Jan. **Map** p248 D5.

Not to be confused with the PAC (*see p156*), this astoundingly handsome venue showcases artists such as MM Campos Pons, Pietro Finelli, Robert Gligorov, Miriam Cabessa and Ofri Cnaani. Note: the street numbering in foro Buonaparte is misleading – number 60 is closest to the corso Garibaldi end.

Galleria Ponte Rosso

Via Brera 2, North (02 86461053/www.ponte rosso.com). Metro Lanza/bus 61/tram 3, 4, 12. **Open** 10.30am-12.30pm, 3.30-7pm Tue-Sat. Closed July, Aug. **Map** p248 D6.

Founded in 1973, the Ponte Rosso has long given space to Lombardy painters and the movements they started, from the early 1900s to the present day. Among the extensive list of artists who have been exhibited here are Giuseppe Novello, Cristoforo De Amicis and Carlo Dalla Zorza.

Giò Marconi

Via Tadino 15, East (02 2940 4373/www.gio marconi.com). Metro Lima or Porta Venezia/ bus 60/tram 5, 33. **Open** 10.30am-12.30pm, 3-7pm Tue-Sat. Closed Aug, late Dec-early Jan. **Map** p249 G4.

This three-level space caters to all tastes, exhibiting everything from Italian post-war art to the latest video installations. **Photo** *p156*.

Lia Rumma

Via Solferino 44, North (02 2900 0101/www.galleria liarumma.com). Metro Moscova/bus 41, 43, 94. **Open** 11am-1pm, 3-7pm Tue-Sat. Closed 1wk Aug. **Map** p248 D4.

Lia Rumma is the sister space of the renowned gallery in Naples. Established and emerging international artists alike are displayed in the long, corridor-like premises.

Nuages

Via del Lauro 10, North (02 7200 4482/www. nuages.net). Metro Cairoli or Lanza/tram 3, 4, 12. **Open** 2-7pm Tue-Fri; 10am-1pm, 2-7pm Sat. Closed Aug. **Map** p248 D6/p252 D6.

Lorenzo Mattotti, Tullio Pericoli and Gianluigi Toccafondo are among the Italian artists exhibited here; international stars have included Milton Glaser, Sempé, Folon and Art Spiegelman.

Galleria Carla Sozzani. See p154.

Arts & Entertainment

Modern master: **Giò Marconi**. *See p155.*

PAC (Padiglione d'Arte Contemporanea)

Via Palestro 14, East (02 7600 9085/www.comune.
milano.it/pac). Metro Palestro or Turati/bus 61, 94.
Open varies (depending on exhibition). Closed Mon
& 2wks Aug. **Admission** €6; €3 concessions; free
under-8s. **No credit cards. Map** p249 F5.
The PAC tries to fill the void left by the lack of a
contemporary art museum in Milan and generally
features well-established international artists.
Designed by Ignazio Gardella (1905-99) in the 1950s,
it was rebuilt by the original architect after it was
almost destroyed by a deadly mafia bomb in 1993.

Photology

Via della Moscova 25, North (02 659 5285/
www.photology.com). Metro Moscova/bus 94. **Open**
11am-7pm Tue-Sat. Closed Aug. **Map** p249 E4.
Shows at this long-established photo gallery tend to
be split 50/50 between Italian and other artists.
Among the photographers represented are Mario
Giacomelli and Gian Paolo Barbieri, while shows by
Luigi Ghirri and Giacoma Costa have also been held.

Pianissimo Contemporary Art

Via Lambrate 24, East (339 6598 192 mobile/
www.pianissimo.it). Metro Lambrate/bus 62, 921.
Open 3-7pm Tue-Sat. Closed Aug.
This ultra-contemporary spot is one of a group of
spaces forming in the somewhat seedy neighbourhood near Lambrate station. Focusing on sculpture
and installations, it hosts one artist at a time –
recently Roberto Ago and Alessandro del Pont.

Spaziotemporaneo

Via Solferino 56, North (02 659 8056). Metro
Moscova/bus 41, 43, 94. **Open** 4-7.30pm Tue-Sat.
Closed mid July-Aug, 1wk Dec. **Map** p248 D5.

Established by Patrizia Serra in 1983, this gallery
shows work by foreign and Italian artists, especially
those of the generation who]ve moved beyond arte
povera and realism to experiment with avant-garde
materials. Valerio Anceschi, for example, recently
exhibited sculptures of ribbon-like soldered iron.

Studio Guenzani

Via Eustachi 10, East (02 2940 9251). Bus 60,
62/tram 5, 11, 23. **Open** 3-7.30pm Tue-Sat;
morning by appointment. Closed Aug. **Map** p249 H5.
Claudio Guenzani has shown the likes of Cindy
Sherman and Hiroshi Sugimoto, and has strong links
with Milanese artists, including painter Margherita
Manzelli and photographer Gabriele Basilico.
Other locations: via Melzo 5, East (02 2940 9251).

Viafarini

Via Farini 35, North (02 6680 4473/www.viafarini.
org). Metro Porta Garibaldi/bus 41, 51, 70/tram
3, 4, 7, 11, 29, 30. **Open** 3-7pm Tue-Sat; morning
by appointment. Closed Aug. **Map** p248 D2.
More than just a gallery, this space – run in con-
junction with the city council – provides facilities for
researching contemporary art in Milan. There's an
art library and an archive on young working artists.

Zonca & Zonca

Via Ciovasso 4, North (02 7200 3377/www.
zoncaezonca.com). Metro Cairoli or Lanza/bus 61/
tram 3, 4, 12. **Open** 10am-1pm, 3.30-7.30pm Mon-
Fri; Sat by appointment. Closed mid July-early Sept.
Map p248 D6/p252 D6.
This space merges Italian modernism with super-
contemporary art. Selections by Gianfranco Zonca,
which have included work by Lucio Fontana and
Mimmo Rotella, are offset by his daughter Elena's
taste for cutting-edge installation and photography.

Gay & Lesbian

The scene may be scattered (with straight crossovers), but, like everything else in Milan, it's sexy and stylish.

Squeeze into popular one-nighter **Join the Gap**. See p158.

The most international of Italian cities, Milan has a lot to offer gay and lesbian travellers. The no-nonsense, mind-your-own-business attitude of the Milanese allows gay venues to spring up and flourish without too much interference, while the gay-friendly fashion and design industries bring cosmopolitan style to a scene that attracts people from all over the country. However, there is a downside: with so many locals flaunting the trademark 'Milanese cool' and keeping themselves to themselves, finding out where to go when you arrive can be a challenge. This is compounded by the fact that, apart from via Sammartini, there is no obvious 'gay' area in the city.

It's worth persevering. As well as devoted gay and lesbian venues, the city is peppered with gay-friendly bars and restaurants. These tend to come in and out of fashion quickly, so it's best to check monthly magazine *Pride* to find out what's flavour of the month. Some of the best clubs entail a taxi trip to the suburbs – but you can at least expect lots of cute locals when you get there. Happy hunting!

PRACTICALITIES

Milan's gay clubs, saunas and some bars require clients to have a membership card issued by Arcigay, Italy's leading gay and lesbian organisation (*see p227*). The Arcigay card can be bought at most venues that require it, is valid for a year and costs €14. If you're only in town for a short time, a one-month visitor's card is available for €7.

Another indispensable tool for going out in Milan is the free map produced by gay publisher Echo, which has a comprehensive list of clubs, shops, saunas and cruising areas, with contact details. You can find it, along with *Pride* and other magazines, in most gay venues and at bookstore Libreria Babele (*see p122*).

Note that many clubs run themed nights or are one-nighters at straight venues, and all are subject to change – so before heading out, it's a good idea to phone or check the website to find out what's going on and when. Also, some clubs offer discounts with flyers, so keep an eye out around town, and check websites for printable versions.

Gay Milan

Unsurprisingly, Milan has plenty of fashionable spots where it's all about buff bodies and flaunting the latest gear. But there's also scope for those who hate all the posing, or have a penchant for leather and/or dark rooms.

Bars, clubs & discos

For other top gay-friendly nights, *see p168* **Plastic** *and p169* **Magazzini Generali**.

Afterline

Via Sammartini 25, North (02 669 4476/www.gay street.it). Metro Centrale FS/bus 81, 200, 727/tram 2, 5, 9, 33. **Open** 9pm-2am Mon-Wed, Sun; 9pm-3am Thur-Sat. **Admission** free Mon- Wed, Sun; €6 (incl 1 drink) Thur-Sat. **No credit cards. Map** p249 G2.
This discopub in via Sammartini has been going strong for more than a decade. A popular place for the younger crowd to relax, drink and dance, it runs themed nights for the boys and is a great place to kick off an evening before heading to the clubs.

Billy

Amnesia, via Gatto, at viale Forlanini, East (mobile 335 832 7777/www.billyclub.it). Bus 38. **Open** noon-5am Sat. Closed Aug. **Admission** €16-€20 incl 1 drink. **Credit** AmEx, MC, V.
Milan's most popular gay club has international appeal, with guest DJs from abroad. In addition, its close links with the fashion trade make it the place for trendsetters. In the summer it moves to one of the clubs near the Idroscalo leisure park.

Binario I

Via Plezzo 16, East (02 2159 7436). Metro Lambrate/bus 72. **Open** 11pm-4am Sat. Closed July, Aug. **Admission** €12-€15. **No credit cards.**
This popular club is conveniently located next to Royal Hammam sauna (*see p160*). It's arranged on three levels, so you can survey the crush on the dancefloor from the balcony or chill out downstairs, where there's also a dark room. It's a good alternative to the more fashion-conscious Billy (*see above*). The music is on the fun side of commercial (disco, Madonna and the like).

Glitter Lo Chalet

HD, via Caruso 11, at via Tajani, East (02 718 990). Tram 5. **Open** noon-4am Sat. Closed July, Aug. **Admission** €12 incl 1 drink. **No credit cards.**
Formerly at Cafè Dali, Glitter is now at HD until further notice (the club also runs a low-key gay night on Tuesdays). A mixed gay/lesbian/straight crowd dances to 1980s sounds, electronica, Britpop and trash. The staff keep things lively with shows and impromptu performances.

G Lounge

Via Larga 8, Centre (02 805 3042/www. glounge.it). Metro Duomo or Missori/bus 54, 60, 65/tram 12, 23, 27. **Open** 7am-9pm Mon;

7am-2am Tue-Fri; 6pm-2am Sat, Sun. Closed 3wks Aug. **Admission** free. **Credit** AmEx, DC, MC, V. **Map** p251 E7/p252 E7.
This cavernous venue has an interesting history, having been both a former Fascist HQ and a billiard hall. Today it caters to a much more fashionable crowd. During the day it serves sandwiches and drinks to lunchtime workers; in the evening the downstairs bar opens and the glamorous atmosphere is enhanced by loungey music and a small dancefloor. As with many bars, it's gay-friendly rather than exclusively gay; Saturday is the best night to meet the like-minded.

Join the Gap

Borgo del Tempo Perso, via Fabio Massimo 36, East (02 569 4755). Metro Corvetto or Porto di Mare. **Open** 7pm-2am Sun. Closed July, Aug. **Admission** €12-€15 incl 1 drink. **Credit** AmEx, DC, MC, V.
Run by CIG (Centro di Iniziativa Gay), this very popular club is a Sunday-night follow-up to Billy, with a similar, though slightly younger, crowd. The baroque interior contrasts with the buzz. Get there early – the buffet gives way to a floor show and classic tracks for a jam-packed evening. **Photo** *p157*.

Lelephant

Via Melzo 22, East (02 2951 8768/www.lelephant.it). Metro Porta Venezia/tram 9, 29, 30. **Open** 6pm-2am Tue-Sun. Closed 3wks Aug. **No credit cards. Map** p249 G5.
A focal point for a mixed straight/gay crowd, Lelephant – with its eclectic collection of chairs and ever-changing decor – offers expertly mixed cocktails and an excellent early-evening buffet. Always full, it is particularly recommended for its Sunday-night happy hour (*see also p118*).

Nuova Idea

Via de Castillia 30, North (02 6900 7859). Metro Gioia/bus 42, 82, 83/tram 30, 33. **Open** 10.30pm-4am Thur-Sat. Closed July, Aug. **Admission** €10-€16. **No credit cards. Map** p249 E3.
Still going strong after 30 years, this Milan institution is unusual in that it has two dancefloors: one for ballroom dancing (complete with a live orchestra at weekends) and one for disco. Frequented by a mixed age group, it is also popular with the area's transvestite crowd.

Pervert Gold

Rolling Stone, Corso XXII Marzo 32 (02 733 172/ www.rollingstone.it). Bus 45, 73/tram 12, 27. **Open** 11pm-5am 2nd, 4th Sun of mth. **Admission** €30 (incl 1 drink). **Credit** AmEx, MC, V. **Map** p251 H7.
Another gem from club organisers Pervert, this night is unmissable. The stage shows amazing animations worthy of a theatre, inspired by a famous film or opera. The crowd is older than at Sodoma, but the music is just as hard, with regular DJs Obi Baby, Lorenzo Lsp and international guests such as Fischerspooner. Remember to check the location as it frequently changes: call 338 105 1232.

Popstarz

Gasoline Club, via Bonnet 11A, North (mobile 339 7745 797/www.discogasoline.it). Metro Garibaldi/ bus 94/tram 29, 30. **Open** 10.30pm-5am Thur. Closed mid June-Aug. **Admission** €15 incl 1 drink. **Credit** MC, V. **Map** p248 D3.

One of the best gay-oriented nights in Milan. There's no snobbery here: beautiful girls, transvestites, muscular men, gays and lesbians all pack out the dancefloor, while resident DJs Nancy Posh and Tommy Boys play electro, '80s and contemporary pop.

Ricci

Piazza della Repubblica 27, North (02 6698 2536). Metro Repubblica/bus 2, 11/tram 2, 9, 33. **Open** 7.30am-2am Mon-Sat; 7.30am-8.30pm Sun. Closed 1wk Aug. **No credit cards. Map** p249 F4.

Effectively a café and cake shop, Ricci is a welcome oasis in an area not known for bars. During the day it serves office workers and leisured ladies, but at night it fills up with the young and trendy. It's especially popular in summer, when it gets so crowded people spill out on to the street.

Sodoma

Hollywood, corso Como 15 (02 659 8996/www. discotecahollywood.com). Metro Garibaldi/tram 11, 29, 30, 33. **Open** 10.30pm-4am Wed. Closed July, Aug. **Admission** €20 incl drink. **Credit** AmEx, DC, MC, V. **Map** p248 D3.

Organised by Pervert, Sodoma is the best night at Hollywood, the only one where people are not there to see and to be seen. Resident DJs include Obi Baby and Nino Lopez, who keep the dancefloor busy with young boys in sunglasses and cheerful transvestites.

Studio Know How

Via Antonio da Recanate 7, North (02 6739 1224). Metro Centrale FS/bus 81, 200, 727/tram 2, 5, 9, 33. **Open** 9.30am-7.30pm Mon-Sat. Closed 2wks Aug. **Credit** AmEx, DC, MC, V. **Map** p249 F3.

Billing itself as Italy's only entirely gay shop, Studio Know How has a magnificent choice of videos and DVDs. For those who like things a bit harder, there's a large selection of games and sex toys too.

Zip After Hour

Zip Club, corso Sempione 76 (02 331 4904). Bus 57/tram 1, 19, 33. **Open** 4am-11am Sat. Closed June-Aug. **Admission** with 1-yr card €25. **No credit cards. Map** p248 A3.

It's hard to find somewhere to dance in Milan after 5am. Currently, one of the few options is Zip, a wacky club near Bullona Station. Most of the people here are transvestites, but gay and hetero night owls love the place too. Music is techno and hard electro, and the dark room is legendary. It's a private club, so bring an ID card or passport to secure entry.

Cruising bars

Cruising bars are becoming increasingly popular in Milan. Dark rooms are nothing new, of course, but entire clubs built on the premise

Rhabar. *See p160.*

of swift and easy sex without even putting a token toe on the dancefloor are. Often housed in anonymous blocks (sometimes the only clue to their existence is a tiny plaque at the entrance), these establishments offer total discretion, and you'll be safe in the knowledge you're among like-minded people.

Cruising Canyon

Via Paisello 4, East (02 2040 4201). Metro Loreto/ bus 90, 91, 92. **Open** 24hrs daily. **Admission** €8-€10. **Credit** AmEx, MC, V.

For cruising at its simplest, this round-the-clock bar has an erotic cinema, labyrinth, dark rooms and cubicles, as well as a witty mock-up of the *'fossa'* cruising area just outside Parco Sempione. The lack of a bar and its smoky atmosphere can be a bit offputting, but there is plenty of space to move around, chill out and check out who's there.

Depot

Via dei Valtorta 19, North (02 289 2920/www. depotmilano.com). Metro Turro/bus 199. **Open** 10pm-3am Mon-Thur; 10pm-6am Fri, Sat; 3pm-2am Sun. Closed Aug. **Admission** €20-€25 (couple), €18-€20 (single). **No credit cards.**

Not for the faint-hearted, this intimate cruising bar on three floors welcomes those in search of close encounters of a harder kind. It offers themed nights, from leather to sneaker-sportswear fetish, as well as naked parties. Generally, it attracts a slightly older crowd, but don't be put off by its dark exterior – the guys inside are welcoming and friendly.

Flexo
Via Oropa 3, East (02 2682 6709/www.flexoclub.it). Metro Cimiano. **Open** 10pm-3.30am Mon-Thur; 10pm-6am Fri, Sat. **Admission** €5 Mon-Wed; €10 (incl 1 drink) Fri, Sat (€5 after 4am). **Credit** AmEx, DC, MC, V.

A very popular cruising bar in the north-east suburbs. There's a large bar area to meet friends and mingle, while upstairs the action gets a little harder, with cubicles and a labyrinth. At the weekend, Flexo teams up with Metro Cimiano sauna (*see below*), offering joint entry prices. There are naked parties on Tuesday, Thursday and Saturday, plus other themed nights.

Saunas

Metro Centrale
Via Schiapparelli 1, North (02 6671 9089/www. metroclub.it). Metro Centrale FS/bus 42, 53, 60, 90, 91/tram 2, 5, 33. **Open** noon-2am daily. **Admission** €15 (€12.50 after 8pm). **Credit** MC, V. **Map** 249 G2.

Metro Centrale is spread out over two floors, with jacuzzis, a steam bath, a massage room and a Finnish sauna. For your private viewing pleasure, there are videos in the chill-out rooms, as well as an internet hook-up. Free condoms are handed out at the door. There are discounts for under-26s. **Other locations: Metro Cimiano** Via Oropa 3, East (02 2851 0528).

Royal Hammam
Via Plezzo 16, East (02 2641 2189). Metro Lambrate/bus 72. **Open** 2pm-2am Tue-Thur; 24hrs Fri-Sun. Closed 1wk Aug. **Admission** €16. **Credit** MC, V.

The superb facilities at Milan's newest and best-equipped sauna include a large pool (open-air in summer), jacuzzis and steam baths, and a restaurant. At weekends it is open 24 hours, from 2pm on Thursday through to midnight on Sunday.

Thermas
Via Bezzecca 9, East (02 545 0355/www.thermas club.com). Bus 60/tram 27, 29, 30, 84. **Open** noon-midnight Mon-Wed, Sat, Sun; noon-2am Thur, Fri. Closed 2wks Aug. **Admission** €15; €13 Tue & after 8pm daily. **No credit cards**. **Map** p251 G7.

Spartan but clean, Thermas is frequented by a diverse crowd of all ages ranging from corporate executives to the ordinary lad on the street. Its offerings include a bar, steam bath, small body-building room, cooling-off area and recliners for relaxing on. Discounts for the under-25s.

Lesbian Milan

While gay clubs are relatively plentiful in Milan, the city offers a lot less to lesbians. But the scene is picking up with the new Rhabar, the reopening of Cicip & Ciciap and one-nighters such Kick-off at Black Hole. Highbrow bi-monthly lesbian magazine *Towanda* includes book reviews, political commentary and art critiques, as well as news on lesbian holiday spots and events organised by Arcilesbica (*see p227*). As for nightlife, Kick-off co-ordinates events and parties at a variety of bars and clubs (details at www.kickoff.biz). A good general resource for everything from events and chatrooms to job listings is www.listalesbica.it.

Bars, clubs & discos

Cicip & Ciciap
Via Gorani 9, Centre (02 8699 5410/www.ricicip. org). Metro Cordusio/bus 50, 58, 199/tram 18, 19. **Open** 7pm-1am Wed-Sun. **No credit cards**. **Map** p250 C7/p252 C7.

This historic and political centre for women has recently reopened, hosting discussion groups for women of all ages, though it's popular with the politically and non-politically minded alike. The centre also has a bar and a reasonably priced restaurant.

Kick-off at Black Hole
Via Cena 1, East (02 7104 0220/www.kickoff.biz). Bus 92/tram 12. **Open** 11.30pm-4am Fri. Closed July, Aug. **Admission** €12-€14 incl 1 drink. **No credit cards**.

This disco in an area well served by gay venues hosts a popular lesbian disco on Friday nights. The sleek modern space has two dancefloors, and an outdoor garden that's open in summer. Music is a mix of commercial R&B, house and pop.

Rhabar
Alzaia Naviglio Grande 150, South (mobile 338 8266 160/www.rhabar.it). Tram 2. **Open** 6pm-2am daily. Closed 10 days Aug. **No credit cards**.

This comfortable, welcoming canal-side bar/disco hosts a variety of themed nights and live music. The modern Moroccan-influenced decor will appeal to younger, style-conscious women. **Photo** p159.

Sottomarino Giallo
Via Donatello 2, East (339 545 4127/www.sotto marinogiallo.it). Metro Loreto or Piola/bus 55, 56, 90, 91/tram 11, 33. **Open** 11pm-3am Wed, alternate Thur, Sun; 11pm-4am Fri; 11pm-5am Sat. Closed 3wks Aug. **Admission** €10 incl 1 drink. **No credit cards**.

A long-established club on two levels, with a cosy lounge upstairs and a disco downstairs playing mainstream music. It's popular with all ages. Saturdays are strictly women-only, Fridays are mainly women, Thursdays are mixed gay and lesbian, while the rest of the week the club caters to a straight crowd.

Music

High notes – and high drama.

It's only rock 'n' roll... the Rolling Stones play **Stadio Meazza**. *See p164.*

See p164.

Milan's position as the country's business capital extends to the music industry, with all the major Italian record labels headquartered here. The reasons for the city's musical dominance are historical. The presence of La Scala opera house from the late 18th century onwards led to the growth of the sheet-music industry, particularly with Ricordi (which remained an Italian company until it was bought by Germany's BMG in the 1990s). In the mid 1900s the Galleria del Corso (an elegant arcade off the corso Vittorio Emanuele II) developed as Milan's equivalent of Tin Pan Alley. To this day, Sugar, an independent label responsible for the international phenomenon, Andrea Bocelli, has its offices here (above the Messaggerie Musicali book and record store, which it also owns).

The fact that so many record labels are based in Milan means that a lot of artists are obliged to live there, often against their will. Indeed, a dislike of the city seems to have inspired several songs. In 2001 a Roman artist, Alex Britti, recorded the melancholic *Milano*, which

describes a lonely Sunday spent wandering around in search of something to do. The following year, the rap group Articolo 31 recorded *Milano Milano*, which sums up the ambiguous feelings that many residents have: 'Whenever I go away, I want to come back,' the group sang, 'but as soon as I come back, I want to escape.'

The Milanese do indeed like nothing more than to get away, but for those who stick around there's a lively music scene, both at the weekend and during the week. Let's face it: it's not on the scale of London or any big American city, but there will often be something going to suit you, whatever your taste in music. Most important Italian artists perform in Milan at some stage, and the city is also on the concert circuit for many international acts.

INFORMATION AND TICKETS

Trying to find out about upcoming concerts in Milan can be frustrating. Italians do not plan things far in advance, and most venues do not publish a programme. So when it comes to upcoming concerts, the best sources are the

Arts & Entertainment

Melodrama at La Scala

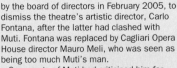

The last few years at La Scala have been eventful, to say the least. In 2001 the company left the theatre it has called home since 1778, taking up temporary residence at the modern Teatro degli Arcimboldi in the north of the city (*see p165*), so that much-needed restoration work could be carried out. As the €61-million revamp drew to a finish, the company made a partial return for the opening of the 2004-5 season and a complete return for 2005-6.

What planners hadn't been able to foresee was the dramatic upheaval that would take place in 2005, when the company's music director and chief conductor of 20 years, Riccardo Muti, resigned. Muti's official reason for leaving was 'the vulgar show of hostility' by his colleagues. Strikes and calls for his resignation had followed the decision, made

by the board of directors in February 2005, to dismiss the theatre's artistic director, Carlo Fontana, after the latter had clashed with Muti. Fontana was replaced by Cagliari Opera House director Mauro Meli, who was seen as being too much Muti's man.

Opponents of Muti had criticised him for being dictatorial. Film and opera director Franco Zeffirelli, for one, described La Scala's programme under Muti as 'one horrendous production after another; constipated, anal and with no explosion of vitality on stage'.

Defenders of Muti, on the other hand, saw him as a misunderstood genius and a victim of La Scala's highly unionised 800-strong workforce. Indeed, what was striking about the story was how, in true Italian style, even a dispute at an opera house could become a political issue: generally speaking, left-wingers joined the 'Muti Out' campaign, while right-wingers, including Silvio Berlusconi's Forza Italia party and the city's then mayor (and, by the same token, president of La Scala's board of directors) Gabriele Albertini, took up the maestro's defence. In fact, a few days after Muti's resignation, two of his presumed political allies followed suit. Fedele Confalonieri, president of Silvio Berlusconi's Mediaset media empire, resigned from La Scala's board of directors, as did Marco Tronchetti Provera, boss of the powerful Pirelli tyre company and Telecom Italia.

weekly supplements published by two national dailies, *Corriere della Sera* (with its *ViviMilano* supplement on Wednesday) and *La Repubblica* (which includes a handy *Tutto Milano* booklet in its Thursday edition). Three free distribution dailies – *Metro*, *City* and *Leggo* – all of which can be found in metro stations in the morning, contain information regarding shows taking place in town that evening. Keep an eye out for posters around town too, though don't be surprised if you've already missed something that sounded great.

Also, a word of warning about tickets. As with theatres, it's often simpler to use central booking agencies like Ticketone (www.ticketone.it); indeed, the venues' websites themselves tend to point visitors in that direction. If you don't fancy the internet

in Italian, then Ticketone has a box office at the Teatro dal Verme in via San Giovani sul Muro (*see p165*). You can also pick up tickets for concerts in large bookshops and music stores like Messaggerie Musicali (*see p123*), Ricordi Media Store (*see p141*), La Feltrinelli (*see p122*) and FNAC (via Torino, at via della Palla 2, Centre, 02 8699 5209).

OPENING TIMES AND TRANSPORT

In the listings below we have tried giving fixed box office opening times where possible, as well as performance times and regular opening times (for bars and clubs). Note, however, that the main act may not come on stage until an hour or two after the performance is billed as starting. Note too that some venues are in out-of-the-way neighbourhoods, and even if you

Arts & Entertainment

One thing is true: most opera-goers disliked trekking out to the Arcimboldi and are only too happy to be back at La Scala's central location. Although supporters of Muti see him as being irreplaceable, many opera buffs feel that his departure, along with the return to the old premises, has led to much-needed improvement. In practical terms, the renovation work has created more storage space, thanks to a controversial new 'fly tower', visible from piazza della Scala. In theory at least, this means it's easier to make scene changes as the tower allows a stage set to slide up and down as well as sideways – meaning it's now possible to stage three performances a day. As for the traditional complaint that you get a pretty poor view of the stage from a lot of La Scala seats, not much appears to have changed.

In artistic terms, the departure of Muti could mark the dawning of a new era. He has yet to be officially replaced, although the name of Riccardo Chailly, of Orchestra Verdi (which plays at the city's Auditorium), has been mooted. The short-lived tenure of La Scala's artistic director Mauro Meli ended in May 2005. He was succeeded by Stephane Lissner, a Frenchman best known for his work at the Aix Festival in Provence.

One of Lissner's first moves was to invite a young Englishman, Daniel Harding, to conduct the inaugural opera of the 2005-6. Harding, who had worked with Lissner at Aix, picked up his baton for a production of Mozart's *Idomeneo* on 7 December 2005. He was the first ever Englishman to conduct an opening night at La Scala and, surprisingly for an opera audience known for booing unwelcome novelties, his performance received rapturous applause.

In fact, the opening night, which takes place on the holiday of the city's patron saint, Sant'Ambrogio, manages to bring out many of the political, artistic and business dramas that make La Scala the place that it is. Every winter, as the makers and shakers arrive at the opera house in their fur coats, protesters and strikers gather in the piazza outside in order to give them a loud welcome. We may live in the post-modern, post-rock'n'roll world, but in Italy the border between real life and opera is still blurred.

arrive by public transport, chances are it will have stopped running by the time the concert is over. You'd do well, therefore, to get a cab home (in smaller venues staff will be happy to book one for you).

Mega venues

Forum

Via D Vittorio 6, Assago, South (premium line 199 128 800/www.forumnet.it). Metro Famagosta then bus to Assago. **Open** times vary. **Tickets** prices vary. **No credit cards**.

This large sports and music venue, which opened in 1990, should be getting its own subway stop one of these years, but until then it will continue to be hard to reach (and get back from) by public transport. The acoustics aren't great either, but it's the sort of place where big Italian (like Eros Ramazzotti and Laura Pausini) and international (Coldplay and Depeche Mode) acts play. Next door (and part of the same complex) is the more intimate Teatro della Luna, where the intriguing Australian Pink Floyd performed a while back. As there's no numbered seating, it's a good idea to arrive early.

Mazda Palace

Via Sant'Elia 33, West (02 3340 0551/www.mazda palace.it). Metro Lampugnano. **Open** *Box office* 9.30am-1pm, 2.30-6pm Mon-Fri. **Tickets** prices vary. **No credit cards**.

In early 1985 Milan was hit by freakishly heavy snowfall, which destroyed the city's indoor sports arena. The 9,000-seat Mazda Place (originally known as the Palatrussardi) was rapidly built to replace it. Frank Sinatra was the first to play here, in 1986, and he has been followed by the likes of Paul

Blue Note.

McCartney, Elton John, Bob Dylan and the Foo Fighters. This venue has the added advantage of a metro station, which makes it less of a pain to get to than a lot of Milan concert venues, though the area can be a bit dodgy at night.

Stadio Meazza (San Siro)

Viale Piccolomini 5, West (02 4871 3713). Metro Lotto/tram 16. **Open** times vary. **Tickets** prices vary. **No credit cards.**
The city-owned soccer stadium San Siro is shared by the Milan and Inter clubs throughout the year, but during the summer months it is the scene of the occasional mega concert. Typical names would include Bruce Springsteen, the Rolling Stones and U2, as well as Italian stadium acts like Vasco Rossi, Renato Zero and Luciano Ligabue. *Photo p161.*

Medium to large

Alcatraz

Via Valtellina 25, North (02 6901 6352/http://alcatrazmilano.com). Bus 82, 90, 91, 92/tram 3. **Open** times vary. **Tickets** prices vary. **No credit cards. Map** p248 D1.
Another largish site that doubles as a disco (Friday and Saturday) and concert venue (mainly Monday and Thursday). Housed in a converted industrial space, it is located in a reasonably accessible part of town. It features both Italian and international acts such as James Blunt, Paul Weller and Kanye West.

Rolling Stone

Corso XXII Marzo 32, East (02 733 172/www.rollingstone.it). Bus 45, 73/tram 12, 27. **Open** times vary. **Tickets** free-€35. **Credit** AmEx, MC, V. **Map** p251 H7.

This large disco hosts several concerts a month. It has a capacity of 1,650, making it a good venue for established acts such as Jamie Cullum and David Gray. *See also p168.*

More intimate

Blues House

Via Sant' Uguzzone 26, North (02 2700 3621/www.blueshouse.it). Metro Villa San Giovanni. **Open** 9pm-2am Mon, Wed-Sun. **Tickets** €8 incl 1st drink. **No credit cards.**
Situated towards the northern end of viale Monza, this venue may be a little off the beaten track, but for blues fans it's a gem. Here guitar wizards like Poppa Chubby and John Moony have played in front of small, but appreciative audiences. Chances are you'll also get to buy your heroes a beer at the bar after the show.

La Casa 139

Via Ripamonti 139, South (02 4548 8267/www.lacasa139.com). Bus 95, 99/tram 24, 34. **Open** Mon-Sat. **Tickets** prices vary, entrance with ARCI membership (small charge to join on the door). **No credit cards. Map** p251 F11.
This multi-functional club seems to host just about everything: concerts, DJ sets, exhibitions, conferences and private parties. Its music tends to feature up-and-coming Italian, as well as occasional foreign, acts (like the Belgian band Austin Lace).

Transilvania Live

Via Paravia 59, West (mobile 339 746 7251/www.transilvania.it). Bus 95/tram 24, 34. **Open** 9pm-3am daily. **Tickets** prices vary. **No credit cards.**
If you want to take a walk on the dark side, then Transilvania Live is probably the place. This ghoulish Gothic club is something of a Milan institution and here you can catch acts like the Swedish heavy metal female band Crucified Barbara, and the wild, post-punk London rockers Steranko.

Jazz

Italian jazz generally enjoys a good reputation locally. In addition to old timers like Paolo Conte and Enrico Rava (another one, Romano Mussolini, son of Il Duce, died in February 2006), there's an exciting new generation that includes trumpeter Paolo Fresu and pianists Stefano Bollani and Giovanni Allevi. Milan's clubs provide a perfect setting for sitting back, relaxing and enjoying the music, even though the cliché 'smoke-filled' no longer applies, thanks to the cigarette ban.

Blue Note

Via Borsieri 37, North (02 6901 6888/premium rate info line 899 700 022/www.bluenotemilano.com). Metro Porta Garibaldi or Zara/bus 82, 83/tram 4, 7, 11. **Open** 8.30pm-1am Tue-Sat; 8.30-11pm Sun. *Box office* 2-7pm Mon; 2pm-midnight

Arts & Entertainment

Tue-Sat; 7-10pm Sun. **Tickets** €25-€30. **Credit** AmEx, DC, MC, V. **Map** p249 E2.
The Blue Note club, restaurant and bar is the largest and most prestigious of the Milan jazz venues, being part of an international franchise. There are two shows nightly from Tuesday to Saturday and one on a Sunday, and the range of music is broad: recent guests have included Suzanne Vega and the London Community Gospel Choir. **Photo** *p164*.

Nordest Caffè

Via Borsieri 35, North (02 6900 1910/www.nordest caffe.it). Metro Porta Garibaldi or Zara/bus 82, 83/tram 4, 11. **Open** 8am-1am Mon-Fri; 8.30am-8.30pm Sat, Sun. Closed 1wk Aug. **No credit cards**. **Map** p249 E2.
This pleasant wine bar hosts local jazz artists on Wednesday and Thursday evenings (from 10pm in winter and from 7.30pm in summer). Entrance is free, although the first drink costs €7.50.

La Salumeria della Musica

Via Pasinetti 2, South (02 5680 7350/www. lasalumeriadellamusica.com). Tram 24. **Open** times vary. **Tickets** prices vary. **No credit cards**.
This venue (literally translated as the 'Delicatessen of Music') prides itself on having been listed by *Down Beat* magazine among the world's 100 best jazz clubs. A wide variety of musical genres is played here and it is also used for literary and other cultural events. Norah Jones and Joss Stone have both had showcases here. Shows tend to start around 9.30pm.

Le Scimmie

Via Ascanio Sforza 49, South (02 8940 2874/www. scimmie.it). Metro Porta Genova/tram 3, 15. **Open** 7pm-3am Mon-Sat. **Admission** free (1 drink min at tables). **Credit** AmEx, DC, MC, V. **Map** p250 C10.
This intimate club and restaurant, which is located in the lively Navigli area, describes itself as 'the temple of Milan jazz'. It also features other types of music (rock, blues, reggae), as well as English-language stand-up comedy (*see p176* **Grin and Beer it**). In addition to the interior area, there's a boat that's moored on the canal. Katie Melua recently climbed aboard for a showcase.

Opera & classical

Auditorium di Milano

Largo Mahler 1, South (02 8338 9201/www. auditoriumdimilano.org or www.orchestrasinfonica. milano.it). Bus 59, 90, 91/tram 3, 15. **Open** times vary. **Tickets** €10-€50. **Credit** AmEx, DC, MC, V. **Map** p250 C10.
Located at the intersection of corso San Gottardo, close to the canals, this relatively new venue has received the thumbs-up from music fans. Opened in 1999, the 1,400-seat auditorium is the home of the city's highly respected Orchestra Verdi. Performances are usually on a Thursday and Friday night, with a matinée on a Sunday.

Conservatorio di Musica Giuseppe Verdi

Via Conservatorio 12, East (02 762 1101/www. consmilano.it). Metro San Babila/bus 54, 61, 84/ tram 12, 27, 23. **Open** Box office & library 8am-8pm Mon-Fri. *Performances* 9pm Mon-Fri. **Tickets** €15-€20. **No credit cards**. **Map** p251 F6/p252 F6.
This prestigious institution was founded in 1808 in a former Lateran convent. Many key figures in Italian music studied here – although, ironically, the young Giuseppe Verdi was rejected – and it still plays a fundamental role in Italian musical life today. There are two concert halls: the smaller Sala Puccini for chamber music and the bigger Sala Verdi for symphonic and choral music, both with reasonably varied programmes. The library (free entry) houses over 35,000 volumes and 460,000 musical works, including manuscripts by Mozart, Donizetti, Bellini and Verdi. Rare string instruments are housed under glass cases along the corridor.

Teatro alla Scala

Piazza della Scala, Centre (02 7200 3744/www. teatroallascala.org). Metro Duomo/tram 1, 2. **Open** times vary. **Tickets** prices vary. **Credit** AmEx, DC, MC, V. **Map** p251 E6/p252 E6.
The world-famous opera house is still coming to terms with the return to its old home (and other changes – *see p162* **Melodrama at La Scala**). Finding tickets for Italian opera remains extremely difficult, but if you're prepared to watch non-Italian opera or to attend concerts, then it isn't as tricky.

Teatro dal Verme

Via Giovanni sul Muro 2, North (02 8790 5201) Metro Cairoli/bus 57, 58, 61/tram 1, 4, 14, 27. **Open** Box office 11am-9pm Tue-Sat; 11am-1pm Sun. **Tickets** prices vary. **Credit** AmEx, MC, V. **Map** p248 D6/p252 D6.
Originally built in 1872, this theatre became a cinema after World War II. It finally reopened as a music venue in 2001 after a 20-year renovation process, by which time another concert hall (the Auditorium; *see above*) had already opened. Performances start at 9pm on a Thursday, and there are also afternoon concerts (I Pomeriggi Musicali) at 5pm on Saturdays or Sundays.

Teatro degli Arcimboldi

Viale dell'Innovazione 1, North (02 7200 3744/ Ticketone premium rate booking line 899 500 022/www.teatroarcimboldi.org). Metro Precotto then shuttle bus/bus 44, 162/tram 7. **Open** times vary. **Tickets** prices vary. **Credit** AmEx, DC, MC, V.
Since fulfilling its original role as the temporary home of La Scala, the Teatro degli Arcimboldi di Milano (TAM) is still trying to decide what to do in life. Under the artistic directorship of Paolo Arcà, it continues to host dance and orchestral events, but it also features concerts by the likes of Woody Allen and Pink Floyd's Dave Gilmour. Designed by Vittorio Gregotti, this 2,400-seat auditorium is also worth checking out for its love-it-or-hate-it architecture.

Arts & Entertainment

Nightlife

Dress up and get down.

Casablanca Café. See p167.

If Milan is just one stop on your tour of Italy, it's a good idea to get the partying out of your system here: you'll be hard pressed to find a better selection of nightclubs anywhere else, and, as you might imagine, a city with a responsibility for looking hip and young can put on a pretty good show after midnight.

You don't have to be young or hip, however, to enjoy it. Few Milanese bother to show up to work before 9am, so post-dinner partying is pretty common at any age. You just have to find the place that fits your style.

One of the city's nightlife hubs is the northern end of corso Como. This is home to the mainstays **Hollywood**, **Casablanca Café**, **Tocqueville 13** and a handful of others that cram the neighbourhood near the Garibaldi metro stop. At the southern edge of town, **Magazzini Generali** is the bread and butter for natives. Dozens of smaller and spicier locales are sprinkled everywhere in between, though relatively few new ones have opened in the past few years. One highly touted exception is Giorgio Armani's pet project, **Armani Privé**, which opened in 2005 to mixed reviews. For a shot at rubbing shoulders with famous soccer players, meanwhile, try corso Como on a

Sunday night. Otherwise, **Lime Light**, co-owned by *calciatori* (footballers), is a good star-gazing venue.

At most clubs, payment follows a familiar routine: if you make it past face control, you'll be given a ticket (*tessera*) at the door, each drink will be hole-punched into it and you'll pay as you leave. Hang on to that card: the fine for losing it is stiff. Most clubs serve dinner before the business of the night begins in earnest: food is unlikely to be great, but it will definitely be more than palatable, and there is often live jazz music during dinner. Taking a table usually ensures access to the *privé* (a fancy term for a restricted-access chill-out room). Most clubs close at 4am, or else when the last group of people leaves.

INFORMATION

Zero2 ('Zerodue') is a free mini-sized fortnightly magazine that's indispensable for finding out what's going on where and when. Look for it at venues around town. Websites www.2night.it and www.milano2night.it have events listings in Italian; there's also www.mymi.it, which produces a free, quarterly guide to urban living called *Kult*, available in most bars and clubs.

Duomo & Centre

Armani Privé
Via Pisoni 1 (02 6231 2655). Metro
Montenapoleone/bus 54, 61/tram 1, 12. **Open**
10.30pm-3am Tue-Sat. Closed Aug. **Admission**
free; 1st drink €20. **Credit** AmEx, DC, MC, V.
Map p249 E5.
Giorgio Armani knows how to accessorise, and the
latest add-on to his empire is this club, situated
beneath his sushi restaurant, Armani/Nobu (*see*
p105). Since its opening, veteran fashionistas have
lamented the apparent slide of the status of the clientele – but its velvet ropes draw a clamouring crowd
nonetheless. Not surprisingly, it helps a lot if you get
there early and are on the guest list.

La Banque
Via B Porrone 6 (02 8699 6565/www.labanque.it).
Metro Cordusio/bus 50, 58/tram 1, 3, 12, 19, 24.
Open 6pm-5am daily. Closed Aug. **Admission**
€13-€16 incl 1 drink. **Credit** AmEx, MC, V.
Map p248 D6/p252 D6.
Staid and central, this sleekly decorated club is the
kind of place that attracts guys who wear a suit to
go clubbing. On weekdays it opens for *aperitivi*
(happy hour) at 6pm, and it serves an elegant dinner from 8pm to midnight every night. Remember,
though: you'll be turned away if you're not decked
out smartly (don't even think about wearing train-
ers, for a start).

Sforzesco & North

Alcatraz
Via Valtellina 25 (02 6901 6352/www.alcatraz
milano.com). Bus 82, 90, 91, 92/tram 3. **Open**
11pm-4am Fri, Sat. Closed July, Aug. **Admission**
€12 incl 1 drink. **Credit** MC, V. **Map** p248 D1.
During the week this ex-industrial building hosts
live music; on weekends it turns into a dance club.
Friday nights feature house and 'revival' music;
Saturdays are all rock 'n' roll.

Casablanca Café
Corso Como 14 (02 6269 0186/www.casablanca
cafe.it). Metro Garibaldi/tram 11, 29, 30, 33.
Open 8.30pm-4am Mon, Fri, Sat; 7pm-4am Tue-
Thur, Sun. Closed Aug. **Admission** €13-€16
incl 1 drink. **Credit** AmEx, MC, V. **Map** p248 D3.
This disco-bar and restaurant has a strict door policy, so get ready to be scrutinised. The DJ plays commercial house and there's some dancing, but that's
not what the Casablanca is about. *Milanesi* come
here for a spot of people-watching in the Moroccan-
theme back room before hitting some of the more
serious clubs. **Photo** *p166*.

De Sade
Via G Piazzi 4 (02 688 8898/www.desade.it). Bus 82,
90, 91, 92/tram 3. **Open** 9.30pm-4am Wed, Fri-Sun.
Closed June-Aug. **Admission** €15-€20 incl 1 drink.
Credit MC, V. **Map** p248 D1.

The name says it all: dress as wildly as you dare and
don't be surprised if the most glamorous women
head for the men's loo. Different nights cater to different clientele, so check the website first.

Gasoline Club
Via Bonnet 11A (mobile 339 7745 797/www.
discogasoline.it). Metro Garibaldi/bus 94/tram 29,
30. **Open** 10.30pm-5am Thur-Sat. Closed mid June-
Aug. **Admission** €12-€16 incl 1 drink. **Credit** MC,
V. **Map** p248 D3.
Situated near hip corso Como, this small club fea-
tures everything from 1980s pop to deep house.
Don't miss the brilliant Popstarz on a Thursday,
which is popular with the gay crowd (*see p159*).

Hollywood
Corso Como 15 (02 659 8996/www.discoteca
hollywood.com). Metro Garibaldi/tram 11, 29, 30,
33. **Open** 10.30pm-4am Wed-Sun. Closed July, Aug.
Admission €18-€25 incl 1 drink. **Credit** AmEx,
DC, MC, V. **Map** p248 D3.
There's a high model-to-mortal ratio in this locale:
suck in your cheeks and look bored if you want
to stand a chance of fitting in. Friday is student
night, Sunday is the time to spot soccer players and
their buxom brides, Tuesday is hip hop, Wednesday
is called Sodoma, attracting a huge, sexed-up crowd
(*see p159*), and Thursday is straight house music.
Music is largely commercial.

Leoncavallo
Via Watteau 7 (02 670 5185/www.leoncavallo.org).
Bus 43/tram 1. **Open** 8.30pm-1am Mon-Thur, Sun;
8.30pm-4am Fri, Sat. **Admission** free; occasional
small charge. **No credit cards.**
The Leonka (as locals call it) is an institution for the
city's left-wing youth. A very active *centro sociale*,
it hosts talking shops and protest meetings in the
afternoon and more underground entertainment at
night, with DJs playing sets until the wee hours.
Drinks are cheap, as is the late-serving cafeteria.

Old Fashion Café
Viale E Alemagna 6 (02 805 6231/www.oldfashion.it).
Metro Cadorna/bus 61/tram 1, 27. **Open** 9pm-4am
Mon-Tue, Thur-Sat; 8pm-4am Wed; noon-4pm, 7pm-
1am Sun. **Admission** €10-€20 incl 1 drink. **Credit**
AmEx, MC, V. **Map** p248 D5.
Central and hip, the Old Fashion Café draws a
crowd throughout the week. If beautiful people
are what you're after, Mondays and Saturdays are
best; Wednesday is student night. Sunday brunch
is good. **Photo** *p169*.

Soul To Soul
Via San Marco 33A (02 2900 6350). Metro
Moscova/bus 41, 43. **Open** 9.30pm-4am Thur-Sat;
7pm-2am Sun. **Admission** free with €20 annual
membership. **No credit cards. Map** p248 D4.
Playing hip hop and R&B, this small basement disco
is a refreshing antidote to Milan's homogenous dancing scene. The place gets pretty hot and sweaty, and
it's definitely a long way from chic, but if commercial house is wearing you down, give it a go.

Midnight munchies

Once upon a time in Milan, late-night sandwich counters were the domain of drunks, prostitutes, travel writers and other cadaveric characters who wandered the streets at 3am. But that stigma is fading. Now endearingly referred to by the Spanish term *chiringuito* – a nod to the culture that perfected the art of nocturnal eating – these same sandwich counters have become bona fide locales where well-dressed party-goers and seedy snackers alike share the fluorescent lighting and greasy fare that define pre-dawn culture in Milan. You won't find them in the *Yellow Pages*, of course – these mobile units have no phones or addresses, and they rely on diesel generators for electricity – but you can be pretty sure to find them in their usual haunts, mostly parked near discos.

One of the most popular sits at the northern end of corso Como, right outside the exits of Casablanca Café, Hollywood (for both, *see p167*) and Tocqueville 13 (*see below*).

Another is cheekily parked by the taxi rank in Parco Sempione, near the exit of Old Fashion Café (*see p167*). In the general vicinity of Rolling Stone and Plastic (for both, *see below*), by the courthouse, is an old-school purveyor of hot dogs. Then there's the sandwich stand at the south end of corso Genova, by the Navigli... the list goes on. Our favourite, though, is the caravan that often pops up by the Lima metro station in winter time, on corso Buenos Aires. Invariably outfitted with a well-worn hog's carcass on the counter, it provides the main ingredient for delicious *porchetta* sandwiches.

The latest mutation of this odd breed of eaterie is the summertime *chiringuito*, slinging thirst-slaking watermelon slices to sweat-soaked dancers. These carts hang out by the most popular summer venues, especially by the Idroscalo near Linate airport, home to Café Solaire and Punta dell'Est (for both, *see p169*) – and, incidentally, a relentless horde of mosquitoes.

Tocqueville 13

Via Tocqueville 13 (02 2900 2973/www.tocque ville13.it). Metro Garibaldi/tram 11, 29, 30, 33. **Open** 9.30pm-4am Tue-Sat; 8.30pm-4am Sun. Closed July, Aug. **Admission** €13-€20 incl 1 drink. **Credit** AmEx, MC, V. **Map** p248 D4.
Totally renovated and given a sleeker look in 2005, Tocqueville 13 attracts footballers, models and local VIPs (they're likely to be tucked away in the *privé*, of course). Expect the unexpected, music-wise, or check the website to see what's on that week as the line-up changes constantly. Dinner is served in the evening from 9.30pm, and if you eat, you too can be privy to the *privé*.

San Babila & East

Plastic

Viale Umbria 120 (02 733 996/www.clubplastic.biz). Bus 92/tram 12. **Open** midnight-5am Fri, Sat, 1 or 2 Thur per mth; 8pm-2am Sun. Closed July, Aug. **Admission** €10-€20 incl 1 drink. **No credit cards. Map** p251 H7.
At this enduringly trendy spot – possibly the best club in Milan – you can dance 'til late to an agreeable mix of sounds (electro, indie, rock, Italian trash, '80s pop). It's a popular (not only) gay destination and a prime place to spot some of the city's loveliest drag queens. Electro DJs spin the tunes once a month at Plastic On Thursday – try to catch it. Oh, and be sure to dress to impress, or you'll never make it past the bouncers.

Rolling Stone

Corso XXII Marzo 32 (02 733 172/www.rolling stone.it). Bus 45, 73/tram 12, 27. **Open** 11pm-5am Fri, Sat. **Admission** €12-€15 incl 1 drink. **Credit** AmEx, MC, V. **Map** p251 H7.
Milan's leading rock venue spreads over three floors and offers gigs during the week and dancing on Fridays and Saturdays. The sounds vary from floor to floor and include hip hop, ragga and Latin music.

Porta Romana & South

Café Atlantique

Viale Umbria 42 (199 111 111/www.cafeatlantique. com). Bus 90, 91, 92. **Open** 9pm-4am Tue-Sat; 7.30pm-4am Sun. Closed July, Aug. **Admission** €10-€25 incl 1 drink. **Credit** MC, V. **Map** p251 H9.
If you don't seriously dress up, you'll never get through the door here. Positioned beneath an incredible modern chandelier, the circular bar in the centre of the main room is one of the best places in the city to watch Milan's 'I'm too cool' crowd, or *fighetti*.

Lime Light

Via Castelbarco 11 (02 5831 0682). Bus 79, 90, 91. **Open** 11pm-4am Wed, Fri, Sat. Closed July, Aug. **Admission** €10-€15 incl 1 drink. **Map** p250 D9.
This club seems to suffer from a personality disorder: not only is it a venue for live music, it also opens its doors to students (on Wednesdays, commercial music) and private parties. For cutting-edge music, go elsewhere, but you can't deny it's a crowd magnet.

Magazzini Generali

Via Pietrasanta 14 (02 5521 1313). Bus 90, 91/tram 24. **Open** 11.30pm-4am Wed, Fri, Sat. Closed June-Aug. **Admission** €20 Fri; €15 Sat. Free Wed. **Credit** MC, V. **Map** p251 F10.

With a capacity of about 1,000, Magazzini hosts musical acts of every genre as well as popular club nights. Avoid Wednesdays unless you're after a student crowd. JetLag on Fridays is a Milanese classic: heavily gay but not exclusively so, with muscular go-go dancers and house, techno, electro and minimal music (guests include Tiga, Tiefschwarz, Jeff Mills and the resident DJ Lele Sacchi). Saturdays are more commercial and attract a younger set.

Rocket

Via Pezzotti 52 (02 8950 3509/www.therocket.it). Bus 79, 95/tram 3, 15. **Open** 10pm-2am daily. Closed Aug. **Admission** free. **No credit cards**. **Map** p250 D11.

More than two years after it opened, Rocket is still fresh on everyone's lips. This DJ bar became popular thanks to a simple (yet rare, in Milan) formula: the entry is free, the sounds are excellent (rock, electro, classic) and the bartender mixes brilliant cocktails. Try to catch Miss Barbarella – who belts out Italian '80s pop – on a Tuesday.

6essanta5inque Metri Quadri

Via Casale 54 (02 3651 1124/www.65metri quadri.it). Metro Porta Genova/bus 47, 74/tram 2. **Open** 10pm-2am daily. Closed Aug. **Admission** free. **No credit cards**. **Map** p250 B9.

Though it's small in size (65sq m, to be precise), '*il 65*' is big on ideas. The dancefloor gets wild, and guest DJs crank up techno, electro and house tunes once a month (Luomo, Abe Duque and Mr Fingers are ones to watch out for). Come on a Friday night for People.

Summer venues

Most of the action on summer nights is at the Idroscalo, a huge man-made lake near Linate airport. It's is not the easiest place to reach by public transport, so start saving for a cab now. At the southern entrance, **Café Solaire** is one of the most popular summer party places. Nearby is **Punta dell'Est**, another club worth checking out. Back in the city, **Borgo del Tempo Perso** is also a busy summer hangout, with DJs, drinks and dancing in its two gardens and inside. From Friday to Sunday it hosts **Karma**, attracting an in-the-know crowd.

In summer the Navigli area is closed to traffic after 8.30pm, and canal-side bars and cafés stay open until late. Brera, corso Como and Porta Ticinese also come out on to the pavement.

Borgo del Tempo Perso/Karma

Via Fabio Massimo 36, East (02 569 4755/www. borgodeltempoperso.com). Metro Corvetto or Porto di Mare. **Open** May-Sept 11.30pm-4am Thur-Sun (Borgo), Tue, Fri-Sun (Karma). Oct-Apr 8.30pm-4am Thur; 9.30pm-4am Fri, Sat; 8pm-2am Sun. **Admission** €15-€20 incl 1 drink. **Credit** AmEx, DC, MC, V.

Café Solaire

Gate 7, Circonvallazione Idroscalo, Segrate, East (02 5530 5169/www.cafesolaire.it). **Open** May-Sept 9.30pm-4am Thur-Sat; 6pm-2am Sun. **Admission** €10-€18 incl 1 drink. **Credit** MC, V.

Punta dell'Est

Circonvallazione Idroscalo, Segrate, East (02 607 1253). **Open** June-Sept 11pm-4am. **Admission** €10-€25. **No credit cards**.

Old Fashion Café. *See p167.*

Sport & Fitness

How the beautiful people stay so slim.

Once upon a time, keeping fit in Italy as a tourist meant taking the stairs instead of the lift, as there were very few 'proper' fitness centres. Even during the 1970s and '80s, when the idealised waistline shrank by inches, exercise was something the Milanese did with a football, or maybe with some legwarmers in front of the TV. Indeed, it's only in the last decade that regular gym-going has taken off, and even now there isn't much choice for the casual visitor.

In Milan, sweating and pumping iron are taken in equal doses with spa-soaking and meditating in chill-out rooms. Virtually every other conceivable way of getting fit indoors – dancing, spinning, judo, swimming, yoga, boxing, squash, and more – is offered in the sprawling complexes, so much so that they have become essentially the only place where the moneyed Milanese burn off their aperitifs (when they're not out of town, on the slopes or at the beach, that is). This is only natural in a city whose tight and busy streets, flat, inland geography and generally poor air quality make outdoor exercise a near impossibility.

Cycling

There are three main cycle paths in Milan, each passing historic sites and patches of natural beauty. The longest path crosses the whole city, from the waterfalls of the Martesana canal in the north-east, along much of the canal's length, through Parco Sempione and Brera to Porta Genova in the south-west.

The paths along the Naviglio Pavese and the Naviglio Grande lead south to the towns of Pavia and Abbiategrasso. The former track passes locks designed by Leonardo da Vinci, but is rough riding: you'll need a mountain bike to handle the bumps. The latter track is a dream, often consisting of finished jogging surfaces and populated mostly by fellow cyclists. Abbiategrasso, just an hour away at racing speed, is quite bland, but the path continues up past verdant stretches with views of the Alps. A further 15 kilometres (9.5 miles) down the road, heading south-west, is the medieval town of Vigevano.

See also p171 **On yer bike**. For bike hire, *see p223*.

Football

Stadio Giuseppe Meazza – aka **San Siro** (named after the neighbourhood; *see also p96*) – is perhaps the most renowned stadium in Italy. Third-ring seats are pretty far away from the pitch, but unlike Rome's Stadio Olimpico, for example, the field is not surrounded by an athletics track, which means the stands are closer to the action. San Siro's other attraction is ease of exit: apparently, no stadium in the world can fill up or empty out as quickly.

Most importantly, the San Siro is home to two of Italy's top teams, AC Milan and Inter Milan. The former was established in 1899 by a group of British expats, who found themselves with few outlets for English sports in a cycling-mad city. So successful was AC Milan that in 1908 the Italian Football Federation harshly decided to exclude foreign players from the championship. The internationals on AC's roster formed their own club and called it Football Club Internazionale, or Inter. Eventually, they won the right to compete in the championship and a rivalry that stands to this day was born.

Once upon a time, team affiliations cleaved fairly neatly down political lines. From the 1950s up until Silvio Berlusconi bought a nearly bankrupt AC in 1986, *milanisti* were known as *cacciaviti* (screwdrivers), a reference to the club's blue-collar fan base. In the tumultuous 1970s, the club represented the hard left, and the red of their red-and-black strip signalled their communist leanings. Inter, on the other hand – with regal blue-and-black stripes – has always been associated with the bourgeoisie. The Moratti family of oil barons have presided over the club for most of the 20th century.

The two teams face each other in the San Siro stadium twice a year, once in autumn and once in winter or spring. If you're lucky enough to secure a ticket to one of these matches, make sure you turn up a good hour ahead of time to secure your spot. Each team's *curva*, or end zone, is the most raucous (ironically, the safest places are away from the police, as they're the most common target for missiles).

At the **Museo Inter e Milan**, located by Gate 21 of the stadium (02 404 2432, www.sansirotour.com), you can admire memorabilia, brush up on your Italian football

On yer bike

It's widely assumed that the pink pages of *Gazzetta dello Sport* exist in order to feed the national passion for football, yet the sport that gave birth to the *Gazzetta* is not football at all, but rather Italy's first love, and enduring mistress: the bicycle.

In the early part of the 20th century, when football was a boy's game played on parish fields, the men at café tables talked about the exploits of the country's cycling champions, played out every May in Italy's answer to the Tour de France, the Giro d'Italia. The Milan-based paper launched the first edition of the Giro in 1909, starting in Milan's piazzale Loreto (to the north-east of the city), and it has dressed the tour's leader in a pink jersey ever since. The ultimate winner is decided in the Alps to the north of Milan. As you head out of town and into the Lombard countryside, it's easy to see why this area is the capital of the sport in Italy: sprinkling the landscape are the headquarters of such enduring cycling marques as Bianchi, Campagnolo and De Rosa.

Every Sunday morning, hundreds of cycling enthusiasts in colourful lycra make the exodus from the city on northbound avenues and into the hills. Newcomers and visitors would do well to simply wait on piazzale Loreto or the adjoining viale Monza at about 7am and ask if they can tag along.

You haven't brought your gear? No problem: the city is home to some excellent family-run bike stores that are worth a visit, both for their products but also for the expertise of the people behind the counter (who might even have a father who has raced in the Giro d'Italia).

Located to the west of Milan, at the city's Vigorelli velodrome, **Alberto Masi** runs his eponymous shop (via Arona 19, 02 3310 1647, www.albertomasi.it, closed Sun, Aug), which was founded by his father, Faliero, who rode twice in the Giro d'Italia in the 1930s.

Masi Senior then went on to build bikes for many of the greatest riders of the 20th century, Aldo Bini, Fausto Coppi, Eddy Merckx and Jacque Anquetil among them.

Another family affair, the **Detto Pietro** store (viale Vittorio Veneto 8, East, 02 2940 5018, www.dettopietro.com, closed Sun, 2wks Aug) continues a tradition that began in 1895, when the Detto family manufactured the world's first bicycle shoes (an early pair still hangs on the wall). Besides clothing and shoes, the Dettos make a pretty mean frame. Over on corso Garibaldi, **Cicli Rossignoli** (No.71, North, 02 804960, www.rossignoli.it), was built up by the owner of the original store, Ettore Rossignoli, from the rubble of the family's original shops, which were bombed during World War II. It's now one of the best-regarded cycling shops in the city. Located, appropriately, near the bicycle-shop-turned-hip-bar Le Biciclette, **I Signori del Ciclismo** (via Gaudenzio Ferrari 8, South, 02 8940 1498, www.isignoridelciclismo.it, closed Sun, 3wks Aug) is a superb neighbourhood shop run by friendly and competent cyclists who can fix any problem in a hurry. The selection of racing bikes includes lovely ones by De Rosa.

trivia and take a tour of the stadium. On match days, a ticket for the game allows entrance to the museum from three hours before kick-off.

TICKETS

AC Milan vs Inter matches generally sell out way in advance, though touts outside the stadium will sell you a ticket… at a price. Tickets to AC Milan home games are sold at **Milan Point** (via San Gottardo 2, entrance in piazza XXIV Maggio, South, 02 8942 2711, closed Sun). For Inter home games, try any branch of **Banca Popolare di Milano** (a central one is at via Meravigli 2, 02 8646 0598, www.bpm.it, closed Sat, Sun). The sky's the limit when it comes to prices, though cheap ones start at €11.

Stadio Giuseppe Meazza (San Siro)
Via Piccolomini 5, West (02 404 2432/02 4879 8253/www.sansirotour.com). Metro Lotto/tram 24.

Golf

The countryside around Milan has some of the most beautiful golf courses in Italy. However, almost all require membership. A notable exception is Golf Le Rovedine, the only public course in Lombardy.

Golf Le Rovedine
Via Karl Marx 18, Noverasco di Opera, South (02 5760 6420/www.rovedine.com). Metro Porta Romana then tram 24. **Open** *Mar-Nov* 8am-8pm daily. *Dec-Feb* 8am-6pm daily. Closed 2wks Aug, 2wks Dec-Jan. **Rates** €40 Mon-Fri; €65 Sat, Sun. **Credit** AmEx, DC, MC, V.
This basic, par-72 course is 7km (4.5 miles) outside the city. It draws a crowd in good weather, especially at weekends, so booking is always advisable.

Gyms

Nowadays much of Milanese fitness revolves around gyms, or *centri di benessere* (health and fitness centres). Facilities commonly include dance studios, sunbeds, nutritionists, pools, hairdressers, saunas, climbing walls and equipment stores. For tourists, however, they can be pricey and/or out of the way, so hotel gyms are often a better bet. For the city's best spas, see p139 **Shopping and flopping**.

Downtown Palestre
Piazza Cavour 2, North (02 7601 1485/www.down townpalestre.it). Metro Turati/bus 61, 94/tram 1, 2. **Open** 7am-midnight Mon-Fri; 10am-9pm Sat, Sun. Closed 2wks Aug. **Rates** €50 per day; €170 per mth. **Credit** AmEx, MC, V. **Map** p249 E5.
Downtown's clientele consists of the rich, the famous and the very beautiful, including models keeping catwalk-trim for the spring and autumn fashion shows. In addition to a variety of classes, there are two floors of gym equipment, including treadmills and stairclimbers, while a spa and beauty centre (02 7631 7233) offers all kinds of pampering treatments. Note that the other branch closes an hour earlier. **Other locations:** piazza Diaz 6, Centre (02 863 1181).

Skorpion Club
Corso Vittorio Emanuele 24, East (02 781 424). Metro San Babila/bus 54, 60, 65/tram 12, 27. **Open** 7am-10pm Mon-Fri; 10am-7pm Sun. **Rates** €70 per day; €150 per week. Closed Aug. **Credit** AmEx, MC, V. **Map** p251 E6/p252 E6.
Skorpion is the most central gym in Milan and is therefore pricey. It offers a full range of activities, including Turkish baths for men and women. The 11th-floor solarium has a sweeping view of the city.

Tonic Club
Via Mestre 7, East (02 2641 0158/www.tonicnet.it). Metro Udine/bus 55, 75. **Open** 7am-midnight Mon-Fri; 9am-7.30pm Sat, Sun. **Rates** €20 per day; €150 for 10 sessions. **Credit** MC, V.

Tonic is a national chain of gyms, based in large, industrial spaces and generally devoid of the glamour of the clubs closer to the centre. This location has four squash courts and racket rental, plus dance lessons, climbing wall and martial arts training.

Squash

Although old-school *milanesi* still opt for tennis in clubs that require year-long memberships, squash is becoming increasingly popular in Milan: it's quick, played indoors and has a northern European feel. Slower outdoor sports, the city's *squashisti* believe, are best left to the Romans. *See also above* **Tonic Club**.

Vico Squash
Via GB Vico 38, West (02 4800 2762/02 4801 0890/www.vicogroup.it). Metro Sant'Agostino/bus 50, 94/tram 2, 14. **Open** 7am-11pm Mon, Wed; 8.30am-11pm Tue, Thur, Fri; 10am-9pm Sat, Sun. **Rates** €50 per day; €300 per 3mths; €840 per year. **Credit** MC, V. **Map** p250 B7.
With a dozen squash courts, this is the place to practice Milan's favourite new sport.

Swimming pools

While most private gyms have their own pools, many Milanese opt for a pay-as-you-go plan. Public pools are much cheaper, though the open-access swimming schedules can be very complicated. Remember your bathing cap – you won't be allowed to use the pool without one. Times below are for open-access swimming; at other times, pools are usually used for classes.

Piscina Cozzi
Viale Tunisia 35, East (02 659 9703/www.milano sport.it). Metro Porta Venezia or Repubblica/tram 2, 11, 29, 30. **Open** noon-11pm Mon; 7.30am-2.30pm Tue, Thur; 8.30am-4.30pm, 6-9.30pm Wed; 8.30am-4.30pm Fri; 10am-5.30pm Sat, Sun. **Rates** €4 Mon-Fri; €5 Sat, Sun; €40 per 11 visits; €250 annual pass. **No credit cards. Map** p249 F4.
Built in 1934, with a typically grandiose fascist exterior and a Soviet interior, this is one of Milan's most popular and populist pools. It's Olympic-size, but often crowded. Opening hours are extended during the hottest months.

Piscina Solari
Via Montevideo 20, West (02 469 5278/www.milano sport.it). Metro Sant'Agostino/bus 50/tram 14, 29, 30. **Open** 7-9.30am, noon-3pm Mon, Thur; 7-9.30am, 11.30am-3pm, 6.30-11.30pm Tue, Fri; 7-9.30am, 10.30am-3pm, 10-11.30pm Wed; 1-7.30pm Sat; 10am-7.30pm Sun. **Rates** €4 Mon-Fri; €5 Sat, Sun; €40 per 11 visits. **Credit** AmEx, DC, MC, V. **Map** p250 A8.
This is one of the city's more modern-looking public pools, with floor-to-roof windows looking out on to the park, but there are few frills and the staff can be surly. Scuba courses are also available.

Theatre & Dance

Milan's under-funded companies are making dramas out of a cash crisis.

Uplifting performance: **Teatro Smeraldo**. *See p175.*

See p175.

It was once said – a little cruelly, perhaps – that the Italians don't make good actors as they are too busy acting in everyday life. That's as may be, but theatre in Italy has traditionally taken second place to opera as the chief form of stage entertainment. This is especially true of Milan: after all, La Scala is the city's main theatre.

Historically, the growth of a national theatre was also hampered by the dominance of local dialects. It was hard to write for an audience in Italian when only a minority of the population actually spoke the language, although in the latter half of the 19th century, unification began to change that. The lack of home-grown theatre could also explain why so much programming involves translations of international authors, although this is also testament to Italy's receptiveness to other cultures.

Nevertheless, Italian – and Milanese – theatre has produced some giants of its own over the years. Nobel Prize winner Dario Fo, for example, is best known for the 1970 international smash hit *The Accidental Death of an Anarchist*, based on real events in the city (*see p80*). Fo, who

moved from Lago Maggiore to Milan as a young man, cut his teeth performing cabaret in the city. He and his wife Franca Rame don't tread the boards in Milan much these days (a pity, as their stage shows were memorable), preferring to dedicate their energies to less noble pursuits like running for mayor.

Milan theatre's other legend is the late, great Giorgio Strehler (1921-97), who is justly honoured with a theatre in his own name. A highly influential director, he is credited with, among other things, introducing the rest of the world, and indeed Italy, to the works of the Venetian playwright Carlo Goldoni.

As elsewhere, theatre in Milan is divided into high- and lowbrow. Sadly, several theatres go in for lightweight entertainment, which is often a vehicle for TV stars whose physical attributes are more impressive than their acting ability. This criticism does not, however, apply to the stars of the *Zelig* stand-up show, which is one of the country's better TV programmes.

The more 'cultural' theatre, on the other hand, is struggling with an acute cash shortage.

In 2005 the government cut theatre funding in half, and what little there is, in addition to being too little, is often too late. The money is allocated for the season that is already in progress, but it rarely gets handed over until the season is actually finished.

Milan also offers a range of contemporary dance options. **CRT Teatro Dell'Arte** has a Short Formats Festival, while the **Teatro Smeraldo**, which is mainly a musical venue, hosts organisations like the Parsons Dance Company and the circus group Les Farfadais. As a venue, however, pride of place goes to **La Scala** (*see p162* **Melodrama at La Scala**).

INFORMATION AND TICKETS

Individual theatres put on several productions during the course of the year. In London's West End or on Broadway, a show will run as long as it draws an audience: in Milan, it tends to run for a pre-established fortnight. Therefore, if you hear about a show that sounds appealing, you need to book pretty much immediately, otherwise it will pass you by.

Milan's theatre season, like just about everything else in the city, grinds to a halt in the summer months. It's also worth remembering that Milan theatres are 'dark' on a Monday night, while Sundays usually feature afternoon matinées and, in one or two cases, morning shows.

Until a few years ago, buying tickets for Milanese theatre shows was far from straightforward. Audience members were expected to queue at the theatre box office at selected times several days ahead of the date in question and, as a result, they would often spend as much time buying the tickets as seeing the show itself. This frustrating state of affairs is thankfully beginning to change as Italian theatres are coming to terms with such revolutionary concepts as phone bookings, a few decades after the rest of the western world. Yet many theatres still refuse to accept credit cards, even if the growth of central online booking agencies like TicketOne (www.ticketone.com) and Vivaticket by Charta (www.vivaticket.it) has improved the situation. The online agencies do accept credit cards and most theatre website sites will direct you towards them.

Should you be staying in Milan for a while, you might be interested in the **Invito a Teatro** scheme. For €68 you can choose eight shows to see over a single season at 16 city theatres, including nine listed in this chapter (labelled with an asterisk *). The pass is available from the theatres themselves or from TicketOne in the Spazio Oberdan centre on viale Vittorio Veneto 2 (02 7740 6384).

Venues & companies

*CRT

Teatro Dell'Arte *Via Alemagna 6, West. Metro Cadorna/bus 61/tram 1, 29, 30*. **Map** p248 B5. **CRT Salone** *Via Dini 7, South. Metro Abbiategrasso/tram 3, 15*. **Both** *02 8901 1644/www.teatrocrt.it*. **Season** Oct-May. **Open** *Box office* 11.30am-7pm Mon-Sat; 3-4pm Sun. **Performances** *Teatro Dell'Arte* 8.45pm Tue-Sun; 4pm Sun. *CRT Salone* 9pm Tue-Sat; 4pm Sun. **Tickets** €18; €9-€12 concessions. **Credit** MC, V.

This company, which was founded in the 1970s, has two locations. One is adjacent to the Palazzo dell'Arte, on the edge of Parco Sempione, while the other, the CRT Salone, is in via Dini, on the south side of town. CRT stands for Centro di Ricerca per il Teatro (Centre for Theatre Research) and it is considered Italy's leading forum for theatrical experimentation. Its programme combines contemporary drama, opera and classical theatre. Dance is also a feature: its Short Formats Dance Festival in October features over a dozen European companies.

*Teatro Arsenale

Via Correnti 11, South (02 8321 999/www.teatro arsenale.org). Metro Sant'Ambrogio/bus 94/tram 2, 3, 14. **Season** Sept-June. **Open** *Box office* 6-8pm Tue-Fri; 2-8pm Sat; 3.45-4.30pm Sun. **Performances** 9.15pm Tue-Sat; 4.30pm Sun. **Tickets** €15; €11 concessions. **No credit cards**. **Map** p250 C7/p252 C7.

This theatre is housed in a deconsecrated 13th-century church at the far (ie, non-Duomo) end of via Torino. The company, directed by Annig Raimondi, tends to specialise in either contemporary work or older material by authors not generally known for theatre (such as Sartre, Copi and Céline).

*Teatro Carcano

Corso di Porta Romana 63, South (02 5518 1377/ www.teatrocarcano.com). Metro Crocetta/bus 77, 94/tram 16. **Season** Oct-May. **Open** *Box office* 10am-6.30pm Mon; 10am-8pm Tue-Sat; 1-6.30pm Sun. **Tickets** €23-€32. **No credit cards**. **Map** p251 E8.

This theatre opened its doors in 1803 (a couple of years before Napoleon had himself crowned king of Italy) and was subsequently the setting for the debut performances of operas by Bellini and Donizetti. Not surprisingly, productions tend to concentrate on theatre classics (such as Shakespeare, Sophocles, Molière and Pirandello) and are of high quality. It also has a programme of events for children.

Teatro Ciak

Via Sangallo 33, East (02 7611 0093/www.teatro ciak.it). Bus 38, 54, 93/tram 5. **Season** Sept-May. **Open** *Box office* 10am-6.30pm Mon-Sat; 3pm-9pm Sun. **Performances** 9pm Tue-Sun. **Tickets** €12-€26. **Credit** MC, V.

Leo Wachter – who organised the first Beatles concert in Italy – turned this cinema into a theatre in 1977. Today Ciak (which is the onomatopoeic sound made by a clapperboard at the start of film-ing) works closely with two musical venues, Teatro Smeraldo and the Ventaglio Nazionale, and tends to concentrate on cabaret and comedy; several stars from the cult stand-up show *Zelig* perform here. Ciak also does a line in dance and musical comedy.

*Teatro dell'Elfo

Via Ciro Menotti 11, East (02 716 791/www. elfo.org). Bus 54, 61/tram 5, 11. **Season** Oct-June. **Open** *Box office* (at Teatro Leonardo da Vinci, Via Ampere 1, 02 2668 1166) 11.30am-8pm Mon-Sat. **Phone reservations** (02 716 791) 2.30-6.30pm Mon-Fri. **Tickets** €19 (€11 Tue); €9.50-€12 concessions. **No credit cards. Map** p249 H6.

This is the home of the Teatridithalia Elfo compa-ny, which also performs at the Teatro Leonardo da Vinci (*see below*). The group was founded in 1973 by, among others, a young Gabriele Salvatores, who went on to direct movies such as the award-winning *Mediterraneo*. Teatridithalia Elfo has a reputation for non-traditional, hard-hitting theatre. Note that the company should be moving to more spacious premises in corso Buenos Aires in 2008.

*Teatro Franco Parenti

Via Cadolini 19, South (02 5518 7056/www.teatro francoparenti.com). Bus 90, 91, 92/tram 16. **Season** Oct-late May. **Open** *Box office* Via Giorgio Vasari (02 5999 5700) 10am-6.30pm Mon-Sat; 11am-12.30pm Sun. *Box office* Via Cadolini 2.30-6.30pm Mon-Sat; 11am-12.30pm Sun. **Tickets** €25; €9-€12.50 concessions. **Performances** 9pm Tue-Sat; 4.30pm Sun. **Credit** MC, V.

The original theatre in via Vasari is closed for renovation until the 2007-8 season. In the meantime, the company is using temporary premises in a nearby converted factory on via Cadolini. Director Andrée Ruth Shammah is renowned for his tireless fund-raising and for producing a varied programme of quality. To give an idea, the 2005-6 calendar included work by Beckett, Pinter, Pirandello and the Neapolitan legend Eduardo de Filippo.

*Teatro Leonardo da Vinci

Via Ampère 1, at piazza Leonardo da Vinci, East (02 2668 1166/www.elfo.org). Metro Piola/bus 62, 90, 91/tram 11, 23. **Season** Oct-June. **Open** *Box office* 11.30am-8pm Mon-Sat. **Tickets** €19 (€11 Tue); €9.50-€12 concessions. **No credit cards.**

This is the home of the Quelli di Grock, an experi-mental theatre company established in 1976. One of its founders, Maurizio Nichetti, went on to become an acclaimed film director. The theatre originally concentrated on mime, clowns and dance, but it has recently gone in for reinterpretations of classics, such as Molière, Goldoni, Beckett and Shakespeare. It also runs a theatre school (at another location) and hosts the Teatridithalia Elfo company (*see above*).

*Teatro Litta

Corso Magenta 24, West (02 8645 4545/www. teatrolitta.it). Metro Cadorna/bus 18, 50, 54/tram 19, 24. **Season** late Sept-late May. **Open** *Box office*

2.30-7pm Mon-Sat. **Performances** 8.30pm Tue-Sat; 4.30pm Sun. **Tickets** €17; €8.50-€12 concessions. **Credit** MC, V. **Map** p249 C6/p252 C6.

This theatre is housed in a splendid baroque build-ing in an elegant part of Milan. The company, on the other hand, is young and endeavours to present the work of contemporary authors or rethink the clas-sics. A recent production of *Macbeth*, for example, divided the character in two: Mac was a DJ, Beth his loser girlfriend.

Teatro Manzoni

Via Manzoni 42, Centre (02 763 6901/www.teatro manzoni.it). Metro Montenapoleone/bus 61, 94/tram 1, 2. **Season** Oct-June. **Open** *Box office* 10am-7pm Mon-Sat; 11am-5pm Sun. **Performances** 8.45pm Tue-Sat; 11am (concerts), 3.30pm Sun. **Tickets** €28-€30. **Credit** MC, V. **Map** p249 E5.

This theatre is part of the vast media empire of Silvio Berlusconi. The programme tends to feature TV stars in light comedy for an audience that has been described as 'the bourgeoisie in fur coats', but the 2005-6 line-up also included some Pirandello and Joe Orton's *What the Butler Saw*. The theatre does Sunday morning concerts: Bobby 'Don't Worry Be Happy' McFerrin performed at one such show.

Teatro Nuovo

Piazza San Babila, Centre (02 7600 0086/www. teatronuovo.it). Metro San Babila/bus 37, 54, 60/tram 2, 3, 14, 27. **Season** Oct-May. **Open** *Box office* 11am-6pm Tue-Sun; 11am-1pm, 4.30-6pm Sun. **Performances** 8.45pm Tue-Sat; 4pm Sun. **Tickets** prices vary. **Credit** MC, V. **Map** p249 F6/p252 F6.

In spite of its central address, this theatre is hard to find, located downstairs among the shopping arcade colonnades at San Babila. The programme tends to feature comedies and musicals that are often vehi-cles for TV starlets. The company also performs work by Sandro Mayer, whose gossip mag publica-tions often combine scantily clad women with national religious legend Padre Pio.

*Teatro Out Off

Via Mac Mahon 16, North (02 3453 2140/www. teatrooutoff.it). Tram 12, 14. **Season** Nov-early July. **Open** *Box office* 11pm-1am, 7-8.30pm Mon-Fri; 11am-1pm, 4-8.30pm Sat; 3-4pm Sun. **Performances** 8.45pm Tue-Sat; 4pm Sun. **Tickets** €15. **No credit cards. Map** p248 A2.

This company, which opened for business in 1976, moved to new premises (a converted cinema) in November 2004. Over the years it has acquired a rep-utation for serious theatre, with works by Arthur Miller, Edward Bond, Tennessee Williams and Pier Paolo Pasolini, the film director murdered in 1975.

Teatro Smeraldo

Piazza XXV Aprile 10, North (02 2900 6767/ www.smeraldo.it). Metro Garibaldi or Moscova/ bus 43/tram 11, 29, 30, 33. **Season** Sept-June. **Open** *Box office* 10am-6.30pm Mon-Sat; 10am-1pm Sun. **Performances** 8.45pm Tue-Sat; 4pm Sun. **Tickets** €30 (€15 concessions); €26 Wed (€13 concessions). **No credit cards. Map** p248 D4.

Arts & Entertainment

This 2,000-seater is one of the city's largest theatres, although it tends to concentrate on music and dance, rather than drama. The calendar is eclectic, to say the least: Michael Bolton, Tracy Chapman, ballet (*Giselle*, for example) and the popular Italian comedy trio, Aldo, Giovanni and Giacomo. **Photo** *p173*.

*Piccolo Theatre Group

Piccolo Teatro Strehler *Largo Greppi, North.* **Metro** *Lanza/bus 43, 57, 61, 70/tram 1, 3, 4, 12, 14.* **Map** p248 D5.
Piccolo Teatro Studio *Via Rivoli 6, North. Metro Lanza/bus 43, 57, 61, 70/tram 1, 3, 4, 12, 14.* **Map** p248 D5.
Piccolo Teatro Grassi *Via Rovello 2, Centre. Metro Cordusio/bus 199/tram 1, 3, 12, 14, 16, 27, 19.* **Map** p250 D6/p252 D6.
All *02 7233 3222/www.piccoloteatro.org.* **Season** Sept-July. **Open** *Box office* 10am-6.45pm Mon-Sat;

1-6.30pm Sun. **Performances** 7.30pm Tue, Sat; 8.30pm Wed-Fri; 4pm Sun. **Tickets** prices vary. **Credit** AmEx, DC, MC, V.
Named in honour of the great late director Giorgio Strehler, the Piccolo Teatro Strehler is generally acknowledged as city's top theatre. Its director, Luca Ronconi, is highly respected, while the fact that the theatre is publicly owned means that it is one of the very few to receive adequate funding. There are actually three theatres: the Teatro Strehler and the Teatro Studio are at the main site (which looks like a smaller, red-brick version of London's National Theatre), while the Piccolo Teatro Grassi is in via Rovello (a stone's throw from the Duomo). It's also one of the few to offer spectators the chance to see works in English. A year-round festival features productions by the likes of Peter Brook, performed with surtitles in Italian over the stage.

Grin and Beer it

English-language stand-up in Milan? It's no joke: Paris-based Brit Karel Beer (pronounced Bear) is bringing British and other English-speaking comedians to the city with his Beer Necessities agency. Beer began importing laughs to Europe in 1995, when he persuaded Eddie Izzard to perform in Paris. English-language stand-up has since become a feature at the French capital's La Java club, and Beer has expanded his scheme to include Milan, which also has a sizeable expat community. Ross Noble was the first to perform here back in May 2003, and he has been followed by fellow Irishmen Ardal O'Hanlon and Dylan Moran, plus English comedian Shazia Mirza and Australia's Julia Morris. As Beer, an actor who does his own brief comic turn as he introduces the main act, puts it: 'I think we've had representatives of just about every English-speaking country, with the possible exception of Wales.'

Apparently, established comics love playing the low-profile venue, Le Scimmie, and even

get a kick out of putting Milan on their tour posters. The club has even attracted royalty – well, if you count Los Angeles-based Floridian Lord Carrett, that is, who performed here on his European tour in early 2006. Carrett dresses like Jerry Lee Lewis circa 1956, complete with coiffeur and leopard suit. His nostalgia for the '50s also extends to humour, and he cites the comedians who played the Catskill Mountains 'Borscht Belt' resorts as a major influence.

Le Scimmie itself, a small jazz club and restaurant in Milan's lively Navigli district, provides an intimate setting for comedians to work their wit (on average there's a stand-up show once a month). The audience is largely made up of British and American expats, although Italian friends and partners often come along for the ride. Knowing about the shows ahead of time is a challenge, as the only local listings publication that covers them is the English-language *Hello Milano*. Beer tends to work on a word-of-mouth basis, encouraging the punters to visit his website and sign up for his mailing list, while reservations can also be made on his mobile phone (see below). Tickets typically cost €20 (€17 for students), with the first drink free.

For information on stand-up acts coming to Le Scimmie, call Karel Beer on 349 0777 547, email italia@anythingmatters.com or see www.anythingmatters.com/italia.

Le Scimmie

Via Ascanio Sforza 49, South (02 8940 2874/www.scimmie.it). Metro Porta Genova/tram 3, 15. **Open** 7pm-3am Mon-Sat. **Credit** AmEx, DC, MC, V. **Map** p250 C10.

Arts & Entertainment

Trips Out of Town

Getting Started

Cities or scenery? Combine the two for the ultimate getaway.

The charm of laid-back **Varenna**. *See p206*.

Just outside Milan lies a region packed with pretty villages and breathtaking scenery. The highlight is undoubtedly the lake region – Lombardy's most visited attraction. Italy at its most romantic takes the form of lakes Maggiore, Como and Garda (and the smallish Lake Orta, which is big in beauty and cannot be omitted from this guide even though it's located in neighbouring Piedmont). Each lake is detailed in a separate chapter with itineraries that begin at the southernmost point and continue clockwise around the shores.

Lombardy is also home to several towns that make ideal day-trip destinations from Milan. Majestically built high on a hill, Bergamo prides itself as a world apart. Stressed-out Milanese come here to escape the city and to step back in time. Monza, meanwhile, is home to the famed

racetrack that hosts an annual Formula One race, but it also has several historic cities – not to mention swathes of natural parkland – on its doorstep.

Getting around Lombardy

Each chapter in this section contains information on how to get to each destination from Milan, both by car and by public transport, and on getting around within the surrounding area, but the following general information is also useful.

The Lombardy regional council's website (www.infopoint.it) has a journey planner (in Italian), as well as listings of all forms of public transport, including timetables.

Regional bus services

Around 40 national bus services pass through Stazione Garibaldi. In general they serve destinations not covered by train services.

Regional rail services

As the city's largest train station, Stazione Centrale serves most locations in Lombardy; many services also operate from the station at Porta Garibaldi. There's also a private railway service, Ferrovie Nord, which leaves from Milan's Stazione Nord near Cadorna metro station.

Driving

Once you've exited Milan's *tangenziale* (ring road) at the relevant junction, the excellent *autostrade* (motorways) will whisk you efficiently (though at a cost) from A to B, though they may be short on scenery. Alternatively, there is a far-reaching and, on the whole, well-maintained network of *strade statali* (SS; state highways), which provide a more picturesque view of the region. *Strade provinciali* (SP; provincial roads) are not always in tip-top condition and don't necessarily take the most straightforward route from A to B, but they will undoubtedly provide some memorable Lombard driving moments.

For general driving information, including car hire, *see p221*.

Food and travel

Though Milan itself boasts the culinary experience that is Peck (*see p107* **The taste maker**), the rest of Lombardy is home to a number of destination restaurants that are worth a trip in their own right. Here is a selection of our favourites. Some of them fall outside the areas covered in the guide, but we think they merit the detour.

Milan

Il Luogo di Aimo e Nadia

Via Montecuccoli 6, Milan (02 416 886/ www.aimoenadia.com). Metro Primaticcio/ bus 63, 64. **Meals served** *12.30-2pm, 8-10pm Mon-Fri; 8-10pm Sat. Closed 1wk Jan, Aug.* **Average** *€100.* **Credit** *AmEx, DC, MC, V.*
The final stop for Italy's best ingredients. Black truffle from Norcia, chestnuts from Piedmont and oversized prawns from Sanremo are deftly transformed here. Conversation-prone waiters and a colourful collection of contemporary art mean the menu is not the restaurant's only charm, but with dishes such as *riccioli con ragù di vitello e parmigiano* (pasta with veal sauce and parmesan) it's definitely one of them.

Lake Como

Vecchia Varenna

Contrada Scoscesa 14, Varenna (0341 830 793/www.vecchiavarenna.it). **Meals served** *12.30-2pm, 8-10pm Tue-Sun. Closed Jan.* **Average** *€50.* **Credit** *MC, V.*
The excitement at Vecchia Varenna is twofold: excellent food and stunning views of the lake (which is so close you can almost touch the water). The speciality is freshwater fish, including roasted pink trout with garlic. Refreshingly informal and with enough scenery to contemplate over a very long lunch.

Bergamo

L'Osteria di via Solata

Via Solata 8, Città Alta, Bergamo (035 271 993/www.osteriaviasolata.it). **Meals served** *12.30-2pm, 7.30-10pm Mon, Wed-Sat; 12.30-2pm Sun. Closed 3wks Aug.* **Average** *€75.* **Credit** *AmEx, DC, MC, V.*
Traditional recipes are interpreted with a contemporary twist by chef and sommelier Ezio Gritti. The menu features *gnocchetti* with

pigeon ragu; spaghetti with oysters, pine nuts and basil; and lamb fillet with figs in chocolate sauce. Finish with white chocolate mousse or *semifreddo* with rose petals. Extra marks for presentation and the intimate dining room.

Near Brescia

Castello Malvezzi

Via Colle San Giuseppe 1, Mompiano Brescia (030 200 4224/www.castellomalvezzi.it). **Meals served** *7.30-10.30pm Wed-Fri; 12.30-2pm, 7.30-10.30pm Sat, Sun. Closed 3wks Jan, 2wks Aug.* **Average** *€50.* **Credit** *AmEx, DC, MC, V.*
This gorgeous castle with sumptuously elegant interiors hosts wine-and-food pairing events and theme-food nights. A Franco-Italo cooking team is behind such dishes as spaghetti with prawns and a basil sauce, fish 'mosaic' and chateaubriand with bearnaise sauce.

Gualtiero Marchesi

Via Vittorio Emanuele 11, Erbusco (030 776 0562/www.marchesi.it). **Meals served** *12.30-2pm, 7.30-10pm Tue-Sat; 12.30-2pm Sun. Closed 4wks Jan-Feb.* **Average** *€120.* **Credit** *AmEx, DC, MC, V.*
Chef Gualtiero looms large in Lombardy's epicurean diary and still nabs top scores for his tried and true classic: *riso oro e zafferano* (risotto with saffron and gold leaf). Other dishes come close, though – try the *raviolo aperto* (handmade raviolo with meat, fish and vegetables) and *seppia al nero* (black cuttlefish). A word of warning: the romantic dining room has squeezed marriage proposals out of the most adamant bachelors.

Near Mantova

Dal Pescatore

Località Runate, Canneto sull'Oglio (0376 723 001/www.dalpescatore.com). **Meals served** *8-10pm Wed; noon-2pm, 8-10pm Thur-Sun. Closed 2wks Jan, 3wks Aug.* **Average** *€120-€140.* **Credit** *AmEx, DC, MC, V.*
Located in an idyllic country home, Nadia and Antonio Santini's gastronomic wonderland always features prominently on lists of Italy's best restaurants. Standout dishes include *crema di patate di montagna con calamaretti* (cream of mountain potatoes with baby squid). *See also p31.*

Trips Out of Town

Monza & the Brianza

Speed freaks and nature lovers alike will be in their element.

Villa Reale in Parco di Monza, being restored to its former glory. *See p182.*

In an attempt to hold back the expanding monster that is Milan, city limits have been drawn where no obvious break in the urban sprawl exists. The result is a ring of independent townlets that fail to provide a clear indication of where Milan ends and suburbia begins.

Towns like Cormano and Bollate to the north, Rho and Pero to the west, Buccinasco to the south, and Segrate and Peschiera Borromeo to the east conspire to make Milan seem never-ending. But the sprawl does not, cannot, extend for ever. And where it begins to break up, life becomes pretty, pleasant and plain – in the flattest, greenest sense.

Monza

The rolling hills that begin north of Milan in the Brianza countryside have largely been given over to unattractive industry, but many elegant villas and *palazzi* remain.

Monza is undoubtedly the Brianza's biggest draw. Once a metropolitan centre that rivalled Milan in size and importance, the city still retains something of its medieval character in the 13th-century town hall, or **Arengario**, and the magnificent **Duomo** (piazza Duomo, 039 323 404, closed Mon). Lombard queen Theodolinda had a chapel dedicated to St John

the Baptist built in the late sixth century where the Duomo now stands. Scant traces of this early Christian building still remain; the Duomo we see today is a mainly 14th-century structure with later additions. The lunettes above the door of the white marble Gothic façade show Theodolinda and her offspring presenting what is known as the Iron Crown to John the Baptist. In the **Cappella di Teodolinda**, located to the left of the high altar, you will see the fifth-century gem-encrusted crown – made of gold, though believed to contain an iron nail from Christ's cross – used to crown Italy's kings from the Middle Ages up to Napoleon. Around this chapel's walls are 15th-century paintings by Franceschino, Gregorio and Giovanni Zavattari depicting scenes from Theodolinda's life. Her remains are in a sarcophagus behind the altar.

A door off the left nave leads to the cemetery and the **Museo Serpero**, where treasures from the town's heyday are kept, including articles donated to the original chapel by Theodolinda and Pope Gregory the Great. Among the queen's gifts is a gilded, gem-studded missal. Theodolinda's crown – rather like a bejewelled pillbox hat – is kept here, as is a gilded silver hen with seven chicks, made some time between the fourth and seventh centuries and said to represent the seven provinces of Lombardy.

On track

In January 1922 a group of car enthusiasts gathered at the headquarters of the Milan Automobile Club and set about choosing an appropriate way to commemorate its 25-year anniversary. Several ideas were mooted, but ultimately these speed-loving gentlemen had only one thought on their minds: to create an Italian Grand Prix.

They wanted a modern racing circuit that would be big, bad and (most important of all) better than the well-established Grand Prix that their rivals, the French Automobile Club, had set up near Le Mans, on a track called the Circuit de la Sarthe, in 1906.

The Villa Reale park in Monza was chosen as the best site for the Autodromo, and work began on 15 May that year. In just 110 days, a crew of 3,500 workers created the first ten-kilometre (6.2-mile) racetrack on an area of 3.4 square kilometres (1.3 square miles).

It was only the beginning. Over its 80-year-plus lifespan, the Autodromo has had more makeovers than a Hollywood star. The track has changed from macadam to concrete to high temperature-resistant asphalt over the decades, and at one point even included curves paved with porphyry stones. When

not being used for racing, it is open to the public, and it's not unusual to see people speeding around the circuit on everything from roller skates to motorcycles.

Today the Autodromo is a year-round attraction. In terms of races, the main draw is undoubtedly the annual Formula One racing weekend (usually in September), which brings several hundred thousands of spectators. Recent years have seen Juan Pablo Montoya, Rubens Barrichello and Michael Schumacher take the chequered flag. The long, fast straights and sweeping Curva Parabolica, combined with the enthusiasm of the *tifosi* (Ferrari fans), make for an exciting race for both drivers and spectators. In addition, the complex, set within a large, verdant park, boasts camping facilities, an Olympic swimming pool and a car museum.

Autodromo Nazionale Monza

Parco di Monza, via Vedano 5 (039 24 821/ www.monzanet.it). **Open** (for driving) usually 9am-12.30pm, 2-5pm Sat, Sun (check website first). **Admission** (for driving) €30 per hr. **Credit** AmEx, DC, MC, V. Check the website for racing fixtures and details of how to reach the track.

Formula One fun.

Trips Out of Town

North of the centre, the vast **Parco di Monza** contains the **Villa Reale** (built 1771-80; viale Regina Margherita 2, 039 322 086, closed for refurbishment until 2008) – originally the summer residence of the archduke of Austria – a golf course and the **Autodromo Nazionale Monza**, the world-famous Formula One motor-racing track (*see p181* **On track**).

Extending further north from the park through forests of oak, ash, chestnut and conifers, the **Parco Naturale della Valle del Lambro** covers 65 square kilometres (25 square miles) along the banks of the River Lambro. Stop in at the park headquarters at Triuggio for maps before starting out on an eight-kilometre (five-mile) hiking or bike circuit that cuts through the densely wooded valleys of the Lambro – but be warned: the route is not always clearly marked. On a mix of dirt roads, trails and asphalt roads, you'll pass several 18th- and 19th-century villas, as well as the sprawling Renaissance complex of the Jesuit-owned Villa Sacro Cuore, though none of it is open to the public.

Around Monza

North of Monza is **Biassono**. Its town hall, Villa Verri, is a perfect example of the early 18th-century *barocchetto* style, while its **Museo Civico** (via San Martino 1, 039 220 1077, closed Mon-Thur, Sun; open only by appointment Fri, admission free) has reconstructions of Brianza farm life through the ages. In **Carate Brianza**, the Villa Cusani Confalonieri (not open to the public) is a 17th-century remodelling of a late 16th-century castle. The church of **Santi Ambrogio e Simpliciano** (0362 900 164, closed noon-2pm daily) has outstanding canvases by Daniele Crespi and Francesco Hayez. In **Agliate**, the early 11th-century basilica of **Santi Pietro e Paolo** (036 29 871, open 8am-1pm, 4.30-7pm daily) is built in river stone set in a herringbone pattern, as is its baptistery, a rare nine-sided structure.

To the east of Monza, **Arcore** is now indelibly linked in the Italian psyche to Silvio Berlusconi, who resides in a high-gated villa here. But there is also the 18th-century **Villa Borromeo d'Adda** (039 601 2248, only the grounds are open to the public), just one of the magnificent properties owned by this important Renaissance family. The Borromeos also owned land in **Oreno**, three kilometres (two miles) to the east, where the **Villa Borromeo** estate (via Piave 12, 039 669 004, open by appointment only) boasts a hunting lodge with remarkable 15th-century frescoes of hunting scenes.

Despite being a thriving manufacturing centre, **Vimercate** has preserved much of its original charm. In the town hall (**Palazzo Trotti**), an 18th-century fresco cycle stretches over 11 rooms. The basilica of **Santo Stefano** was built between the 10th and 11th centuries on earlier foundations. Along via Cavour, off the central piazza Roma, are several 15th-century *palazzi* and the little Romanesque **Oratorio di Sant'Antonio**, with frescoes from 1450. At the end of the street, the **Ponte di San Rocco**, built from recycled Roman remains, was part of the medieval fortifications.

North of Vimercate, the **Parco Regionale di Montevecchia e della Valle del Curone** (039 993 0384) is a weekend favourite with the Milanese. It has several short walks through the hillside terraces planted with rosemary and sage. Call park volunteers on 039 531 1275 to arrange a visit.

Getting there

By bus
ATM buses 723, 724 and 727 from Milan's Stazione Centrale or 721, 820 and 821 from Sesto FS metro station cover the short hop to Monza, Vimercate and other Brianza destinations.

By car
For Monza, take viale Zara out of Milan, which becomes viale Fulvio Testi. Journey time 15mins to 1hr, depending on traffic. From Monza, local roads are well signed for Biassono, Carate Brianza, Arcore, Oreno and Vimercate. Vimercate can also be reached via the A15 *autostrada*.

By train
Mainline trains for Monza leave Milan's Stazione Centrale or Porta Garibaldi about every 15mins. Trains also leave hourly (every half hour during rush hours) from both stations for Arcore, on the Milan–Sondrio line. Triuggio, headquarters for the Parco Lambro, is on the Sesto–Lecco line, with trains every hour.

Getting around

The easiest, most efficient way to visit the area around Milan is to rent a car (for car hire, *see p223*). But efficient public transport exists for most of the destinations covered in this chapter.

Tourist information

Pro Monza (IAT)
Palazzo Comunale, piazza Carducci (039 323 222/ www.comune.monza.mi.it). Open 9am-noon, 3-6pm Mon-Fri; 9am-noon Sat.

Ufficio Cultura Arcore
Via Gorizia 20 (039 6013 263). Open 9.30am-noon Mon, Wed, Fri, Sat.

Bergamo

This pretty medieval city is a calming counterpoint to its noisy neighbour, Milan.

Piazza Vecchia. *See p185.*

It's just an hour from the hustle and bustle of downtown Milan, yet the small (some might say provincial) city of Bergamo is a world away from its busy neighbour. This is where stressed-out *milanesi* come to escape when their daily grind gets too much. And with Ryanair's cheap flights to the city's Orio al Serio airport, it's a feasible weekend city break from England too.

Surrounded by the valleys and lakes to the north-east of Milan, Bergamo has an inviting air of relaxation. The city is divided into two: old Bergamo, or **Città Alta** (Upper City), and the modern **Città Bassa** (Lower City). The latter, the working heart of city, is not without its own attractions. In particular, both the *palazzi*-lined via Pignolo – one of the old approaches to Città Alta – and the impressive **Pinacoteca Accademia Carrara** (piazza G Carrara 82A, 035 399 640, www.accademiacarrara.bergamo.it, closed Mon), with its extensive art collection stretching from Raphael to Rubens, are well worth a visit. But it's the imposing **Città Alta**, the walled medieval town on a hill that presides majestically over the business district below, that is Bergamo's main draw.

Come Sunday afternoon, Città Alta's ancient main thoroughfares, via Gombito and via Bartolomeo Colleoni, teem with life as people flock here to amble down the area's cobbled alleys, lose themselves in the glorious mountain views and be transported back in time as they eat velvety ice-creams in the shadows of the medieval architecture.

Sightseeing

Città Alta

Small but perfectly formed, the beautiful old town is very easy to explore. While you could comfortably walk the length of Città Alta in 15 minutes, it's worth taking much longer to admire the fairytale medieval buildings.

Viale Vittorio Emanuele II, the main thoroughfare up to Città Alta, passes through the city's defensive walls at Porta Sant'Agostino, built in 1575 by the Venetians and still featuring the lion of St Mark. But the Venetians were not the first to build walls in Bergamo: there is evidence that the Etruscans had fortified sites on the hills, and there are remnants of 14th-century defensive systems, such as La Rocca and La Cittadella.

To the left of Porta Sant'Agostino is the viale delle Mura promenade, built in the 1880s. This tree-lined street follows a good portion of the walls, passing by two more of Città Alta's four extant gates: San Giacomo and Sant'Alessandro. (The fourth gate – San Lorenzo, or Garibaldi – is off the tourist track, at the end of via della Fara.)

Head into the heart of Città Alta along via Porta Dipinta, just inside the Porta Sant'Agostino. This takes you past the **Torre di Sub Foppis** – a piece of the pre-Venetian defensive system and part of the gate that guarded the street – and the church of **San Michele al Pozzo Bianco** (035 247 651), to the left. Set off the street on a little square, this church dates back to the eighth century, but subsequent renovations mean the façade is less than a century old, while most of the interior is from the 1400s. Inside, the walls of the single-naved church are covered in magnificent

frescoes, including scenes from the life of Mary by Lorenzo Lotto, in the chapel to the left of the high altar. Via Porta Dipinta is named after another gate into Città Alta, which sported pre-1500 frescoes. Unfortunately this 'painted gate' was torn down in 1815 in an ill-judged fit of urban development; a small plaque about halfway along the street marks the spot where it once stood.

At the top of via Porta Dipinta itself, lined with beautiful *palazzi* built in the 16th and 17th centuries by successful *bergamaschi*, is **piazza Mercato delle Scarpe**, one of Città Alta's important hubs. On the southern side of the square is the late 19th-century funicular railway, the lazy way up from Città Bassa. Stretching to the north-west is via Gombito, lined with small shops and bars. A few steps into via Gombito, turn off to the right, up via Rocca, to enjoy the valley views from the grounds of **La Rocca** (piazzale Brigata Legnano, 035 226 332, closed Mon). Standing

here, on the 14th-century remains of the city's Venetian defences, you can also see the stadium of the local football team, Atalanta.

Further up via Gombito, at the intersection with via Lupo, stands the **Torre Gombito** (not open to the public), which dates back to the Guelph-Ghibelline struggles of the 12th century.

Beyond the tower, via Gombito eventually opens out into the lovely, spacious **piazza Vecchia**. The medieval buildings on the square's eastern side house the offices of the local university. On the south-western side of the square, the magnificent **Palazzo della Ragione** (035 210 204) is used as an exhibition space. Originally constructed in the 12th century, the palazzo has seen many changes. The covered staircase leading to the principal meeting room was added in 1453, and the street-level loggia dates from 1520. Inside, the fresco-covered *sala superiore* provides an impressive backdrop for temporary exhibitions. Also here are Donato Bramante's frescoes of *Tre Filosofi* (1477).

The neo-classical **Palazzo Nuovo**, on the north-east of piazza Vecchia, is home to the municipal archives and library. Towering nearly 53 metres (173 feet) above the square is the 12th-century **Torre Civica** (035 247 116, Apr-Oct closed Mon, Nov-Mar call ahead for reservation). Climb to the top for wonderful views over the old town.

A passage through the loggia of the Palazzo della Ragione leads to **piazza Duomo**, which houses some of Bergamo's most important buildings: the Duomo, the basilica of Santa Maria Maggiore and the Cappella Colleoni.

The **Cappella Colleoni**, to the south-west of the square, was built by Venetian general Bartolomeo Colleoni. He had the old sacristy of Santa Maria Maggiore demolished to make way for his mausoleum, which was finished in 1475, a year after his death. Colleoni's tomb and that of his daughter Medea grace the chapel, as do frescoes (1733) by Giambattista Tiepolo. On the gate outside the chapel, the Colleoni coat of arms has been polished to a bright sheen by hands rubbing it for luck. The coat of arms, it should be noted, bears three testicles – as did Colleoni, according to legend.

The **Duomo** (035 210 223, currently closed for refurbishment) is officially known as Cattedrale di Sant'Alessandro. Construction, to a design by Antonio 'Il Filarete' Averlino), began in 1459, on a spot previously occupied by an early Christian church. The project passed through the hands of several architects before completion in 1886. Among the mostly 18th-century works surrounding the main altar is Giambattista Tiepolo's *Martyrdom of St John*

the Bishop. The statue of Pope John XXIII at the Duomo's entrance is a reminder of the importance of the *bergamasco* pope to the city.

Next door to the Duomo is the impressive **Santa Maria Maggiore** (035 223 327). Construction began in 1157 on the site of an earlier church, and did not end until 1521, when the Porta della Fontana was completed. Each period of construction offers something of beauty, from the presbytery (1187), to the prothyum (1350), to the new sacristy (late 15th century). The most stunning aspect, however, is the series of wooden inlay works on the presbytery stalls. These exquisite 16th-century carvings, designed by Venetian artist Lorenzo Lotto, who emigrated to the city in 1513, tell stories from the Old Testament; they also contain detailed comments in the form of alchemic symbols.

Behind Santa Maria Maggiore, via Arena leads to the **Museo Donizettiano** (via Arena 9, 035 399 269, closed Mon Apr-Sept, closed Mon & afternoons Oct-Mar), dedicated to Bergamo-born opera composer Gaetano Donizetti (1797-1848).

Beyond piazza Vecchia, via Gombito becomes via Bartolomeo Colleoni and leads to piazza Mascheroni, home to **La Cittadella**. Built in the 14th century to defend Città Alta from attacks from the west, the citadel now plays host to colourful weekend markets (mainly on a Sunday, but occasional Saturdays too). Rising above the square is the pretty **Torre della Campanella**. Built in 1355, the bell tower wasn't actually finished until the 19th century, hence the relatively modern-looking clock face.

Continuing through piazza Cittadella takes you out of the historic Città Alta to Colle Aperto, an open space just inside the Porta Sant'Alessandro overlooking the foothills of the Alps. If you fancy a drink, reward your sight-seeing efforts with a pastry from **La Marianna** (*see p187*). Alternatively, sit on a bench and take in the panorama. However, these views are nothing compared to the breathtaking sights to be had from **Il Castello**, the city's former ramparts, now a public park.

To reach Il Castello, follow the Colle Aperto through the Porta Sant'Alessandro. On the other side of this stone gate is Città Alta's second funicular, which takes you up to via al Castello, at the base of the park. Those feeling energetic can make their way on foot, up steep via San Vigilio. It's a 15-minute amble up to the top but your efforts are rewarded along the way with the picture-perfect views of the old town, and at your destination with vistas of the Apennines and Alps – including Monte Rosa, the second-highest mountain in Europe.

Lago d'Iseo

Nestled in the mountains of eastern Bergamo and western Brescia (it forms part of the boundary of the two provinces), Lago d'Iseo not only mirrors majestic mountains and hosts fishermen and boaters; it also holds one of the jewels of Lombardy: Monte Isola, the largest lake island in Italy.

THE BERGAMO SHORE

Sarnico, at the south-western tip of the lake, has been inhabited since prehistoric times. These days, particularly in summer, 'occupied' might be a better word. When weekend waterskiers and windsurfers descend on the waters and the lake front gets crowded with campers in town for supplies and *gelato*, escape into the winding streets of the medieval centre for some window-shopping.

At the northern end of the lake is **Lovere**, which was historically important for its strategic position – guarding the passage from the lake to the textile-producing heart of the Valcamonica region. These days café-lined *piazze* and elegant *palazzi* along the shore bear witness to the prosperity this small town has enjoyed over the centuries. Behind, different levels, connected by stairs and alleys, rise up from the water and run along the hillside.

THE BRESCIA SHORE

Across from Lovere sits **Pisogne**, which has long been known for its rich iron ore deposits and its via Valeriana – the Roman road linking Brescia with the Valcamonica. Today there's a relative lack of tourists here, making it the perfect territory for a quiet stroll in the small medieval *borgo* behind the uncrowded lakefront piazza del Mercato, which contains the 13th-century Torre del Vescovo.

From Marone, a narrow road (SP32) climbs through a series of hairpin turns to **Zone**, a hamlet surrounded by mountain peaks and offering glimpses of the lake. In Zone's small nature reserve, erosion has left boulders stranded atop towering pinnacles; trails around them allow a closer look. At the entrance to the park, the isolated 15th-century church of San Giorgio boasts stunning frescoes.

Further south, **Iseo** is the lake's principal and most cosmopolitan town. But despite its focus on modern-day tourism, Iseo manages to retain a peculiar timelessness thanks to its labyrinth of narrow alleys, the 12th-century Pieve di Sant'Andrea church and the 14th-century Castello Oldofredi, now the library.

MONTE ISOLA

The ferry from Sulzano to **Peschiera Maraglio** on **Monte Isola** only takes a few minutes, but carries visitors to a very different world. Besides Peschiera Maraglio, the car-less island is home to a number of other small, characterful villages. At **Sensole**, on the south-western corner, the microclimate allows for olive-growing; the quaintly traditional **Menzino**, **Sanchignano** and **Siviano** occupy the western coast; and at the top of the mountain, the Madonna della Ceriola sanctuary offers unparalleled views of the lake.

Where to stay & eat

In Iseo, **Il Volto** does a wonderful blend of *haute cuisine* and regional comfort food (via Mirolte 33, 030 981 462, closed all day Wed, Thur lunch & 2wks July, average €50). The 29-room hotel **Relais Mirabella** (via Mirabella 34, Clusane sul Lago, Iseo, 030 989 8051, www.relaismirabella.it, closed Jan-Mar, doubles €110-€135) offers lovely lake views.

Getting there & around

By boat

Ferries run (035 971 483, www.navigazione laghi.it) from Sulzano to Peschiera Maraglio, and from Iseo to Peschiera.

By bus

From Bergamo, SAB (035 289 011) runs frequent services to Lovere and Sarnico.

By car

From Bergamo, take the A4 towards Brescia; exit at Grumello del Monte and follow signs for Lago d'Iseo.

By train

From Bergamo, take the Brescia train and change at Palazzolo; six trains a day run each way between Palazzolo and the Paratico line (summer only).

Tourist information

IAT Iseo

Lungolago Marconi 2C, Iseo (030 980 209/ www.provincia.brescia.it/turismo). **Open** Easter-Sept 9am-12.30pm, 3.30-6.30pm daily. Oct-Easter 9am-12.30pm, 3-6pm Mon-Fri; 9am-12.30pm Sat.

Where to eat & drink

Bergamasco cuisine is for hearty appetites. Starters focus on cold cuts, particularly home-made *salame* and *lardo*, creamy white slices of pork fat (it's better than it sounds), while main courses tend towards roasts and braised dishes, often served with polenta (*see p188* **Corn star**). The city is also home to some stunning *pasticcerie*. If you fancy a splurge, try L'Osteria di via Solata (*see p179* **Food and travel**).

Al Donizetti

Via Gombito 17A (035 242 661/www.donizetti.it). **Meals served** 12.30-2.30pm, 7.30-11pm. **Average** €15-€25. **Credit** MC, V.

This little wine bar off the main drag specialises in local salamis and cheeses. Take a table in the cosy restaurant or, if the sun's out, under the Renaissance-style arcade outside. Alternatively, do as the locals do and nip in for a quick snack at the counter.

Antica Trattoria la Colombina

Via Borgo Canale 12 (035 261 402). **Meals served** 12.15-2.15pm, 7.45-10.15pm Wed-Sun. Closed 3wks Jan, 3wks June-July. **Average** €30. **Credit** AmEx, DC, MC, V.

This historic trattoria just outside the Città Alta walls has impeccable food and marvellous views that are well worth the walk up.

Bar Ristorante La Marianna

Colle Aperto 4 (035 247 997/www.lamarianna.it). **Open** *Bar/pasticceria* 7am-1pm Tue-Sun. *Restaurant* 12.30-2.30pm, 8-10.30pm Tue-Sun. Closed 2wks Jan. **Average** €50. **Credit** AmEx, MC, V.

Situated just outside the heart of the old city, this family-friendly *pasticceria* (with a garden, open in good weather) is where those in the know come for post-sightseeing snacks and ice-creams.

Cantina di Via Colleoni

Via Bartolomeo Colleoni 5 (035 215 864). **Open** 12.30-2.30pm, 7.30-10.30pm Wed-Mon. Closed 2wks end Jan, 2wks end Aug. **Average** €25. **Credit** AmEx, MC, V.

Enjoy warming Tuscan and Piedmontese wines in this popular, stylish wine bar.

Cavour Pasticceria

Via Gombito 7A (035 243 418/www.davittorio.com). **Open** 7.30am-midnight Mon, Tue, Thur-Sat; 8am-midnight Sun. Closed 3wks Aug. **Credit** AmEx, DC, MC, V.

Indulge yourself with a coffee and pastry in the quasi-Austrian splendour of this elegant café. Prices aren't the lowest, but the surroundings compensate.

Da Ornella

Via Gombito 15 (035 232 736). **Meals served** noon-3pm, 7-11pm Mon-Wed, Fri-Sun. **Average** €22. **Credit** AmEx, DC, MC, V.

Large servings of trad food are Ornella's mainstay. The mixed grilled meats platter is great for sharing.

Il Fornaio

Via Bartolomeo Colleoni 3 (035 249 376). **Open** 8am-3pm Mon; 8am-8pm Tue-Sun. Closed 3wks end June. **No credit cards**.

This busy bakery offers a never-ending array of pizza and focaccia (sold by weight), as well as freshly made sandwiches and other goodies. Choose your pizza then pay at the till while they heat it up.

Nessi

Via Gombito 34 (035 247 073). **Open** 8.30am-8pm Mon-Fri, Sun; 8.30pm-midnight Sat. Closed July. **No credit cards**.

A welcoming *pasticceria* perfect for a snack on the hoof. Enjoy the excellent cakes and focaccias at the standing area at the back at no extra charge. See if you can spot the gushing personal endorsement from local football hero Maurizio Ganz.

Ristorante Pizzeria Da Franco

Via Bartolomeo Colleoni 8 (035 238 565/www.da francobergamocitta.it). **Meals served** 7-10.30pm Tue-Sun. **Average** €15. **Credit** AmEx, MC, V.

Laid-back and deservedly popular, this friendly restaurant serves a varied menu of local and Italian cuisine to a mixed and – by the time they've finished their meal – happily sated crowd. Great value too.

Ristorante Pizzeria San Vigilio

Via San Vigilio 34 (035 253 188/www.ristorante pizzeriasanvigilio.it). **Meals served** noon-2.30pm, 7-10.45pm daily. Closed Wed Nov-Mar. **Average** €35. **Credit** AmEx, MC, V.

Perched up near Il Castello on the higher reaches of Città Alta, this smart hilltop bar/restaurant/pizzeria provides spectacular views over lower Bergamo's verdant valley from its cliffside terrace.

Where to stay

Agnello d'Oro (via Gombito 22, 035 249 883, www.agnellodoro.it, doubles €92) in Città Alta is a central as it gets. The building dates back to the 16th century, the 20 rooms are small but comfortable, and the reception area is a mind-boggling bazaar. Across from the Cittadella, the **Albergo San Lorenzo** (piazza Mascheroni 9A, 035 237 383, www.hotelsanlorenzobg.it, doubles €160) has some of the few Roman ruins left in Bergamo (they were excavated while the hotel was building its parking lot).

If you don't mind staying in Città Bassa, the **Best Western Hotel Premier Cappello d'Oro** (viale Papa Giovanni XXIII 12, 035 232 503, www.hotelcappellodoro.it, doubles €95-€220) strives – with some success – to combine modern comforts with tradition. The **Jolly Hotel Bergamo** (via Paleocapa 1G, 035 227 1811, www.jollyhotels.it, doubles €210), meanwhile, is conveniently located close to the train station and often has cheap last-minute deals.

Getting there

By air

For information about Bergamo's Orio al Serio airport, about 45km (28 miles) from Milan, *see p218*.

By bus

Autostradale buses (035 244 354, www.autostradale.it) leave Milan's Stazione Porta Garibaldi for Bergamo every 30mins. Journey time is about 1hr.

By car

Take the A4 *autostrada* from Milan east towards Venice; exit at Bergamo.

By train

Services run from Milan's Stazione Centrale via Treviglio, and from Stazione Porta Garibaldi via

Carnate. The Carnate service is more regular and crosses the Adda river over the dramatic Ponte di Paderno (848 888 088). Journey time is about 1hr.

Getting around

Bergamo buses are operated by ATB (035 364 211). Tickets (€1) must be bought before boarding. They are sold at tobacconists and some newsstands around town.

Tourist information

IAT Città Alta

Via Gombito 13, Città Alta (035 242 226/www. comune.bergamo.it). **Open** 9am-12.30pm, 2-5.30pm daily.

Corn star

Look in the window of any *pasticceria* in Bergamo, and there'll be a round yellow cake topped with chocolate bits looking right back at you. These are *polenta e osei*, or 'polenta and little birds'. Yet they're made neither of polenta nor, thankfully, birds. Instead, these little sponge cakes rolled in fondant are an affectionate tribute to the medieval dish of the same name that – you guessed it – was exactly what its name suggests.

To the untrained eye, polenta looks like mash gone wrong. But this stodgy savoury porridge has been eaten with passion for

centuries. Traditionally it was the food of the poor, and over the centuries it has fed everyone from the Roman Emperor's foot soldiers to the Pope – polenta was the favourite dish of local-boy-made-good Pope John XXIII.

Made from spelt, millet and buckwheat – and since the introduction of corn to Europe at the tail end of the Middle Ages, cornmeal – polenta was traditionally cooked in a rounded copper pot (*paiolo*) over an open fire (the copper to help distribute the heat; the rounded-off bottom to keep it from sticking). If the larder was empty, the polenta was eaten on its own or, as was the case with that old Bergamo speciality, with grilled wild songbirds such as thrush. The lucky few ate it with game (both the furry and feathered kind) as the grains were perfect for mopping up the meat's rich juices.

Though killing wild songbirds is somewhat frowned upon these days, polenta is still an intrinsic part of the Bergamo diet. In fact, the local speciality is so cherished that in 1976 the Order of the Knights of Polenta was founded here. From running annual polenta festivals to devising new recipes, these apron-fronted polenta guardians continue to hold true to their noble charter and remain dedicated to 'upholding, defending, and promoting' the tasty mush.

Grilled, fried, boiled or baked, this staple is, undeniably, the most humble of foods. But served alongside succulent meats and sausages or enriched with cream and cheese such as *branzi* or gorgonzola, it is a treat to sate the stomach and comfort the soul.

Lago d'Orta

Come here for film-set scenery and cut-price teapots.

If you're determined to visit one of Lombardy's lakes but can't face the crowds attracted to the more famous ones, Lago d'Orta is for you. Located west of Lago Maggiore, in the Piedmont region, this smallish stretch of water (measuring just 18.2 square kilometres/seven square miles) is the only northern lake you can take in at a single glance. Most of its attractions – from the romantic, medieval town of Orta San Giulio, to its picture-postcard-sized island and lakeside museums – can be seen in a couple of days. People come here to steep themselves in the area's natural beauties and well-preserved history, but that's not to say the locals are stuck in their ways. The lakeside town of Omegna is the unlikely home of Alessi, whose factory produces icons of Italian design (*see p190* **Alessi's cave**).

Orta San Giulio

Visitors to the medieval lakeside town of Orta San Giulio could be forgiven for thinking they have somehow stumbled on to the set of a romantic film. A dramatic pathway sweeps from the main waterside square (piazza Motta)

to the yellow-stained church of **Santa Maria Assunta** (1485), and crumbling villas flank the shorelines stretching out from the town. Back in the café-lined square, models are often found posing for photoshoots beneath the *loggia* stilts of the 16th-century **Palazzo della Comunità** (the former town hall). It's no wonder Orta is popular for weddings (if you get the urge to tie the knot, there's even a resident British wedding organiser, Philippa Lane, mobile 338 461 0665).

Perched above the town, in the wooded **Sacro Monte** nature reserve, are 20 small chapels (1591-1770) containing remarkably lifelike terracotta tableaux depicting scenes from the life of St Francis. A pleasant pilgrims' path (30 minutes) winds uphill from piazza Motta, leading to the 17th-century **Chiesa di San Nicolao** and the Sacro Monte. Alternatively, you can drive to the top.

Where to stay, eat & shop

The luxurious **Villa Crespi** (via Fava 18, 0322 911 902, www.villacrespi.it, closed early Jan-Feb, doubles €175-€500) is an over-the-top Moorish villa on the road from the station. The villa's restaurant (average €70) – under young Neapolitan chef Antonino Cannavacciuolo – is ranked as one of Italy's best, so it is wise to book well ahead.

The historic four-star **Hotel San Rocco** (via Gippini 11, 0322 911 977, www.hotelsanrocco.it, doubles €160-€225) offers lakeside rooms and dining (average €50), as does the three-star **Leon d'Oro** (piazza Motta 43, 0322 911 991, www.albergoleondoro.it, closed Jan, doubles €110-€180), where tables are spread over an outdoor terrace (average €25-€35).

The 500-year-old wine bar **Osteria al Boeuc** (via Bersani 28, 0322 915 854, closed Tue Apr-Dec & Mon-Wed Jan-Mar, average €15) serves bruschetta, cheese, cold cuts,

salsiccia ubriaca ('drunken' sausage) and over 350 wines. If what's on the menu particularly titillates your taste buds, drop into the Boeuc's food store next door, **La Dispensa**.

The intimate **Taverna Antico Agnello** (via Olina 18, 0322 90 259, closed Tue & Dec-Jan, average €40) serves creative regional food in a cosy dining room.

Finally, lovers of local crafts shouldn't miss **Penelope** (piazza Motta 26, 0322 905 600) for hand-woven kitchen linens printed with antique wooden stamps and natural dyes.

Tourist information

Distretto dei Laghi

Via Panoramica, Orta San Giulio (0322 905 614/ www.distrettolaghi.it). **Open** 9am-1pm, 2-6pm Wed-Sun.

Alessi's cave

Away from its mystical monasteries and romantic alleyways, Lago d'Orta has a more modern side. Tucked away at the end of the lake, at Crusinallo, are the factory, offices, museum and outlet store of Alessi, the company whose slick household objects crop up in stylish kitchens and bathrooms around the world. Known for its glistening steam kettles and Philippe Starck-designed spindly legged juice squeezers, the company began life in 1921 as a humble producer of homewares in brass, nickel and silver. During the 1960s and '70s, the big designers were drafted in, and the company morphed into a global brand. Today, visitors can't miss the aqua-and-orange factory with a giant sculpture of Alessi's archetypal, squat 1940s teapot outside.

Understandably, the company is a little reluctant to let all and sundry through its gates. Although the on-site museum is jam-packed with more than 22,000 design objects, only industry specialists (designers, students and professionals, strictly by appointment) are allowed a glimpse inside. Fortunately, there is rather more chance of being let loose in the factory outlet. Head here for Alessi pieces at knock-down prices and join the legions of style hounds who can't survive for another minute without one more Alessi gewgaw shimmering in their homes.

Alessi Outlet Store

Via Privata Alessi, Crusinallo (0323 868 611). **Open** 2-6pm Mon; 9.30am-6pm Tue-Sat. **Credit** AmEx, DC, MC, V.

Isola San Giulio

According to legend, St Julius (San Giulio) drifted over to this island using his cloak, then got down to banishing its thriving population of snakes and dragons. These days you can reach the enchanting island and its basilica (founded in AD 4 or 5) by taxi boat from piazza Motta at Orta San Giulio (mobile 333 605 0288). From here you can also book a 20- or 30-minute tour of the lake (€6-€8), or if you're feeling sporty, row yourself across (boat hire €10 per hour). Once on the lake you might notice a curious phenomenon: unlike all the other pre-Alpine lakes and rivers, Orta's waters flow north.

Inside the basilica, a black marble pulpit has rare Saxon-influenced carvings, while frescoes from many centuries battle for space around its walls. A circular pathway (via del Silenziao) runs around the island, past the cloistered Benedictine convent and many romantic villas.

If you're here for St Julius's feast day (31 January), rap on the convent door to get a bag of *pane San Giulio* (dried fruit, nut and chocolate bread) for a small donation. (This treat is for sale in mainland bakeries all year round.) There is no hotel on the island, but there is an eaterie, **Ristorante San Giulio** (via Basilica 4, 0322 90 234, www.orta.net/ sangiulio, closed Mon Apr-Oct, Mon-Sat Nov-Mar, average €25-€30), though atmosphere outstrips quality here.

Around the lake

Perched on the hill above Orta San Giulio, **Vacciago di Ameno** houses the **Collezione Calderara di Arte Contemporanea** (via Bardelli 9, 0323 89 622, closed Mon mid

May-mid Oct, open only by appointment mid Oct-mid May). This museum was transformed from a late 17th-century home by Antonio Calderara (1903-78) and of the 327 paintings and sculptures inside, 56 are by Calderara himself. The impressive collection documents the international avant-garde from the 1950s and '60s, with an emphasis on kinetic art, geometric abstractionism and visual poetry.

Pettenasco stands on the lake shore north of Orta. Its Romanesque church tower started life attached to the church of Sant'Audenzio, a pal of San Giulio, as well as Pettenasco's town prefect in AD 300. The intricate woodwork for which the town was once famous is commemorated at the **Museo dell'Arte della Tornitura del Legno** (via Vittorio Veneto, 0323 89 622, closed Mon & Oct-May), which displays tools, wooden objects and machines collected from the town's old factories.

Named after the battle cry uttered by Julius Caesar (*Heu moenia!* – 'Woe to you, walls!') before he ploughed through the defences of the city, **Omegna** was the site of tremendous battles during World War II. Today the town – the biggest on the lake – manufactures metal kitchenware products. In the **Forum Omegna** cultural centre (parco Maulini 1, 0323 866 141, www.forumomegna.org, closed Sun am), a museum documents the area's industrial history. A gift shop sells discounted items from local manufacturers Alessi, Bialetti (the inventor of the espresso coffee maker), Calderoni (cutlery), Lagostina (pans) and others.

Seven kilometres (4.5 miles) west and up from Omegna, **Quarna Sotto** offers great views of the lake, plus one of the area's wildest museums. Around the late 1800s, the town was famous around the world for its wood and metal wind instruments. The **Museo Etnografico** (via Roma, 0323 89 622, closed Mon mid June-Sept, open only by appointment Oct-mid June) honours this tradition with graphic explanations of manufacturing methods. But this lovingly curated gem also has displays on housing design, local costume and domestic arts, as well as a water mill.

From **Pella**, on the lake's western shore, a signposted road climbs uphill for ten kilometres (six miles) to the church of Madonna del Sasso. En route, the hamlet of **Artò** has antique wash-houses, sundials and a building adorned with a 16th-century fresco, and **Boleto** is a picture, with its cobbled lanes and church. At the top, the **Madonna del Sasso** church (0323 896 229, open irregular hours daily), built between 1730 and 1748, sits 638 metres (2,127 feet) above the lake on a granite outcrop. In thanks for some miracle, a successful local cobbler arranged for the bones of San Donato to be transferred here

from the San Callisto catacombs in Rome. The holy skeleton, resting oddly on its side, lies in a transparent casket to the left of the altar. Most of the frescoes are the work of local artist Lorenzo Peracino, while the painting above the pink, grey and black marble altar is the *Pietà* (1547) by Fermo Stella da Caravaggio.

Where to eat & stay

The **Hotel Panoramico Ristorante** in Boleto (via Frua 31, 0322 981 312, www.hotelpanoramico.it, closed Nov and mid Jan-Mar, doubles €70-€85) has plain but comfortable rooms and a restaurant (average €28) with two outdoor terraces and wonderful views of the lake.

Tourist information

Pro Loco di Omegna

Piazza XXIV Aprile 17 (0323 61 930/www.proloco omegna.vb.it). **Open** 9am-12.30pm, 2.30-5.30pm Mon-Fri; 9am-12.30pm Sat.

Getting there

By car

Take the motorway for the lakes (Ai Laghi). When it divides, head for Malpensa/Varese/Sesto Calende, then join the A26 in the direction of Gravellona Toce. Exit at Borgomanero, then follow the signs to Gozzano and Lago d'Orta.

By train

Mainline service from Stazione Centrale or Porta Garibaldi to Novara, then local service stopping at Orta/Miasino, Pettenasco and Omegna. Note: all stations except Omegna are located up steep hills above the towns, 15-20mins walk from the lake. You can pre-book a taxi through Lago d'Orta Autonoleggio (338 986 4839 mobile).

Getting around

By boat

Navigazione Lago d'Orta (0322 844 862) operates a boat service around the lake, stopping at Orta, Isola San Giulio, Pettenasco, Gozzano and elsewhere (daily Easter-mid Oct; Sat, Sun in Oct, Nov; Sun only in Jan). The best departure points are Pella, where there's ample parking, and Omegna. A full day's ticket is €6.50. No credit cards. Another option is to book a tour in a motor taxi from the Servizio Pubblico Motoscafi (333 605 0288 mobile) at Orta San Giulio.

By car

The two-lane road surrounding the lake is 33km (21 miles) long, with a smooth surface. A car is essential for visiting the towns above the lake shore. Orta San Giulio's town centre is closed to traffic; cars must be left in the pay parking lots at the edge of town.

Trips Out of Town

Lago Maggiore

Misnomer aside, it's a major attraction.

Although, as the name suggests, Maggiore is big, it actually comes second in size to Garda. Some 65 kilometres (40 miles) long, and covering 215 square kilometres (84 square miles), Lago Maggiore has a circumference of 166 kilometres (103 miles), the width going from a minimum of two kilometres (across from Arona), to a maximum of 12 kilometres (7.5 miles) between Stresa and Portotravaglia. Picturesque from just about any angle, Lago Maggiore offers open vistas, magnificent gardens, whimsical landmarks, intriguing islands and historic towns set against the Alps, the latter especially in the more northerly sector, which lies in Switzerland. Indeed, even on the Italian side, the lake has two allegiances. The eastern shore is in Lombardy, while the western side belongs to Piedmont.

The area around Lago Maggiore was inhabited in the Bronze and Iron Ages and by the Middle Ages, much of it was under the control of the powerful Visconti and, later, the Borromeo families. It is to them that the lake

owes some of its most celebrated landmarks, including the island gardens, fortresses and the looming statue of celebrated son Carlo Borromeo. The lake later became a stop-off point on the grand tours of the 18th and 19th centuries, with its mild climate and enchanting position attracting Italian nobility, the budding industrial bourgeoisie and wealthy foreigners, many of whom built themselves sumptuous lakefront villas and gardens.

The Piedmont shore

Although the lake is handsome on the eastern side, it's the western shore that attracts most visitors. From Arona to Cannobio, small towns alternate with majestic villas and gardens, many of which are only visible from the water.

At the southern tip of Lago Maggiore is **Arona**, a lively commercial town with a pretty, historic centre. San Carlo Borromeo was born here and a 17th-century, 35-metre (117-foot) tall copper statue of the saintly local hero, built using the same technique later employed to construct the Statue of Liberty, stands high on a hill above the town (piazzale San Carlo, closed Mon-Fri Nov-Mar). Those with steely nerves can climb a narrow internal spiral staircase and ten-metre (32-foot) vertical ladder to the statue's head to peer at the lake through the saint's eyes.

A few kilometres north, the smaller town of **Meina** has some attractive private residences, although derelict hotels and villas give the place a somewhat dilapidated air. A dark chapter of Italian history mars the town's apparent serenity. In September 1943 Nazi troops shot 16 Jewish guests at a local hotel.

Further north, **Lesa** is home to a museum of mementoes of author Alessandro Manzoni's stay (Museo Manzoniano, Villa Stampa, via la Fontana, 0322 76 421, open only Sat, Sun July & Aug).

Above **Belgirate**'s tiny historic centre is the church of Santa Maria del Suffragio (closed Mon-Sat), lavishly adorned with frescoes by the school of Bernardino Luini, the local 16th-century artist.

Stresa stands on the Golfo Borromeo, which, with its islands, forms the heart of the lake. The town became famous after Dickens and Byron gave it rave reviews; Hemingway also set part of *A Farewell to Arms* here. During the belle époque, Stresa's grandiose hotels, refined attractions and casino rivalled those of Monte Carlo and the Venice Lido. **Villa Pallavicino** (Strada Statale 33, Località Stresa, 0323 31 533, www.parcozoopallavicino.it, closed Nov-Feb) has a vast English-style garden and a zoo.

The 1,491-metre-high (4,970-feet) summit of **Montagna Mottarone** can be reached by cable car or a five-hour hike from Stresa. It becomes a ski resort in winter and, on a clear day, you can enjoy a stunning view of the Alps, several lakes, and – on really exceptional days, as far as Milan and Turin. The cable car also stops at the **Giardino Alpinia** (0323 20 163, closed Mon & mid Oct-mid Apr), which boasts hundreds of alpine plant species.

From Stresa, ferries and water taxis take tourists to the three islands collectively known as the **Isole Borromee**: Isola Bella, Isola Madre and Isola dei Pescatori. So popular are these excursions that the islands can become unpleasantly crowded in high season. The Borromeo feudal lords took possession of these islands in the 16th century. The **Isola Bella** (0323 30 556, closed Nov-mid Mar) was named

© Copyright Time Out Group 2006

Trips Out of Town

in honour of Isabella d'Adda, whose husband Carlo Borromeo III began transforming the island in 1632. The island's baroque **Palazzo Borromeo** (where Napoleon and Josephine slept after his conquest of northern Italy) has a stately Italian-style garden with albino peacocks. The Isola dei Pescatori is a strip of narrow lanes and whitewashed houses, ending in a park with benches and shady trees. The 16th-century **Palazzo Borromeo** on the **Isola Madre** (the largest of the three Isole Borromee) has an 18th-century puppet theatre and is surrounded by a magnificent English-style garden (summer 0323 31 261, winter 0323 305 56, closed Nov-Feb).

Beyond Stresa, **Baveno** is home to the tenth-century church of the saints Gervasio e Protasio. The octagonal baptistery dates from the fifth century. The local pink marble is exported worldwide.

The reed thickets in the Riserva Naturale (nature reserve) at **Fondotoce** (0323 496 596, www.parchilagomaggiore.it) at the mouth of the Toce river, are a nesting ground for many birds. Some of the hiking and bike trails here lead to the smaller Lago di Mergozzo. Marble used in the construction of Milan's Duomo was extracted nearby at Candoglia.

Verbania, the provincial capital, is made up of several towns unified in 1939. **Pallanza** is renowned for its gardens and has an attractive lakeside promenade abundant with flowers. The gardens of **Villa Giulia** (corso Sanitello 10, 0323 503 249) at the end of the promenade have views over the privately owned islet San Giovanni Battista, where composer Arturo Toscanini spent his holidays (Villa Giulia itself is closed the public).

The garden at **Villa Taranto** (via Vittorio Veneto 111, 0323 556 667/404 555, www. villataranto.it, closed Nov-Mar), between Pallanza and Intra, was laid out by captain Neil McEacharn, who bought the property in 1931, and contains over 20,000 species of plants. **Intra** boasted a booming textile manufacturing industry in the 19th century.

One of Europe's largest wilderness areas, the **Parco Nazionale della Val Grande** stretches behind Verbania and is reached from the town of **Cicogna** in the hills above. Dozens of hiking and bike trails lead to meadows, gorges and peaks where chamois goats far outnumber hikers (information office: via Sanremigio 19, Verbania, 0323 557 960, www.parcovalgrande.it, closed Sat, Sun).

Heading towards Switzerland, the Intra-Cannobio road is one of the lake's loveliest. Bordered by weathered stone walls, it winds round the shoreline, passing through quiet, genteel towns and offering views of ruined castles on tiny islands and, across the water, the mountainsides of the sparsely inhabited eastern shore.

North of Intra is **Ghiffa**. Here, the **Museo dell'Arte del Cappello** (corso Belvedere 279, 0323 59 174/59 209, closed Nov-Mar & Mon-Fri Apr-Oct) commemorates the once-thriving local trade of felt hat manufacturing. The **Riserva Naturale Sacro Monte della Santa Trinità** (information office: via Santissima Trinità 48, 0323 59 870, www.sacromonteghiffa.it, closed Sat, Sun), extending behind Ghiffa, has well-marked hiking trails.

Emerging from the waters off the shores of **Cannero Riviera** are the evocative ruins of the Malpaga castles, built on two rocky islets between the 13th and 15th centuries. At one time they were inhabited by pirates who plundered and pillaged the local towns.

The last major stop before the Swiss border is **Cannobio**, a handsome town that features a pleasant promenade lined with cafés and restaurants. Nearby, the Orrido di Sant'Anna is a dramatic gorge plunging into dark depths and crossed by stone bridges. The 17th-century church of Sant'Anna (closed winter) sits perilously on one edge.

Where to eat

In Arona, enjoy excellent grilled vegetables with smoked cheese at the stylish **Caffè della Sera** (lungolago Marconi, 85, 0322 241 567, closed dinner & 2wks Jan-Feb, average €30).

In a villa just outside Lesa is the elegant restaurant **Antico Maniero** (via alla Campagna 1, 0322 7411, www.anticomaniero. com, reservations only, closed Mon, lunch Tue-Sat & Nov, average €60); the fish ravioli at the **Triangolo** in Stresa (via Roma 61, 0323 32 736, closed Tue Sept-July, Dec-Jan, average €35) is superb and compensates for the lack of a view.

In Verbania-Suna, the lively **Osteria Boccon Di Vino** (via Troubetzkoy 86, 0323 504 039, closed lunch Wed, all Thur & Jan, average €30) serves local fare and fine wine, while the cuisine at the elegant **Monastero** (via Castelfidardo 5-7, 0323 502 544, closed Mon, Tue & 2wks Aug, average €50) draws diners from miles around.

At Mergozzo, the central **Ristorante Vecchio Olmo** (piazza Cavour 2, 0323 80 335, closed Thur Sept-June, average €25) has a good-value set menu and excellent fish and home-made pasta.

In Pallanza, **Milano** (corso Zanitello 2, 0323 556 816, closed dinner Mon, all Tue & mid Nov-mid Feb, average €60) serves classic dishes and excellent fish on its lakeside terrace.

Luxe on the lake: Stresa's **Grand Hotel des Iles Borromées**.

In the village of Bee in the hills behind Verbania, the **Chi Ghinn – Locanda e Ristoro** (via Maggiore 21, 0323 56 430, 0323 56 326, closed lunch Wed, all Tue & early Jan-Feb, average €35) has a terrace where local lake-caught delicacies such as crayfish are served.

In Cannobio, **Lo Scalo** (piazza Vittorio Emanuele III 32, 0323 71 480, closed lunch Tue, all Mon & 5wks Jan-Feb, average €45) serves meals made from fresh market produce and freshly baked bread.

Where to stay

At the pleasant **Hotel Giardino** (corso della Repubblica 1, Arona, 0322 45 994, www. giardinoarona.com, doubles €70-€85) half of the rooms have lake views, and some are equipped with jacuzzis.

In Lesa, **Villa Lidia** (via Giuseppe Ferrari 7-9, 0322 7095, mobile 347 993 1607, doubles €75) is a charming three-room B&B.

Among Stresa's most sumptuous five-star belle époque hotels are the **Grand Hotel des Iles Borromées** (corso Umberto I 67, 0323 938 938, www.stresa.net/hotel/borromees, closed mid Dec-mid Jan, doubles €399), where Ernest Hemingway once stayed. There's also the **Hotel Regina Palace** (corso Umberto I 33, 0323 936 936, closed 2wks Dec-Jan, doubles €260-€350), which was used as a location for Gina Lollobrigida's 1950 film *Miss Italia*.

The **Lido Palace Hotel Baveno** (SS Sempione 30, 0323 924 444, www.lidopalace. com, closed Oct-Apr, doubles €130-€205) has an enviable view over the Borromeo islands; luxury suites feature jacuzzis.

In Pallanza, the small **Albergo Villa Azalea** (salita San Remigio 4, 0323 556 692, www.albergovillaazalea.com, closed Nov-mid Mar, doubles €64-€74) is set high in the hills. On the waterfront, the **Hotel Pace** (via Cietti 1, 0323 557 217, closed Nov-Apr, doubles €85-€100) has ten comfortable rooms. The **Grand Hotel Majestic** (via Vittorio Veneto 32, 0323 504305, www.grandhotelmajestic.it, closed Oct, doubles €180-€250) is a handsome belle époque hotel offering breathtaking views of the Isole Boromee. It also has a spa.

In Cannobio, the **Hotel Pironi** (via Marconi 35, 0323 70 624, www.pironihotel.it, closed mid Nov-mid Mar, doubles €115-€150) offers modern comforts in a former 15th-century monastery with frescoed ceilings. A couple of kilometres south, the **Hotel del Lago** (via Nazionale 2, Carmine, 0323 70 595, www. enotecalago.com, closed Nov-Mar, doubles €95-€120) has ten rooms (most with a view over the lake), a private beach and a restaurant serving classic cuisine (average €50). In Cannero Riviera, **La Rondinella** (via Sacchetti 50, 0323 788 098, www.hotel-la-rondinella.it, closed 3wks Jan, doubles €78-€90) features 13 rooms in a 1930s villa furnished with antiques.

Tourist information

APT Arona

Piazza Duca d'Aosta (0322 243 601/www.comune. arona.no.it). **Open** *Apr-Sept* 9am-12.30pm, 3-6pm Mon-Sat. *Oct-Mar* 9am-noon, 3-6pm Mon-Fri.

IAT Stresa

Piazza Marconi 16 (0323 30 150). **Open** *Apr-Oct* 10am-12.30pm, 3-6.30pm daily. *Nov-Mar* 10am-12.30pm, 3-6.30pm Mon-Fri; 10am-12.30pm Sat.

IAT Verbania

Corso Zanitello 6-8 (0323 503 249/www.verbania-turismo.it). **Open** *Apr-Sept* 9am-12.30pm, 3-6pm Mon-Sat; 9am-12.30pm Sun. *Oct-Mar* 9am-12.30pm, 3-6pm Mon-Fri.

Pro Loco IAT Cannobio

Viale Vittorio Veneto 4 (0323 71 212/www.procannobio.it). **Open** *Apr-Sept* 9am-noon, 4-7pm Mon-Sat; 9am-noon Sun. *Oct-Mar* 9am-noon, 4.30-7pm Mon-Wed, Fri, Sat; 9am-noon Sun.

The Swiss shore

Mellowed stone, elegant villas and a certain shabby gentility give way to modern buildings and an air of efficiency over on the Swiss side of Lago Maggiore; the bustling towns and smart boutiques make it worth a visit, though.

Brissago's reputation rests on its production of fine cigars. During the summer months, boats operated by Navigazione Lago Maggiore (*see p197*) serve the **Isola di San Pancrazio**, with its **Parco Botanico** (0041 91 791 4361, closed Nov-late Mar).

North-east of Brissago is the ancient fishing village of **Ascona**, which hosts an important European jazz festival (end June-early July, www.jazzascona.ch) and, from August to October, classical music events (www.settimane-musicali.ch).

Locarno, at the lake's northern tip, hosts a prestigious film festival (www.pardo.ch) every August. The remains of a 14th-century tower are a reminder that the Visconti family once ruled here. Two attractions worth a visit are the Pinacoteca (art gallery) inside the 17th-century Casa Rusca (piazza Sant'Antonio, 0041 91 756 3185/172, www.locarno.ch, closed Mon & 2wks Jan) and the **Museo Archeologico** (via al Castello, 0041 91 756 3170, closed Mon & Nov-Mar). To reach the art-filled **Madonna del Sasso** church, either take the funicular or walk up the steep hill flanked by the Stations of the Cross.

Take note that, in theory, you will need your passport when crossing the border into Switzerland, though in practice people are often just waved through.

Where to eat, drink & stay

In Brissago, the family-run **Hotel Eden** (via Vamara 26, 0041 91 793 1255, www.hotel-eden-brissago.ch, closed Nov-mid Mar, doubles SF156-SF204) is a pleasant option.

In Ascona, a 13th-century castle houses the **Romantik Castello-Seeschloss** (piazza Motta, 0041 91 791 0161, www.castello-seeschloss.ch, closed Nov-Mar, doubles SF248-SF548).

In Locarno, the lakefront **Treff Hotel Beau Rivage** (viale Verbano 31, 0041 91 743 1355, closed Nov-early Mar, doubles SF162-SF210) is modern and attractive. For a more historic stay, the **Schlosshotel** (via Rusca 9, 0041 91 751 2361, www.schlosshotellocarno.ch, closed Dec-mid Mar, doubles SF160-SF210) occupies part of the Visconti castle.

Centenario (lungolago Motta 17, 0041 91 743 8222, closed Mon & Sun, 3wks Jan & 2wks July, average SF80) is an elegant eaterie in Locarno. In the Valle Maggia, 11km (7 miles) north of Locarno, **Uno Più** (Gordevio, 0041 91 753 1012, closed Dec-Mar, average SF30) serves local seasonal delicacies; there are also six rooms (doubles SF110-SF168).

Tourist information

Ente Turistico Lago Maggiore

Via B Luini 3, Locarno (0041 91 791 0091/www.maggiore.ch). **Open** *Apr-Oct* 9am-6pm Mon-Fri; 10am-6pm Sat; 10am-1.30pm, 2.30-5pm Sun. *Nov-Mar* 9.30am-noon, 1.30-5pm Mon-Fri; 10am-noon, 1.30-5pm Sat.
The tourist office includes a bureau de change.

The Lombardy shore

Despite a couple of unmissable sights, the lake's eastern (Lombard) shore is less of a draw for tourists and has a decidedly low-key feel. The scarcity of public transport serving this side of the lake is no doubt a factor.

In **Luino**, the church of San Pietro has frescoes attributed to local artist Bernardino Luini and a Romanesque bell tower.

To the south, **Laveno** is a busy port, with ferries to Intra (*see p194*).

Perched precipitously on a lip in the rock face 18 metres (60 feet) above the water near Leggiuno is the exquisite 12th-century **Eremo di Santa Caterina del Sasso Ballaro** (0332 647 172, closed Mon-Fri Nov-Feb). Home to Dominican monks and lavishly adorned with frescoes dating from the 14th century, the sanctuary has heart-stopping views across the lake. It can be reached by boat or by 250-odd (steep) steps from the car park.

Angera's **Rocca Borromeo** (via alla Rocca, 0331 931 300, closed late Oct-mid Mar), a towered and crenellated fortress built in the 11th century and expanded and fortified until the 17th, dominates the lake's southern stretches from its clifftop position. In Visconti hands from the 13th century, it became Borromeo property in 1449. One wing contains a rare cycle of 14th-century frescoes by local Lombard artists; another houses a collection of 17th-century dolls and children's toys. The

Borromeo wing features frescoes taken from the family's palazzo in Milan.

The **Museo Archeologico** at **Sesto Calende**, on the lake's southern tip, is usually bypassed for the nearby ninth- to 12th-century abbey of San Donato (0331 923 459, www.prosestocalende.it/Donato.htm), or the Iron Age tombs at Golasecca, which are accessible from the Sesto–Golasecca road.

Where to eat & stay

In Angera, the pleasant **Hotel dei Tigli** (via Paletta 20, 0331 930 836, www.hoteldeitigli.com, closed 3wks Dec-Jan, doubles €110-€130) has period furniture, as well as wireless internet connection in all the rooms. In Sesto Calende, the seven-room **Locanda Sole** (via Ruga del Porto Vecchio 1, 0331 914 273, www. trattorialocandasole.it, doubles €90) is in a centrally located 18th-century house, and has a restaurant with a panoramic terrace that serves fish specialities.

For a truly memorable meal, including exquisite fish, at truly memorable prices, try **Il Sole** at Ranco (piazza Venezia 5, 0331 976 507, www.ilsolediranco.it, closed Mon lunch, all Tue & Dec-mid Feb, average €100); it also has accommodation (doubles €180-€242).

At Laveno, just south of Mombello, the **Hotel Porticciolo** (via Fortino 40, 0332 667 257, www.ilporticciolo.com, closed 2wks Jan-Feb, 1wk Nov, doubles €97-€180) is a charming hotel with a good restaurant (average €45, closed Tue).

An inexpensive option in Laveno itself is the lakefront **Hotel Moderno** (via Garibaldi 15, 0332 668 373, closed Jan & Feb, www. meoblemoderno.it, doubles €60-€70), which has simple, clean rooms.

In Luino, the **Camin Hotel Luino** (viale Dante 35, 0332 530 118, www.camin hotelluino.com, closed 5wks Dec-Jan, doubles €130-€165) is a 19th-century villa with a garden, decorated with art deco furniture. **Casottino Risto Caffè** (via Rossini 6, 0332 537 882, average €20) serves simple, traditional fare.

Tourist information

IAT Laveno-Mombello

Via de' Angeli 18 (0332 666 666/www.laveno-online.it). **Open** *Apr, Sept* 9am-noon Mon-Sat. *May-Aug* 9am-noon, 3-6pm Mon-Sat.

IAT Luino

Via Piero Chiara 1 (0332 530 019/www.varese landoftourism.it). **Open** *Easter-Sept* 9am-noon, 2.30-6.30pm daily. *Oct-Easter* 9am-noon, 2.30-6.30pm Mon-Sat.

Getting there

By boat

Navigazione Lago Maggiore (0322 46 651/Swiss side: 0041 91 751 6140, www.navigazionelaghi.it or www.navlaghi.it) operates boats, and hydrofoils, to most of the towns around the lake, including the Swiss side; seasonal schedules. Local water taxis may be rented at many of the ports, including Stresa.

By bus

Autoservizi Nerini (0323 552 172, www.safduemila. com) and Baldioli (0332 530 271, www.baldioli.it) provide a twice-daily commuter bus service, to the Piedmont and the Lombard shores respectively, from Porta Garibaldi.

On the western shore, Trasporti Nerini (0323 552 172) runs a service between Arona and Verbania; VCO Trasporti (0323 518 711) operates between Verbania to Brissago and Switzerland.

Autolinee Nicora e Baratelli (0332 668 056, www. sila.it) runs regular services between Luino and Laveno on the eastern shore.

On the Swiss side, FART Viaggi (0041 91 751 8731) runs a regular service between Locarno and Brissago.

By car

The A8 motorway gets you from Milan to Sesto Calende. For towns on the lake's western (Piedmont) shores, take the A26 towar ds Gravellona Toce. The S33 skirts the lake to Fondotoce, where it becomes the S34 to Cannobio.

For the eastern shore, take the S629 to Laveno, then the S394, which skirts the lake, to Luino and beyond.

For Locarno, on the lake's Swiss side, take the A9 motorway from Milan to Bellinzona, then follow the signs. The road that meanders along the lake starts as via Cantonale 13, becoming 22 on the eastern side.

By train

For the western (Piedmont) shore, take the Domodossola service from Milan's Stazione Centrale station. This stops at Sesto Calende, Arona (journey time 1hr), Meina, Lesa, Belgirate, Stresa (1hr 30mins), Baveno, Verbania/Pallanza (1hr 40mins), Mergozzo, and Candoglia. Express trains from the Stazione Centrale serve Arona (45mins) and Stresa (1hr).

Rail services to the eastern (Lombardy) shore are relatively scarce. There are direct services from Milan's Porta Garibaldi to Sesto Calende. For Luino or Portotravaglia, take the train to Varese or Domodossola from Milan's Garibaldi or Centrale stations and change at Gallarate. Journey time 1hr 30mins-2hrs.

For Laveno and Luino, take the Ferrovie Nord service from Cadorna station. Journey time 50mins.

For the Swiss shore, take the train to Domodossola from Milan's Stazione Centrale (1hr). Trains run from Domodossola to Locarno along the northern shore. However, rail enthusiasts, as well as lovers of rugged alpine landscapes, will want to opt for the Centovalli, or Hundred Valleys Railway. This 1hr 40min ride covers the 55km (34-mile) stretch of the Val Vigezzo, crossing some 86 bridges. There may or may not be 100 valleys, but this is surely one of the finest mountain railway journeys anywhere in Europe.

Trips Out of Town

Lago di Como

A thing of beauty.

This world-famous beauty spot had been attracting the rich and famous for at least a couple of millennia before George Clooney moved in. Como-born Pliny the Younger (AD 62-112) wrote ecstatically of the 'several villas' he possessed on the lake, singling out two (which he called Comedy and Tragedy) as his special favourites, gushing of one that 'you can quite simply cast your line out of the window without getting out of bed'. In the 19th century, Stendhal, Rossini and Shelley all stayed at Villa Pliniana in Torno. Vincenzo Bellini sojourned at Villa Passalacqua in Moltrasio between 1829 and 1833, during which time he wrote his opera *La Sonnambula*. More recent visitors to Moltrasio have included Elton John and Madonna, who were guests at Gianni Versace's villa, Le Fontanelle.

Whereas most of the people mentioned above would have been visiting by invitation, others in the past did not have the good grace to wait to be asked. The Celts, in about 520 BC, are a good example. According to Livy, they made their way through the Splügen (or possibly the San Bernardino) Pass, decided they liked the Como area, and opted to stay. In 196 BC the Romans took over, setting up a *castrum* (settlement) in what is now downtown Como. Providing a link between central Europe and the Mediterranean, the area was of considerable commercial and strategic importance.

In AD 569 the Lombards decided they wanted a piece of the action and promptly took residence within the walled town. In the 11th century Como started to give as good as it got, and expanded its hold over the surrounding area. But things did not go as planned, and in 1186 Como signed a peace treaty, after which it was allied with Milan.

Defeated militarily, Como succeeded brilliantly on an artistic level. All through the Middle Ages, the skills of its itinerant stonemasons – the *maestri comacini* – were in demand far and wide. Their exquisite carvings embellished brick- and stone-faced walls and façades throughout the region, the rest of northern Italy and beyond.

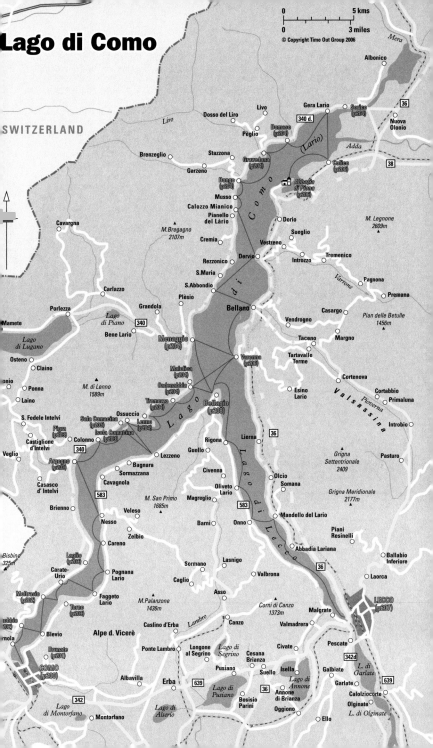

Lago di Como

Como gradually built a reputation as a centre for silk-weaving and by 1769, when Emperor Joseph II of Austria visited, some 155 looms were licensed. The city is still famed for its silk, even if the silkworms are no longer raised on the lake and raw thread is now imported from the Far East.

Lake Como – or Lario, as it has been known since Roman times – extends in an inverted Y shape from the Alps in the north to the plain just 70 kilometres (42 miles) from Milan in the south. Cólico is at the northerly extreme, while the cities of Como and Lecco, some 50 kilometres (30 miles) away, are located at other two ends. The three 'arms' come together to form the promontory of Bellagio.

Despite the fact that the lake has a 178-kilometre (106-mile) perimeter, and is Italy's third largest (and Europe's deepest), it is never more than four and a half kilometres (three miles) wide, which creates a sense of intimacy. Moreover, each of the lake's 'arms' is different. The Como section is relatively narrow; the mountains behind are somewhat uniform, with plenty of little towns and grand villas along the shoreline. The Lecco branch is more rugged, the jagged edges of the Grigne range providing a strong contrast. The northern part features deep valleys and tall mountains, and is the most dramatic.

The scenery is at its most spectacular in the central section of the lake, around the triangle of Bellagio, Menaggio and Varenna (*il triangolo lariano*).

The best time to come? It is a common belief in Italy that lakes in general, not just Como, are *tristi* (sad) from October to March. Make up your own mind, but it's worth noting that some hotels and restaurants may be closed during the winter months.

Como

Como is busy, industrialised and, outside the pretty pedestrianised area, traffic-ridden. If you enjoy open-air markets, come on a Saturday. The entire area around the city walls, as well as several *piazze,* fills with stalls selling fruit and veg, clothes, shoes and antiques; there's even a section devoted to rocks and minerals.

On the lakeside by the ferry jetty, piazza Cavour is one of Como's most popular meeting points. The neo-classical **Mausoleo Voltiano**, or Tempio Voltiano (viale Marconi, 031 574 705, closed Mon), in the **Giardini Pubblici** west of the square, was erected in 1927 to mark the centenary of the death of Alessandro Volta, the Como-born physicist who invented the battery and gave his name to the volt; the museum contains some of his original instruments.

A brilliant fusion of Romanesque, Gothic, Renaissance and baroque, Como's **Duomo** (piazza del Duomo, 031 265 244; **photo** *p201*), begun in 1396, is unique – as well as spectacularly beautiful. Its late-Gothic façade (1455-86) is even more striking for the fact that pride of place is given to two renowned pagans – the Plinies, Older and Younger. Note also Tommaso Rodari's intricate Frog Door (Porta della Rana) leading into the left side of the nave. In the Latin-cross interior, the three-aisled nave is Gothic and the transept Renaissance, while the great octagonal dome was designed by Filippo Juvarra in baroque style in 1744.

Abutting the apse end of the Duomo, in piazza Verdi, stands the 19th-century **Teatro Sociale** (via Bellini 3, 031 270 170, www.teatrosocialecomo.it, closed Sun & Aug), its neo-classical façade adorned with six mighty Corinthian pillars. The theatre had its moment of glory at the end of World War II when its opera season outshone Milan's, if only because La Scala had been badly damaged in bombings.

Further east, in piazza del Popolo, is Giuseppe Terragni's **Casa del Fascio** (1932-6), also known as Palazzo Terragni. A perfect example of Italian Rationalist architecture, with its clean-cut lines, outside and in, the building is currently used by the Guardia di Finanza, the Italian customs and excise police. Visits are possible, though (after 4.30pm Mon-Thur, after 1pm Fri, 10am-1pm Sat, Sun), as long as someone is available to accompany you. Ask at the porters' lodge (*portineria*) and be prepared to leave an ID document for the duration of the visit.

Still further west, on via Sinigaglia, Terragni's **Novocomum** apartment block (1927-9) is another prime example of Italian Rationalist architecture.

San Fedele is in the piazza of the same name. Built some time between the tenth and 12th centuries, the church was named after the saint who brought Christianity to Como in the fourth century. It was Como's cathedral until the Duomo was built at the end of the 14th century. The rose window over the reconstructed main entrance is from the 16th century; the majority of the decorations inside are baroque.

See the remaining stretches of Como's 12th-century walls along viale Battisti to the imposing **Porta Torre** gate (1192). The **Basilica di Sant'Abbondio** (via Sant'Abbondio) is one of the greatest jewels of the Lombard Romanesque. Visiting monks from northern Europe are perhaps responsible for the innovative design of this Benedictine abbey church – including the twin bell towers, a Norman touch – built to replace an earlier structure in the 11th century.

A little off the beaten track, but worth the effort, is the **Museo Didattico della Seta** (Silk Museum, via Castelnuovo 1, 031 303 180, www.museosetacomo.com, closed Mon, Sun, open Sat only by appointment). This lovingly curated museum brings the city's main industry to life. It's housed inside Como's silk-making school, and displays include examples of silk looms through the ages, printing equipment, dyeing processes and numerous examples of the end product.

No trip to Como is complete without a visit to **Brunate**, the village 720 metres (2,400 feet) above Como town. The funicular railway (adjacent to the Como Nord Lago railway station, www.geocities.com/funicolare comobrunate), will take you up there in just under seven minutes, at gradients of up to 55 per cent. However, if this seems like the easy way out, by all means walk it – it will take about an hour and a half to cover the five kilometres (three miles).

It's worth going to Brunate for stunning views over the lake, but also for a stroll around. Outside the perimeter walls you can admire some of the villas built in the 19th and early 20th centuries, when Brunate became a resort for the well-heeled, thanks to the construction of the funicular. The **Grand Hotel Brunate** and the **Grand Hotel Milano**, both of which have now been diverted to other functions, attest to that past glory.

Where to eat & drink

There's good pizza at **Le Colonne Ristorante Pizzeria** (piazza Mazzini 12, 031 266 166, average pizza €10, menu €25). **Breeze Inn Ristorante** (via Natta 29, 031 242 320, www.breeze-inn.com, closed lunch Mon, all Sun, 2wks Aug & 1wk Dec, average €45) serves local specialities in a pleasant setting. Housed in a converted barn, **Il Solito Posto** (via Lambertenghi 9, 031 271 352, closed Mon, 1wk Jan & 1wk Aug, average €40) prepares creative dishes with local ingredients. The café at La Tessitura (*see below*) is another option.

Shopping

Although the raw thread is now imported, Como's reputation as a centre of excellence for silk textile manufacturing and printing lives on. Factories with retail outlets include **Martinetti** (via Torriani 41, 031 269 053, www.martinetti.it, closed Sun & 3wks Aug), which can be reached on foot from piazza Cavour.

It's also worth checking out the collection called **La Tessitura** by Mantero, one of the top names in luxury silk design and production.

Como's **Duomo**. *See p200.*

Accessories for women, men and the home have been created by Mantero's in-house team of international designers using remnants of luxury silk that have been redyed, retextured, rewoven, reprinted or taken from one-off colour samples. La Tessitura's outlet at viale Roosevelt 2A (031 321 666, www.latessitura.com) also has a chic café.

Where to stay

The **Barchetta Excelsior** (piazza Cavour 1, 031 3221, www.hotelbarchetta.it, doubles €190-€350) is located right on the lakeside. In the same square, the **Metropole & Suisse** (piazza Cavour 19, 031 269 444, www.hotel metropolesuisse.com, closed 3wks Dec-Jan, doubles €135-€188) has been going strong since 1892; its restaurant, **L'Imbarcadero** (average €50; set menu €25), is highly regarded. **Le Due Corti** (piazza Vittoria 12-13, 031 328 111, doubles €138-€203) is a romantic spot, while the centrally located **Albergo Ristorante Posta** (via Garibaldi 2, 031 266 012, www.hotelposta.net, doubles €77-€92.50) is another comfortable choice.

Tourist information

IAT Como

Piazza Cavour 17 (031 269 712/www.lakecomo.it). **Open** *June-Sept* 9am-1pm, 2.30-6pm Mon-Sat; 9am-1pm Sun. *Oct-May* 9am-1pm, 2.30-6pm Mon-Sat.

The western shore

The first stop on the commuter-boat service from Como is **Cernobbio**. This town of magnificent villas and private boat jetties is dominated by **Villa d'Este**, originally one of three villas built for Tolomeo Gallio when he was made a cardinal in 1565. In 1814 the villa became the home of Princess Caroline of Brunswick, the estranged wife of Britain's Prince Regent. It was she who decided to remodel the house and gardens, and gave it its current name. There is, in fact, no connection with the famous d'Este family from Ferrara. After Queen Caroline sold the villa, it was eventually acquired by a wealthy Milanese family who had it converted into a hotel in 1873. (*see p206*). The villa became the focus of world attention in March 2006, when it was rumoured that Brad Pitt and Angelina Jolie were to marry here.

Although much of the magnificent 16th-century Italian garden has been lost, the extraordinary water staircase survives – walk up the grass-covered steps as water falls on either side. Framing the staircase are theatrical shell- and pebble-mosaic wings topped with obelisks.

Back on the boat, head north for **Moltrasio**. In spring, a gorge splits this small town in two and fills with a rapidly flowing torrent as the snow above melts. Moltrasio is also home to the 11th-century church of **Santa Agata**, with its fine campanile; next door is the 18th-century **Villa Passalacqua**, which has a stunning Italian garden (closed Mon-Wed, Fri-Sun). The opera composer Vincenzo Bellini wrote *La Sonnambula* while staying here between 1829 and 1833.

There are other important villas in Moltrasio. In 1945 Winston Churchill stayed in **Villa Le Rose**, which has a handsome garden, while

Water gardens

The balmy microclimate of Lake Como has afforded splendid opportunities to gardeners and garden-lovers over the centuries. One of the finest examples is the garden of **Villa del Balbianello**, located just south of Lenno. Built on a headland that protrudes into the lake, a space that offered no scope for a formal Italian garden (or what the Italians call *un giardino all'inglese*), the gardens are what one might call site-specific. They interact with the lake and shoreline rather than follow any set design or concept. The fact that they are approached by water adds to the impact: visitors can feel what it was like to arrive as a guest of the original owners – among them the Cardinal Durini, the families of Porro

Lambertenghi and Arconati Visconti and the explorer Count Guido Monzino. It was the latter who bequeathed Balbianello to the FAI (Fondo Ambiente Italiano), Italy's equivalent of Britain's National Trust.

Renowned for its plane trees clipped into candle shapes, the garden follows a steep slope, where statues alternate with wisteria, and azaleas and rhododendrons provide exhilarating bursts of colour throughout the spring and early summer. Built in the 16th century and extended in the 18th, the villa can be visited by appointment only.

Rhododendrons are also very much in evidence among the 500-plus plant varieties in the 80,000 square metres (861,000

Villa Le Fontanelle was acquired by the late Gianni Versace in 1977. Both can be visited free of charge.

On the opposite shore from Moltrasio is the village of **Torno**, which is also associated with famous guests. In the 19th century Shelley, Stendhal and Rossini all stayed at **Villa Pliniana**. As is typical with many of these dream residences, the villa can only be reached by a footpath or by water – privacy guaranteed.

For many years the village of **Laglio**, just north of Moltrasio, was known primarily for the remains of a prehistoric bear found in the Grotta del Buco dell'Orso. That was BG (Before George). Mr Clooney bought **Villa Oleandra** as his private pad in 2002; as a result, the village has become world-famous. To see the house, cruise by on the boat. To see George, head for the nearest cinema.

Back in Moltrasio, take the fast ferry for Cólico and get off at the first stop, the little resort of **Argegno**. From here, a cable car (031 821 344) makes the journey every day of the year up to **Pigra**, a lofty hamlet with superb views across the lake to Isola Comacina and the Bellagio promontory.

Boats depart daily from the village of **Sala Comacina** (031 821 955, mobile 335 707 4122, www.boatservices.it, no service Nov-Feb) for **Isola Comacina**, the only island on the lake. Just 600 metres (1,970 feet) long, 200 metres (650 feet) wide and two kilometres (one and a quarter miles) in circumference, it has plenty of history to boast about. The Romans and the Byzantines used it as a fortified settlement; the Lombard king Autari seized it in AD 590; Como razed it in the early 12th century. The islanders had backed the Milanese against the town. As Como also had Frederick Barbarossa on its side,

---

square feet) of garden at **Villa Carlotta**, in Tremezzo. Named after princess Charlotte, who received it as a wedding present from her mother princess Marianna of Nassau in 1843, the villa was built in neo-classical style in the early 1700s for the marquis Giorgio Clerici.

Leading to the villa are five terraces, with stairs to either side; the geometric lines are softened by vines, climbing roses and trailing geraniums. The house contains many sculptures, including Antonio Canova's *Cupid and Psyche*.

Villa Melzi and Villa Serbelloni are two extra attractions for visitors to Bellagio. While neither of the houses is open to the public, the gardens are more than worth seeing. **Villa Melzi** (**photo** *left*) boasts a pretty Japanese garden, some splendid water lilies and a Moorish-looking, lapis lazuli-blue coffee house.

Open for guided tours twice a day, the 17th-century **Villa Serbelloni** – which is owned by the Rockefeller Foundation – stands high on the point above Bellagio's town centre. It may be on the site of Pliny the Younger's villa Tragedia (he had another villa called Commedia at Lenno; *see p204*). The trees in the gardens of Villa Serbelloni, added in the 19th century, are worth noting. Although they seem to blend effortlessly into the landscape, these were, in fact, among the first examples of magnolias, oleanders, palms and cedars ever planted in Italy.

Villa del Balbianello
Via Comoedia 8, Lenno (0344 56 110/ www.fondoambiente.it). **Open** 10am-6pm Tue, Thur-Sun. **Admission** *Gardens* €5; *Gardens & villa* €11. **No credit cards**. Boats depart every half hour from the jetty at Lenno (*see p204*), between 9.45am and 3.45pm. On Tue, Sat, Sun and public holidays, a footpath provides access to the gardens from Lenno.

Villa Carlotta
Via Regina 2, Tremezzo (0344 40 405/ www.villacarlotta.it). **Open** *Villa Apr-Sept* 9am-6pm daily. *Mid-Mar, Oct* 9am-noon, 2-4.30pm daily. *Gardens Apr-Sept* 9am-7.30pm daily. *Mid-Mar, Oct* 9am-5pm daily. **Admission** €7.50; €3.75 concessions. **No credit cards**.

Villa Melzi
Lungolario Marconi, Bellagio (031 950 204/ www.bellagiolakecomo.com). **Open** *mid Mar-Oct* 9am-6pm daily. **Admission** €6; €5 concessions. **No credit cards**.

Villa Serbelloni
Piazza della Chiesa, Bellagio (031 951 555/ 031 950 204/www.bellagiolakecomo.com). **Open** *Apr-Oct* 11am, 4pm Tue-Sun. **Admission** €7; €5.50 concessions. **No credit cards**. Only guided tours of the garden are available, at the times given above. You can book tickets at the nearby IAT Bellagio (*see p208*).

Trips Out of Town

this was not a smart move. Bought in 1918 by the king of Belgium, who later donated it to Milan's fine arts academy, the island is now home to a restaurant, a handful of ancient ruined churches and the baroque oratory of **San Giovanni** (St John), the patron saint of Como. This is also why the island is sometimes referred to as the Isola San Giovanni. The festival of Saint John (24 June) provides the occasion for a spectacular fireworks display.

LA TREMEZZINA

Awash with camelias and azaleas and dotted with luxurious villas, La Tremezzina is a gorgeous stretch of coast from Lenno to Menaggio. There are a few faded reminders of an age when British dowagers came to winter (and summer) here: an Anglican church (in Cadenabbia), a Victorian tearoom and even a crazy-golf course.

Lenno may have been the site of Commedia, one of Pliny the Younger's villas (*see p202* **Water gardens**) – the baths of a sumptuous Roman villa were unearthed in the crypt of the town's 11th-century parish church of **Santo Stefano**, which has an octagonal baptistery. Just south of the church, a path leads to the 12th-century abbey of **Acquafredda** (0344 55 208), built by Cistercian monks but now home to some Capuchins. Lenno's jetty is the departure point for boats to the picture-perfect **Villa del Balbianello** (*see p202* **Water gardens**).

In **Tremezzo**, the neo-classical **Villa Carlotta** (*see p202* **Water gardens**) boasts sculptures by Antonio Canova and a massive, spectacular garden.

At **Cadenabbia**, the lake is at its widest. A foot and car ferry plies between here and Bellagio, while another car ferry goes to Varenna. Giuseppe Verdi composed much of *La Traviata* in **Villa Margherita Ricordi** (closed to the public), in the nearby hamlet of **Maiolica**.

Long a bustling commercial town and now an equally bustling resort, pretty pink- and ochre-tinted **Menaggio** has a ruined castle and lovely views across to Bellagio and the eastern shore. Menaggio is 12 kilometres (eight miles) from Lake Lugano (*see also p207* **Luck be a lake tonight**); keen walkers (with the emphasis on keen), might want to consider the hike up to **Monte Bregagno**, from which, on a very clear day, it is possible to see both lakes. A car ferry links Menaggio and Varenna.

THE NORTHERN REACHES

Continuing north towards the peaks overlooking the Valchiavenna valley, you reach the **Tre Pievi** ('three parishes') of Dongo, Gravedona and Sòrico. These formed an independent community in the Middle Ages

and were powerful enough to wrest a special deal at the Treaty of Constance (1183), which put an end to the wars between Frederick Barbarossa and the Italian city-states.

Remembered as the place where Mussolini and his lover Claretta Petacci were captured on 27 April 1945 as they headed for the Swiss border, **Dongo** was also the scene of violence in 1252, when St Peter Martyr was finished off with a hatchet through by Cathar heretics.

A manufacturing town and popular water-sports centre, **Gravedona** was the most important of the Tre Pievi and a key ally of medieval Milan – hence it was razed by Como in the 12th century. The Romanesque church of **Santa Maria del Tiglio** (via Roma) is simple, severe and stunning. **Palazzo Gallio**, also known as Palazzo del Pero, was the second of the three houses commissioned by Tolomeo Gallio from Pellegrino Tibaldi (Villa d'Este, *see p206*, was another).

The fishing village of **Domaso** still produces a white wine mentioned by Pliny the Elder. It is also Lake Como's recognised windsurfing centre. In fortified **Sòrico**, tolls were extracted from travellers arriving on the lake's shores from the Valchiavenna and the Valtellina.

Where to eat

In the hamlet of Piazza Santo Stefano, above Cernobbio, **Trattoria al Glicine** (via Paolo Carcano 1, 031 511 332, closed 2wks Jan, average €40) serves typical Mediterranean cuisine under a wisteria-covered pergola with a splendid view of the lake. In Moltrasio, **Crotto Valdurino** (via Besana 37, 031 290 101, closed Tue, average €20) and **Imperialino** (via Antica Regina 26, 031 346 600, closed 5wks Jan-Feb, average €55) are both reliable.

In Sala Comacina, **La Comacina** (via Statale 14, 0344 55 035, closed Mon & Nov, average €25) offers filling, hearty pasta dishes, while **La Tirlindana** (piazza Matteotti 5, 0344 56 637, www.tirlindana.lariovalle.it, closed Wed Mar-Oct & Mon-Fri Nov-Feb, average €45) is renowned for its delicious ravioli stuffed with lemon-flavoured cheese.

In Lenno, the family-run **Santo Stefano** (piazza XI Febbraio 3, 0344 55 434, closed Mon & mid Jan-mid Feb, average €30) serves the hard-to-find local delicacy *missoltini* (called shad in English, but don't let that put you off) and other lake fish.

Tremezzo has various restaurants linked to the **Grand Hotel Tremezzo Palace** (*see p206*). But, for a change of pace (and price), try **Trattoria del Rana** (via Monte Grappa 27, 0344 40 602, closed Tue & 3wks Oct, average €20), a laid-back eaterie.

Bellagio. *See p208.*

Where to stay

For unbeatable luxury, and if you are happy to dress up for dinner, **Villa d'Este** (viale Regina 40, Cernobbio, 031 3481, www.villadeste.it, closed mid Nov-Feb, doubles €465-€890) is the place. If your budget won't stretch to that, have a drink in the bar (€15) and visit the gardens (*see p202*). You can get a ticket at the entrance.

In Tremezzo, the splendid art nouveau **Grand Hotel Tremezzo Palace** (via Regina 8, 0344 42 491, www.grandhoteltremezzo.com, closed end Nov-end Feb, doubles €229-€880) is another luxury option, with spectacular views over the lake.

In Moltrasio, the **Albergo Posta Ristorante** (piazza San Rocco 5, 031 290 444, www.hotel-posta.it, closed Jan & Feb, doubles €95-€135) is a reliable bet, while Lenno's **San Giorgio** (via Regina 81, 0344 40 415, closed Oct-Mar, doubles €110-€120, breakfast €10.50) is modest but pleasant, in a modern building with a garden.

The private beach at Menaggio's **Grand Hotel Victoria** (lungolago Castelli 9, 0344 32 003, www.centrohotelslagocomo.it, closed Nov-Feb, doubles €120-€240) is a great base for windsurfing.

Tourist information

APT Cernobbio

Piazza Cavour 17 (031 343 211/www.lakecomo.org).
Open *May-Sept* 9am-1pm, 2.30-6pm Mon-Sat; 9am-12.30pm Sun.

IAT Menaggio

Piazza Garibaldi 3 (0344 32 924/www.menaggio.com).
Open *Apr-Sept* 9am-12.30pm, 2.30-6pm daily. *Oct-Mar* 9am-12.30pm, 2.30-6pm Mon-Sat.

Pro Loco Tremezzo

Via Peduzzi 6 (0344 40 493/www.tremezzo.it).
Open *May-Sept* 9am-noon, 3.30-6.30pm Mon-Wed, Fri, Sat.

The eastern shore

Mountains drop precipitously into the lake waters along much of Como's eastern shore, making for considerably lower-density tourist development than across the water.

From **Cólico**, an unprepossessing port town at the far north-eastern end of the lake, the SS36 road plunges through tunnels on its swift way south towards Lecco (*see p207*) and Milan. Opt for the slower lakeside road if you want to see the sights, or take a boat excursion to the nearby **Abbazia di Piona** (0341 940 331, www.cistercensi.info/piona/capitolo.htm). This is on a small promontory separating Lake Como proper from the oddly green Laghetto di Piona. Consecrated as a Cluniac house in 1138, the striking abbey is now home to Cistercians. The complex has a 13th-century cloister with Romanesque and Gothic columns and fragments of earlier frescoes lining its walls, as well as the abbey-church of San Nicolao.

The Pioverna river thunders down the **Orrido di Bellano**, a gorge providing the driving force for the hydroelectricity that has long powered the area's textile industry. You can feel the force for yourself by braving the bridge suspended above the torrent (0341 821 124, www.comune.bellano.lc.it, open daily Apr-Sept, weekends or by appointment Oct-Mar).

Varenna, an ancient fishing village, is the most sedately elegant of the lake's resorts. **Villa Monastero** (0341 295 450, www.villamonastero.org, gardens closed Nov-Mar) began life as a 13th-century convent. Adjacent to Villa Monastero is **Villa Cipressi** (0341 295 450, 0341 830 113, gardens closed Nov-Mar). The late 16th-century pile, built for the Serpenti family, has a spectacular lakeside position and beautiful gardens.

A path leads from Varenna to the **Fiumelatte** ('river of milk'). This is Italy's shortest, most mysterious, and most predictable, river. Its frothy milk-white water rushes for all of 250 metres (833 feet) down the rockface and crashes into the lake from the end of March to the end of October each year – and then stops. Leonardo da Vinci climbed down to find out what happened to it the rest of the year, but neither he nor anyone else has ever discovered the secret. (He made reference to it in the *Codex Atlanticus*.) A 20-minute walk leads to the ruined **Castello di Vezio** (open daily Apr-Sept, closed most days in winter), which boasts a splendid view of the lake. Then you can take the relatively short – but rather steep – set of steps (it takes about 20 minutes) back down to the centre of the town, and have a well-deserved drink in the piazza.

Passenger ferries connect Varenna with Menaggio (*see p204*); a car ferry links it to Cadenabbia (*see p204*) and Bellagio (*see p208*).

Where to stay & eat

In Varenna, romantic **Vecchia Varenna** (contrada Scoscesa 14, 0341 830 793, www.vecchiavarenna.it, closed Mon in May-Oct, Mon & Tue in Nov-Mar, all Jan, average €40) serves excellent fish fresh from the lake on a lovely terrace in summer or in its cosy interior when temperatures drop. Equally

Luck be a lake tonight

Harry Lime in *The Third Man*: 'In Italy for 30 years under the Borgias, they had warfare, terror, bloodshed and murder but they produced Michelangelo, Leonardo da Vinci and the Renaissance. In Switzerland, they had brotherly love, they had 500 years of democracy and peace. And what did that produce? The cuckoo clock.'

Not even Graham Greene could have envisioned a plot of espionage and intrigue such as that concocted in Campione d'Italia, an enclave that is part-Italian, part-Swiss, and entirely unique (if somewhat identity-challenged). It lies on the shore of Lago di Lugano, where 3,000 people live in an area less then three square kilometres (one square mile). They are technically Italian but their currency is the Swiss franc; their cars have Swiss plates. Culturally, they try to strike a balance between the disparate sensibilities of being both Italian and Swiss. There's no hospital, so to be born, they have to go to Lugano or back into Italy at Como. There's no cemetery either, so life's full circle has to be completed elsewhere.

But what this odd place does have is a casino. It's literally the only game in town. The first casino opened in 1917 with the improbable intent of luring spies and diplomats to divulge their wartime secrets once compromised at the roulette wheel. This James Bond-like form of espionage worked. Later, Mussolini saw the casino as a tax generator and had a larger lakeside house of gaming built in the Fascist architectural style.

In 2006 a spanking new one opened that should put Campione squarely on the map – there are still only four casinos in all of Italy. Designed by Swiss star architect Mario Botta, responsible for the recent makeover of La Scala theatre, it's big news for the little village. A cavalcade of buses transports day-tripping gamblers in a little over an hour from downtown Milan. Don't forget your passport as you cross into Switzerland before re-entering this extra-territorial bit of Italy.

Campione has Roman origins and was favoured for its microclimate where vineyards and palm trees flourish not far from snow-capped peaks. It never belonged to Switzerland, though the Swiss tried to lay claim to it. Instead, the enclave quietly went about its life for 1,000 years under the tutelage of Milan's Ambrosian Basilica, to which the land was granted by a benevolent Longobard named Totone around 777. Napoleon suppressed the rule of the monastery and made Campione part of the province of Como, just a few miles away.

Life in this quirky lakeside village runs by the whir of slot machines and baccarat tables; it stays open late to cater to gamblers, and generally sleeps in. Italian police must surrender their arms to Swiss border authorities when crossing into Switzerland, only to be rearmed once in Campione.

In Italian, *campione* means champion, which is how lucky gamblers may feel. It also means 'sample', which is a fitting name for this slice of Italy beyond its borders.

romantic, the 16-room **Hotel du Lac** (via del Prestino 4, 0341 830 238, www.albergodulac. com, closed mid Nov-mid Mar, doubles €160-€225) is a 19th-century palazzo. The **Royal Victoria** (piazza San Giorgio 5, 0341 815 111, www.royalvictoria.com, doubles €120-€210) has period furniture in its public rooms. In addition to its main restaurant (average €30), which is known for good-value, delicate cuisine, the hotel also has the cheaper **Victoria Grill** pizzeria (closed Mon except in summer, average €15).

Tourist information

Proloco Varenna

Piazza Venini 1 (0341 830 367/www.varenna italy.com). **Open** *Oct-Mar* 10am-5pm Sat. *Apr-Sept* 10am-2pm, 3-5pm Sat; 10am-noon Sun.

Lecco, Bellagio & the southern shore

Stunningly located but grimly overshadowed by its iron and steel industry, the city of **Lecco** signifies just one thing to the vast majority of Italians: *I promessi sposi*. As the birthplace of Alessandro Manzoni (1785-1873), author of that seminal novel, it provided the backdrop for the adventures of his characters Renzo and Lucia.

Settled from prehistoric times, Lecco stood on key trading routes, and was an important link in the defences of Milan's Visconti family. Azzone Visconti built an eight-arch bridge (three more arches were added later) over the River Adda in 1336; the bridge survives today and still bears its maker's name. Central piazza Manzoni boasts an impressive statue of the town's most famous son, while piazza Cermenati is the site of the basilica of **San Niccolò**, the city's cathedral.

To find out more about the author Italian schoolchildren love to hate, visit Alessandro's birthplace, **Villa Manzoni** (via Don Guanella 1, 0341 481 247, closed Mon), which houses a collection of memorabilia and manuscripts.

Perched at the tip of the southern promontory, **Bellagio** is simply glorious. Narrow streets lead up the hill from a port lined with impressive reminders of a more elegant age of tourism. Among those who came and were enchanted were Liszt, Stendhal and Flaubert.

Two villas provide the icing on the cake: **Villa Serbelloni** – crowning the hill where one of Pliny the Younger's villas may have stood – and **Villa Melzi**, a Napoleonic pile surrounded by lush gardens (for both, *see p202* **Water gardens**).

Where to eat

For first-rate fish (at top prices) in Lecco, head for **Al Porticciolo** (via Valsecchi 5-7, 0341 498 103, closed Mon, Tue, 2wks Jan & all Aug, average €65). A nice alternative is **Nicolin** (via Ponchielli 54, 0341 422 122, closed Tue & 3wks Aug, average €40), a lively father-and-son operation offering meaty Lombard specialities.

In Bellagio's outskirts, heading towards Como, the family-run **Silvio** hotel and restaurant (via Carcano 12, 031 950 322, www.bellagiosilvio. com, closed mid Nov-mid Dec, 6wks Jan-Feb, average €30) offers lake fish and beautiful views; it also has 21 rooms (doubles €70-€100), and rents apartments (www.bellagioapartments.it).

In Bellagio itself, **Barchetta** (salita Mella 13, 031 951 389, closed Tue & Dec-Feb, average €40) is a romantic location for an intimate dinner under a pergola.

Where to stay

In Bellagio the well-appointed **Hotel du Lac** (piazza Mazzini 32, 031 950 320, www.bellagio hoteldulac.com, closed Nov-end Mar, doubles €180-€230) has been welcoming travellers for 150 years. Check out the owners' new boutique hotel, **Hotel Bellagio** (salita Grande 6, 031 951 966, www.hotelbellagio.it, doubles €80-€150). Nearly every room has a lake view.

Located in an 18th-century palazzo on the lakeshore, the **Florence** (piazza Mazzini 46, 031 950 342, www.bellagiolakecomo.com, closed end Oct-Easter, doubles €135-€220) has charming rooms; book well in advance.

For real luxury, follow in the footsteps of Winston Churchill and John F Kennedy and splash out on a room at the **Grand Hotel**

Villa Serbelloni (via Roma 1, 031 950 216, www.villaserbelloni.com, closed Nov-Mar, doubles €340-€935), where facilities include indoor and outdoor pools, sauna, Turkish bath and day spa, as well as spectacular lake views.

Tourist information

APT Lecco
Via Nazario Sauro 6 (0341 295 720/www.turismo. provincia.lecco.it). **Open** 9am-1pm, 3-6pm daily.

IAT Bellagio
Piazza Mazzini – Pontile Imbarcadero (031 950 204/ www.bellagiolakecomo.com). **Open** *Apr-Oct* 9am-noon, 3-6pm daily. *Nov-Mar* 9am-noon, 3-6pm Mon, Wed-Sat.

Getting there

By car
For Como, take the A8 motorway west out of Milan and fork on to the A9 after Lainate. Alternatively, take the SS35 for Como or the SS36 for Lecco.

By train
Two railway companies serve Como. The state railways (Ferrovie dello Stato, aka Trenitalia) offer hourly services from Milan's Stazione Centrale on the Chiasso–Lugano route. This takes 30mins and comes into San Giovanni station; there's also an hourly service from Porta Garibaldi station.

The Ferrovie Nord service departs every 30mins from Cadorna station for the Como Nord Lago station (journey time 1hr).

For Lecco, there is an hourly service from Porta Garibaldi (journey time 1hr), and one train every two hours (journey time 45mins) from Stazione Centrale.

Getting around

By boat
Navigazione Lago di Como (via per Cernobbio 18, Como, 031 579 211, www.navigazionelaghi.it, office open 8am-noon, 1-5pm daily) operates ferry and hydrofoil services year-round. The boats run very frequently, and there are point-to-point commuter services to Tavernola, Cernobbio, Moltrasio, Torno and Urio at the southern end of the lake; Còlico at the lake's northern tip; and to intermediate towns such as Bellagio, Varenna, Cadenabbia and Menaggio. There are also some car-ferry services. Special tourist cruises are also on offer. If you are travelling between October and Easter, check the schedules on the site as services are often curtailed.

By car
The SS340 and SS583 around the lake's shores are very scenic, but traffic is heavy, especially in summer and at weekends. Progress is quicker, if less picturesque, on the SS36, which follows the eastern shore of the lake. The minor roads up into the hill villages can be challenging, not least because they are favoured by motorcyclists and cyclists.

Lago di Garda

Italy's biggest lake is awash with activity and brimming with history.

It's easy to see what draws the crowds to Lago di Garda – the largest lake in Italy. Surrounded by steep mountains rising sharply from the water's edge, it makes a relaxed alternative to the standard seaside holiday. Although it lacks sandy beaches and crashing breakers, the water is clean and its depth (average 135 metres/443 feet) means it remains cool even in the hottest months, while exhilarating mountain breezes create ideal conditions for windsurfing.

Garda's stony shores bustle with activity, attracting a mix of tourists, thrill-seeking windsurfers and families from neighbouring Brescia and Verona. Despite the sprawl of campsites, hotels and amusement parks that cluster to the south, the resorts that line the lake's shores are all extremely picturesque; each features its own medieval centre, often guarded by a miniature castle. There are several fine Romanesque churches, and Desenzano and Sirmione also contain important Roman remains. The lake may not offer much in the way of romantic solitude, but it has a range of attractions, both cultural and sporting, to satisfy most visitors.

The southern shore

Nestling in Garda's south-western corner, **Desenzano del Garda** is the largest of the lakeside towns. Behind the quaint old port is the arcaded piazza Malvezzi, with its statue of St Angela, and the church of **Santa Maria Maddalena** (open 9am-noon, 4-6pm daily). Inside the church is a striking *Last Supper* signed by Giambattista Tiepolo, although it is painted in a style more reminiscent of his son, Giandomenico, who may have restored *papà*'s work extensively. To the west, along via Crocefisso, are the remains of the third-century **Villa Romana** (No.22, 030 914 3547, www.sopraintendenza-archeologica.lombardia.it, closed Mon; **photo** *p210*). Excavated in 1921, it features some splendid mosaics.

Six kilometres (3.5 miles) to the east lies the lake's main tourist magnet: the medieval spa town of **Sirmione**, protected by the supremely picturesque 13th-century **Rocca Scaligera** (piazza Castello, 030 916 468, closed Mon; **photo** *p213*). This moat-girdled castle gives wonderful views of the lake from its battlements.

Also in Sirmione is the first-century **Grotte di Catullo** (piazza Orti Manara, 030 916 157, closed Mon; **photo** *p216*). Set amid sloping olive groves at the tip of the peninsula, these ruins bear the name of the Roman poet Catullus – although it's unlikely that such a colossal villa actually belonged to him.

Peschiera, at the south-eastern corner of the lake, has a decidedly military feel to it. The town has been fortified since Roman times; in the 19th century the Austrians rebuilt and strengthened its 16th-century Venetian defences. It now houses a huge purifying plant.

Just to the north of the town is **Gardaland** (SS 249 Gardesana Orientale, Castelnuovo del Garda, Località Ronchi, 045 644 9777, 045 644 9555, www.gardaland.it, closed Nov-late Mar except school hols) – Italy's answer to Disneyland. Over three million people visit its Dinosaur Islands and Dolphinariums each year – hence the huge traffic queues that strangle the road system in high season.

Where to stay & eat

In Desenzano, the comfortable **Hotel Tripoli** (piazza Matteotti 18, 030 914 1305, www. hotel-tripoli.it, closed late Dec-late Jan, doubles €90-€115) has lake views. For ice-creams and

cocktails, head to **Bar Agorà** (piazza Malvezzi 10, 030 999 1010, closed Wed & 2wks Nov), with its Gaudi-inspired interior.

In Sirmione, the luxurious **Hotel Fonte Boiola** (viale Marconi 11, 030 990 4922, www.termedisirmione.com, closed 2wks Dec, doubles €100-€154) has a spa, a restaurant and a wonderful garden on the lake. The **Osteria Torcol** (via San Salvatore 30, 030 990 4605, closed Wed, average €25) serves own-made pasta and hot and cold snacks.

Tourist information

IAT Desenzano
Via Porto Vecchio 34 (030 9141 510/www.provincia. brescia.it). **Open** 9am-12.30pm, 3-6pm Mon-Fri; 9am-12.30pm Sat.

IAT Peschiera
Piazzale Betteloni 15 (045 755 1673). **Open** *Mar-Oct* 8am-1pm, 3-6pm Mon-Sat; 8am-1pm Sun. *Nov-Feb* 8am-1pm, 3-6pm Tue, Thur, Fri; 8am-1pm Wed, Sat.

IAT Sirmione
Viale Marconi 2 (030 916 114/www.provincia. brescia.it). **Open** *Apr-Oct* 9am-12.30pm, 3-6pm daily. *Nov-Mar* 9am-12.30pm, 3-6pm Mon-Fri; 9am-12.30pm Sat.

Villa Romana. *See p209.*

The western shore

It is here, on Garda's magnificently rugged western shore, that lakeside tourism really began. Splendid villas dating back to the 18th century dot its shores, two of which once belonged to the poet Gabriele D'Annunzio and Benito Mussolini.

The lakeside road leads north from Desenzano to **Salò** (known in Roman times as Salodium), set in a deep bay. The town's name is irrevocably linked with the puppet republic set up here by the Nazis in 1943 for Mussolini (*see p212* **Benito's betrayal**). But Salò's other, happier, claim to fame is as the birthplace of Gasparo da Salò, also known as Gasparo Bertolotti (1542-1609), who was one of the first great violin-makers.

The fine art nouveau hotels (built in 1910) along the lakefront are mere young pups compared to the many medieval and Renaissance *palazzi* in the centre of this important old town. In piazza del Duomo, the cathedral of the **Annunziata** has a Renaissance portal in its unfinished façade and a splendid Venetian-Gothic interior complete with gilded statues of saints, two paintings by Romanino and a polyptych by Paolo Veneziano. Around the cathedral is the

oldest part of the town, with fine *palazzi* from the 15th to the 18th centuries lining the main street parallel to the lake.

Four kilometres (2.5 miles) further north is **Gardone Riviera**, which is made up of cosmopolitan hotels and holiday villas, including **Villa Alba**. This large neo-classical building – built in the 1880s as a mini-replica of the Parthenon for the Austrian emperor (he never used it) – is now a conference centre.

Gardone's main attraction is the **Giardino Botanico Hruska** (via Roma 2, mobile 336 410 877, www.hellergarden.com, closed Nov-Feb). Laid out from 1910 by Arturo Hruska, a dentist and naturalist, it contains a host of plants from every continent and climate, including magnolias, reeds and ferns.

From Gardone there is a good view of **Isola del Garda**. In the ninth century Charlemagne gave this island to Verona's archbishop (and later saint) Zeno. It remained in ecclesiastical hands until 1798. The extraordinary Venetian Gothic-style villa (the largest on the lake) was built by the noble Borghese family in 1900-3 and is still privately owned (and consequently not open to the public).

On the hill above the Gardone Riviera is the old town of **Gardone di Sopra**, notable mostly as the site of the grandiose **Vittoriale** degli Italiani (via Vittoriale 22, 036 529 6511, www.vittoriale.it, closed Mon). This presumptuously named villa was the residence of late 19th-century poet, novelist, dramatist, man of action and grand poseur Gabriele D'Annunzio. Mussolini authorised the poet to turn the house into a national monument; it was one way for him to exert some kind of control over the only Italian capable of upstaging him. 'If you have a rotten tooth,' said Il Duce of the popular poet and hero, 'either you have it pulled out or you cover it with gold.'

Despite the patriotic name, Il Vittoriale is essentially an extravagant monument to its owner, in which no aspect of his character or achievements is uncelebrated. The villa's interior, with its claustrophobia-inducing clutter, reveals D'Annunzio's numerous rampant enthusiasms: music, literature, art, the Orient and – most rampant of all – sex. Highlights include the spare bedroom with the coffin in which D'Annunzio would meditate Bela Lugosi-style, and the dining room, which is complete with an embalmed and bronzed pet tortoise that died from overeating. The grounds celebrate his more extrovert passions, from theatre (his most famous love affair

was with actress Eleonora Duse) to bellicose heroics – where other people might have garden gnomes, D'Annunzio erected the prow of the battleship *Puglia* to commemorate his quixotic attempt to 'liberate' the city of Fiume (now Rijeka) from Yugoslav rule. Lastly, don't miss (you can't anyway) his monstrous wedding-cake mausoleum.

The grounds also contain the **Museo della Guerra** (War Museum; guided tour, closed Mon), celebrating D'Annunzio's more aggressive adventures: from the ceiling hangs the plane he used to fly over Vienna in 1918.

Continuing north, **Toscolano-Maderno** is a resort with a good beach. Roman and Byzantine traces can be found in the 12th-century Romanesque church of **Sant'Andrea** (piazza San Marco, open 8.30am-noon, 2.30-7pm daily), particularly in the pillar capitals; the church is a miniature version of Verona's San Zeno Maggiore.

Bogliaco, the next village, is home to the grandiose 18th-century **Villa Bettoni** (closed to the public), the second largest villa on the lake, and the place where the ministers of the Salò republic (*see below* **Benito's betrayal**) would meet.

Benito's betrayal

By the time northern Italy's Nazi occupiers installed Mussolini in Villa Feltrinelli in Gargnano (*see p213*), the fascist leader had been humbled by history. Most of his Grand Council had voted to remove him from power on 25 July 1943, by which time Anglo-American forces were firmly installed in Sicily and inflicting crushing blows up the boot of Italy. The king had defected to the Allied side and had Mussolini imprisoned in a mountain stronghold in Abruzzo; it had taken an SS commando team to get him out and whisk him off to the north.

Il Duce's comeback took the vicious, squalid form of the Repubblica di Salò. Mussolini did not choose the place from which he was to 'govern' northern Italy for the next 18 months; he would have preferred to return to Rome for a bloody settling of accounts, but the more pragmatic Germans put their jack-booted feet down and kept him in the more easily controllable north. Just to make sure Mussolini was under no illusions that he was running anything other than a puppet administration, the Germans spread ministries haphazardly around lakeside towns

and made it clear that everything – including Mussolini's letters to his lover Clara Petacci, who had been housed in an ex-convent in Gargnano – was checked over by the SS.

Holed up in Villa Feltrinelli, Mussolini was a pathetic parody of his former self. He drew up futile plans for the war effort, refusing to face the fact that it was now the Nazis running the show. The Salò Republic's one memorable act was the trial and subsequent execution of five members of the Grand Council who had voted Mussolini out of office, including *il Duce*'s son-in-law, Galeazzo Ciano. Mussolini went to great lengths to pretend that the malevolence of others had prevented him from signing a pardon. When his daughter refused to believe him, he whinged that it was his 'destiny to be betrayed by everyone, including my own daughter'.

The beauty of the setting in which these events took place was of little consolation to Mussolini. 'Lakes are a compromise between river and sea,' he moaned, 'and I don't like compromises.' As it turned out, it was beside another lake – Como – that he was to be executed by partisans.

Wonder walls: Sirmione's medieval **Rocca Scaligera**. *See p209.*

DH Lawrence lived in nearby **Gargnano** in 1912-13; his *Twilight in Italy* contains – amid reflections on Italian phallocentricity – some of the most evocative descriptions of the lake ever written. Gargnano's fine 13th-century church of **San Francesco** (open 9am-noon daily) has Gothic cloisters; note the pillar-capitals with carved lemon leaves. By the lake is **Palazzo Feltrinelli**, built in 1894 for a wealthy industrialist family. Now a conference centre for Milan University, during the Republic of Salò, this was Mussolini's administrative headquarters. Il Duce's private residence was in the larger **Villa Feltrinelli**, set in an expansive garden to the north of the town. This has recently been restored as a luxury hotel (www.villafeltrinelli.com).

Beyond Gargnano, the lake narrows and the mountains rise sheer out of the water. The lakeside road, the Gardesana, continues as a series of tunnels, which during World War II were used as bomb-proof factories for weapons and car and aeroplane engines.

Lined by a two-mile beach, **Limone sul Garda** has a small port and an attractive medieval centre with steep, narrow streets and staircases. It's unclear whether the town's name derives from the Latin *limen* (border) or from its extensive lemon plantations dating back to the 13th century and thought to have been the first in Europe. Bare pillars that used to support protective greenhouse cover during the winter months now stand, as DH Lawrence fancifully put it, like 'ruined temples... forlorn in their colonnades and squares... as if they remained from some great race that had once worshipped here'.

The parish church in the main square contains a fine, late 16th-century wooden crucifix. At the northern end of the village, at the top of a steep staircase and amid the lemon groves, is the tiny 14th-century church of **San Rocco**, with a frescoed altarpiece inside a trompe-l'oeil frescoed frame (though the church is often closed, you can normally peek through the window).

Through yet more tunnels, the Gardesana leads to **Riva del Garda**, the largest town in the northern half of the lake. It stands between Monte Brione to the east and the sheer cliffs of Monte Rocchetta to the west, which bring early dusk to the town. Once a major port, from 1813 until 1918 Riva lay in Austrian territory, and saw fighting during World War I. The centre of the town is piazza III Novembre, with the imposing 13th-century **Torre Apponale** (piazza Catena, 0464 554 444, closed Mon except July, Aug), which you can climb, the 14th-century **Palazzo Pretorio** (not open to the public) and picturesque medieval porticoes. An archway beneath the Palazzo Pretorio leads to tiny piazza San Rocco,

Trips Out of Town

where the surviving apse of a church destroyed in World War I has been converted into an open-air chapel. Eastwards from piazza III Novembre is the moat-encircled **Rocca** (fortress), containing the **Museo Civico** (piazza Battisti 3, 0464 573 869, closed Mon Oct-mid July), with collections of archaeology and armour. North, through porta San Michele, viale Roma leads to the **Chiesa dell'Inviolata**, an octagonal 17th-century church designed by a Portuguese architect whose name local history has failed to record; he saw no reason to stint on stucco and gilt, covering every square inch with decoration. Paintings by the prolific Palma il Giovane (1548-1628) adorn the chapels.

More baroque splendour can be found in the Madonna chapel of the **Chiesa dell'Assunta** in via Mazzini (open 8.30am-noon, 3-6.30pm daily), while the energetic can follow a zigzag path up to the **Bastione**, a cylindrical tower (212 metres/707 feet high) built by the Venetians in 1508, which commands spectacular views over the town.

Where to stay & eat

In Salò, the **Gallo Rosso** (vicolo Tomacelli 4, 0365 520 757, closed Wed & Thur lunch, 1wk Jan & 1wk June, average €25) offers good fish-based meals. Near the cathedral is the **Hotel Duomo** (lungolago Zanardelli 91, 036 521 026, www.hotelduomosalo.it, doubles €105-€185), with rooms looking either on to the cathedral or the lake. **Pignino Sera** (via Panoramica 13, 036 522 071, www.contiterzi.it, rates €30-€35 per person) is a farm situated about a kilometre (half a mile) from the centre of Salò. Surrounded by olive groves, and with a splendid lake view, it offers basic accommodation for small groups of people. Five kilometres (3 miles) from Salò, in località San Carlo–Gavardo, **San Carlo** (0365 371 850, closed Mon-Thur, Jan, July, average €25-€30) has rustic fare based on home-grown products.

In Gardone di Sopra, **Agli Angeli** (piazza Garibaldi 2, 036 520 832, closed Tue & mid Nov-mid Feb, average €40) was recommended by Gabriele D'Annunzio to his friends (although he preferred to dine at home).

In Limone, the family-run **Hotel Bellavista** by the lake (via Marconi 20, 0365 954 001, www.gardalake.it/hotelbellavista, closed Nov-Mar, doubles €72-€90) has a pretty garden.

In Riva del Garda, the **Ristorante Al Volt** (via Fiume 73, 0464 552 570, www.ristorantealvolt.com, closed Mon & mid Feb-mid Mar, average €38) serves up excellent meals including fish from the lake. The **Grand Hotel Riva** (piazza Garibaldi 10, 0464 521 800, www.gardaresort.it, doubles €114-€145) is a

large and comfortable hotel by the castle. Its top-floor dining room commands panoramic views of the lake.

Tourist information

IAT Gardone Riviera
Corso Repubblica 8 (036 520 347). Open Apr-Sept 9am-12.30pm, 3-6.30pm daily. Oct-Mar 9am-12.30pm, 2.15-6pm Mon-Fri; 9am-12.30pm Sat.

IAT Salò
Piazza Sant'Antonio (036 521 423/www.comune.salo.bs.it). Open Oct-May 9am-12.30pm, 3-6pm Mon-Fri; 9am-12.30pm Sat. June-Sept 9am-12.30pm, 3-6pm Mon, Tue, Thur-Sat; 9am-12.30pm Wed.

IAT Toscolano-Maderno
Piazza San Marco 1 (036 564 1330/www.provincia.brescia.it). Open June-Sept 9am-12.30pm, 3-6.30pm daily. Oct-May 9am-12.30pm, 2.15-6pm Mon-Sat.

Ingarda Trentino Azienda per il Turismo
Giardini di Porta Orientale 8 (046 455 4444/www.gardatrentino.com). Open Apr-Oct 9am-noon, 3-6.30pm Mon-Sat; 10am-noon, 2-6.30pm Sun. Nov-Mar 9am-noon, 2.30-5.15pm Mon-Fri.

Ufficio Informazioni Gargnano
Piazza Boldini 2 (036 579 1243/www.gargnano sulgarda.com). Open Apr-Sept 9.30am-12.30pm, 3.30-6.30pm Mon,Tue, Fri, Sat; 9.30am-12.30 Wed; 3.30-6.30pm Thur.

The eastern shore

Medieval towns provide aesthetic relief from the campsites and amusement parks found along the lake's eastern shore. Among them, poised on Garda's north-eastern corner, lies pretty **Torbole**, a historic town of strategic importance. In 1439 it witnessed the launch of a fleet of 26 Venetian ships that had been dragged over the mountains for a surprise attack on the Milanese rulers, the Visconti.

Malcesine (15 kilometres/9.5 miles south) is arguably the eastern shore's most delightful stopover, especially notable for the **Castello Scaligero** (via Castello, 045 740 0837/657 0333, closed Nov, only open weekends Dec-Mar). The castle was built, like many in the region, by Verona's ruling Della Scala family, from which the name *scaligero* derives (*see p215* **All in a name**). Situated on a craggy headland looming over the medieval quarter, the castle also has a small museum featuring sketches by Goethe. While drawing them in 1786, the poet was arrested for spying by a suspicious local.

Close to the Gardesana road, is the church of **Santo Stefano**, with its impressive altar (1771) and *Via Crucis* (stations of the Cross).

All in a name

Grab a coffee in one of the medieval piazzas that line the shores of Lake Garda and there's a good chance you'll be sitting in the shadows of the Della Scala family. Generations of Scaligeri, as they were also known, ruled the area for over a century, and these lakeside towns are scattered with the family's imposing remains. Ruined castles at **Malcesine** (see p214), **Lazise** (see p216) and **Torri del Benaco** (see below), to mention a few, bear the names of the lords who built them, and local history is defined by their influence.

The Scaligeri dynasty began in 1260, when the Holy Roman Emperor Frederick II appointed Mastino della Scala to succeed Ezzelino IV as *podestà* (governor) of Verona at the height of the struggle for power between the Papacy (the Guelphs) and the Holy Roman Empire (the Ghibellines). Although the new lord of Verona was loyal to the Emperor, the city was divided by the brutal rivalry between these political factions – strife epitomised in the tragic tale of Romeo (Guelph) and Juliet (Ghibelline), who were said to have lived in the city under Scaligeri rule.

But despite the city's continuing inner turmoil, Verona reached the height of its power under the Scaligeri reign — embracing areas even beyond these lakeside towns under its rule – thanks in particular to Mastino's grandson, Can Francesco della Scala, aka Can Grande (1291-1329), who became lord in 1308. Either by force or by treaty, this formidable statesman brought the cities of Treviso, Padua, Belluno, Mantova and Vicenza, among others, into his fold. Can Grande ruled with a heavy hand, but he was also known as a patron of the arts, granting asylum to the likes of Giotto and Dante.

But the lord's heroic deeds were eventually undone by those who succeeded him. The aggression of Can Grande's direct successor, his nephew Mastino II, provoked a war with a hugely powerful Venetian-Florentine league. After three years of fighting, the Della Scala empire was reduced to just Verona and Vincenza. Attempts to regain prominence by Mastino II's sons and grandsons ended in failure when Verona fell – first to Milan (1387) and then Venice (1405).

This area might have been worse off at the end of the Della Scala reign than it was at the start, but its historic leaders have been well remembered. In Verona (20 kilometres/ 12 miles from Lake Garda), the Santa Maria Antica church houses the family's Gothic tombs, and it's here that Can Grande has been impressively immortalised. Not one to be outdone, even in death, he lies in a breathtaking sarcophagus carved by the renowned Gothic sculptor Bonino da Campione.

Alongside the lake, in via Capitani del Lago, the **Palazzo dei Capitani del Lago** (not open to the public) has a garden courtyard overlooking the lake.

For a blast of Alpine air, take a 15-minute cable-car ride from Malcesine to the top of **Monte Baldo** (€14 return, closed Mar, Nov), a popular ski-resort in winter.

Further down the coast, in **Torri del Benaco**, are remnants of the ancient town walls and the 14th-century **Castello Scaligero** (viale Fratelli Lavanda 2, 045 629 6111, closed Nov). The church of **Santissima Trinità** (in the eponymous square) contains 15th-century frescoes, including a splendid Christ Pantocrator in gleaming floral garb.

Set in a deep bay in the shadow of Monte Garda, the town of **Garda** is home to several notable Renaissance *palazzi*. (For more, take the sunny villa- and garden-lined path along the curving shore towards **Punta San Vigilio** down to the lake.) It was in a (now long-gone) castle on this hill in the 10th century that Queen Adelaide was imprisoned by Berengar II, after he had murdered her husband and she had refused to marry him (or his son Adalbert; sources are divided).

At the tip of the headland is a harbour with a tiny chapel dedicated to **San Vigilio**. From here a path leads up to the 16th-century **Villa Guarienti**; it's privately owned, but a glimpse can be caught of its splendid formal gardens, much loved by Winston Churchill and Laurence Olivier, among others. Nearby is **Locanda San Verolo**, modest in appearance but offering luxury hotel service (045 720 0930, www.sanverolo.it). On the other side of the promontory is the tiny **Baia delle Sirene**, which has a beach.

South of Garda, the waterside footpath is a pleasant and mostly pine-shaded walk as far as **Bardolino**. This small town, famed for its wine, is flanked by gardens leading to the lake and has two fascinating churches. The tiny ninth-century **San Zeno** can be reached by turning eastwards off the Gardesana along the

Grotte di Catullo. See p210.

suburban-looking via San Zeno. **San Severo**, a well-preserved 12th-century building with a good campanile, contains notable 12th- and 14th-century frescoes.

In **Lazise** is another **Castello Scaligero**, now incorporated into the garden of a privately owned villa. South of here lie the delights of Gardaland (*see p210*).

Where to stay & eat

The 34-room **Hotel Gardesana** in Torri del Benaco (piazza Calderini 20, 045 722 5411, www.hotel-gardesana.com, closed Jan, Feb, doubles €90-€154) has a fine lakeside location and has hosted the likes of Winston Churchill.

In Garda, away from the lake, **Stafolet** (via Poiano 9, 045 725 5427, closed Tue, average €20-€25) does good grilled dishes and pizza. The best of the numerous restaurants on the lake is **Miralago** (lungolago Regina Adelaide 52, 045 725 5198, www.zaglio.it, closed Mon, average €25), which offers reasonable fish dishes and pizza.

Hotel **Gardenia** (piazza Serenissima 12, 045 621 0882, www.hotelgardenia.it, doubles €78-€145) in Bardolino offers two swimming pools and views over the lake. The **Ristorante Ai Platani di San Severo** (piazza San Severo 1, 045 721 0038, www.aiplatani.com, closed Wed, average €15-€25) serves reliable local dishes and pizza.

Tourist information

IAT Bardolino
Piazzale Aldo Moro 5 (045 721 0078). **Open** *Apr-Oct* 9am-1pm, 3-6pm Mon-Sat; 9am-1pm Sun. *Nov-Mar* 9am-1pm, 3-6pm Tue, Thur; 9am-1pm Wed, Fri, Sat.

IAT Garda
Lungolago Regina Adelaide 13 (045 627 0384/ www.tourism.verona.it). **Open** *Apr-Oct* 9am-1pm, 3-7pm Mon-Sat; 9am-1pm Sun. *Nov-Mar* 9am-1pm, 3-6pm Mon-Fri; 9am-1pm Sat.

Getting there

By bus
The Brescia–Verona services run by SAIA (030 288 9911, 840 620 001, www.trasportibrescia.it) call at Desenzano (journey time 1hr), Sirmione (journey time 1hr 20mins) and Peschiera (journey time 1hr 30mins).

By car
The Milan–Venice A4 motorway has exits at Desenzano, Sirmione and Peschiera.

By train
Many trains on the Milan–Venice line from Stazione Centrale stop at Desenzano and Peschiera. Journey time around 1hr 30mins.

Getting around

By boat
Hydrofoil and steamer services are frequent in the summer, connecting the most important points on the lake. Throughout the year there is a regular car ferry service (roughly every 40mins) between Toscolano-Maderno and Torri del Benaco. All boat services are operated by Navigazione sul Lago di Garda (030 914 9511, www.navigazionelaghi.it).

By bus
The southern shore (Desenzano, Sirmione, Peschiera) is served by buses from both Brescia and Verona (*see above* **Getting there**). SAIA (030 288 9911, 840 620 001, www.trasportibrescia.it) runs buses from Desenzano to Riva along the western shore; Verona's APT (045 805 7911, www.apt.vr.it) operates services from Peschiera to Riva along the eastern shore.

By car
The road that skirts the lake is called the Gardesana. In summer, expect heavy traffic, particularly around the Gardaland amusement park (*see p210*).

Directory

Directory

Getting Around

Aeroporto di Malpensa

flight information 02 7485 2200/ switchboard 02 74851/www.sea-aeroportimilano.it. **Map** p246.
Milan's main airport is in Somma Lombarda, 50km (30 miles) from the city centre in the province of Varese. Malpensa has two terminals: Terminal 1 is for intercontinental, international and domestic flights; Terminal 2 is mostly for charter flights, although it's also used by a few international services. Airlines that fly to Malpensa from the UK include British Airways (from Heathrow) and Easyjet (from Gatwick).

Aeroporto di Linate

flight information 02 7485 2200/ switchboard 02 74851/www.sea-aeroportimilano.it. **Map** p246.
Milan's national airport is in Segrate, about 7km (4.5 miles) from the centre of town. It handles domestic and continental flights (such as British Airways from Heathrow and Easyjet from Gatwick).

Aeroporto di Orio al Serio

035 326 323/flight information 035 326 111/www.orioaeroporto.it.
Bergamo's airport is in Orio al Serio, about 45km (28 miles) from Milan and 5km (3 miles) from Bergamo. It handles national, continental, intercontinental and charter flights (Ryanair flies here from Luton and Stansted in the UK). When Milan's airports are fog-bound, flights are often rerouted here.

On from Malpensa

By train

02 20 222 (Italian-speaking operator only 7am-8pm)/www.ferrovienord.it/ webmxp. **Tickets** €11 (€13.50 if bought on train); €5.50 4-12s (€8 if bought on train); free under-4s.
The Ferrovie Nord's **Malpensa Express** train runs at 27 and 57 minutes past each hour from 5.57am to 8.57pm (Sunday 9.27pm) daily between Malpensa Airport (Terminal 1) and Cadorna metro station, platform 1 (journey time 40mins),

stopping at Bovisa/Politecnico, Saronno and Busto Arsizio. Tickets can be bought at the Ferrovie Nord desks in the airport and at stations where the Malpensa Express stops as well as all FN stations (there is a surcharge for buying tickets onboard). Tickets must be stamped in the machines on the station platform before boarding.
The train is replaced by a non-stop bus service (50mins) early mornings (4.20am and 5am from Cadorna) and in the evenings after 9pm (until 1.30am from Malpensa). A free shuttle bus runs at 15min intervals between Malpensa's Terminals 1 and 2.

By bus

Two main bus services link Malpensa to Milan. The **Malpensa Bus Express** (information 02 240 7954/02 3391 0794) departs every 30mins (5.55am-10.45pm from Malpensa Terminal 1; 5.15am-9.15pm from Stazione Centrale) and takes approximately 1hr 10mins. Tickets cost €5.50 (€2.75 under-13s; free under-3s) and are available in the arrivals terminals at the airport, in piazza Luigi di Savoia by Stazione Centrale, at the tourist office near the Duomo (*see p233*) or on the bus. The service also stops at Terminal 2 and Fiera MilanoCity (by request from the airport).
Malpensa Shuttle (recorded information in English 02 5858 3185/www.malpensashuttle.it) services depart every 20mins (5.30am-12.15am from Malpensa terminal 1; 5am-11.15pm from Stazione Centrale) and take approximately 50mins. Buses will stop at Fiera MilanoCity and the new Fiera complex at Rho on request. Tickets (€5; €2.50 under-13s; free under-3s) can be purchased in the airport arrivals halls, at the Colombo or Salerno newsstands (both in Milan's Stazione Centrale) or on the bus.
Malpensa Shuttle also runs 10 shuttle bus services a day each way between Malpensa and Linate with request stops at Terminal 2 (journey time 1hr 10mins). Tickets, which can be bought on the bus, cost €9 (€4.50 under-13s; free under-3s).

By taxi

See also p221.

A taxi from Malpensa to Milan costs approximately €85. Journey time is around 45mins. Beware of rush-hour traffic, which can lengthen the trip substantially. Use only white taxis lined up at the ranks and avoid all drivers who solicit business as you exit the terminal.

On from Linate

By bus

There is no train service into Milan from Linate, but the excellent **ATM bus 73** departs every 10mins from Linate Airport and San Babila metro station. Travel time is around 25mins, rising to 40mins at rush hour. An ordinary €1 city bus ticket is valid for the airport service.
Starfly (02 5858 7237) services leave every half hour and link Linate airport and Stazione Centrale (5.05am-10.35pm from Linate; 5.35am-9.35pm from Stazione Centrale). Tickets cost €3 (€1.50 under-13s; free under-3s) and can be purchased from the driver.

By taxi

See also p221.
A taxi to or from Linate will cost approximately €20-€25, depending on what part of town you are travelling from or to.

On from Orio al Serio

By train

Trains depart regularly from Bergamo's station for Milan's Stazione Centrale or Garibaldi. Prices vary, depending on the train, from €3.50-€4. Travelling time is about 1hr. From the airport the ATB bus 1C (www.atb.bergamo.it) will take you to the station in 10mins for €1.55 (a taxi will cost you about €18).

By bus

Autoservizi Zani (035 678 611/ 035 678 678/www.zaniviaggi.it) runs a service from Orio al Serio to Milan Lambrate (piazza Bottini) and Stazione Centrale; coaches run from 8am-1am (with one at 4.30am) from Orio to Stazione Centrale; 8.10am-10pm to Lambrate. The trip takes 50mins and costs €6.70 (€3.35 under-12s if they don't occupy a seat).

Autostradale (information 02 7200 1304/www.autostradale.it) runs buses 4.30am-1am daily from Orio al Serio to the air terminal at Milan's Stazione Centrale; 4am-11.30pm in the other direction. Tickets can be bought on board and cost €6.70 (€3.50 under-12s; free under-2s; 3 tickets €13.40). When fog closes Milan's airports, airlines provide buses to ferry stranded passengers to and from Orio al Serio.

Orio shuttle (035 319 366/ www.orioshuttle.com) runs 5am-12.30am from Orio to Stazione Centrale; 4.10am-23.30pm in the other direction. The trip takes about 1hr. Tickets are €6 (€3 for under-12s; free under-2s) and can be bought on the bus itself, from the office at the station or from Orio shuttle staff at the airport.

Airlines

Alitalia
Flight information, ticket sales & assistance 06 2222/www.alitalia.it. **Open** *Phone enquiries* 24hrs daily. *Piazzale Cadorna 14, West (02 2499 2500). Metro Cadorna/bus 50, 58, 94/tram 1, 27.* **Open** *For ticket purchase, check-in & connection to Malpensa Express train service (see p218)* 9am-6pm Mon-Sat.

British Airways
Flight information & ticket sales 199 712 266/www.britishairways.com. **Open** *Phone enquiries* 9am-6pm Mon-Fri; 9am-5pm Sat.

EasyJet
848 887 766/www.easyjet.com.

Ryanair
050 503 770/www.ryanair.com.

Arriving by bus

There isn't one central bus station in Milan, though many companies now use Porta Garibaldi. A useful site to check timetables is www.orariautobus.it, which provides links to the coach companies that stop in Milan. Two major companies that stop at Garibaldi are **Autostradale** (02 637 901, www.autostradale.it) and **Eurolines** (199 184 616, www.eurolines.it). See p221 for more information about the station.

Arriving by train

International and long-distance train services arrive at and depart from Milan's Stazione Centrale. The station is a pickpocket's paradise, so watch your wallet and luggage carefully. If you arrive late in the

evening, it is advisable to take a taxi to your destination; the metro stops shortly after midnight (*see p219*). Note that Stazione Centrale is being refurbished and taxi ranks have recently been moved to the side of the station. For information on buying train tickets, *see p220*.

Public transport

For transport map, see p256. The services operated by the Azienda Trasporti Milanesi (ATM; www.atm-mi.it) are the mainstay of Milan's transport system, serving both the inner-city *rete urbana* (urban network) and the Greater Milan area. ATM manages a public transport network of three metropolitan railway lines and 120 tram, trolley-bus and bus lines, covering nearly 1,052sq km (406sq miles) and reaching 86 municipalities.

Public transport in Milan is fairly safe, even at night. Watch out for pickpockets in packed buses and subways.

In Milan

There are three underground (metro) lines. These are Linea 1, 2 and 3, aka red (*rossa*), green (*verde*) and yellow (*gialla*) lines. The stations are signposted with a red 'M'. There is a fourth service, the *passante ferroviario* urban railway – shown in blue on transport maps and indicated with a letter 'R' above ground. The *passante* stations are Porta Vittoria, Dateo, Porta Venezia, Repubblica, Garibaldi, Lancetti and Bovisa. As well as providing a link between metro stations within the city, the *passante* serves outlying suburban areas, where it runs overground.

The city centre is circled by three concentric ring roads, each of which is covered by public transport. Buses 50, 58, 61 and 94 travel (portions of) the inner circular route, which passes close to the centre. Trams 29 and 30 circle

the city along the middle route. Buses 90, 91 and 92 travel the outer ring road. Many trams cut across the city, intersecting the ring roads and continuing into outlying or suburban areas. One example is the number 2, which takes you from the Stazione Centrale in the north through many of Milan's most famous tourist spots (via Manzoni, piazza della Scala, piazza Duomo, via Torino, corso Genova, corso Colombo and Porta di Ripa Ticinese in the south.

Metro trains run every 4-5mins from 6am until 12.30am daily; after 9pm, services run only every 10-12mins until about 12.30am. After that there are night buses, which substitute metro lines 1 and 3 until about 2am. All ATM bus and tram services – except night services (*see p220*) – also run between 6am and midnight daily, departing every 5-20mins, depending on the route and time of day. The doors for boarding are clearly marked *entrata*; doors for alighting are marked *uscita*. Some new trams/buses require you to push a button to open the doors. If you wish to alight from a bus, make sure you have pushed one of the red buttons alerting the driver that the next stop is requested (*fermata prenotata*). The driver will speed by without stopping if there's no request and he sees no passengers waiting at the stop.

At each bus stop a sign shows all stops made along the route and includes a timetable for weekdays (*feriali*), Saturdays (*sabato/ pre-festivi*) and Sundays and holidays (*domenica e festivi*). Most stops now have electronic signs telling you how long you have to wait for your bus/ tram. Major changes take place to the timetables in the summer, when Milan empties.

Directory

Radiobus (02 4803 4803, 1pm-2am daily) is a request-only bus service run by ATM that operates throughout the city, from selected bus stops. You can book from three days before, right up to the time of travel. Call to specify your route and the time you want to travel and the bus will meet you at the most convenient stop. The service is rarely busy so it is like travelling around Milan in a luxurious private minibus at a fraction of the cost of a taxi. Tickets are sold at all ATM sale points (€1.50) and on the bus (€3).

Public transport information

Information on routes, tickets and changes can be found at the ATM points in the underground stations at Duomo (7.45am-8.15pm), Cadorna, Loreto, Centrale and Romolo (7.45am-7.15pm) by ringing freephone 800 808181 (also in English) 7.30am-7.30pm or at ATM's website (www.atm-mi.it). We've included a map of the metro system on p256, but you can buy a city map with all the transport options at ATM points and most newsstands for €2.

Night services

The three metro lines operate until 12.30am; buses then ply routes 1 and 3 until 2am. There are also 55 night bus and tram routes, which run from 12.30am to 2.30am. There is no service between 2.30am and 6am.

Tourist services

See also p51 **Guided tours**.

The hop-on, hop-off Ciao Milano tourist tram 20 had been suspended when this guide went to press, but may be reintroduced; check with the tourist information centre (*see p223*).

Tickets & fares

Milan is currently in the process of moving over to magnetic/electronic tickets. When this guide went to press, only the season tickets had been changed but all tickets will change to the new system by the end of 2006. The rules are basically the same: you must buy your ticket before boarding, although on the metro you will have to validate the ticket on entering and exiting. ATM tickets can be bought at underground stations (6am-8pm at staffed desks; from ticket machines at other times), ATM points (Duomo, Loreto, Centrale, Romolo), *tabaccherie*, bars

and most newsstands, as well as Lampugnano, Bisceglie and Famagosta station car parks.

It's a good tip to stock up as tickets are hard to come by, except at the station ticket machines, after 8pm when the majority of bars shut. If you are caught without a ticket at night you will be fined. The fact that nowhere was open to buy one is not seen as a valid reason for not having one.

The same tickets are valid on all ATM bus, tram and metro lines operating within the inner-city *rete urbana* (urban network). Travel to and through other zones requires appropriate tickets.

When you board a tram or bus, stamp tickets in the machines by the rear and/or front doors. If travelling without paying looks an easy option, bear in mind that there are ticket inspectors around: if you are caught you will be fined €100 on the spot. In the underground, stamp the ticket at the barrier (when the new electronic tickets come into effect you will need to swipe your ticket through a machine on entering and exiting).

Children under 1m (3ft) in height travel free of charge. Students, pensioners and the disabled pay lower rates for monthly and yearly tickets.

A single ticket (**biglietto singolo**, €1) is valid for 75mins from when it's stamped, during which it can be used on unlimited ATM trams and buses on the *rete urbana* (inner-city network), plus one trip on the metro. This ticket is also valid on the *passante ferroviario* and on the urban sections of the Ferrovie Nord and Ferrovie dello Stato mainline railways.

A **carnet** (€9.20) is a book of ten tickets, and can be shared by several people.

The **settimanale** (€6.70) is geared towards commuters. It can be used for two trips of up to 75mins in one day, from Monday to Saturday. If one day is not used it can be used on a Sunday.

Abbonamento serale (€1.80) can be used from 8pm to the end of the service.

Abbonamento giornaliero (€3) is valid for 24hrs for unlimited use on all transport in the *rete urbana*.

Abbonamento bigiornaliero (€5.50) is valid for 48hrs for unlimited use on all transport in the *rete urbana*. You will need a passport-sized photo for the following magnetic season tickets:

An **abbonamento settimanale** (€9) is valid for seven days for unlimited use of all transport in the *rete urbana*.

An **abbonamento mensile** (€30) is valid for a month for unlimited

use of all transport within the *rete urbana*, and entitles you to discounts on some concerts and exhibitions.

Greater Milan services

ATM manages a Greater Milan fare system called SITAM (*Sistema Integrato Trasporti Area Milanese* or Milan Area Integrated Transport System). Many extra-urban transport operators with routes running into the city participate in this system. Beyond the *rete urbana* (*see p219*), the area is divided into concentric coloured outer zones – yellow, green, red, blue, brown, orange, purple and grey; fares depend on the number of zones travelled through.

For information on travel to greater Milan destinations ask at the ATM point in the Duomo metro (*see p223*). A guide to fares, the '*Carta della Mobilità*', can be picked up from all ATM points.

Tickets

To travel from what Milanese call '*l'hinterland*' (the suburbs) into the city, or from one suburban area to another, *biglietti interurbani* (inter-urban tickets) and *biglietti cumulativi* (combined tickets) are available. The former can be used exclusively on routes outside the *rete urbana*; the latter can be used both in the suburbs and on the urban network.

The **abbonamento 1 giorno cumulativo Area Grande** (€7.40) is the most useful of the cumulative tickets as it is valid for one day on all ATM routes and most inter-urban SITAM routes.

Rail services

Milan's metropolitan rail network (*see p219*) is heavily used. Regular bus/tram/metro tickets are valid on trains as far as the stations marked *limite tariffe urbana* (urban tariff limit) in red on the map on p256.

For more information on train travel in the Lombardy region, *see p178* and also individual destinations in the Trips Out of Town section. The Lombardy Region's online guide is also very useful for planning journeys, although it is in Italian only (www.infopoint.it).

Mainline train services are operated by the state-run Ferrovie dello Stato (FS, aka Trenitalia) and private company Ferrovie Nord. Note that as from 2006 the main Stazione Centrale will be undergoing refurbishment for at least three years and many facilities will be closing or relocating. Keep up to date with what's going on at www.grandistazioni.it/milano/indexf.cfm.

Train timetables & tickets

Train timetables can be bought at any newsstand. The easiest to read is *Nuovo Grippaudo Orario*, which includes all suburban train timetables, as well as boat schedules for Lake Maggiore, Como and Garda. Train tickets can be bought at stations or travel agents with an FS sign, by credit card over the phone on 892 021 (24hr service) or on the FS website (www.trenitalia.com). The site is well organised and available in English, though making reservations and paying online is still a challenge. Children under 12 pay half fare; children under four travel free if they don't occupy a seat. There are also special deals for family bookings. For information on taking wheelchairs on trains, *see p225*.

Train fares in Italy are much cheaper than in the UK and several options may be available on one route. Be aware that the cheaper the fare, the longer the train takes. It's usually worth paying the extra money to take the InterCity (IC) instead of the *inter-regionale*. EuroCity (EC) or Eurostar (ES) cost more than the IC and are even faster. Reservations are essential on ES trains.

Should you, for whatever reason, have to board a train without a ticket, you should get on at the front and find the conductor straight away. This way, you will have to pay only a €5 extra penalty; if you wait for the ticket collector to find you, you are liable for a fine of up to €25.

Larger stations and ticket machines accept all major credit cards. **Always stamp your train ticket – and any supplements you have – in the yellow machines by each platform before boarding the train: failure to do so can lead to a €25 fine. Eurostar train tickets do not have to be stamped as their booking information is on them and they are valid for that journey only.**

Milan's main stations are listed below. For which station to use for other destinations in Lombardy, see individual destinations.

FS Customer Assistance
02 6371 2016. Open 7am-9pm daily.
FS Informa
892 021. Open 24hrs daily.

FS Disabled Passengers
National number 199 303 060/ Stazione Centrale 02 6707 0958. Open 7am-9pm daily.
FS Lost & Found office
02 6371 2667. Open 6am-midnight daily.

Stazione Centrale
Piazzale Duca D'Aosta, North. Map p249 G3. Connects with metro lines 2 and 3.

Stazione di Cadorna (Ferrovie Nord)
Piazzale Cadorna, West. Map p248 C6. Connects with metro lines 1 and 2 and the Malpensa Express.

Stazione Porta Garibaldi
Piazza Freud, North. Map p248 D3. Connects with metro line 2, the *passante ferroviario* and Milan's bus station.

Stazione Lambrate
Piazza Bottini, East. Connects with metro line 2.

Stazione Porta Genova
Piazza Porta Genova, South. Map p250 B9. Connects with metro line 2.

Taxis

Licensed taxis are white and meter-operated. If anyone comes up to you at the airport, Stazione Centrale or any of the major tourist magnets muttering 'Taxi?', always refuse – they are likely to charge you up to 400% more than the normal rate.

Most of Milan's taxi drivers are honest; if, however, you suspect you're being ripped off, make a note of the driver's name and number from the metal plaque inside the car's rear door. The more openly you do this, the more likely you are to find the fare returning to its proper level. Report complaints to the drivers' co-operative (the number is on the outside of each car) or, in serious cases, the police.

Fares & surcharges
When you pick up a taxi at a rank or hail one in the street, the meter should read zero. As you set off, it will indicate the minimum fare –

€3.10 at time of writing – for the first 200 metres, after which the charge goes up according to time and distance. Minimum fare on Sundays, public holidays and at night (9pm-6am) is €6.10.

Taxi ranks
Ranks are indicated by a white sign with 'Taxi' written in black. In the city centre there are ranks at largo Augusto, via Feltrami, piazzale Cadorna, largo Carrobbio, piazza Cavour, via Cordusio, piazza Duomo, piazza Fontana, via Gonzaga, corso Italia, via Manara, via Pisoni, via Mercato, via Francesco, via Santa Maria Segreta, corso Matteotti, via San Raffaele, via Spaderi, via San Pietro all'Orto and via Verri.

Phone cabs
To phone for a taxi, look under 'Taxi' in the phone book or dial any of the companies listed below. When your call is answered, give the street and number, or the name and location of a bar, club or restaurant where you wish to be picked up. You will be given the taxi code name (always a location and a number) and a time – for example, 'Como 69, tre minuti' ('Como 69, in three minutes'). The meter will start from the moment the taxi sets off to pick you up. If you intend to use a taxi at rush hour, during a major event, or in bad weather, order it well in advance.
Taxi Blu *02 4040.*
Radio Taxi *02 8585.*

Driving

Short-term visitors should have no trouble driving with their home licences, although if they are written in different scripts or less common languages, an international licence can be useful. Driving licences issued in other EU states are valid in Italy and there is no legal obligation to convert them. Other international licences must be converted after the owner has been resident in Italy for one year. Full details can be found on the Automobile Club of Italy's website (ACI; www.aci.it).

Italy's system of points (*punti*) brings the country's road legislation in line with the rest of Europe. Traffic cops will detract a certain number of points for infringements such as speeding, jumping red lights and so on. The important thing to remember is that have 20 points to start with and when you lose them all you have to retake your driving test within 30 days, or your licence will be suspended.

Useful tips

● You are required by law to wear a seatbelt at all times, to carry a warning triangle in your car and to wear a reflective 'lifejacket' if you get out of your car on the road.
● If you are thinking of driving in winter, especially in the mountains, keep a set of snow chains in the car. If you drive on snow, it's advisable to fit them, and if you see a sign saying *'obbligo di catene'* or showing a wheel with chains on it, you have to fit them by law from that point on.
● You are required by law to keep your driving licence, insurance papers, vehicle registration and photo ID documents on you at all times.
● Do not leave anything of value (including a car radio) in your car.
● Flashing your lights means that you intend to pass the driver in front of you, so you want him to pull over into the supposedly slower right lane.
● On motorways Italians flash their hazard warning lights when approaching a traffic jam.
● On motorways drivers are required to keep their headlights on dipped at all times.
● If traffic lights flash amber, stop and give way to the right.
● Green men are few and far between, so pedestrians assume right of way when the traffic lights show green – be careful when turning right at crossroads.
● Watch out for death-defying mopeds and pedestrians. Pedestrians usually assume right of way in the older, quieter streets without clearly designated pavements.
● Italian drivers are not in the habit of stopping for pedestrians at zebra crossings – be aware that the car in front of you won't necessarily stop, and the one behind you won't be expecting to.
● Mobile phones can only be used with earphones or on speaker mode in the car.

Restricted areas

Large sections of the city centre are now pedestrianised and closed to traffic at all times; the many signposts will direct you to the ring roads around the centre, making it difficult to reach the centre by car. If you do manage to slip into

unauthorised areas, you may be fined and your car may be wheel-clamped if you park – you'll have to pay a fine and a charge to have the clamp removed. The best thing is to head for the *autosilos* (guarded car parks; *see p222*) which, if not cheap, are at least safe. If you are in a hired car or have foreign plates and are stopped, mention the name of your hotel, and you will likely be waved on.

Occasional Sundays are designated no-car days. These are heavily advertised beforehand, which is just as well as they are rigidly enforced in the city centre. There are, however, exceptions for moving around outside the inner ring road.

The *corsie veloci* (fast lanes) that form the central parts of the ring roads are strictly for buses and taxis.

Breakdown services

It is advisable to join a national motoring organisation, such as the AA or RAC in Britain or the AAA in the US, before taking a car to Italy. These organisations have reciprocal arrangements with the Automobile Club d'Italia.

If you require extensive repairs and do not know a mechanic, pay a bit more and go to a manufacturer's official dealer, as reliable service at many garages depends on having built up a good client-mechanic relationship over several years. Dealers are listed in the *Pagine Gialle* (*Yellow Pages*) under 'Auto', along with specialist repairers, such as *gommista* (tyre repairs), *marmitte* (exhaust repairs) and *carrozzerie* (bodywork and windscreen repairs). The English-language *Yellow Pages*, available from most major bookshops, has a list of garages where English is spoken.

Automobile Club d'Italia (ACI)

Corso Venezia 43, East (02 77451/ 24hr emergency service 803 116/ 24hr traffic information 1518/ www.acimi.it). Metro Palestro. **Open** 8.30am-12.45pm, 2.15-5pm Mon-Fri. **Map** p249 F6/252 F6.
The ACI has English-speaking staff. Members of associated organisations are entitled to free basic repairs, and to other services at preferential rates. This is still the best place to call in the event of a breakdown, even if you are not a member. You will be charged, but prices are generally reasonable.

Europ Assistance

Customer service 800 013 529/ 24hr assistance (non-members) 803 803/24hr assistance (members) 02 58241/www.europassistance.it.

Piazza Trento 6, South (02 5838 4275). Metro Lodi/bus 90, 91. **Open** 9am-1pm, 2-6pm Mon-Fri. **Credit** AmEx, DC, MC, V. **Map** p251 F10.
Via Albricci 2, Centre (02 5824 2424). Metro Missori/bus 54, 65/ tram 12, 27. **Open** 9am-6pm Mon-Fri. **Credit** AmEx, DC, MC, V. **Map** p251 E7/p252 E7.
Europ Assistance, which operates in 24 countries, has been offering a 24-hour breakdown service in Italy since 1968. Prices are reasonable and the staff speak good English.

Parking

Parking is a nightmare in Milan: the best solution is to leave your car in one of the 20-odd guarded car parks in the downtown area. Alternatively, use the Sosta Milano parking system, which operates throughout most of the city centre and Fiera: parking areas are marked on the road with blue lines. Those with yellow lines are strictly for residents only. Buy tickets (€1.50 for an hour) at newsstands, *tabaccherie* (*see p232*), from some parking attendants or at the ATM points in Duomo and Cadorna, and scratch them to indicate the day and time. Leave the ticket visible on the dashboard. You can have up to a maximum of two hours. Parking is generally free after 8pm except in the city centre within the inner ring road (where €2 will get you five hours). Cars with disabled signs can park free within blue stripes.

Watch out for signs by entrances saying *'passo carrabile'* (access at all times), *'sosta vietata'* (no parking) and road signs denoting spaces for handicapped drivers. The sign *'zona rimozione'* (tow-away area) means no parking and is valid for the length of the street, or until you come to a tow-away sign with a red line through it. If a street or square has no cars parked in it, you can safely assume it's a seriously enforced no-parking zone. Be aware of the weekly street cleaning that operates throughout Milan. Signposts along the road will tell you when that road and its nearby streets are to be cleaned and this means from midnight onwards of that day. If your car is found parked on the road at that time, expect a €35 fine. Avoid it by parking in neighbouring streets or on the pavement. In some areas, self-appointed *parcheggiatori* will look after your car for a small fee; although this practice is illegal, it's often worth coughing up to ensure that your tyres remain intact.

Autosilo Diaz
*Piazza Diaz, Centre (02 8646 0077).
Metro Duomo/bus 54/tram 15.* **Open**
7am-2am daily. **Rates** €2.50/hr;
€28.50/24hrs. **Credit** AmEx, DC,
MC, V. **Map** p251 E7/p252 E7.

Garage Meravigli
*Via Camperio 4, North (02 8646
1784). Metro Cairoli/bus 54, 58/
tram 1, 19, 24.* **Open** 7am-midnight
(entry until 7pm) Mon-Sat. **Rates**
€5/hr; €31.20/24hrs. **Map** p248 D6/
p252 D6.

Garage Zeus
*Corso Europa 2, Centre (02 7602
2220). Metro San Babila/bus 65, 73/
tram 12.* **Open** 24hrs daily. **Rates**
€5 1st hr then €3/hr; €35/24hrs;
€333/mth. **Map** p251 E7/p252 E7.

Mediolanum Parking
*Largo Corsia dei Servi 15, Centre
(02 7600 8467). Metro San Babila/
bus 65/tram 12.* **Open** 7am-1am
daily. **Rates** €2.50 1st hr then
€2/hr; €28.50/24 hrs.

Rinascente
*Via Agnello, Centre (02 885 2419).
Metro Duomo.* **Open** 7.30am-1.30am
daily. **Rates** €9/3hrs; €11/4hrs; €1
each additional hr. **Credit** AmEx,
DC, MC, V. **Map** p251 E6/p252 E6.

Car pounds
If you can't find your car, chances are
it has been towed away. There is an
information office at via Beccaria 19,
open 24hrs a day; ring it on 02 7727
0280/2 quoting your number plate to
find out which car pound it has been
taken to. There is fine of €62 for
recovering your car, on top of fines.

Fuel
Petrol stations sell regular petrol
(*benzina*), unleaded petrol (*senza
piombo* or *verde*) and diesel (*gasolio*).
Liquid propane gas is GPL. Most
stations offer full service on weekdays,
but are often closed at lunchtimes.
At night and on Sundays many have
self-service pumps that accept €5,
€10 or €20 notes in good condition.
Few stations accept credit cards.

Car hire
To hire a car you must be over 21 –
in some cases 23 – and have held
a licence for at least a year. It's
advisable to take out collision
damage waiver (CDW) and personal
accident insurance (PAI) on top
of basic third party insurance.
Companies that do not offer CDW
are best avoided.

Avis
*National booking line 06 452 108
391.* **Open** 24hrs daily.
Linate airport (02 715 123).
Open 7.30am-midnight daily.
Malpensa airport (02 585 8481).
Open 7am-midnight daily.
*Stazione Centrale, North (02 669
0280).* **Open** 8am-8pm Mon-Fri;
8am-4pm Sat. **Map** p249 G3.
*Piazza Diaz 6, Centre (02 8901
0645). Metro Duomo/bus 54.*
Open 8am-7pm Mon-Fri; 8am-4pm
Sat. **Map** p251 E7/p252 E7.
All **Credit** AmEx, DC, MC, V.

Hertz
*National booking line 199 11221/
199 113 311.* **Open** 8am-11pm daily.
Linate airport (02 7020 0256/97).
Open 7.30am-12.30am daily.
*Malpensa airport (02 5858 1312/
0210).* **Open** 7.30am-midnight daily.
*Piazza Duca d'Aosta 9, Stazione
Centrale, North (02 6698 5151/
6153).* **Open** 8am-8pm Mon-Fri;
8am-2pm Sat, Sun. **Map** p249 G3.
*Via Alcuino 16, West (02 3360
3073). Metro Lotto/bus 48, 78.*
Open 8am-7.30pm Mon-Fri; 8am-
1pm Sat.
*Via Visconti di Modrone 4, East (02
7639 8096).* **Open** 8am-7pm Mon-
Fri; 8am-12.30pm Sat. Map p251 F7/
p252 F7.
All **Credit** AmEx, DC, MC, V.

Bicycles & motorbikes
For more info on cycling in
Milan and bike shops, *see also
p171* **On yer bike**.

Aggressive drivers,
numerous tram tracks and
cobbled streets mean Milan is
less than kind to bikes and
cyclists. But, as a result of
cycle paths and the increasing
pedestrianisation of Milan, life
is getting a little easier. The
main paths are from the centre
along via Melchiorre Gioia
going north, Porta
Romagna/corso Lodi going
south-east, via Dezza and
Monte Rosa going west and
along the Navigli going south;
there's also one in Parco
Sempione. Be warned,
however, that there are gaps
in the paths, where you'll have
to brave the traffic. Bikes are
allowed on the metro and
trains – with various Italian-
style limitations (*see below*).

Metro: bikes are allowed after
8pm weekdays; from 10am onwards
Saturdays; all day Sundays and
holidays and August. There is an
extra €1 charge and access is in
the second, fifth and last carriage
of the train.
Trains: at a price (€3.50) you can
take your bike on all direct, regional
and inter-regional trains.
The **Ciclobby club** (02 6931 1624,
www.associazioni.milano.it/ciclobby)
organises bike tours in interesting
areas every Sunday for members
and non-members. The **Circolo
Ricreativo Culturale Arci** (via
Rovetta 14, North, 02 284 6323,
www.arciquartiere.org) organises
cycle tours out of Milan every
Sunday in spring and autumn
for members.

Bike & motorbike hire
To hire a scooter or moped
(*motorino*) you'll need a credit card,
an identity document and a cash
deposit. Helmets are required on
all kinds of scooters, motorbikes
or mopeds; the police are very
strict about enforcing this.
For bicycles, it is normally enough
to leave an identity document. For
mopeds up to 50cc you need to be
over 14; a driver's licence is required
for anything over 50cc.

AWS Bicimotor
*Via Ponte Seveso 33, North (02
6707 2145). Metro Centrale FS
or Sondrio/bus 90, 91, 92/tram 2.*
Open 9am-1pm, 3-7pm Tue-Sat.
Rates €11/24hrs (€100 deposit).
Credit MC, V. **Map** p249 F2.
City and mountain bike rental.

Biancoblu
*Via Gallarate 33, West (02 308
2430/www.biancoblu.com). Tram 14,
19, 33.* **Open** 9am-12.30pm, 2.30-
7pm Mon-Fri; 9am-12.30pm Sat; 8-
10am, 6-8pm Sat, Sun for pre-booked
bikes.* **Credit** AmEx, DC, MC, V.
Motorbikes and electric bikes for
rent.

Cicli Rossignoli
*Corso Garibaldi 65-71, North (02
804 960). Metro Moscova/bus 41,
43, 91/tram 3, 4.* **Open** 2.30-7.30pm
Mon; 9am-12.30pm, 2.30-7.30pm Tue-
Sat. **Rates** €6/half day; €10/day;
€18/wkd (€100 deposit). **Credit** MC,
V. **Map** p248 D4.
City and mountain bikes.

Mototouring
*Via del Ricordo 31, East (02 2720
1556/www.mototouring.com). Metro
Crescenzago then bus 53.* **Open** 9am-
6pm Mon-Sat. **Credit** AmEx, DC,
MC, V.
Bikes, motorbikes and scooters.

Directory

Resources A-Z

Age restrictions

The age of consent is 14 for both heterosexuals and homosexuals. Beer and wine can be bought at bars from the age of 16, spirits from 18. Cigarettes cannot legally be sold to under-16s. Anyone aged 14 or over can ride a moped or scooter of 50cc; no licence is needed (though this may change in the near future). You must be over 18 to drive and over 21 to hire a car.

Business

If you're doing business in Milan, a call or visit to the commercial section of your embassy or consulate (*see p226*) is a good first move. As ever in Italy, any personal recommendations will smooth your way immensely: use them shamelessly and mercilessly.

American Chamber of Commerce
Via Cantù 1, Centre (02 869 0661/ www.amcham.it). Metro Cordusio or Duomo/bus 50/tram 19, 24, 27. **Open** 9am-12.30pm, 2-5.30pm Mon-Fri. **Map** p250 D7/p252 D7.

British Chamber of Commerce
Via Dante 12, North (02 877 798/ www.britchamitaly.com). Metro Cairoli/bus 43, 70/tram 1, 24, 27. **Open** 9am-1pm, 2-5pm Mon-Fri. **Map** p248 D6/p252 D6.

Business centres

Conservatorio 22
Via Conservatorio 22, East (freephone 800 895 562/02 77 291/www.cogesta.it). Metro San Babila/bus 54, 61. **Open** 8.30am-6pm. **Map** p251 F6/p252 F6.

Executive Service Network
Via Vincenzo Monti 8, West (freephone 800 938 373/02 467 121/www.executivenetwork.it). Metro Cadorna or Conciliazione/bus 61, 68/tram 1, 19, 27. **Open** 8.30am-6pm Mon-Fri. **Map** p250 B6.

Tiempo Group
Via Giovanni da Udine 34, North (freephone 800 246 868/02 3809 3456/www.tiemponord.it). Bus 40, 69/tram 14, 19, 33. **Open** 9am-8pm Mon-Sat.

Conventions & conferences

Business-oriented Milan offers excellent conference facilities in all categories and locations. The city moves and shakes with over 900 conventions each year at the Fiera MilanoCity in the centre or at the new Fiera in Rho, just outside Milan (reachable by underground line 1). Company conferences can be held in magnificent historic buildings such as the Milan Chamber of Commerce's very central Palazzo Affari Ai Giureconsulti (piazza Mercanti 2, Centre, 02 8515 5873) or its equally delightful Palazzo Turati (via Meravigli 9B, North, 02 8518 5875), or in the very modern Magna Pars (via Tortona 15, South, 02 8940 1384), near the fashionable Navigli district. Alternatively, most of the major hotels can cater for events.

If you don't wish to handle the practical details yourself, a number of agencies will smooth the way for you. The Italcongressi (www. italcongressi.com) is based in Rome, but has a lot of useful information on regional conference organisers and interpreters.

AIM Group
Via Ripamonti 129 (02 566 011/ www.aimgroup.it).

FBAI Promotion Entertainment Group
Via Ascanio Sforza 81A (02 8480 0065/www.fbaipromotion.it).

Milan Conference Bureau
www.milanconference.com.

Couriers

International
DHL *199 199 345/www.dhl.it.*
Federal Express *freephone 800 123 800/www.fedex.com.*
TNT *803 868/www.tntitaly.it.*
UPS *freephone 800 877 877/www.ups.com.*

Local
Rinaldi L'Espresso *02 760 311.*
Shadow *02 8912 5505.*

Interpreters & translators

See *traduttori e interpreti* in the *Pagine Gialle* (*Yellow Pages*). Executive Service Network (*see above*) can also arrange a translation service.

International Association of Conference Interpreters (AIIC)
www.aiic.net.
Communication Trend Italia
02 669 1338/www.cti-communication.it.
Language Consulting Congressi
02 8057 846/02 864 156/www.lcc.it.

Customs

Travellers arriving from other EU countries do not have to declare goods imported into or exported out of Italy for personal use, up to the following limits:

800 cigarettes or 200 cigars or 1kg tobacco; ten litres of alcoholic drinks (above 22%); 90 litres of wine (including 60 litres of sparkling wine) and 110 litres of beer. Visitors are also allowed to carry up to €12,500 in cash.

For those arriving from non-EU countries, the following limits apply: 200 cigarettes or 100 small cigars or 50 cigars or 250g (8.8oz) of tobacco; one litre of spirits (over 22% alcohol) or two litres of wine; 50g (1.76oz) of perfume or various goods up to the value of €175. Visitors are also allowed to carry up to €12,500 in cash.

Disabled

The best source of information is AIAS (Associazione Italiana Assistenza Spastici). Most literature is in Italian (for example their booklet *Milano Facile*) but the website (*see below*) has up-to-date information on Milan and Lombardy in English. Or you can send a specific request to aiasmi.vacanze@tiscalinet.it to receive information in English.

The city council also operates a *sportello disabili* (disabled desk), where helpful information is dispensed, in Italian only. It can also provide a booklet in English, *Region of Lombardy Disability Advice Centre: Information and Services*.

AIAS Milano Onlus
02 330 2021/www.milanopertutti.it).

Sportello disabili
Regione Lombardia, via Fabio Filzi 22, North (02 6765 4740/ sportello_disabili@regione.lombardia. it). Metro Centrale FS, Gioia or Repubblica/tram 2, 9, 33. **Open** 9am-5pm Mon-Thur; 9am-3pm Fri; 9am-1.30pm Sat. **Map** p249 F3.

Hotels & restaurants

AIAS (*see above*) keeps an updated list of wheelchair-accessible hotels: see the website for listings. *See also pp36-48* for details of hotels with disabled facilities.

Few restaurants or bars are fully accessible, though staff will be more than willing to help you in most of them. The situation improves in the summer, when tables are placed outside. AIAS has listings of accessible bars and restaurants in all zones of Milan – see under *Cerca locale* on its website.

Sightseeing

Pavements in Milan's centre are narrow, and negotiating cobbled streets is a challenge. On the upside, most street corners have pram/wheelchair ramps, and well-designed ramps and lifts and disabled toilets have been installed in many of the city's museums. Visit the AIAS website (*see above*) for details on reccommended itineraries around the city for disabled people.

Toilets

While the law requires all public facilities to have disabled toilets, many of those in old buildings have yet to pay attention to the rules. The more modern-looking the bar, restaurant, convention facility or museum, the more likely it is to have renovated and appropriately adapted all of its public facilities.

Transport

Some city transport lines are equipped for disabled travellers. The newer Linea 3 metro line is fully accessible by elevators, while the older lines 1 and 2 still have some limitations; the stations currently fitted with lifts are:
Linea (Line) 1: Sesto FS; Duomo; Cadorna; Molino Dorino; Pero; Rho Fiera; Bisceglie.
Linea (Line) 2: Abbiategrasso, Famogosta; Cadorna; Garibaldi; Centrale.

Other stations have wheelchair lifts fitted to the stairs; ask the guard at the ticket barrier for assistance. For more information, call the freephone number 800 808 181 or visit the ATM information points (*see p220*). The evening Radiobus service (*see p220*) is supplied with lifts for wheelchairs and spoken messages for the blind. A number of the city's buses and trams provide easy access for disabled people.

In stations and airports a rubber strip along the floor of passageways and corridors has been laid to help orientate blind or partially sighted people.

The Ferrovie dello Stato (*see p220*) is slowly phasing in easy-access carriages. Trains with wheelchair facilities are indicated by a wheelchair symbol on timetables. Many medium- and long-distance trains have one carriage equipped to transport two wheelchairs plus companion. The CAD Centro Assistenza Disabili (disabled assistance 02 6707 0958 for Milan, or 199 303 060 nationwide) at Centrale, Cadorna or Garibaldi stations will arrange help for boarding or alighting from trains. Call well in advance to organise assistance in Milan and other major Italian cities If travelling at night (10pm-6am), call 12 hours before. For assistance on international trains, the request must be made two days in advance. Full details of trains and services for the disabled can be found in *Services for Disabled Passengers* published by Trenitalia and available at Stazione Centrale.

Transport to both Linate (bus 73) and Malpensa (Malpensa Express) airports (*see p218*) is wheelchair accessible. Book taxis in advance, specifying if you need a car large enough to cope with a wheelchair (*carrozzella*). Alternatively, the following services use small vans and seating for up to eight; try to book at least 48 hours ahead.

A.la.t.Ha
02 4225 7216/www.alatha.it. **Open** by appointment.

CTA
02 355 9360/02 357 4768. **Open** 7.30am-6pm Mon-Fri.

Missione Handicap
02 453 1236. **Open** 7.30am-6pm Mon-Fri.

Wheelchair hire

Farmacie (pharmacies, *see p227*) either rent wheelchairs or can direct you to specialised wheelchair rental services.

Directory

Drugs

The drugs law in Italy has recently changed. It is illegal to grow, produce, manufacture, sell, distribute or deliver any type of drug, either hard or soft. If you are found in possession of amounts considered to be for personal use (for example, 500mg cannabis or 750mg cocaine), you will be fined. Carry over these amounts and you risk a jail sentence. Sniffer dogs are a fixture at most ports of entry into Italy.

Electricity

Most wiring systems work on 220v, which is compatible with British-bought appliances. With US 110v equipment you need a current transformer. A few systems in old buildings are 125v. Socket sizes, especially in older buildings, are not always standard, but two-pin adaptor plugs (*riduttori*) can be bought at any electrical shop (*elettricità*).

Embassies & consulates

Listed below are the Milan consulates of the main English-speaking countries. A full list is found under *Consolati* in the *Pagine Gialle* (*Yellow Pages*).

Australia

Via Borgogna 2, Centre (02 777 041). Metro San Babila/bus 54, 60, 61, 73. **Open** 9am-5pm Mon-Thur; 9am-4.15pm Fri. **Map** p249 F6/p252 F6.

South Africa

Vicolo San Giovanni sul Muro 4, Centre (02 885 8581). Metro Cairoli/tram 1, 16. **Open** 8.30am-4.45pm Mon-Fri. **Map** p248 D6/p252 D6.

UK

Via San Paolo 7, Centre (02 723 001). Metro Duomo or San Babila/bus 15, 60, 73. **Open** 9.15am-12.15pm, 2.30-4.30pm Mon-Fri. **Map** p251 E6/p252 E6.

US

Via Principe Amedeo 2-10, North (02 290 351). Metro Turati/tram 1, 2, 94. **Open** 8.30am-4.30pm Mon-Fri. **Map** p249 E5.

Emergencies

See also below **Health**; *p230* **Money**; *p230* **Police**; *p231* **Safety & security**.

Thefts or losses should be reported immediately at the nearest police station (*see p230*). You should report the loss of your passport to your embassy or consulate (*see above*). Report the loss of a credit card or travellers' cheques immediately to your credit card company (*see p230*).

National emergency numbers

Ambulance *Ambulanza 118.*
Fire service *Vigili del Fuoco 115.*
Police *Carabinieri (English helpline) 112; Polizia di Stato 113.*
Child helpline *114*
Car breakdown (*see also p222*)
Automobile Club d'Italia (ACI) *803 116 24; Europ Assistance freephone 803 803.*

Domestic emergencies

If you need to report a malfunction, these emergency lines are open 24 hours a day.
Electricity *AEM 02 2521; Enel 803500.*
Gas *AEM 02 5255.*
Telephone *Telecom Italia 187.*
Water *02 8477 2000*

Gay & lesbian

For bars and nightlife, *see chapter* **Gay & Lesbian**.

Arcigay

Via Bezzecca 3, East (02 5412 2225/helpline 02 5412 2227/www.arcigaymilano.org). Bus 45, 66, 73/tram 27. **Open** 3-8pm Mon-Fri; 3.30-7.30pm Sun. Closed 1wk Aug, 1wk Dec. **Map** p251 H7.
The Bologna-based Arcigay and Arcilesbica (*see below*), Italy's main gay and lesbian associations, are important sources of information. Arcigay runs an excellent website, a helpline and issues the Arcigay card (*see p157*), which is becoming increasingly essential for getting into Milan's gay venues. The Milan office

is open on Sunday afternoons to welcome new members and answer questions. There is a small library stocked with gay-related books, magazines and videos.

Arcilesbica

Corso Garibaldi 91, North (02 2901 4027/www.arcilesbica.it). Moscova/bus 41, 43, 94/tram 3, 4, 12, 14. **Open** for events only. **Map** p248 D4.
While less active than its brother group Arcigay, this is nevertheless Italy's main political organisation for lesbians. Its website includes a calendar of activities, from workshops to film screenings. There is also a helpline open 7-9pm on Thursdays (02 6311 8654).

Collettivi Donne Milanesi

Corso Garibaldi 91, North (02 2901 4027/www.women.it/cdm). Metro Moscova/bus 41, 43, 94/tram 3, 4, 12, 14. **Open** for events only. **Map** p248 D4.
A lesbian group organising events, political evenings and film screenings in association with Arcigay.

Health

Emergency health care is available for all travellers through the Italian national health system. By law, hospital accident-and-emergency departments (*see below*) must treat all emergency cases free. Before travelling to Milan, EU citizens should obtain the EHIC (European Health Insurance Card), available in the UK on 0845 606 2030, from post offices and online at www.ehic.org. This is equivalent to the Lombardy *Carta Regionale dei Servizi* and allows you to consult a national health service doctor free of charge. *See also p228* **Insurance**.

Accident & emergency

Should you be in need of urgent medical care, head to the *Pronto Soccorso* (casualty department) of one of the hospitals listed below, all of which offer 24hr emergency services. If your child needs emergency treatment, go to the casualty department of the Ospedale dei Bambini Vittore Buzzi or the Ospedale Maggiore.

Ospedale dei Bambini Vittore Buzzi

Via Castelvetro 32, North (02 5799 5363). Bus 43, 57/tram 12, 14. **Map** p248 A3.
Obstetric as well as paediatric casualty departments.

Ospedale Fatebenefratelli

Corso Porta Nuova 23, North (02 63 631). Metro Turati/bus 41, 43. **Map** p249 E4.

Ospedale Maggiore di Milano Policlinico Mangiagalli e Regina Elena di Milano

Ospedale Maggiore *Via Francesco Sforza 28-35, South (02 5503 32/ 09/switchboard 02 55 031/paediatric 02 5799 2694/297. Metro Crocetta, Missori or San Babila/bus 60, 73, 77, 94/tram 12, 16, 24, 27, 23.* **Map** p251 E7.
Ospedale Mangiagalli *Via della Commenda 12, South (switchboard 02 57991). Metro Crocetta or Missori/bus 77, 94/tram 4, 12, 24.* **Map** p251 F8.

Ospedale Niguarda

Piazza Ospedale Maggiore 3, North (02 64 441/poison centre 02 6610 1029 24hrs/www. ospedaleniguarda.it). Bus 5, 40, 51, 83/tram 4.
The Niguarda is renowned throughout Italy for its poison department.

Complementary medicine

A wide range of homeopathic remedies is available from the majority of pharmacies around town (*see below*).

Contraception & abortion

Condoms (*preservativi*) are on sale near checkouts in supermarkets, or over the counter in pharmacies (*see below*). The contraceptive pill (*pillola anticoncezionale*) is available on prescription. The morning-after pill can be obtained at hospital casualty departments (*see above*) – the doctor on duty will write a prescription that you then take to a pharmacy to be filled.
Abortion is available on financial hardship or health grounds, and legal only when performed in public hospitals.

Each district has a family-planning clinic (*consultorio familiare*), run by the local health authority. EU citizens with an EHIC card (*see p226*) are entitled to use them, paying the same charges for services as locals. They are listed in the phone book under *Consultorio Familiare*; or visit www.asl.milano.it/DipAssi/ consultorio.asp.
Gynaecological advice can also be had at the following clinics or at the international health centres listed below.

AIED

Via Vitruvio 43, East (02 6671 4156). Metro Lima/bus 60/tram 5, 33. **Open** 9.30am-7pm Mon-Fri. **Map** p249 G3.

Centro Diagnostico Italiano

Via Saint Bon 20, West (02 483 171). Metro Inganni/bus 18, 49, 58, 67. **Open** 7.30am-7.30pm Mon Fri; 7.30am-noon Sat.

Dentists

Most dentists (see *Dentisti* in the *Yellow Pages*) in Italy work privately. You may wait for months for a dental appointment in a public hospital. Treatment is not cheap and may not be covered by your health insurance. For serious dental emergencies, go to the hospital casualty departments listed above. Check with your consulate for international health clinics where English-speaking dentists can help you. The English *Yellow Pages* (online at www.intoitaly.it) lists English-speaking dentists.

Doctors

EU nationals with an EHIC card (*see p226*) can consult a national health service doctor free of charge. Drugs that he or she prescribes can be bought from chemists at prices set by the Health Ministry. If you need tests or specialist outpatient treatment, this too will be charged at fixed rates (known in Italian as '*il ticket*').
Non-EU nationals who need to consult national health service doctors will be charged a small fee at the doctor's discretion.
Pharmacists (*see below*) are generally useful sources of information: they will recommend local doctors and provide you with addresses of laboratories to have tests done.
Milan's long-established international health clinics have highly qualified medical staff, can do tests and also deal with emergency situations.

American International Medical Center (AIMC)

Via Mercalli 11, South (02 5831 9808/www.iht.it/aimc). Metro Missori/bus 94/tram 15. **Open** 9am-6pm Mon-Fri. **Map** p251 E8.

International Health Centre

Galleria Strasburgo 3, Centre (02 7634 0720). Metro Duomo or San Babila/bus 61. **Open** 8.45am-7pm Mon-Fri. **Map** p251 F7/p252 F7.

Milan Clinic

Via Cerva 25, Centre (02 7601 6047). Metro San Babila/bus 60, 65, 73. **Open** 9am-6pm Mon-Thur; 9am-5pm Fri. **Map** p251 F7/p252 F7.

Helplines & agencies

ALA

02 8951 6464. **Open** 9.30am-1.30pm Mon-Fri.
STD, HIV and AIDS helpline.

CADMI (Help Centre for Maltreated Women)

02 5501 5519. **Open** 10am-1pm, 2.30-6pm Mon-Thur.
Sexual violence and rape helpline. There is normally an English-speaking volunteer available.

Sexual violence first aid helpline

Ospedale Mangiagalli 02 5799 2489. **Open** 24hrs.

Hospitals

Milan's public hospitals (*see p226* **Accident & emergency**) offer good to excellent treatment for most illnesses.

Opticians

See p141.

Pharmacies & prescriptions

Pharmacies (*farmacie*, identified by a green cross) give informal medical advice for straightforward ailments, and also make up prescriptions. Most pharmacies also sell homeopathic medicines, and all will check your height/weight/blood pressure on request. Over-the-counter drugs such as aspirin are considerably more expensive in Italy than in the UK or US. Anyone who requires regular medication should bring adequate supplies of their drugs with them.

Directory

Also, make sure you know the generic name of any medicines you need, since they may be available in Italy under different names.

Normal opening hours are 8.30am-12.30pm and 3.30-7.30pm Monday to Saturday. Outside of normal hours, a duty rota system operates. Night service typically operates 8pm-8.30am. A list by the door of any pharmacy indicates the nearest open ones; this is also published in the paper, or call 800 801 185 to find your nearest open pharmacy. At duty pharmacies there is a surcharge of €3.87 per client (not per item) when the main shop is shut. The pharmacy at **Stazione Centrale** (North, 02 669 0739) is open 24 hours, while **Carlo Erba** (piazza del Duomo 21, Centre, 02 7202 3120) is open from 8pm to 8.30am nightly, but closes for a few hours each day.

ID

You are required by law to carry photo ID with you at all times. You will be asked to produce it if you are stopped by traffic police (who will demand your driving licence, which you must carry when you are in charge of a motor vehicle). You will also need ID when you check into a hotel.

Insurance

See also p226 **Health** *and* *p230* **Police**.

EU nationals are entitled to reciprocal medical care in Italy, provided they have an EHIC card (*see p226*). This will cover you for emergencies, but using it involves having to deal with the intricacies of the Italian state health system. For short-term visitors it may be better to take out health cover under private travel insurance, so you can choose your health-care provider.

Non-EU citizens should buy private medical insurance for all eventualities.

If you rent a vehicle, motorcycle or moped, it's worth paying the extra charge for full insurance cover. Likewise, sign the collision damage waiver when hiring a car. *See also p223* **Car hire**.

Internet & email

At most of the cheaper hotels you can plug your modem into the phone system; upmarket ones have broadband or wireless (WiFi) access, though you will usually be charged a daily rate for this (sometimes through a third party, though connection is usually simple, if not cheap). Italian providers offering free internet access (once you register) include: Caltanet (www.caltanet.it), Libero (www.libero.it), Tiscali (www.tiscali.it) and Kataweb (www.kataweb.it).

Internet access

There are many internet points throughout the city; the following is a selection. **Biblioteca Sormani** (*see below*) offers free internet access.

FNAC
Via Torino, at via Palla 2, Centre (02 869 541). Metro Duomo/tram 2, 3, 14. **Open** 9am-8pm Mon-Sat; 10am-8pm Sun. **Rates** €3/hr; €2.50/hr with FNAC card. **Map** p250 D7/p252 D7.

Gr@zia Internet Café
Piazza Duca d'Aosta 14, North (02 6700 543). Metro Centrale FS/bus 60/tram 5, 33. **Open** 8am-2am daily. **Rates** €4/hr. **Map** p249 F3.

Internet Enjoy
Alzaia Naviglio Pavese 2, South (02 835 7225). Metro Porta Genova/bus 59, 71/tram 9, 29, 30. **Open** 9am-midnight Mon-Sat; 2pm-midnight Sun. **Rates** €1.80/hr. **Map** p250 C9.

Viamatica
Corso Colombo 9, South (02 5811 8100). Metro Porta Genova/tram 9, 29, 30. **Open** 10am-10pm Mon-Sat; 1-9pm Sun. **Rates** €4/hr; €8/3hrs. **Map** p250 B8.

Left luggage

Most hotels will look after your luggage for you for a few hours after you have checked out. The left-luggage depot at Stazione Centrale (02 6371 2667) operates 6am-midnight daily; at Malpensa airport Terminal 1 (02 5858 0069) 7am-9pm daily; Linate airport (02 7012 4451) 7am-9.30pm daily.

Legal help

The first stop if you find yourself in need of legal help should always be your consulate; *see p226*. You may be directed to local law firms with English-speaking staff. Milan is also home to many associates of English and American law firms.

Libraries

Milan has some 40 libraries with public access, the most useful and central of which are listed below. Visit www.comune.milano.it/biblioteche for a full list. You will need to show ID (such as your passport) to gain entry to gain entry to most libraries.

Biblioteca del Conservatorio Giuseppe Verdi
Via Conservatorio 12, East (02 762 1101/www.consmilano.it). Metro San Babila/bus 54, 61. **Open** 2-8pm Mon-Wed (book distribution 3-6pm); 8am-2pm Thur-Sat (book distribution 9am-noon); 8am-2pm (book distribution 9am-noon) Sept, Oct, July. **Map** p251 F6/p252 F6.
Attached to Milan's conservatory, this has a huge collection of music-related books and manuscripts.

Biblioteca Nazionale Braidense
Via Brera 28, North (02 8646 0907/www.braidense.it). Metro Lanza or Montenapoleone/bus 61, 94/tram 1, 2, 3, 4, 12, 27. **Open** 8.30am-6.15pm Mon-Fri; 9am-1.45pm Sat. **Map** p248 D5/p252 D5.
The National Library contains over a million books, plus manuscripts, periodicals, 19th-century prints and antique books. Consultation is free; only Lombardy residents can borrow.

Biblioteca Sormani
Corso di Porta Vittoria 6, South (freephone 800 880 066/02 8846 3397/www.comune.milano.it/bibliotec he). Metro Missori or San Babila/bus 54, 60, 65, 73, 84, 94/tram 12, 23, 27. **Open** 9am-7.30pm Mon-Sat. **Map** p251 F7/p252 F7.
Milan's central public library has over 600,000 works, including Stendhal's library, audio recordings and a great choice of daily papers. Entrance and consultation is free for over-14s only; only Lombardy residents can borrow.

English-language libraries

CSSU (Centro di Studi sugli Stati Uniti)

Piazza Sant'Alessandro 1, Centre (02 5031 3593). Metro Missori/bus 15/tram 2, 3, 14. **Open** 10am-5pm Mon-Thur. **Map** p250 D7/p252 D7.
Housed in Milan University, this library hosts a collection of over 10,000 English-language volumes, focusing on US literature, history and social and political issues. Consultation is free for everyone, but borrowing is confined to University staff and students.

Università Cattolica del Sacro Cuore

Largo Gemelli 1, West (freephone 800 209 902/02 72341/ Bibliopoint 02 7234 3849). Metro Sant'Ambrogio/bus 50, 58, 94. **Open** 9am-8pm Mon-Fri; 9am-1pm Sat. **Map** p250 C7.
A well-stocked university library of over one million books, many in English. A free three-day pass is available from Bibliopoint, the office on the ground floor of the University's Gregorianum building.

Lost property

Ufficio Oggetti Rinvenuti

Via Friuli 30, South (02 8845 3900/ 08/09). Bus 62, 90, 92/tram 4. **Open** 8.30am-4pm Mon-Fri. **Map** p251 H9.
Milan city council's lost property office lists everything found the previous week on its website (www.comune.milano.it) – look under *Oggetti rinvenuti*.

Ufficio Oggetti Smarriti Ferrovie dello Stato

Stazione Centrale, Galleria delle Partenze (in the left-luggage office), North (02 6371 2212). Metro Centrale FS/bus 53/tram 2. **Open** 6am-midnight daily. **Map** p249 G3.
Anything lost on trains should eventually end up here.

Media

Magazines

With the naked female form emblazoned across their covers most weeks, Italy's serious news magazines are not immediately distinguishable from the large selection of soft porn on newsstands.

Panorama and *L'Espresso* provide a generally high-standard round-up of the week's news; national newspaper *Corriere della Sera*'s Saturday colour supplement, *Io Donna*, is a meaty read and, despite the name, isn't just for women. For tabloid-style scandal, try *Gente* and *Oggi*, *Chi* or the execrable *Eva 3000*, *Novella 2000* and *Cronaca Vera*.
  The biggest-selling title of them all, however, is *Famiglia Cristiana* – available from newsstands or most churches – which alternates Vatican line-toeing with Vatican-baiting, depending on relations between the Holy See and the idiosyncratic Paoline monks who produce it.

National daily newspapers

Italian newspapers can be a frustrating read. Long, indigestible political stories with very little background explanation predominate. On the plus side, they are delightfully unsnobbish and happily blend serious news, leaders by internationally known commentators, and well-written, often surreal, crime and human-interest stories.
  Sports coverage in the dailies is extensive and thorough, but if you're not sated there are the mass-circulation sports papers *Corriere dello Sport*, *Gazzetta dello Sport* and *Tuttosport*. Milan's businessmen are major purchasers of the three big financial dailies, *Il Sole 24 Ore*, *Italia Oggi* and *MilanoFinanza*.

Corriere della Sera

www.corriere.it
To the centre of centre-left, the Milan-based *Corriere della Sera* is good on crime and foreign news. It includes a daily Milan section, which is useful for information on films and cultural events, not to mention strikes, roadworks and so on. Its *ViviMilano* supplement (Wednesday) has weekly listings.

Il Giorno

www.ilgiorno.it
Owned by Silvio Berlusconi's family, *Il Giorno* is understandably pro-government… often to a nauseating (when not risible) extent.

La Repubblica

www.repubblica.it
This left-ish daily is good on the mafia and the Vatican, and comes up with the occasional major scoop on its business pages. It has a Milan section and, on Thursdays, a weekly listings magazine, *TuttoMilano*.

La Stampa

www.lastampa.it
Part of the massive empire of Turin's Agnelli family, *La Stampa* has good (though inevitably pro-Agnelli) business reporting.

Local dailies

The free newspaper phenomenon hit Italy about five years ago. Milan has three: the first was *Metro*. *City* is published by *Corriere della Sera*. Another is *Leggo*. All include brief news items and are good for people trying to practise their Italian.

Foreign press

The *Financial Times*, *International Herald Tribune* (with *Italy Daily* supplement), *Wall Street Journal*, *USA Today*, and most British and European dailies can be found on the day of issue at central newsstands; some US dailies appear a day late.

Comics

A suprising number of grown-up comics exist in Italy, which are supported loyally by their fans. *Dylan Dog* comics are set in London and feature a Rupert Everett-lookalike hero who combats ghosts and spirits throughout the UK; other heroes include the criminologist Julia (with more than a passing resemblance to Audrey Hepburn), Nathan Never, Tex and Brendan. You'll find people reading them everywhere and, if you are so inclined, they are a fun way to learn a bit of Italian.

Listings & small ads

Easy Milano

www.easymilano.it
Free biweekly classified-ad mag for the English-speaking community, distributed at consulates and expat hangouts in Milan.

Hello Milano

www.hellomilano.it
A free monthly in English with event and exhibition listings, distributed at the tourist office (*see p233*).

The Informer

www.informer.it
Although not specifically Milanese, this long-established publication is based in Milan. It offers useful advice on dealing with red tape and a good small ads section. Worth reading if you are thinking of moving to Italy.

Directory

Secondamano

www.secondamano.it
The mother of all classifieds
(in Italian). Includes ads for car,
household and other second-hand
sales, plus flat rents and shares.
Available daily at newsstands.
It also has shops around the city
where you can place adverts.

Urban

It's worth having a look a this free
monthly newsprint publication even
if you don't read Italian; it provides
listings of new bars and restaurants
in Milan, as well as Rome, Turin and
Bologna. Find it in racks outside
trendy shops, restaurants and clubs.

Radio

The three state-owned stations (**RAI
1**, 90.6FM; **RAI 2**, 93.7FM; **RAI 3**,
99.4FM) play classical and light
music, and also feature endless chat
shows and regular, excellent news
bulletins. If you can't stand babbling
DJs, try **LifeGate Radio**
105.1/88.7FM. For UK and US chart
hits, mixed with home-grown
offerings, try the following:
Gamma Radio 97.1FM
Radio DeeJay 97.7-107FM
Radio Lombardia 100.3FM
(regional radio with news and
magazine programmes)
Radio Monte Carlo 105.3-5FM
Radio 105 99.100FM
Radio Reporter 103.7FM

Television

Italy has six major networks (three
owned by state broadcaster RAI, RAI
1 being the most mainstream and
RAI 3 the more 'radical') and three
belonging to Mediaset, owned by
Silvio Berlusconi). Many smaller,
local stations provide hours of
compulsively awful channel-zapping
fun. However, La7 is recommended
for its independent stance. The
standard of television news and
current affairs programmes varies,
but most offer a breadth of coverage
that makes British TV news look like
a parish magazine. All channels dub
programmes into Italian, but MTV
often shows American sitcoms and
other programmes in English with
Italian subtitles, and the advent of
Sky and digital terrestrial
broadcasting means that in many
hotels (and homes) there is more
variety in terms of foreign channels,
especially those dedicated to news.

Money

Italy's currency is the euro.
There are euro banknotes of

€5, €10, €20, €100, €200 and
€500, and coins worth €1
and €2 as well as 1, 2, 5, 10,
20 and 50 cents (c). Euros
from any euro-zone country
are valid in Italy.

ATMs

Most banks and some post offices
have 24-hour cashpoint (Bancomat)
machines; the vast majority of
them accept Visa, MasterCard and
other cards.

Banking hours

Most banks are open 8.30am-1.30pm
and 2.45-4.15pm Monday to Friday.
Banks are closed on public holidays.

Bureaux de change

Commission rates vary considerably.
Banks usually offer better exchange
rates than private bureaux de change
(*uffici di cambio*). Beware places
displaying 'no commission' signs,
as the rate of exchange will almost
certainly be bad. Main post offices
(*see below*) also have exchange
bureaux, though they don't accept
travellers' cheques. Many city centre
bank branches have automatic cash-
exchange machines, which accept
notes in most major currencies (in
good condition). Take a passport or
other identity document whenever
you're dealing with money,
particularly to change travellers'
cheques or withdraw money on a
credit card.

American Express

*Via Larga 4, Centre (02 7210 4010).
Metro Missori/bus 54/tram 12, 15,
27.* **Open** 9am-5.30pm Mon-Fri.
Map p251 E7/p252 E7.

Credit cards

The Italians have a traditional
fondness for cash, but persuading
them to take plastic has become a
lot easier in the last few years.
Practically all hotels of two stars
and above now accept at least some
of the major credit cards. If your
credit card has been lost or stolen,
phone one of the emergency
numbers listed below. All lines
have English-speaking staff and
are open 24 hours a day.
American Express 06 72 900 347
*(see also above)/lost travellers'
cheques 800 872 000.*
Diners Club *800 864 064.*
MasterCard *800 870 866.*
Visa *800 819 014/lost travellers'
cheques 800 874 155.*

Tax

See also p234 **Working in Milan.**
For VAT rebates on goods purchased
in Italy, *see p122*.
   Sales tax (IVA) is charged at
varying rates on most goods and
services, and is almost invariably
quoted as an integral part of prices,
though there are a few top-end hotels
that will quote prices without IVA.
Some tradespeople will also offer you
rates without it – the implication is
that if you are willing to hand over
cash and not demand a receipt in
return, you'll be paying around 20
per cent (ie the amount you would
have spent on IVA) less than the real
fee – but note that both you and the
tradesperson risk hefty fines should
you be rumbled by the police. Bear in
mind that you are legally required to
keep a receipt from any purchase; you
may have to show it to the Guardia
di Finanza (customs and excise
police) when you leave the country.

Police

Polizia locale, the city police
(rather like traffic wardens),
deal with traffic and minor
problems that upset the
smooth running of the city.
They have a headquarters
in via Beccaria 19 (Centre,
02 77271). The main *polizia
di stato* station, the Questura
Centrale, is at via
Fatebenefratelli 11 (North,
02 62261). The addresses of
others are listed in phone
books under *Polizia* and
Carabinieri respectively.
Incidents can be reported to
either force.

Postal services

For international and local
courier services, *see p224*.
   Italy's equivalent to first-
class post, *posta prioritaria*,
generally works very well:
it promises delivery within
24 hours in Italy, three days
for EU countries and four
or five for the rest of the
world. More often than not,
it succeeds. There's a 60c
minimum cost for Italy, or
62c to the rest of Europe.
This is also the minimum price
of a stamp for Europe. The 45c

stamps are for second-class letters to Italy only.

Stamps for all letters are sold at post offices and *tabaccherie* (*see p232*) only. Most post boxes are red and have two slots, one marked *Per la città* (for Milan) and the other *Per tutte le altre destinazioni* (all other destinations).

The CAI-Postacelere service (available only at main post offices) costs somewhat more than *posta prioritaria* and delivers at the same speed, the only advantage being that you can track the progress of your letter on its website (www.poste.it) or by phone (info line 803 160, 8am-8pm Mon-Sat). Registered mail (*raccomandata*), available only at post offices, has a €2.80 minimum cost in Italy and Europe.

There have been big changes in the management of the Italian post office system in the last few years and this is reflected in the services they offer (fax, money transfers, banking facilities); for the traveller the most important is that many now have longer opening hours (8am-7pm), while the rest keep to the more traditional 8am-2pm Monday to Friday, and 8.30am-noon on Saturday and any day preceding a public holiday. Each post office displays a list of the nearest one open when it is closed.

For postal information of any kind, phone the central information office (803 160) or visit www.poste.it.

Posta Centrale

Via Cordusio 4, Centre (02 7248 2126). Metro Cordusio/tram 2, 3, 4, 12, 14, 24, 27. **Open** 8am-7pm Mon-Sat. **Map** p250 D6/p252 D6.

Ufficio Posta

Piazza Duca d'Aosta, North (02 67395). Metro Centrale FS/bus 90, 91, 92/tram 1, 5, 33. **Open** 8am-7pm Mon-Sat. **Map** p249 F3.
This is the temporary address while the Stazione Centrale undergoes renovation work.

Religion

Anglican

All Saint's Church, via Solferino 17, North (02 655 2258). Metro Moscova/bus 43, 94. **Service** usually 7.15pm Wed; 10.30am Sun. **Map** p248 D4.

Catholic

San Carlo, piazza Santa Maria del Carmine 2, North (02 8646 3365). Metro Lanza/bus 61/tram 3, 4, 12. **Service** in English 10.45am Sun. **Map** p248 D6/p252 D6.

Jewish

Central Synagogue, via Guastalla 19, East (02 551 2029). Bus 60, 77. **Service** times vary; call for details. **Map** p251 F7/p252 F7.

Methodist

Chiesa Evangelica Metodista di Milano, via Porro Lambertenghi 28, North (02 607 2631), Metro Garibaldi/bus 42, 51, 70, 83, 91, 92/tram 4, 11. **Service** 11.45 (in English) Sun; 11am (bilingual English/Italian) 1st Sun of mth.

Russian Orthodox

San Nicola, via San Gregorio 5, East (02 204 6996). Metro Lima or Repubblica/tram 1, 5. **Service** 10am Sun. **Map** p249 G4.

Zen Buddhist

Via Agnesi 18, South (02 5830 6763). Metro Porta Romana/bus 62/tram 9, 29, 30. **Service** times vary; call for details. **Map** p251 F9.

Safety & security

Milan is, by and large, fairly safe. However, as in any large city, petty crime is a fact of life, so take the usual precautions with your personal belongings. Tourists who stand out as such are most susceptible to small-time theft and pickpocketing. Pickpockets often work in pairs or groups, targeting tourist areas, public transport routes and the international arrival area of the airports. Everyone – and lone females especially – should be careful in the Stazione Centrale, parklands and Arco della Pace areas in the evenings.

A few basic precautions will greatly reduce a street thief's chances:

● Don't carry wallets in back pockets, particularly on buses. If you have a bag or camera with a long strap, wear it across your chest and not dangling from one shoulder.
● Keep bags closed, with your hand on them. Whenever you sit down, do not leave bags or coats on the ground or the back of a chair where you cannot keep an eye on them.
● When walking down a street, remember to hold cameras and bags on the side of you towards the wall, so you're less likely to become the prey of drive-by motorcycle thieves.
● If you see groups of ragged children brandishing pieces of cardboard, avoid them or walk by quickly, keeping tight hold on your valuables. They will wave the cardboard to confuse you while their accomplices pick pockets or bags. If you are the victim of a crime, call the police helpline (*see p226*) or go to the nearest police station and say you want to report a *furto* (theft) or *scippo* (bag snatching). A *denuncia* (written statement) of the incident will be made for you. You will need this to make an insurance claim.

Smoking

The groups of people you find outside bars and restaurants will often consist of hardened smokers obeying Italy's rules on lighting up. Smoking is not permitted in any indoor public place and this includes all bars, nightclubs and restaurants. Smoking zones may be provided by owners and a sign on the door will generally inform you if this is the case, but these areas are few and far between. The no-smoking rule is strictly enforced and you will incur a hefty fine if you disobey. For where to buy cigarettes, *see p232* **Tabaccherie**.

Study

See also p228 **Libraries**.

Students staying in Italy for more than eight days need to get hold of a *Permesso di Soggiorno* (permit to stay). This can be obtained at the Ufficio Stranieri at the police station (*questura*) at via Montebello 26 (North, 02 62261). You will need any documents relating to your course, four passport photos, a *marca da bollo* for €14.62 and, if you come from outside the EU, an insurance policy to cover medical fees during your stay. If you are an EU citizen your medical fees will be covered by your EHIC card (*see p226*).

Milan has a state university and polytechnic, a highly regarded language institute, two private universities, including the prestigious Bocconi, a fine art academy and a renowned music academy. Most of these offer international programmes and have agreements with foreign universities. Consult university websites to see what's on offer. EU citizens have the same right to study at Italian universities as Italian nationals. However, you will need to have your school diplomas translated and authenticated at the Italian consulate in your own country before presenting them to the *Ufficio Studenti Stranieri* (foreign students' department) of any university.

Outside Milan, there are also universities in Bergamo (www.unibg.it), Brescia (www.unibs.it), Pavia (www.unipv.it) and Castellanza (www.liuc.it).

The Open University also offers degree-level study programmes in English with tutors throughout Italy. Visit www.open.ac.uk or contact Jane Pollard on 02 813 8048.

Accademia di Belle Arti di Brera
www.accademiadibrera.milano.it.
Il Conservatorio di Milano
www.consmilano.it.
Libera Università di Lingue e Comunicazione IULM
www.iulm.it.
Politecnico di Milano
www.polimi.it/english.
Universita' Cattolica del Sacro Cuore
www.unicatt.it/ucsc_EV.asp.
Università Commerciale Luigi Bocconi
www.uni-bocconi.it.
Università degli Studi di Milano
www.unimi.it.

Language schools

Look under *Scuole di lingua* in the *Yellow Pages*. The Società Dante Alighieri (02 669 2816) and Linguedue (02 2951 9972) are recommended for foreigners learning Italian.

Tabaccherie

Tabaccherie or *tabaccai* (identified by signs with a white T on a black or blue background) are the only places to buy tobacco products legally. They also sell stamps, phone cards and lottery tickets. Where a *tabaccheria* is located close to a tram, metro or bus stop, it may also sell transport tickets. If not, this duty may have fallen to the newsstand (*edicola*). Most *tabaccherie* keep proper shop hours; many, however, are attached to bars or have external vending machines so you can satisfy your nicotine cravings well into the night.

Telephones

Dialling & codes

Landline numbers in Milan begin with the area code 02, and this must be used whether you call from within or outside the city. Phone numbers within Milan generally have seven or eight digits, although some numbers (such as the central operator of a large firm) may have six or fewer.

All numbers beginning with 800 are freephone lines (until recently, these began 176 or 167: you will still find old-style numbers listed; replace the prefix with 800). For numbers beginning 199 (often for customer services or information) you will be charged a local rate from anywhere in the country. Be very wary of calling any number that begins with 899 (often chatlines) as the cost can be as high as €2-€3 a minute and some have fixed rates of up to €15. These numbers can be called from within Italy only; some only function within one phone district.

Rates

Rates have tumbled since competition has hit the phone system. The biggest Italian telephone company, Telecom Italia, charges about 20c a minute (45c for calls to mobiles), plus

44c when the caller picks up, for any call to Europe at any time of day. Local and inter-regional calls have off-peak prices from 6pm to 8am and all day Saturday, Sunday and bank holidays. Avoid using phones in hotels, as rates are extortionate.

Public phones

As the Italians are Europe's most enthusiastic mobile-phone users, it's not surprising the number of public phones has declined considerably in recent years. Some bars have pay phones, but if you need to make a long call go to the Telecom Italia phone centre in the Galleria Vittorio Emanuele II or one of many other cheap phone centres throughout the city. Most public phones only accept phone cards (*schede telefoniche*); a few also accept major credit cards and cash. Phone cards are available from *tabaccherie* (*see above*) and some newsstands and bars. Beware: they have expiry dates.

International calls

To make an international phone call from Italy, dial 00, then the country code: Australia 61; Canada 1; Republic of Ireland 353; New Zealand 64; South Africa 27; UK 44; US 1. Then dial the area code (for calls to the UK, omit the initial zero of the area code) and then the number. To phone Milan from abroad, dial the international code (00 in the UK), then 39 for Italy and 02 for Milan, followed by the number.

Operator services

To make a reverse charge (collect) call, to ask for a connection, or for a real-time translation of the call into English (€9.78 plus €7/min) dial the operator.
Directory enquiries *1214 or 892 892.*
Operator (also international) *170.*
International directory enquiries *4176.*
Wake-up calls *4114.*
An automatic message will ask you to dial in the time you want your call – in four figures, using the 24hr clock – followed by your phone number.

Mobile phones

Italian mobile phone numbers begin with 3. GSM phones operate on both 900 and 1800 bands. British, Australian and New Zealand mobiles work here, as do tri- and quad-band US mobiles. Mobile phones can be rented from the following places:

Easy Line/Global Phone Network

Via Fratelli Bronzetti 1, East (02 7012 0181). Bus 60, 62/tram 12, 27. **Open** 9am-1pm, 2-6pm Mon-Sat. **Credit** AmEx, DC, MC, V. **Map** p251 H7.

Future Service

Corso Lodi 83, South (02 5681 5129). Metro Brenta. **Open** 9am-1pm, 3-7.30pm Mon-Sat. **Credit** AmEx, DC, MC, V. **Map** p251 G9.

Fax

Faxes can be sent to some countries (but not to the UK) from the Posta Centrale (*see p231*), from around €2.50 per page. Otherwise, try phone centres, some *cartolibrerie* (stationers) or photocopying outlets, but be aware that the cost may be higher.

Telegrams & telexes

These can be sent from the Posta Centrale (*see p231*), or you can dictate telegrams over the phone. Dial 186 from a private phone and a message in Italian will tell you to dial the number of the phone you're phoning from. A telephonist will then take your message.

Time

Italy is one hour ahead of London, six ahead of New York, eight behind Sydney. Clocks are moved forward by one hour in early spring and back in late autumn, as with other EU countries.

Tipping

Many of the larger restaurants now include a service charge of ten to 15 per cent. Tips are not expected in family-run restaurants, though a euro or two is appreciated. A cover charge (*coperto*) for the table and bread will automatically be added to your bill; check whether the service charge (*servizio*) is already included and calculate your tip based on any amounts already added and the quality of service. Ten per cent is considered generous. Taxi drivers will be happy if you round the fare up to the nearest whole euro.

Toilets

By law, Italian bars are obliged to let anyone use their toilets. Buying something will ensure the loo isn't 'out of order'. Don't expect a bar's toilets to be clean or have toilet paper. There are toilets at or near most major tourist sites, in some metro stations and at the Cadorna railway station; most have attendants and you'll have to pay a small fee.

Tourist information

Friendly smiles, patience and printed information are rather thin on the ground in Milan's main tourist office by the Duomo, although the office near piazza Castello is rather more helpful (and less busy). Their Welcome Card (€8) will get you discounts on selected sites and tours, and their publication *Milano Mese* has masses of information on exhibitions, concerts, and events in English and Italian.

Tourist information centres

Via Marconi 1, Centre (02 7252 4301/www.milanoinfotourist.com). Metro Duomo/tram 2, 3, 4, 12, 14, 24, 27. **Open** 9am-1pm, 2-6pm daily. **Map** p251 E7/p252 E7.
Note that this office will be relocating during the lifetime of this guide – it's likely to move across the piazza del Duomo into the via Silvio Pellico.
Via Beltrami, at piazza Castello 1, North (02 8058 0614/5). Metro Cadorna, Cairoli or Lanza/bus 43, 57, 61, 70, 94/tram 1, 3, 4, 12, 14, 27. **Open** 9am-6pm Mon-Sat. **Map** p248 D6.
Stazione Centrale, North (02 725 241/www.milanoinfotourist.com). **Open** 9am-1pm, 2-6pm Mon-Sat; 9am-5pm Sun. **Map** p249 G3.

Tours

For guided tours, *see p51*.

Visas

EU nationals do not require a visa to visit Italy; neither do citizens of the US, Canada, Australia and New Zealand for stays of up to three months. For EU citizens, a passport or identity card valid for travel abroad is sufficient; all non-EU citizens must have full passports. All visitors should declare their presence to the police within eight days of arrival. If you're staying in a hotel, this will be done for you. If not, contact the Questura Centrale (main police station; *see p230*) for advice.

Water

There are public drinking fountains throughout Milan and in most cases the water is perfectly acceptable to drink. If you have any doubts, opt for bottled water. In bars, specify whether you want *acqua minerale naturale* (still) or *gassata* (fizzy).

When to go

Climate

The low-lying Po valley is bound on the north by the Alps and the south-west by the Appennines, which keeps all that moisture firmly where it is. Hence the notoriously thick fog that can bring traffic in the area around Milan to a halt. Winter in many parts of Lombardy can be bitter, with winds zipping down from the Alps. Milan, though, is almost wind-free, which makes it feel milder. Snow is uncommon. Spring can be rainy but is quite short, quickly turning to summer, which tends to be muggy and mosquito-ridden. If you are coming in July or August, ensure your hotel has air-conditioning. September is a very pleasant month in Milan, but rain may intrude in late October and November.

Public holidays

On public holidays (*giorni festivi*), banks and businesses are closed, although (with the exception of May Day, Assumption and Christmas Day) bars and restaurants and the shops in the city centre tend to stay open. Public transport is practically non-existent on 1 May and Christmas afternoon. Holidays falling on a Saturday or Sunday are not celebrated the following Monday;

Directory

however, if a holiday falls on a Thursday or a Tuesday, many people will take the Friday/Monday off as well, a practice known as *fare il ponte* ('doing a bridge'), although this doesn't mean offices are closed on these days.

Public holidays are as follows: New Year's Day (*Capodanno*), 1 January; Epiphany (*Epifania*), 6 January; Easter Monday (*Pasquetta*); Liberation Day, 25 April; May Day, 1 May; Republic Day, 2 June; Feast of the Assumption (*Ferragosto*), 15 August; All Saints' (*Tutti Santi*), 1 November; Feast of Sant'Ambrogio (Milan's patron saint), 7 December; Immaculate Conception (*Festa dell'Immacolata*), 8 December; Christmas Day (*Natale*), 25 December; Boxing Day (*Santo Stefano*), 26 December.

Women

Foreign women will be the object of attention in Italy, no matter where they go. Most Italian men are attentive, interested and courteous. You are unlikely to encounter any aggressive behaviour. Having said that, take the usual precautions. Avoid outlying areas and don't wander by yourself at night except in lively central zones. There are prostitutes and pushers in the area around Stazione Centrale after dark. They are unlikely to hassle you, but will make your late-night movements less than

picturesque. A taxi (*see p221*) is a good idea if you're crossing the city late at night.

Working in Milan

Anyone looking to stay for longer periods in Milan for work is obliged to procure a series of forms and permits. EU citizens should have no problem getting the required documentation once they are in Italy, but non-EU citizens are strongly advised to enquire at their local Italian embassy or consulate before travelling. There are agencies that specialise in obtaining documents for you – for a price, of course (see *Pratiche e certificati – Agenzie* in the *Pagine Gialle/Yellow Pages*). An important address for all these tasks is the town hall:

Municipio di Milano

Via Larga 12, Centre (02 8846 2062). Metro Missori/bus 54/tram 12, 15. **Open** 8.30am-1pm, 2.30-6pm Mon-Fri. **Map** p251 E7/p252 E7.

Permesso di soggiorno

If you are staying in Italy for longer than three months, you will need a *permesso di soggiorno* ('permit to stay'), which is usually granted with

the minimum of fuss to EC nationals. In theory, you should apply for one within eight days of arriving. Go to the Ufficio Stranieri at the police station (questura) at via Montebello 26 (North, 02 62261) with four passport photos, a *marca da bollo* for €14.62 and, if you have one, a letter from your employer giving the reason for your stay. If you don't have such a letter, explain that you are looking for work; you may be asked for evidence of how you intend to support yourself in the meantime. For non-EC nationals the procedure tends to be more rigorous.

Residenza

This is your registered address in Italy. It can be obtained from the Ufficio Stranieri in the town hall (Municipio di Milano, *see above*). You will need your *permesso di soggiorno* (*see above*) and passport, plus copies of each. Someone will come round to your flat to check you live there before they issue you with a certificate.

Codice fiscale

A *codice fiscale* (tax code) is essential for opening a bank account or setting up utilities contracts. Take your passport and *permesso di soggiorno* (*see above*) to your local tax office (*agenzia delle Entrate*). Fill in a form and you can pick it up a few days later. It can be posted on request.

Addresses of tax offices can be found under *Agenzia delle Entrate* in the phone book or by looking them up at www1.agenziaentrate.it/ servizi/mappe/info.php. Call the Ministry of Economy and Finance's information line (freephone 848 800 333) or consult www.agenzia entrate.it for further information.

Jobs

Casual employment can be hard to come by, especially for non-EU citizens, as document requirements are more complicated. English-language schools often look for mother-tongue teachers; some (but not always the best) will demand qualifications and/or experience. Expat periodicals (*see p229*) have 'help wanted' ads, as does *Secondamano*. The Friday edition of *Corriere della Sera* has a jobs supplement, where many larger companies and headhunters place ads. Temporary agencies, of which there are now many, offer call centre, secretarial and manual jobs and many companies now require a working knowledge of English as well as Italian.

Weather report

Month	Average temperature		Average rainfall	
	ºC	ºF	mm	in
January	3.5	38.3	65	2.6
February	5	41	50	2
March	9	48.2	75	3
April	13.5	56.3	95	3.7
May	18.5	65.3	120	4.7
June	22	71.6	85	3.4
July	24.5	76.1	75	3
August	24	75.2	85	3.4
September	19	66.2	100	4
October	14	57.2	115	4.5
November	9	48.2	85	3.4
December	4.5	40.1	60	2.4

Directory

Further Reference

Books

Classics

Catullus *Poems* Uncannily modern musings from Lake Garda's most famous Roman.

Pliny the Elder *Natural History* Observations of an old Como native.

Fiction

D'Annunzio, Gabriele *The Child of Pleasure* Autobiographical novel by a *bon viveur* and *grand poseur* (*see p212*).

Eco, Umberto *Foucault's Pendulum* Milan takes on a sinister air in this esoteric novel by the renowned Italian professor.

Fo, Dario *Accidental Death of an Anarchist* Darkly hilarious take on the fatal 'tumble' of an anarchist from a Milanese police HQ window during an interrogation.

Hemingway, Ernest *A Farewell to Arms* Part of this love 'n' war epic is set in Milan.

Manzoni, Alessandro *I promessi sposi* (*The Betrothed*) The seminal Lombard novel (*see p59*), so ubiquitous you begin to wonder whether it isn't the only Lombard novel.

Non-fiction & travel

Burnett, Stanton H and Mantovani, Luca *The Italian Guillotine: Operation Clean Hands and the Overthrow of Italy's First Republic* A fine account of *Tangentopoli*, the scandal that brought Milan to its knees in the early 1990s, and its consequences.

Foot, John *Milan Since the Miracle: City, Culture and Identity* Intriguing study of the city's recent history and culture.

Grundy, Isobel *Lady Mary Wortley Montagu* This 18th-century English traveller spent many years in and around Lovere on Lake Garda.

Lawrence, DH *Twilight in Italy* Contains wonderful descriptions of Lake Garda.

Wharton, Edith *Italian Backgrounds* A clever, spirited refutation of the 'there's nothing to see in Milan' argument.

Film

Bitter Rice (*Riso Amaro*, Giuseppe De Santis, 1948) Passion and exploitation among Lombardy's rice-paddy workers.

Incantesimo Napoletano (Paolo Genovese & Luca Miniero, 1999) A Neapolitan girl rejects her local heritage and embraces all things Milanese.

Miracle in Milan (*Miracolo a Milano*, Vittorio De Sica, 1950) A magical neo-realist tale about a young orphan who brings light to Milan's beggars.

A Month by the Lake (John Irvin, 1994) The beauty of Lake Como compensates for the turgid tug-of-love in the plot.

1900 (Bernardo Bertolucci, 1976) This two-part epic on the conflict between fascism and communism was shot around Cremona.

La Notte (Michelangelo Antonioni, 1961) The middle section of Antonioni's trilogy on bourgeois alienation, *La Notte* covers 24 hours in the break-down of a 'typical' middle-class marriage.

Piso Pisello (Peter Del Monte, 1982) A Milanese teenager becomes a father and decides to raise the child alone in this oddball comedy.

Rocco and his Brothers (*Rocco e i suoi fratelli*, Luchino Visconti, 1960) Five Sicilian brothers and their mother

struggle to earn a living in industrial Milan.

The Tree of the Wooden Clogs (*L'albero degli zoccoli*, Ermanno Olmi, 1978) This film about substinence farming at the turn of the century was made with non-professional actors speaking in the *bergamasco* dialect.

Music

Verdi, Giuseppe (1813-1901) Lombard *per eccellenza*, Verdi gave many of his operas local themes or settings: *The Lombards at the First Crusade* (1843), *The Battle of Legnano* (1849) and *Rigoletto* (1851; set in Mantova). Many more reflect the tribulations of nations oppressed by foreign rulers, a sore point in Milan in Verdi's time.

Websites

www.beniculturali.it The Cultural Heritage ministry's site (Italian only) lists all state-owned museums, galleries, and provides details on temporary exhibitions and initiatives such as the Settimana dei Beni Culturali (*see p144*).

www.hellomilano.it Comprehensive English-language city guide.

www.infopoint.it Local transport information site (Italian only): type in departure point and destination and it will provide timetables.

www.milanotonight.it Italian-only site offering reader reviews of restaurants, bars and the like, all divided by area. Also has a small gay section.

www.cultura.regione.lombardia.it Information (Italian only) on every point of cultural interest in the Milan province and Lombardy region respectively.

Directory

Vocabulary

Italians always appreciate attempts to speak their language, however incompetent those attempts may be.

Note that there are two forms of address in the second person singular (you) in Italian: the formal *lei*, which should be used with strangers and older people; and the informal *tu*. The personal pronoun is usually omitted.

Italian is pronounced as it is spelled.

Pronunciation

a – as in ask.
e – like a in age (closed e) or e in sell.
i – like ea in east.
o – as in hotel (closed o) or in hot.
u – as in boot.

In front of e and i, c and g sound like check and giraffe respectively. A c before a, o and u sounds as in cat; g before a, o and u sounds as in get. An h after any consonant makes it hard. Before a vowel, the h is silent.
gl sounds like lli in million.
gn sounds like ny in canyon.
qu sounds as in quick.
r is always rolled.
s has two sounds, as in soap or rose.
sc sounds like sh in shame.
sch sounds like sc in scout.
z can be sounded ts or dz.

Useful phrases

hello/goodbye (informal) – ciao
good morning – buon giorno
good evening – buona sera
good night – buona notte
please – per favore, per piacere
thank you – grazie
you're welcome – prego
excuse me, sorry – mi scusi (formal), scusa (informal)
I'm sorry, but... – mi dispiace, ma...
I don't speak Italian (very well) – non parlo (molto bene) l'italiano
I don't/didn't understand – non capisco/non ho capito
where's the toilet? – dov'è la toilette/il bagno? (toilets are sometimes marked 'servizi')
open – aperto
closed – chiuso
entrance – entrata/ingresso
exit – uscita
help! – aiuto!
there's a fire! – c'è un incendio!
I want a doctor/policeman – Voglio un dottore/poliziotto
Leave me alone, please – Mi lasci in pace

Times & timetables

could you tell me the time, please? – mi sa (formal)/sai (informal) dire l'ora, per favore?
it's – o'clock – sono le (...)
it's half past – sono le (...) e mezza
when does it open? – a che ora apre?

Directions

(turn) left – (giri a) sinistra
(it's on the) right – è a destra
straight on – sempre diritto
where is...? – dov'è...?
could you show me the way to the Duomo? – mi potrebbe indicare la strada per il Duomo?
is it near/far? – è vicino/lontano?

Transport

car – macchina
bus – autobus
underground/subway – metro(politana)
coach – pullman
taxi – tassì, taxi
train – treno
tram – tram
plane – aereo
bus stop – fermata (d'autobus)
station – stazione
platform – binario
ticket/s – biglietto/biglietti
one way – solo andata
return – andata e ritorno
(I'd like) a ticket for – (vorrei) un biglietto per...
fine – multa
I'm sorry, I didn't know I had to stamp it – mi dispiace, non sapevo che lo dovevo timbrare

Communications

phone – telefono
stamp – francobollo
how much is a stamp for England/Australia/the United States? – quanto viene un francobollo per l'Inghilterra/l'Australia/ gli Stati Uniti?
can I send a fax? – posso mandare un fax?
can I make a phone call? – posso fare una telefonata?
postcard – cartolina

Shopping

I'd like to try the blue sandals/black shoes/brown boots – vorrei provare i sandali blu/le scarpe nere/gli stivali marroni
do you have it/them in other colours? – ce l'ha in altri colori?
I take (shoe) size... – porto il numero...
I take (dress) size... – porto la taglia...
it's too loose/too tight/just right – mi sta largo/stretto/bene
can you give me a little more/less? – mi dia un po' di più/meno
100 grams of... – un etto di...
300 grams of... – tre etti di...
one kilo of... – un kilo/chilo di...
five kilos of... – cinque chili di...
a litre/two litres of... – un litro/due litri di...

Accommodation

a reservation – una prenotazione
I'd like to book a single/twin/double room – vorrei prenotare una camera singola/doppia/matrimoniale
I'd prefer a room with a bath/shower/window over the courtyard – preferirei una camera con vasca da bagno/doccia/finestra sul cortile
is service included? – è compreso il servizio?

Eating & drinking

I'd like to book a table for four at 8pm – vorrei prenotare un tavolo per quattro alle otto
I don't eat meat; what do you recommend? – non mangio carne; cosa mi consiglia?
this is lukewarm; can you heat it up? – è tiepido; lo può riscaldare?
this wine is corked; could you bring me another bottle? – questo vino sa di tappo; mi può portare un'altra bottiglia, per favore?
that was poor/good/(really) delicious – era mediocre/buono/(davvero) ottimo
the bill – il conto
is service included? – è incluso il servizio?
I think there's a mistake in this bill – credo che il conto sia sbagliato
See also p108 On the menu.

Days & nights

Monday – lunedì; Tuesday – martedì; Wednesday – mercoledì; Thursday – giovedì; Friday – venerdì; Saturday – sabato; Sunday – domenica; yesterday – ieri; today – oggi; tomorrow – domani; morning – mattina; afternoon – pomeriggio; evening – sera; night – notte; weekend – fine settimana or, more usually, weekend; have a good weekend! – buon fine settimana!

Numbers & money

0 zero; 1 uno; 2 due; 3 tre; 4 quattro; 5 cinque; 6 sei; 7 sette; 8 otto; 9 nove; 10 dieci; 11 undici; 12 dodici; 13 tredici; 14 quattordici; 15 quindici; 16 sedici; 17 diciasette; 18 diciotto; 19 diciannove; 20 venti; 30 trenta; 40 quaranta; 50 cinquanta; 60 sessanta; 70 settanta; 80 ottanta; 90 novanta; 100 cento; 200 duecento; 1,000 mille.
how much is it? – quanto costa?
do you take credit cards? – accettate carte di credito?
can I pay in pounds/dollars, with traveller's cheques? – posso pagare in sterline/dollari/con i traveller's cheques?

Index

Advertisers' Index

Please refer to the relevant pages
for contact details

National border	- - - -
Province border	- - -
Motorway (*autostrada*)	=
Main road	
Lake/river/canal	
Place of interest	
Church	+
Park	
Hospital/university	
Pedestrianised area	
Car park	P
Tourist information	*i*
Metro station	M

Maps

Lombardy

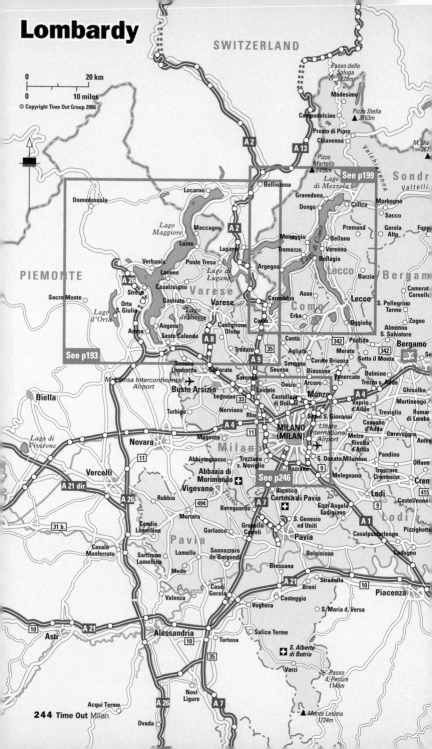

0   20 km

0   10 miles

© Copyright Time Out Group 2006

SWITZERLAND

Passo dello Spluga 2128m

Madesimo

Pizzo Stella ▲3163m

Campodolcino

Prosto di Piuro

Chiavenna

M. Dis ▲367

Valchiavenna

Pizzo Martello ▲2459m

Lago di Mezzola

See p199

Sondr

Valtelli

Locarno

Bellinzona

Gravedona

Dongo

Colico

Morbegno

Sacco

Domodossola

Lago Maggiore

Maccagno

Luino

Luvino

Menaggio

Tremezzo

Premana

Gerola Alta

Fopp

Verbania

Lugano

Ponte Tresa

Bellano

Varenna

Laveno

Lago di Lugano

Argegno

Bellagio

PIEMONTE

Stresa

Casalzuigno

Varese

Cernobbio

Asso

Lecco

Lecco

Barzio

Bergam

Camerat Cornello

Sacro Monte

Orta S. Giulio

Gavirate

Varese

Como

S. Pellegrino Terme

Lago d'Orta

Lago di Varese

Erba

Oggiono

Zogno

Almenno S. Salvatore

Angera

Castiglione Olona

Cantù

Pontida

Bergamo

Arona

Sesto Calende

Tradate

342

Agliate

Merate

342

Sotto il Monte

Sommaria

Galtarate

Saronno

Seregno

Carate Brianza

Vimercate

Dalmine

Trezzo s. Adda

Ghisalba

Busto Arsizio

Legnano

Lainate

Desio

Biassono

Arcore

Monza

Vaprio d'Adda

Treviglio

Martinengo

Romar di Lomba

Turbigo

Nerviano

Rho

Sesto S. Giovanni

Melzo

Rivolta d'Adda

Cassano d'Adda

Caravaggio

Antes

Biella

Magenta

MILANO (MILAN)

Linate International Airport

S. Donato Milanese

Pandino

Offane

Troscore Cremasco

Cren

Novara

Milan

Abbiategrasso

Trezzano s. Naviglio

Rozzano

Melegnano

Lodi

415

Vercelli

Abbazia di Morimondo

See p246

Binasco

Sant'Angelo Lodigiano

Lodi

Lodi

Vigevano

Ticino

Certosa di Pavia

S. Genesio ed Uniti

Casalpusterlengo

Robbio

Bereguardo

Gropello Cairoli

Pavia

Pizzighettone

Candia Lomellina

Mortara

Garlasco

Belgioioso

Cadogno

Casale Monferrato

Sartirana Lomellina

Lomello

Sannazzaro de' Burgondi

Pavia

Po

Bressana

Stradella

Piacenza

Mede

Casei Gerola

Broni

10

Valenza

Voghera

Casteggio

S. Maria d. Versa

Asti

Alessandria

Tortona

Salice Terme

S. Alberto di Butrio

Acqui Terme

Novi Ligure

Varzi

Passo d. Penice 1145m

Ovada

▲ Monte Lesima 1724m

Greater Mila

COMO

Meda

SEREGNO | **LECCO**

Lambro

Gallarate

COMO A9

A8

SS 336 | LAINATE | Autodromo | Villasanta

Aeroporto Intercontinentale della Malpensa

Busto Arsizio

LISSONE

DESIO

Bovisio Masciago

SS 527

Duomo

SARONNO

SS 35

MONZA

Senago

SS 233

Paderno Dugnano

S. Fruttuoso

Lainate

Garbagnate Mil.

Seveso

Arese

Cusano Milanino

CINISELLO BALSAMO

A4

BOLLATE

Cormano

A4

Brugherio

VARESE-MALPENSA

SS 33

BRESSO

SESTO SAN GIOVANNI

RHO

Fiera Milano

Novate Milanese

Cologno Monzese

Naviglio Marte

A8

TORINO

A4

Pero

Certosa di Garegnano

Olona

Bicocca

Crescenzago

SS 11

Vimodrone

NOVARA

SS 11

Lampugnano

Bovisa

A51

Lambro

Segra

Settimo Milanese

A50

Stadio Meazza

Fiera

Piazzale Loreto

Idroscalo

BAGGIO

Castello Sforzesco

Duomo

Aeroporto Internazionale Linate

Cusago

Cesano Boscone

Lorenteggio

See p247

Peschiera Borromee

CORSICO

Rogoredo

S. Donato Milanese

Naviglio Grande

Assago

Abbazia di Chiaravalle

SS 494

SS 35

SS 415

A50

S. Giuliano Milanese

Abbazia di Mirasole

Rozzano

Abbazia di Viboldone

SS 9

Opera

Melegnano

ABBIATEGRASSO

Naviglio Pavese

A1

Binasco

Lacchiarella

0   8 kms

0   5 miles

© Copyright Time Out Group 2006

GENOVA

PAVIA

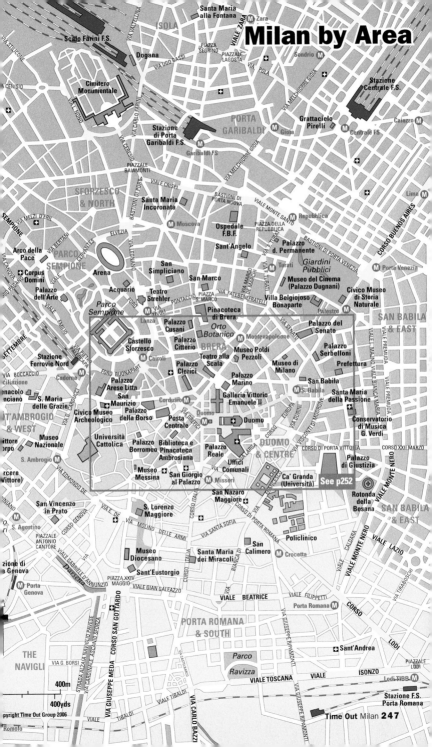

Milan by Area

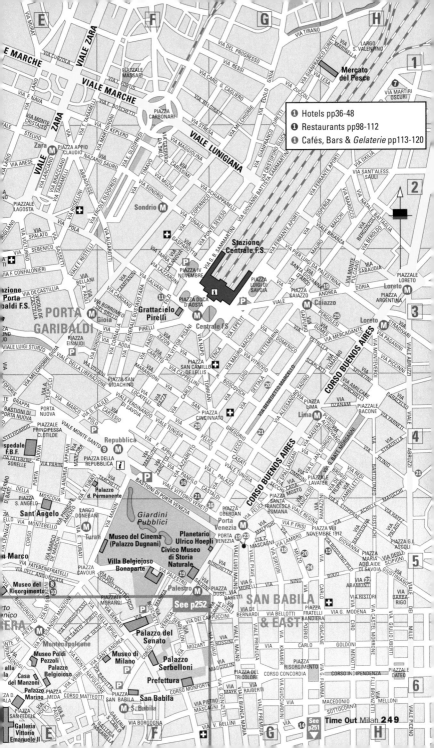

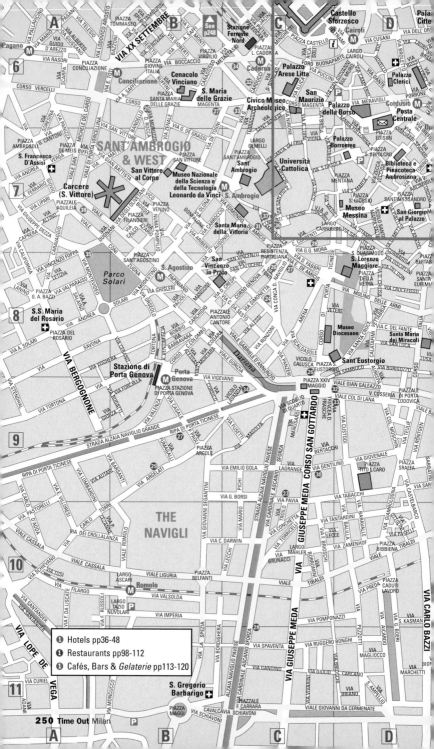

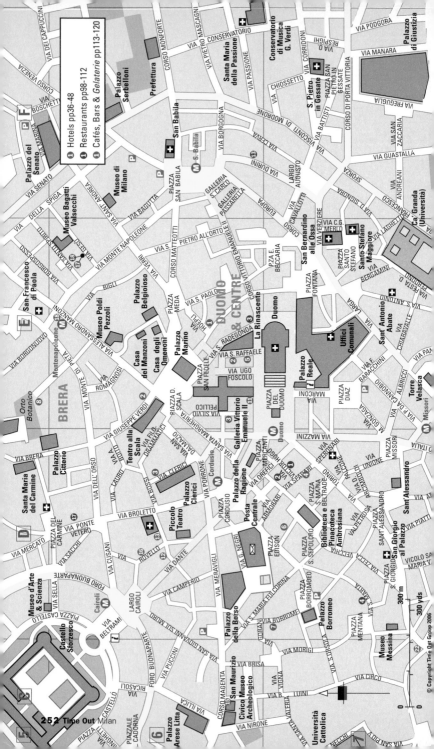

Hotels pp36-48

Restaurants pp98-112

Cafés, Bars & *Gelaterie* pp113-120

Street Index

Rete metropolitana e tratte ferroviarie urbane / Underground network and urban railway system

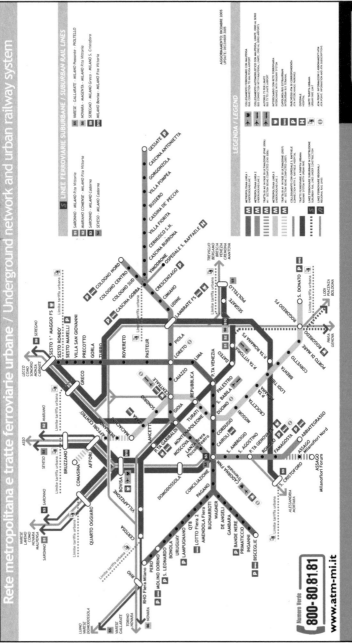